# Central Themes in
# Early Modern Philosophy

# Central Themes in Early Modern Philosophy

Essays Presented to Jonathan Bennett

*Edited by*

J. A. COVER
Purdue University

MARK KULSTAD
Rice University

HACKETT PUBLISHING COMPANY, INC.
Indianapolis and Cambridge

Cover design by Dan Kirklin

Interior design by Jan A. Cover

For further information, please address

    Hackett Publishing Company, Inc.
    P.O. Box 44937
    Indianapolis, Indiana 46244-0937

99 98 97 96 95 94 93 92 91 90   1 2 3 4 5 6 7 8 9 10

**Library of Congress Cataloging-in-Publication Data**

Central themes in early modern philosophy : essays presented to
   Jonathan Bennett / edited by J. A. Cover, Mark Kulstad.
      p.  cm.
   Includes bibliographical references and index.
   ISBN 0-87220-110-4 (alk. paper)
   ISBN 0-87220-109-0 (pbk.: alk. paper)
   1. Philosophy, Modern--17th century. 2. Philosophy, Modern--
18th century.  I. Bennett, Jonathan Francis. II. Cover, J. A. (Jan
Arthur), 1958- . III. Kulstad, Mark, 1947- .
B801.C46  1990
190'.9'032--dc20                          90-44730
                                          CIP

# CONTENTS

Dedication    vii
Preface    ix
Abbreviations    xi

1. MARGARET D. WILSON
   *Descartes on the Representationality of Sensation*    1

2. R. S. WOOLHOUSE
   *Spinoza and Descartes and
   the Existence of Extended Substance*    23

3. G. H. R. PARKINSON
   *Definition, Essence, and
   Understanding in Spinoza*    49

4. DON GARRETT
   ETHICS IP5: *Shared Attributes and
   the Basis of Spinoza's Monism*    69

5. EDWIN CURLEY
   *Notes on a Neglected Masterpiece (II):
   The* THEOLOGICAL-POLITICAL TREATISE
   *as a Prolegomenon to the* ETHICS    109

6. ROBERT C. SLEIGH, JR.
   *Leibniz on Malebranche on Causality*    161

7. MARTHA BRANDT BOLTON
   *Leibniz and Locke on the
   Knowledge of Necessary Truths*    195

8. NICHOLAS JOLLEY
   *Berkeley and Malebranche
   on Causality and Volition*    227

9. ANNETTE BAIER
   *Real Humean Causes*    245

10. PATRICIA KITCHER
    *Apperception and Epistemic Responsibility*    273

Notes on Contributors    305
Index of Names and Topics    307

# DEDICATION

Jonathan Francis Bennett was born in Greymouth, New Zealand, on 17 February 1930. He received his M.A. from the University of New Zealand in 1952 and his B. Phil. in 1955 from Oxford University. He has been Lecturer in Moral Sciences at Cambridge University and Professor of Philosophy at the University of British Columbia; he is currently Professor of Philosophy at Syracuse University. In addition to teaching at Haverford College and Simon Fraser University, Jonathan Bennett has had visiting appointments at Cornell University, the University of Michigan, the University of Pittsburgh, and Princeton University. He has served as President of the American Philosophical Association (Eastern Division) and is a Fellow of the American Academy of Arts and Sciences. He is the coeditor and translator of two editions and the author of seven books and about eighty articles.

This volume consists of new essays in the history of seventeenth- and eighteenth-century philosophy, presented to Jonathan Bennett on the occasion of his sixtieth birthday.

Since the appearance of his first book on Kant nearly twenty-five years ago, work in the history of early modern philosophy has reflected the influence of Professor Bennett's distinctive approach to the great historical figures. Always tough-minded, lively, refreshingly bold, Bennett's work has taught a generation of philosophers how serious scholarship and careful argument can bring those figures into the arena of contemporary philosophical discussion. We do not get intellectual biography from him, but history of philosophy done in the way Bennett does all of his philosophy: with care, with intelligence, with the belief that fair criticism is often high praise. Collectively, the essays in this volume offer a new discussion of central themes in early modern metaphysics and epistemology; individually, each reflects Professor Bennett's overriding concern to expound and argue with important historical texts. These essays are presented to him with gratitude and admiration.

# PREFACE

The honorary occasion of this book is underscored by its contents. All of the articles are new, written expressly for this volume. Contributors were asked to write on topics of their own choosing. An idea of the breadth and unity of the resulting volume can be gotten from a quick perusal of the table of contents. Those qualities at once befit and reflect the content Professor Bennett's own work, celebrated here: The extent of his influence can be gauged by a look at the index.

But the *articles* are the book. These essays provide a cross-sampling of the important current work in the history of seventeenth- and eighteenth-century philosophy, particularly in the areas of metaphysics and epistemology. Every major figure (by one reckoning at least) from Descartes to Kant is considered. Some are treated in a number of essays, with the contribution to research on Spinoza being especially noteworthy. There is a lesser clustering around Descartes, Malebranche, and Leibniz, each of whom figures centrally in two essays apiece. A diverse range of themes is also addressed—from doctrines of substance, to essence, to the knowledge of necessary truths, to epistemic responsibility. Here the issue of causality deserves special mention: three articles direct themselves squarely to this important topic, grappling with the issue as it appears in the hands of Leibniz, Malebranche, Berkeley, and Hume.

Readers are encouraged to have a preliminary glance over the list of volume-wide abbreviations on pp. xi-xiii, before starting their reading. While the list is somewhat long, adopting it as a piece of apparatus helps to unify the volume and improve its usefulness as a research tool; abbreviations also make reading more enjoyable by reducing the number of endnotes.

We have received support, encouragement, and advice from a number of individuals and institutions. Partial subsidy for publication of this volume was received from the offices of the Dean of the College of Arts and Sciences and the Vice-President for Research at Syracuse University, here gratefully acknowledged. Financial assistance was also received from the office of the Dean of the School of Humanities at Rice University, in addition to the support of services from the Departments of Philosophy at Syracuse, Rice, and Purdue University. Technical help was received from Academic Computing Services at Syracuse.

Special thanks go to William P. Alston and Robert C. Sleigh, Jr. for serving as Editorial Advisors to the volume. We are indebted to Mark Brown, Samuel Gorovitz, Allen Matusow, Sue McDougal, Minranda Robinson, Stewart Thau, and Peter van Inwagen for their help at various stages. Manfred Kuehn and Alan Schwerin assisted as manuscript reviewers; Greg E. Ealick and Victoria Pasley corrected penultimate proofs for us.

We want to thank the good people at Hackett Publishing Company (especially Frances Hackett, James Hullett, and Dan Kirklin) for their willingness to undertake this project and for their editorial advice and encouragement.

Finally, we acknowledge the help of Cathy Ladd at Syracuse, who contributed invaluable computer expertise and hours of her labor to this project, some of it coming— quite heroically—during a time when she was burdened by the pain and inconvenience of a serious injury.

Although the initial idea and impulse behind this volume were Cover's, all facets of the editorial work were a collaborative effort. Preliminary and ongoing logistical correspondence with the contributors was undertaken by Kulstad, as was the initial round of computer work; funding, dealings with Hackett, and the second round of computer work were handled by Cover. The formal ceremony in Syracuse at which this volume was officially announced was arranged and conducted by Cover. Front-matter was prepared by Cover. The index was prepared first by Cover, then fine-tuned by Kulstad. Editing of the manuscript was shared equally. The order of our names on the cover and title page is alphabetical, not by seniority.

# ABBREVIATIONS

The following abbreviations apply to works cited in more than one article of the volume. Additional abbreviations employed in the volume but not listed below are explained in footnotes to the particular article in which they figure.

AT       *Oeuvres de Descartes*, edited by C. Adam and P. Tannery. Paris, 1897-1913. Reprint. Paris: J. Vrin, 1964-75. Cited by volume and page.

CS       *The Collected Works of Spinoza*, volume I, edited and translated by Edwin Curley. Princeton: Princeton University Press, 1985.

CSM       *The Philosophical Writings of Descartes*, translated by John Cottingham, Robert Stoothoff, and Dugald Murdoch. 2 volumes. Cambridge: Cambridge University Press, 1985. Cited by volume and page.

E       *Ethica*. Baruch Spinoza. Roman numerals refer to parts; A = axiom; P = proposition; D (following roman numeral) = definition; arabic numerals refer to axioms, propositions, definitions, etc.; D (following P and arabic numeral) = demonstration of a proposition; C, S, L are corollary, scholium, and lemma respectively; Post, Exp, Pref, and App are postulate, explanation, Preface, and Appendix respectively. Where this method of reference will not easily locate the passage cited, and where useful elsewhere in citations from Ep, KV, TdIE, and TTP, volume, page, and sometimes line numbers (e.g. II/195 or III/12/17-18) of the Gebhardt edition are added.

*Enquiry*       *Enquiry Concerning Human Understanding*. David Hume. References are to the edition by L. A. Selby-Bigge and P. H. Nidditch, Oxford: Oxford University Press, 1975.

Ep   *Epistolae* (Spinoza's Correspondence). Cited by letter.

*Essay*  *An Essay Concerning Human Understanding*. John Locke. References are to the edition by P. H. Nidditch, Oxford: Oxford University Press, 1975. Cited by book, chapter, and section (e.g. II, xxvii, 10) and, where useful, by page and line(s) (e.g. 529:27-33) in the Nidditch edition.

G   *Die philosophischen Schriften von G. W. Leibniz*. Edited by C. J. Gerhardt. 7 volumes. Berlin, 1875-90. Reprint. Hildesheim: Georg Olms, 1965. Cited by volume and page.

K   *Descartes: Philosophical Letters*, edited and translated by Anthony Kenny. Oxford: Oxford University Press, 1970.

KV   *Korte Verhandeling van God, de Mensch, en des zelfs Welstand* (= *Short Treatise*). Baruch Spinoza. Cited by part, chapter, and section (Sigwart's).

L   *G. W. Leibniz. Philosophical Papers and Letters*. Edited and translated by Leroy E. Loemker. 2d ed. Dordrecht: D. Reidel, 1969.

LO   *The Search after Truth/Elucidations of the Search after Truth*. Nicholas Malebranche. Edited and translated, with philosophical commentary, by Thomas M. Lennon and Paul J. Olscamp. Columbus: Ohio State University Press, 1980.

MP   *G. W. Leibniz. Philosophical Writings*. Edited and translated by Mary Morris and G. H. R. Parkinson. London: Dent, 1973.

NE   *The New Essays on Human Understanding*. G. W. Leibniz. The translation by Peter Remnant and Jonathan Bennett (Cambridge: Cambridge University Press, 1981) employs the Academy pagination.

*Theodicy* *Theodicy*. G. W. Leibniz. Cited by section number (indicated by '§' or 'section') as given in G VI and the following English translation: *Theodicy*. Translated by E. M. Huggard. New Haven: Yale University Press, 1952. Reprint. La Salle, Ill.: Open Court, 1985. When the sections are not from the three main parts of the *Theodicy*, a title designating the appropriate sub-unit is given also. Occasionally, section numbers are not suitable, and citations are given by page in G VI.

TdIE       *Tractatus de Intellectus Emendatione.* Baruch Spinoza. Cited
           by section (Bruder's).

TTP        *Tractatus Theologico-Politicus.* Baruch Spinoza. Cited by
           chapter and section (Bruder's).

In addition to these abbreviations for citing original texts, '*Study*' and
'LBH' are standardly used in citations to (respectively) Jonathan
Bennett's *A Study of Spinoza's Ethics* (Indianapolis and Cambridge:
Hackett Publishing Company, 1984) and *Locke, Berkeley, Hume:
Central Themes* (Oxford: Oxford University Press, 1971).

# DESCARTES ON THE
# REPRESENTATIONALITY OF SENSATION

*Margaret D. Wilson*

Throughout his writings Descartes identifies our ordinary experiences of color, odor, heat and cold, and other so-called sensible qualities as mere sensations which have a purely mental status. He consistently and emphatically denies that they "resemble" any quality that does or can exist in physical reality. Yet in the Third Meditation he seems to construe such sensations as "ideas of" cold and the like, which *misrepresent* "what cold is" to the mind. Their "falsity" consists in representing what is not a real physical quality as if it were. He presents this view as a corollary of the assumption that *all* "thoughts" are "as if of things."

In the Fourth set of Objections to the *Meditations* Antoine Arnauld strongly challenges the cogency of Descartes's position on sensation. Descartes's reply to Arnauld is both fairly detailed and extremely bewildering. In fact, on the surface it seems to involve a clumsy retraction of the view that sensations are in some way misrepresentations of cold, heat, etc.[1]

In later writings—the *Principles of Philosophy, Passions of the Soul*, and certain letters—Descartes provides further comments on the status of sensations, in relation to extramental reality, that bear on the issue of whether or not he continues to regard sensations as "representative" (or misrepresentative) "of things." This later material appears to suggest some alteration in Descartes's doctrine on the subject.

1

Descartes's position on the representationality of sensation (including the "passions") is important to a number of interpretive issues. Within the Cartesian system, sensations and passions are included among our "thoughts" (*cogitationes*); and the various Latin and French terms for 'sensation' are used more or less interchangeably with 'ideas of sense'. So, claims about Descartes's general position on the relation of thought and representation (or "intensionality"), and on the nature of ideas, really need to take account of his treatment of the sensations and passions, as a sort of problem-posing test case. Further, the issue is obviously relevant to the recently disputed question of whether or not Descartes regards the passive emotions as "cognitive." It is central, as well, to his position on the "primary-secondary quality distinction," on the mind-body union, and on the relation of mind to matter generally. Unfortunately, Descartes's various statements on this subject are exceptionally difficult to understand clearly, even considered individually; and the interpretation problem becomes even harder when one tries to figure out what is going on from one work to another.

In the first three parts of this paper I will (a) present the Third Meditation position more fully; (b) examine Arnauld's objection; and (c) try to make sense of Descartes's reply. I will propose a distinction between senses of 'represent' (or 'idea of') which, I suggest, helps to clarify the difference between Arnauld's and Descartes's positions, while making it easier to interpret the Cartesian texts as intelligible and consistent. In the fourth section I will use the same distinction to help reconcile with these texts seemingly conflicting statements from the *Principles of Philosophy* about whether sensations represent. The final section is concerned with Descartes's position on the representationality of the passive emotions.[2]

## 1

In an often-cited passage from the Third Meditation Descartes ties the concept of 'idea' in the strict sense to some notion of representation, or apprehending a "thing as subject of my thought."

> Of my thoughts some are as if images of things
> (*tanquam rerum imagines*), to which alone the term
> 'idea' is strictly appropriate: as when I think of man, or
> Chimaera, or Heaven, or Angel, or God. Others,
> though, have certain other forms besides: as when I
> will, when I fear, when I affirm, when I deny, I al-
> ways indeed apprehend some thing (*aliquam rem ap-
> prehendo*) as the subject of my thought, but I also
> comprehend by thought something more than the
> similitude of this thing; and of these some are called
> volitions, or affects, but others judgments. (AT VII,
> 37)[3]

The point that ideas are necessarily "of things" is underscored in later stages of his discussion. For instance,
Descartes observes that, although all ideas, considered just
as modes of thought, are equal, nevertheless "some are very
different from others" insofar as "one represents one thing,
another another."[4]

He further relies on the notion that all ideas are "as if of
things" in developing the concept of *material falsity*, specifically in relation to sensation. He asserts that "confused and
obscure" ideas, notably his sensations of "light and colors,
sounds, odors, tastes, heat and cold, and the other tactile
qualities," fail to allow him to determine whether they "are
the ideas of certain things or not of things" (*sint rerum
quarundam ideae, an non rerum*): possibly they are in fact
"of" non-things, of "privations" (AT VII, 43-44). But since
all ideas are "as if of things" (*tanquam rerum*), even these
"confused" ideas *seem* to represent things: thus they provide
"material for error:"

> For although . . . falsity properly so-called, or formal
> falsity, can only be found in judgements, there is nev-
> ertheless a certain other material falsity in ideas, when
> they represent what is not a thing as if a thing (*non rem
> tanquam rem repraesentant*). Thus, for example, the
> ideas that I have of heat and cold are so little clear and

distinct, that from them I cannot tell whether cold is only the privation of heat, or heat the privation of cold, or each is a real quality, or neither. And because there can be no ideas that are not as if of things (*nisi tanquam rerum*), if indeed it is true that cold is nothing else than the privation of heat, the idea which represents it to me as something real and positive (*idea quae mihi illud tanquam reale quid & positivum repraesentat*) will not improperly be called false, and so of the others. (AT VII, 43-44)

These statements clearly imply that our sensations are representative in two respects. First they are *ideas of* cold, heat and so forth (whatever these may be, and whether or not they are "real qualities"). Second, they present heat, cold, etc. to us *in a certain way, as being such-and-such*; specifically (since all ideas are "as if of things") they represent them to us as "real and positive qualities." But it may not in fact be true that both cold and heat are real and positive properties—or for that matter that either one is. In that case the relevant sensory idea tends to mislead us, or provide "material" for erroneous judgment.

It is important to remember that the issue whether certain putative qualities are "real" is distinct, in Descartes's writings, from the issue about whether anything possessing the qualities in question actually exists. Thus, Burman records that Descartes elaborated on the "material falsity" passage as follows:

There is . . . material for error, even if I refer [my ideas] to no things outside me, since I can err with respect to their nature itself. For instance, if I consider the idea of color, and say that it is a thing, a quality, or rather that the color itself, which is represented by this idea, is such (*tale quid esse*); or if I say that white is a quality, even if I refer that idea to no thing outside myself, and say or suppose that nothing is white, I can nevertheless err in the abstract, and about whiteness itself and its nature or idea. (AT V, 152)

Descartes also emphasizes the distinction between reality and existence at least twice in the *Meditations*.[5]

At this point one might well want to know more about the notion of "non-thing," insofar as it is distinguished from "non-existent thing." Can a non-thing really be an "it"? Is it intelligible to speculate about what this "it" is? ("If cold is nothing else than the privation of heat, then the idea which represents it to me . . . .") What exactly is the relation between the notion of "non-thing" and that of "privation," anyway?[6] And (most important in the present context), in what sense does a non-thing qualify to be *represented* at all—whether as a "thing" or, for that matter, as a non-thing?

As it happens, none of these questions (except possibly the last) figures in Arnauld's attack on the notion of material falsity. He appears to accept, for instance, that cold could be a non-thing (or anyway, a privation), and that we can intelligibly discuss what an idea "of it" could or could not be. What he particularly objects to is the notion of *misrepresentation* on which Descartes relies in characterizing the ideas of sensible qualities. In the following discussion I will focus on questions Arnauld does raise (to which Descartes replies), setting aside problems specifically concerned with the notion of a "non-thing" and its role in the material falsity passage.[7]

2

According to Arnauld, "if cold is merely a privation, then there cannot be an idea of cold which represents it to me as a positive thing (*quae illud mihi tanquam rem positivam repraesentet*) . . . ." He elaborates:

> For what is the idea of cold? Cold itself in so far as it exists objectively in the intellect. But if cold is a privation, it cannot be objectively in the intellect by means of an idea whose objective being is a positive entity. Therefore, if cold is only a privation, there can never be a positive idea of it, and hence no (idea) which is materially false. (AT VII, 206)

Arnauld's claim is that a positive idea cannot in any sense represent a privation. To say that the idea is positive is to say that it represents something "real and positive." For what it "represents" is just the "objective being which it contains" (207). (Note that Arnauld is not denying that we can falsely *judge* that cold is something positive; his objection is partly directed toward establishing that Descartes has confused what is possible on the level of judgement with what is possible on the level of ideas alone. In this case our error would consist in judging that the positive idea "is the idea of cold" (206-07).) "Finally," Arnauld concludes:

> What does the idea of cold, which you say is materially false, exhibit to your mind? A privation? Then it is true. A positive entity? Then it is not the idea of cold. (207)[8]

There is some room for doubt about what Arnauld's main point is, exactly. Is he maintaining just that a positive idea cannot represent (or "exhibit") a privation? Or does he mean to endorse either or both of the following stronger claims:

(a)  A privation cannot be represented by any idea at all (since for an idea to represent is just for it to exhibit some reality to the mind, or contain some reality objectively);

(b)  For anything **n**, of which it is true that **n is P**, then any idea which exhibits something to the mind *as not-P* cannot be an idea of **n**?

It may seem at first that Arnauld does implicitly endorse (a). For he does suggest that for an idea to represent *is* for it to exhibit some reality to the mind. If so, the non-real could hardly be represented by any idea at all; and there is no indication that Arnauld means to distinguish the non-real and the privative (any more than Descartes himself does).[9] At the same time, however, Arnauld is prepared to advance the hypothesis that the idea of cold "exhibits a privation to the mind"—a possibility incompatible with (a).

It does appear fairly unproblematic, at any rate (and this is the important point here), that Arnauld is committed to (b), on some interpretation or other. For he rests his claim that a positive idea cannot represent a privation on the notion that a privation *is not* something positive. And there is nothing to indicate that privations are somehow special cases in this regard. In other words, he seems to take it that (in some sense) nothing can count as a representation of **n** that represents **n** *as other than* **n** in fact *is*.

It is hard to guess how broad an interpretation of (b) Arnauld would be prepared to endorse. Take Descartes's example, in Meditation III, of the "two different ideas of the sun" which he finds in himself. One of these, he says, is "as if acquired from the senses": through it the sun appears very small. The other is derived from astronomical reasoning: through it the sun is exhibited as larger than the earth. Surely, he concludes, "both cannot be similar to the same sun existing outside me"; and "reason persuades that that idea is utterly dissimilar to it which seems to emanate most directly from the sun itself" (AT VII, 39). Would Arnauld go so far as to hold that, if the sun is in fact larger than the earth, there can be no idea "of it" through which it appears very small?

Although Arnauld's comments provide no basis for a sure answer to such questions, I do want to suggest that his objection appears to rest on an assumption about representation which divides him from Descartes to greater or lesser degree (depending how exactly we interpret his implicit endorsement of (b)). Insofar as Arnauld assumes (with whatever qualification) that for an idea to be an idea of **n**, or to represent **n**, it cannot *present* **n** as other than **n** in fact is, he seems to rely on what we might call a purely presentational notion of representation. Descartes, as I will now try to bring out further, in examining the Fourth Replies, has what we may call a hybrid notion. For him the representationality of ideas does consist *partly* in presentational content. However, an idea's being an idea of **n**—its representing **n**—does *not* preclude that the idea presents **n** as other than it is. I will speak of Descartes's notion of representation as partially "referential," as a way of expressing the non-presentational element. (Later on, though, I will argue that the "referential" component of Cartesian representation is hard to explain clearly.) Recognizing this distinction between Arnauld's and

Descartes's assumptions helps quite a bit, I will try to show, in making sense of Descartes's reply to Arnauld's criticisms. (One must also, however, be prepared to be very flexible in interpreting his words.) In addition (as I will explain later) it helps to reconcile (with each other and with the Third Meditation) two passages from the *Principles of Philosophy* (I.68 and I.71) in which Descartes appears both to affirm and to deny that sensations "represent" something "outside thought."

Before I move on to the Fourth Replies, let me try to clarify just a bit more the distinction with respect to aspects of representation that I intend to attribute to Descartes. I'm going to hold that (in Descartes's writings) the expressions, 'I have an idea of **n**', and 'my idea **i** represents something **P**' are both ambiguous, in similar ways, reflecting the "hybrid" nature of his conception of representation. Suppose that my mind is in fact an immaterial substance, though (at my present stage of philosophical development) I can only conceive of my mind as an attribute of my body. Then my idea of my mind is in one sense the idea of, and represents, an immaterial substance; in another sense it is not the idea of, and does not represent (to me) an immaterial substance. I introduce the following terms to distinguish the "senses" in question: in the example just given my idea *referentially represents* an immaterial substance; it *presents* a bodily attribute. (Again, I am not going to claim that the notion of referential representation is ultimately a clear one; only that the distinction in question helps to explain the texts.)[10]

## 3

Descartes's initial response to Arnauld's rejection of the notion of material falsity (specifically with respect to the "idea of cold") basically conforms to his Third Meditation statement:

> . . . whether cold is a positive thing, or a privation, doesn't make any difference to the idea I have of it, but it remains in me the same that I have always had; and I say that this [idea] provides me with material for error,

if cold truly is a privation and does not have as much reality as heat; because, considering the ideas respectively of cold and of heat just as I receive them both from the senses, I cannot see (*non possum advertere*) that more reality is exhibited to me by one than by the other. (AT VII, 232-33)

On the reading I propose, Descartes's point should be that neither idea *presents* more reality than the other, though one may well referentially represent more reality than the other, i.e., may referentially represent a real quality rather than a privation.

Descartes goes on to reject Arnauld's claim that "the idea of cold is cold itself insofar as it is objectively in the understanding" (233). We need, he says, to make a distinction:

for it often happens in obscure and confused ideas, among which those of heat and cold are included, that they are referred to something other than that of which they are truly the ideas (*ut ad aliud quid referantur quam ad id cujus revera ideae sunt*).

"Thus," he continues,

if cold is only a privation, the idea of cold is not cold itself, insofar as it is objectively in the understanding, but something else which I wrongly take for this privation (*sed aliud quid quod perperam pro ista privatione sumitur*); that is, a certain sensation which has no being outside the understanding. (233)

The idea is, referentially, the idea *of cold*; it *presents,* however, something else: a mere, if "positive", sensation. It thus "provides the material" for my error of judging that what is (positively if obscurely) presented to me is what the idea refers to, namely cold (which is in fact, in the real world, a privation).[11] What the idea referentially represents is not what it presentationally represents: that is why Descartes can say that the idea of cold is referred to something other than that of which it is in fact the idea. He is

not, in other words, *categorically* accepting Arnauld's claim
that if cold is a privation, a positive idea is not the idea of
cold. He is merely agreeing that the idea would not be
*presentationally* the idea of cold as it "is" in nature, or *quam
res* (namely, a privation). A similar point is at issue in the
next paragraph, when Descartes implies that the source of
error in our judgements about sensible qualities is that ideas
of sense are "referred to something to which [they do] not
conform." (233)[12]

A few lines later Descartes comes back to the original
objection:

> But [he] asks what that idea of cold represents to me,
> which I say is materially false: "For if," he says, "it
> exhibits a privation, then it is true; if a positive being,
> then it is not the idea of cold."

Descartes now rather startlingly *agrees* with the objection:
"*Recte*," he says. But, he continues,

> . . . I call that idea materially false only for this reason,
> that, since it is obscure and confused, I cannot decide
> whether what it exhibits to me as outside my sense is
> positive, or not; and thus I have occasion to judge that
> it is something positive, although perhaps it is only a
> privation. (234)

Although Descartes seems to give away the store here, I
think he has merely expressed himself ineptly. He does not
really intend to retract his position that a particular "positive"
sensation counts as the "idea of cold," even if cold is in fact
a privation. Despite apparent verbal indications to the contrary, he is really continuing on his original track: the sensation of cold referentially represents cold (let's suppose, a
privation)—but fails to *present* cold as it is (namely, as a
privation). In the latter respect only it is not the idea of cold,
"but something else, which I wrongly take for this privation."

On my proposed reading of the Fourth Replies, Descartes
continues to assume that an idea of **n** might represent
(present) **n** as other than **n** is. One of course then wants to
ask, what *is* it for an idea to be an idea of (say) cold, if it is
*not* to present cold as it is (say, as a privation)?[13]

In view of some recent theories of reference and perception, one might hope for a *causal* account of "referential" or non-presentational representation: an idea, that is, referentially represents its cause (or cause under normal conditions), whatever that might be. Thus, for my idea of cold referentially to represent a certain physical state is just for that idea to be caused—in the "right" way—by that state, whatever it might be. On the hypothesis we have been following out—that cold is a privation—this approach would presumably require accepting the notion of privative causes. This sounds odd, but might in the end be tolerable. (Certainly Descartes does often seem to assume that the external reality "represented" by a sensation may just be the cause of that sensation; and who's to say that negative or inhibitory factors can't reasonably be ascribed causative significance?)

There is a more serious problem with this proposal, however. For Descartes (as I mentioned earlier) thinks that *nonexistents* can be referentially represented. My (materially false) ideas of cold and white are ideas of cold and white, it seems, even if no physical things exist, and hence even if there are no instantiations of these qualities as they really are. I am pessimistic that such "entities" can be cast as "causes."[14]

A similar objection would apply as well if we tried to construe referential representation as *demonstrative*. For according to Descartes I can refer a sensation to "a part of the physical world" which in a quite ordinary sense fails to exist. To mention one of his favorite examples, I can point to where an amputated limb should be, in indicating the "location" of a pain. (So "what is going on *there*" will not always "pick out" the real state of the world which my sensation represents referentially.)[15]

On the whole I suspect that the causal account was influential in Descartes's thought, even if he was unable to develop it fully, to create a theory immune to counter-examples. Beyond this observation, I'm unable further to clarify the hybrid conception of representation I've attributed to Descartes. I can only claim that it, or something like it, does seem necessary to make good sense of his response to Arnauld's objection. Further, as I'll now try to show, this

understanding helps to bring what he says about sensation in
the *Principles* into some kind of alignment with his earlier
remarks.

## 4

Although Descartes does not say directly, in the Third
Meditation, that all "*thoughts*" (as opposed to ideas properly
so called) are "as if of things," his wording does suggest this
position. Some thoughts are *just* "as if images of things";
others have other "forms" *besides*. So, it might seem to follow, Descartes does not wish to admit that there are
"thoughts" that don't have the "of-a-thing" character *at least*.
And he has indeed been interpreted in this way.[16] Works
later than the *Meditations*, however, provide some reason to
question whether this interpretation is correct. I have in mind
his treatment of sensations (again, experiences of pain,
color, odor and sound, etc.) in the *Principles of Philosophy*,
and his account of passive emotions in *Principles* and in the
*Passions of the Soul*. At one time I thought that the discussion of *Principles* I.68-71 indeed suggested a deep change in
Descartes's position on the representationality of sensation.[17]
However, I now think that the change is not so great after
all. If we read the *Principles* passages in light of the
distinction I have just proposed, they come out saying
something at least fairly close to the position on sensation in
the Third Meditation and Fourth Replies. I will try to establish this point first, then move on (in the next section) to
murkier question of whether—or in what sense—Descartes
construes the passive emotions, too, as "representational."

The following statement from I.71 provides the strongest
apparent evidence that Descartes has come to deny that sensations do represent (are as if of things):

> . . . In early childhood our mind was so tightly bound
> to the body that it had no leisure for any other
> thoughts, except only those by which it sensed what
> affected the body: and it did not yet refer these to any-
> thing located outside itself, but only sensed pain where
> something occurred harmful to the body; where some-

> thing beneficial occurred, it felt pleasure; and where
> something affected the body without much harm or
> benefit, for the different parts in which and ways in
> which the body was affected, it had certain different
> sensations, namely those which we call the sensations
> of taste, odor, sound, heat, cold, light, color and the
> like, *which represent nothing located outside thought.*
> (*Principles* I.71; emphasis added)

Later on, Descartes explains, the mind realized that its sensations were caused by external objects, and mistakenly attributed heat, color, odor, etc. to the objects. In doing so it
failed to recognize the different natures of the mere sensations on the one hand, and sizes, shapes, motions and the
like on the other hand: the latter only "were exhibited to it not
as sensations, but as certain things, or modes of things, existing, or at least capable of existing, outside thought."

Yet a little earlier he has indicated, more visibly in keeping
with the Third Meditation, that sensations might be said to
"represent" external states in some very limited sense. The
problem with sensations (he seems to say here) is just that
we "cannot tell" *what* they represent. An inattentive person,
he remarks, may persuade himself that sensations of color or
pain give him some notion of external physical qualities, because he may suppose that there is in the object something
similar to what he experiences;

> but if he examines what it might be, which this sensa-
> tion of color or pain represents, as if existing in the
> colored body or painful part, he will notice that he is
> wholly ignorant of it. (*Principles* I.68)

In line with what I have just proposed about the Fourth
Replies, I suggest that we read these passages as expressing
the following view. First, nothing is *intelligibly presented* to
the mind in ordinary sense experience "of" colors, odors,
and so on. Second, we nevertheless tend to take the presentational content of sense experience to be something real, to
refer *it* to external reality. (The story of how we happen to
do this is different from that found in the *Meditations*,

though, since it does not rely on the claim that "all ideas are as if of things," or the notion of material falsity.) Third, the sensations may correctly be said to have some *referential* representativeness, though what they represent in this sense is wholly indeterminate from their presentational content. They are, in other words, "as if images of things," but wholly *confused* images. This reading is borne out by a remark towards the end of the *Principles*, when Descartes remarks that color, sound, and the like are not distinctly imagined or understood; rather, "their images in our thought are always confused, and we do not know what they are (*semper . . . eorum imagines in cogitatione nostra sunt confusae, nec quidnam illa sint scimus*)" (*Principles* IV.200).[18]

## 5

Descartes's treatment of the passive emotions provides another interesting set of problems for the interpreter of his position on the representationality of thought. In particular, it provides an even harder case than his treatment of sensation in the *Principles* for anyone who would hold that for Descartes any thought is necessarily representative, or involves a representative element.[19]

These days it has become common to hold that emotions are always, or nearly always, partially or even wholly cognitive states, essentially involving representation (presentation) of an object. For example, *fear* can only be understood as a state of the fearing being that essentially involves a judgement that something is dangerous to that being. Descartes is sometimes cited as a proponent of the opposed, erroneous view that emotions are mere feelings (perhaps "contingently" connected with an object which causes them).[20]

This interpretation may well seem to conflict directly with the statement from the Third Meditation that I quoted at the outset, in which Descartes mentions fear in particular, and the "affects" in general, as examples of "thoughts" which "always" include the apprehension of some "subject" of the thought, but also have "other forms besides."[21] But of course we cannot immediately exclude the possibility that

Descartes changed his view about the affects, when he came to consider these states of mind more systematically in later works.

In the *Passions*, too, however, Descartes very often phrases his accounts of the various different passive emotions in terms of the soul's responses to objects it thinks of (responses caused and "fortified" by particular physiological changes). Here are a few examples:

*Wonder*
When the first encounter with some object surprises us, and we judge it to be novel, or very different from that which we knew before . . . , that causes us to wonder at it and be astonished by it. (II.53)

*Love and Hatred*
. . . [W]hen a thing is represented to us as good for us, that is, as beneficial to us, that makes us have Love for it; and when it is represented as bad or harmful, that excites Hatred in us. (II.56)

*Concerning Pity*
Pity is a type of Sadness, mixed with Love or good will toward those whom we see suffer something bad, which we consider them not to deserve. Thus it is contrary to Envy, because of its object, and to Mockery, because it considers [the object] in another way. (III.185)

I will not try to settle here the question, just how far such passages go towards establishing that Descartes does think of passive emotions as *typically* tied, in a definitional or "non-contingent" way with mental presentations of (putative) external objects. (Clearly they do go *some* way to supporting such a reading.) What must be noted is that, first, Descartes explicitly acknowledges in both the *Passions* and *Principles* the existence of emotions that *lack*, so to speak, objective content. For instance, thick and sluggish blood produces a feeling of sadness, "although [the soul] perhaps does not know why it should be sad" (*Principles* IV.190; cf. *Passions*

II.51). Further, in both works, Descartes does characterize passive emotions as feelings or "sensations" (*sensus, sentiments*), regardless of whether or not they include the thought of an object. Unlike the sensations of color, taste, etc., and even hunger and thirst, they are not "referred" to material reality: rather they are referred only, or particularly, to the soul (*Passions* I.23-25; 27; cf. *Principles* IV.189-90). And here I take that expression to mean that they are *attributed* to that in which, as thoughts, they occur; in this respect they do not refer beyond themselves. Does the fact that the passions actually present themselves as *internal states of the soul*—are not *referred to objects*, combined with the fact that some of them do not even require the conscious *presentation of objects*, show that this category of "thoughts," at least, includes some that have no representative aspect at all? Is there any use in invoking here the distinction between presentation and reference?

The objectless internal sensations probably do provide the best basis for questioning whether Descartes conceives thought as necessarily, or invariably, representational.[22] I doubt, though, that they provide a conclusive counter-example. My main reservation has to do with the fact that Descartes characterizes the internal sensations, like the external ones, as "confused thoughts" or "confused and obscure perceptions" (*Principles* IV.190; *Passions* I.27-8). If to call "external" sensations "confused" is to suggest (as Descartes does in the *Principles*) that they referentially represent something, but do not intelligibly present it, perhaps we should understand the term in the same sense, when it's used of the sensations that he calls "internal" in the *Passions*. Perhaps, for instance, an "objectless" sadness referentially represents and confusedly presents a bad condition of our own blood, even though the presentation is *so* confused that even the *sense* of external reference is lost. (This sort of sadness must be distinguished, of course, from the sadness we feel when it occurs to us *that* our blood may be diseased).[23]

As far as I know, there is no passage that directly confirms such a reading—and none that refutes it, either.[24] However, a remark from a late (February, 1647) letter to Chanut tells, I think, somewhat in favor of the view I am suggesting—that even the "objectless" affects are in some degenerate sense representations of physiological conditions. (It also provides an interesting insight into Descartes's conception of the relation between the sensational and "cognitive" components of emotion where both are in fact present.) Descartes is discussing the relation between rational love (such as love of God or of knowledge), which can occur wholly independently of any embodiment, and sensuous love. He writes:

> [Sensual love] is nothing but a confused thought, excited in the soul by some motion of the nerves, which disposes it to the other, clearer thought which constitutes rational love. Just as in thirst the sensation of dryness in the throat is a confused thought which disposes us to the desire for drink, but is not that desire itself; so, in love a mysterious heat is felt around the heart, and a great abundance of blood in the lungs, which make us open our arms as if to embrace something, and this makes the soul inclined to join itself voluntarily to the object which is present. But *the thought by which the soul feels the heat* is different from the thought which joins it to this object; and it even sometimes happens that this sensation of love occurs in us without our will being impelled to love anything, because we do not discover any object we think worthy of it. (To Chanut, February, 1647; AT IV, 602-3; emphasis added.)

My conclusion, then, is that it is possible to defend attributing to Descartes a thoroughgoing conception of "thought" as representational, even down to the hardest case, the objectless passions. But the case gets more and more tenuous— and doubtless changes character—as one progresses from ordinary thoughts about this or that, to the treatment of sensation in Meditation III, to the treatment of sensation in later works, and finally to the treatment of the sensuous component in emotion—particularly the objectless affects.

## NOTES

1  In my book, *Descartes* (London: Routledge & Kegan Paul, 1978), I uncharitably dismissed Descartes's response as "a model of confusion confounded." (I discuss the Arnauld-Descartes exchange on representation, and related issues, at pp. 100-119.) The present account is intended to supplement, and on some points correct, that earlier one. See also Anthony Kenny, "Descartes on Ideas," in Doney, *Descartes: A Collection of Critical Essays* (Garden City, NY: Doubleday, 1967), for a detailed, highly critical treatment of aspects of Descartes's position dealt with in the present paper. (Kenny's discussion also forms a part of his book, *Descartes* (New York; Random House, 1968).)

   Some of the same ground is covered by Alan Gewirth in his well-known paper "Clearness and Distinctness in Descartes," also in Doney (but originally published in 1943). My approach resembles Gewirth's in being primarily constructive, rather than critical, but I try out different distinctions and terminology. For another related discussion see Vere Chappell, "The Theory of Ideas" in A. Rorty, *Essays on Descartes' Meditations* (Berkeley: University of California Press, 1986). (Chappell focuses on a passage from the Preface to the *Meditations* in which Descartes says that an 'idea' in one sense is a representing entity; in another sense 'idea' is what is represented—i.e. a represented content. I focus on other passages, in which (as Chappell grants) Descartes appears straightforwardly to assume that *what* ideas normally represent are simply things, states, etc.)

2  Much of what I will say corresponds quite closely to views expressed by Jean-Marie Beyssade in "Descartes on Material Falsity"—a paper read to the April, 1989 conference on "Ideas" in early modern philosophy, the University of Iowa, Iowa City. What I see as a convergence in our viewpoints is, however, coincidental: we did not know of each other's recent work on this subject in advance of preparing our respective essays.

3  I translate *'tanquam'* awkwardly as 'as if' in order to be able to translate it the same way in all contexts. ('Like', for instance, wouldn't work under this condition: Descartes's claim that "all ideas are *tanquam rerum*" (see below) can be translated "all ideas are as if of things," but (obviously) not "all ideas are like things."

4  The "difference" in question here is not individuation of one idea from another, but rather difference of status on a three-tiered scale of "degree of (objective) reality": ideas which represent—or "exhibit"—substances stand higher than those which represent modes, and one that represents God, or infinite substance, above those representing only finite substances.

5  AT VII, 46, 64. In *Descartes* (*op. cit.*, pp. 107-8) I suggest that a "real thing" in the sense relevant here is a possible existent, noting Descartes's claim (AT VII, 116) that possible existence is contained in the "concept or idea" of whatever is clearly and distinctly conceived. Unfortunately this suggestion doesn't help with the problem, touched on briefly below, of how a "non-thing" can be *represented*.

6  For what it's worth, Descartes does remark later in the Third Meditation that he "perceives" rest and darkness by the "negation" of motion and light (respectively) (AT VII, 45). Presumably, then, rest and darkness are privations, and are perceived by Descartes as privations. Either this does not count as having an idea of a non-thing that represents it as a non-thing, or Descartes is here violating the principle that all ideas are "as if of things." My own view is that Descartes *should* allow that the *content* of a distinct idea can be a privation, but not a non-thing. (I believe the underlying conception of reality is—or is tied to—distinct conceivability, and I take it that Descartes needs to be able to say that (relative) rest as well as motion is a distinctly conceivable physical state.) In other words, he should not conflate the two terms. There can be no doubt that he does, however.

7  I will not be able to discuss all of Arnauld's objections, however. Among the points that I will not touch on here is his claim that allowing positive content to an idea which Descartes allows might "arise from nothing" (as he says in passing about ideas of sensible qualities) violates Descartes's principle that an idea's "objective reality" requires a cause of at least equal "formal reality." I have discussed this issue at length in my book *Descartes* (*op. cit.*, ch. 3).

8  In the course of his exposition Arnauld draws some relevant morals from Descartes's argument, later in the Third Meditation, that the idea of God, as an infinitely perfect being, cannot but be true. I omit consideration of these remarks in the interest of keeping the discussion reasonably focused.

9   See note 5, above.
10  I don't claim either that the notion of presentational represen-
    tation is free of problems. Roughly, though, it coincides with
    what the mind takes itself to be aware of. (If I think I see a
    tanager, then I can be ascribed a presentational representation
    of a tanager, regardless of what may actually be going on in
    the world or (otherwise) in me.) As Peter Markie has sug-
    gested to me, the notion may be close to that of "narrow con-
    tent" in the jargon of contemporary philosophy of mind.
11  In the First Replies Descartes accepts that the idea of the sun
    "is the sun itself existing in the understanding." He makes
    clear, however, that the content existing in the understanding
    has "existing in the understanding" as an intrinsic denomina-
    tion, whereas the sun in the heavens is only extrinsically re-
    lated to the mind. He does not there address the question
    whether (or under what circumstances) a *misrepresentation* of
    the sun can count as "the sun itself existing in the understand-
    ing."
12  Later in the paragraph (AT VII, 234) Descartes says that
    "confused ideas coming from the senses," such as the ideas of
    color and of cold, "exhibit nothing real." I take him to mean
    that what is exhibited—namely the sensation itself—is not, as
    presented or exhibited, something real. This is the same posi-
    tion he takes in the *Principles*, which I discuss in the next sec-
    tion.
13  Cf. Kenny, "Descartes on Ideas," *op. cit.*, p. 245.
14  At the beginning of Meditation VI Descartes defends the claim
    that he can't form in imagination the idea of a chiliagon, by
    noting that,
        If I . . . want to think of a chiliagon, . . . I well under-
        stand this to be a figure consisting of a thousand sides, as
        I understand a triangle to be a figure consisting of three;
        but I do not in the same way imagine those thousand
        sides, or intuit them as if present. And although, because
        I am in the habit of always imagining something, when I
        think of a corporeal thing, I perhaps represent some figure
        confusedly to myself, it is nevertheless obvious that this
        is not a chiliagon, because it is in no respect different
        from what I also represent to myself, if I should think of a
        myriagon or some other figure with more sides. (AT VII,
        72)

What interests me in this passage is the suggestion that an "idea" (sc. in imagination) of a chiliagon, to be an idea of a chiliagon, has to be distinguishable (so to speak by inspection) from an idea of a myriagon. This suggests that such an idea's referentially representing a *does* depend on the idea's somehow *presentationally* exhibiting a. At present I regard this passage as presenting a problem for the interpretation of Descartes that I'm trying to support.

15 Calvin Normore stressed the phantom limb case as a problem for my proposed reading, in commenting on an earlier version of the paper. I'm not at all sure that the issue I deal with here captures the full force of his objection.

16 Norman Malcolm, "Thoughtless Brutes," Presidential Address delivered before the Sixty-ninth Annual Eastern Meeting of the American Philosophical Association, December 28, 1972; Alan Donagan, *Spinoza* (Chicago: University of Chicago Press, 1988), pp. 37-38.

17 See *Descartes, op. cit.*, pp. 116-19.

18 Sometimes Descartes talks of external qualities that give rise to sensations as the "objects" of the sensations: cf. *Principles* I.194 (F.v.); *Le Monde* (AT XI, 5): " . . . if the sense of hearing brought (*rapportoit*) to our thought the true image of its object, it would have to be the case that it made us conceive the movement of the parts of the air which tremble against our ears at the time, rather than making us conceive sound."

19 I take it to be clear that Descartes does regard the active or "interior" emotions—those caused in the soul by the soul itself—as always having an "object."

20 See, for instance, the editors' introduction to *What is an Emotion*, edited by Cheshire Calhoun and Robert C. Solomon (New York: Oxford University Press, 1984), pp. 10-11.

My discussion of the *Passions* has benefitted from, and in places follows rather closely, a paper by Ronald A. Nash, which as far as I know is not yet published. Because I haven't seen a final version of his paper, I won't try to comment in more detail on the relation of our views at this time.

21 I am assuming that, as traditional interpretation holds, "subject" here means "object" which a thought is "of," rather than subject to which it belongs. See, though, Third Replies, AT VII, 175, where "subject of a thought" has to be understood in the latter sense.

22   In the language of the Third Meditation, we could say that
     they are *mere* forms, detached from ideas.
23   Does this reading imply that the objectless affects are, after all,
     themselves *ideas*? I think I have to say yes to this question
     (which was brought to my attention by Nydia Lara), though I
     acknowledge that Descartes himself does not (as far as I
     know) call them ideas; and also that construing them as such
     creates problems for the Third Meditation distinction between
     ideas and "other forms" that merely attach (so to speak) to
     ideas.
24   William Lyons, while identifying Descartes as a proponent of
     "the feeling theory" of the emotions, evidently takes *Passions*
     I.36 to show that Descartes regarded the passions as *percep-
     tions of* physiological states (*Emotion* (Cambridge: Cambridge
     University Press, 1980), pp. 2-4). I think that construing
     emotions as "perceptions" of anything at all is at odds with
     construing them as simply "feelings," but (more to the point in
     the present context) I think Lyons' reading of *Passions* I.36 is
     untenable. *There* Descartes says only that certain physiological
     conditions are "ordained by nature to make" the soul experi-
     ence certain passions.

# SPINOZA AND DESCARTES AND THE EXISTENCE OF EXTENDED SUBSTANCE

*R. S. Woolhouse*


According to Descartes a substance has "one principal property which constitutes its nature and essence";[1] and there are two such principal properties for him: extension, and thought. "[E]xtension in length, breadth and depth constitutes the nature of corporeal substance; and thought constitutes the nature of thinking substance" (*Principles* I.53 (CSM I, 210)). This gives two kinds of substance and, for Descartes, any particular substance must be of one, and only one, of these two kinds: either thinking substance (or mind), or extended substance (or corporeal substance, or body).

There are, in Descartes's view, many instances of thinking substance, many minds. Most of these are our minds, or ourselves, finite minds dependent for their existence on God their creator. But one of them is God himself, who is also the only uncreated substance, the only substance which "exists in such a way as to depend on no other thing for its existence" (*Principles* I.51 (CSM I, 210)).

It is in some ways different with extended substance. One difference is that there is no uncreated extended substance. The extended corporeal world, of our bodies and those bodies around us, is created by God and, as Descartes says on more than one occasion, there is nothing corporeal about God, the only uncreated substance.[2]

Another difference is that although there are many minds there are not many extended substances. What we might think of as separate corporeal substances—our own bodies

23

and those of others, the trees and animals around us—are
not so. They are merely parts of the extended corporeal substance that God created. Whether one should say that
'extended substance' is a count term (as is 'thinking substance') and that there is "*one* extended substance," or
whether one should say it is a mass term and that there is just
"extended substance" is uncertain. I think that for Descartes,
as indeed for Spinoza, it strictly is the latter. But both he and
Spinoza do use it in both ways, and I shall follow them in
this (I hope harmless) unclarity.

There is a considerable consensus that Descartes and
Spinoza can be compared and contrasted as follows. Like
Descartes, Spinoza thinks in terms of principal properties
(though he calls them "attributes") which constitute the
essence of substance. Like Descartes, Spinoza holds that
God exists, is a substance, and is a thinking substance. Like
Descartes, Spinoza holds that there is one and only one extended substance; for, with Descartes, Spinoza holds that
our bodies and the things that surround them are not themselves extended substances but rather modes of extended
substance.

But Spinoza does not agree with Descartes that there are
any thinking substances other than God. What for Descartes
are finite created thinking substances, i.e., ourselves, or our
own minds, are, for Spinoza, modes of the one thinking
substance. That is to say, Spinoza does for mental substance, as well as for extended substance, what Descartes
does for extended substance.

Furthermore, while agreeing with Descartes that God exists, is a substance, and is a thinking substance, and while
agreeing with him that there is one and only one extended
substance, Spinoza does not agree that the one and only one
extended substance is a different substance from God,
Spinoza's one thinking substance. Spinoza holds that there
is one and only one substance, which is God; and that this
one substance is both an extended substance and a thinking
substance.[3]

Now having in mind the Cartesian idea that the one extended substance is the corporeal world, and noting that for
Spinoza God is the one extended substance, it is tempting to

do two associated things. First, to identify Spinoza's extended substance and Descartes's extended substance; and, second, to take Spinoza's view to be that the corporeal world is the one extended substance and is God.

H. H. Joachim does both of these things when he writes: "Spinoza follows Descartes . . . in calling the corporeal or material universe 'res extensa'. But the 'res extensa' is no creation of God: it is God."[4] This says that Spinoza's extended substance is Descartes's extended substance, and is the corporeal world; and also says that for Spinoza this extended substance is God. The second idea is repeated when Joachim goes on to say that Spinoza's "God . . . is . . . an extended thing—a corporeal universe."[5]

The idea that Spinoza identifies his extended substance, his God, with the corporeal extended world, goes back to his own time and has persisted since then. According to Malebranche, "not being able to understand the divine power and how God by his will alone could create the universe, [Spinoza] has taken this universe for his God," while according to John Harris, one of the early Boyle lecturers, Spinoza holds "that the Deity is the whole Mass of Beings or of Matter in the Universe."[6] Similarly Samuel Clarke, another Boyle lecturer, said that "*Spinoza* . . . taught that there is no Difference of Substances, but that the whole and every Part of *the Material World* is a Necessarily-existing Being; and that there is no other God, but the Universe."[7]

Frederick Pollock, in the last century, said that for Spinoza the "world of things extended in space . . . is . . . Substance perceived under the Attribute of Extension";[8] William Grant, in this century, that Spinoza "made extension (space), matter, and God one . . . [and] conflated God, extension, matter, and space";[9] and, most recently, Roger Scruton said that Spinoza has the ideas that "God is not distinct from the world but identical with it" and that "[n]othing exists save the one substance . . . which constitutes the world."[10]

Despite this long and continuing tradition it seems to me that it is quite wrong to identify Spinoza's extended substance with Descartes's extended substance and hence with the extended corporeal world. Moreover, since Spinoza's

God undoubtedly is his extended substance, it is equally wrong to identify Spinoza's God with the extended corporeal world. Spinoza's God, his extended substance, is quite other than Descartes's extended substance, the extended corporeal world.

Though it does not explicitly discuss it as such, Jonathan Bennett's *Study of Spinoza's Ethics*[11] has a position on this matter. As we might have expected from the power and hard-edged clarity of the book, the position is not an idle adoption but is written-in and enmeshed with others. The result is that, beyond providing another example of the view I aim to reject, Bennett provides it as part of a consistent and worked-out picture.

At first sight it may not seem that Bennett's Spinoza does identify his one extended substance, his God, with the corporeal world. Spinoza, it first appears, "is committed to agreeing that space is the one extended substance, though he does not put it quite like that and for all I know would decline to do so . . . [and] would certainly refuse to say that space is God" (*Study*, p. 91). But one step in Bennett's proof that Spinoza says that space is extended substance is that for Spinoza, as for Descartes, space and body or matter do not really differ (*Study*, p. 101). And Spinoza's refusal to say that space is God is inferred from the idea that 'space' is Spinoza's name for his single substance "when it is thought of as extended," while 'God' is a name for it "when it is not being thought of under one attribute in particular" (*Study*, p. 91).

Since this idea, that Spinoza's God is to be identified with the extended corporeal world, and so (in effect) with Cartesian extended substance, is contemporary with Spinoza himself we know his own reaction to it. It was one of forthright rejection.

In 1671 Lambert de Velthuysen, future author of a book critical of Spinoza's *Ethics*, wrote to Jacob Ostens giving, as he had been asked, his opinion of the *Tractatus Theologico-Politicus*. In this work, said Velthuysen,

> all things are declared to emanate from God with inevitable necessity, or rather, . . . he declares that this

whole universe is God . . . . For I fear that our author
is not very far removed from this opinion; at least there
is not much difference between declaring that all things
emanate necessarily from the nature of God and that
the Universe itself is God.[12]

Velthuysen's letter quickly passed from Ostens to Spinoza
himself, and though in reply to Ostens Spinoza does not explain what the difference is between what he thinks (that
things *emanate from* God) and what Velthuysen says he
thinks (that they *are* God) he is caustically certain that there
is one. Inviting Ostens to pass this issue by and to consider
instead some further things which Velthuysen "no less spite-
fully adds" and which "you will certainly not find anywhere
in my Treatise," Spinoza says "I do not here inquire why it
is the same, or not very different, to assert that all things emanate necessarily from the nature of God, and that the universe is God" (Ep 43, W 257).

   In correspondence four or five years later there is a similarly forthright rejection of the idea that God, Spinoza's extended substance, is to be identified with the corporeal universe. In various letters Henry Oldenburg cautioned Spinoza
not to proceed with his plan to publish the *Ethics*. The
*Tractatus Theologico-Politicus* had, Oldenburg said, already
led people to suppose that Spinoza's philosophical ideas are
harmful to religion. In response to Spinoza's request "to
point out to me the passages in the *Tractatus Theologico-
Politicus* which have caused uneasiness to learned men" (Ep
68, W 335), he said that in the first place are "those which
seem to speak ambiguously about God and Nature; many are
of opinion that you have confused these two" (Ep 71, W
340). Spinoza's reaction could hardly be clearer: "those who
think that the *Tractatus Theologico-Politicus* rests on this,
namely, that God and Nature (by which they mean a certain
mass, or corporeal matter) are one and the same, are entirely
mistaken" (Ep 73, W 343).

   At least one important thing that lies behind the mistaken
idea that Spinoza does not distinguish God, or the one extended substance, from the corporeal world is his rejection
of the Cartesian view that God is the transitive cause of the

corporeal world.[13] In Descartes's case, because of the nature
of transitive causation, and because his God is not corporeal,
it seems obvious that there is a difference between God and
the corporeal world. But Spinoza's own positive view, that
God is an immanent cause, fogs the difference between the
cause and the effect, a fogginess exacerbated by the fact that
Spinoza's God, as the cause of the extended corporeal
world, is itself an extended corporeal substance (not a purely
thinking substance, as is Descartes's) (E IP3D).

At any rate, it is apparent that it was the obscurity of the
causal relation between Spinoza's God and the corporeal
world that led Velthuysen to think that Spinoza identifies the
two. It is quite apparent, too, that this lay behind the exchange with Oldenburg also. For, in leading up to the just
quoted forthright denial that God is to be identified with the
corporeal world, Spinoza explains that "I hold an opinion
about God and Nature very different from that which
Modern Christians are wont to defend." "I maintain," he
says, "that God is, as they say, the immanent cause of all
things, but not the transitive cause . . . I assert that all things
live and move in God" (Ep 73, W 343).

It follows, of course, that one thing that needs to come
out of my suggestion that it is a mistake to identify Spinoza's
extended substance with Descartes's extended substance
(and so with the corporeal world) is something that will explain or throw light on Spinoza's idea that God (and God *as
extended*) is the immanent cause of the extended corporeal
world. I will not, however, say anything about this here.

So Spinoza's own explicit testimony encourages my idea
that it is a mistake to identify his extended substance with
Descartes's extended substance, the extended corporeal
world. My account of just what that suggested mistake is is
that it rests on failing to realise that the ways in which the
extended substances of Descartes and Spinoza exist, what
might be called called their "modes of existence," are radically different. I suggest that when Descartes says "God exists," and "(an) extended substance exists" he means something radically different from what Spinoza means when *he*
says "God exists," and "(an) extended substance exists."

Propositions about the existence of substance or of God mean something quite different for each of them.[14]

What I have in mind can be explained by reference to some ideas and distinctions to be found in Descartes and Leibniz. They are there in Spinoza too, and it might seem needlessly indirect to look at Descartes and Leibniz first. But in Spinoza they are so closely bound up with the very point to be made that it will be better to approach from the side.

In the *Fifth Meditation* Descartes says that "I find within me countless ideas of things which even though they may not exist anywhere outside me still cannot be called nothing; for . . . they are not my invention but have their own true and immutable natures." He goes on to say that "[w]hen, for example, I imagine a triangle, even if perhaps no such figure exists, or has ever existed, anywhere outside my thought, there is still a determinate nature, or essence, or form of the triangle which is immutable and eternal, and not invented by me or dependent on my mind" (CSM II, 44-45).

I take it that the phrases 'exist outside me' and 'exist outside my thought' which occur in this passage mean the same and that they mean "exist in the corporeal world"; so, for there to be no triangle "existing outside me or my thought" is for there to be no triangular thing or triangular arrangement of things in the corporeal world.[15] Given this, we might think that the other side of the contrast is "inside my thought," and that therefore the contrast is between the corporeal instantiation of a triangle and the mental idea of one. But this is not so. The "essence, nature, form" of a triangle is not a mental idea, but is itself something of which we can have an idea. This is clear from the just-quoted passage in the *Fifth Meditation* where Descartes talks of "ideas of things which . . . cannot be called nothing . . . [and] are not my invention but have their own true and immutable natures."

My understanding of Descartes here agrees with that of Kenny, who also points out that there are ideas to which there are no corresponding natures.[16] That is there are, as Descartes says, "ideas which do not contain true and immutable natures but merely ones which are invented and put together by the intellect."[17] Such ideas of ones "own invention" are those of a siren, or a hippogriff or a winged horse (CSM II, 26). At least some of these fictitious ideas will be ones to which it is impossible that there correspond any natures. To take an example from Leibniz, we may think that there is such a thing as a regular ten-faced solid but we would be wrong (NE 293). On the other hand, presumably there are natures to which there are no corresponding ideas: certainly I have not always had an idea of the true and immutable nature of a triangle.

Descartes's distinction between eternal and immutable natures which have a kind of existence different from that of their instantiations in the corporeal world can be found in Leibniz. Suggesting that propositions about the existence of some thing should not all be understood in the same way, for some of them are "essential" and some "existential," Leibniz says that "'A man liable to sin exists', i.e. is actually an entity" is existential, whereas 'A plane figure having a constant relation to some one point exists' is essential. As a gloss on the second, the essential one, he says "I say 'exists': that is, it can be understood, it can be conceived, that among various figures there is one which also has this nature, just as if I were to say 'A plane figure having a constant relation to some one point is an entity or thing."[18] So for it to be true that a man liable to sin exists (understanding this existentially), there has actually to be in the corporeal world some man who is liable to sin. For it to be true that a plane figure having a constant relation to some one point exists (understanding this essentially) there need not actually be in the corporeal world some circular thing or circular arrangement of things. For the circle to exist it is sufficient that geometrical considerations allow of the possibility of things being figured in that way. The distinction Leibniz makes here between two kinds of existence is made elsewhere too, as in the *New Essays* where an "essence" is distinguished from a "thing [which] actually occurs in the world" (NE 293-94).

Just as with Descartes's "natures" so with Leibniz's "everlasting essences" (NE 296) we should be careful not to understand them as our *ideas* of instantiations of those natures or essences in the corporeal world. They are, as he says, "independent of our thinking" (NE 293). We can have ideas which we mistakenly think correspond to an essence, as when "something . . . appeared to be . . . [an essence] but really is not—as that of a regular decahedron, a regular solid bounded by ten planes or surfaces, would be" (NE 293) or, "for example when the parallelism of parabolas it contemplated, through the delusion that two parabolas can be found which are parallel to one another, like two straight lines or two circles."[19] On the other hand we can come to form ideas of already existing essences, "the inventor's idea . . . has as its archetype a real possibility, or a divine idea" (NE 268).

There is more to be said about the mode of existence of Descartes's and Leibniz's "essences" or "natures." As this last quotation from Leibniz indicates, their existence (at least for him) is, as "divine ideas", in God's mind. But it will be best to have got closer to Spinoza before returning to this.

This distinction between the mode of existence of essences or natures, and that of instantiations or embodiments of these natures, raises this question: When Descartes and Spinoza each say "God exists" or "extended substance exists" are they to be understood "existentially," in analogy with Leibniz's "a man liable to sin exists"; or are they to be understood "essentially," in analogy with Leibniz's "a figure bearing a constant relation to some one point exists"?

When *Descartes* says these things it is plain that *he* is to be understood "existentially". His ontological proof of the existence of God draws a parallel between the immutable nature or essence of God, and that of a triangle, and aims to show that that nature or essence is instantiated at least once (*Principles* I.14 (CSM I, 197-98)). The Divine essence differs from all others, of course, in that it alone is necessarily instantiated; God's existence differs from that of all other things in that it alone is necessary existence. But, necessary though it be, Descartes's God is like a corporeal triangle in being the instantiation of an immutable essence or nature.

Descartes similarly intends his claim that "(an) extended substance exists" as an existential one. The mode of existence of his extended substance is like that of an instantiation of an immutable nature or essence. In the *Principles* there is clearly a distinction between our having a "clear and distinct perception of, some kind of matter, which is extended in length, breadth and depth" and "there exist[ing] something extended in length, breadth, and depth . . . that we call 'body' or 'matter'."[20]

When Spinoza says these things the case is, I suggest, quite different. That is what my claim, that Spinoza's extended substance or his God is not to be identified with Descartes's extended substance, the extended corporeal world, is based on. When Spinoza says that "God exists" or "extended substance exists" *he*, unlike Descartes, is *not* to be understood "existentially". *He*, unlike Descartes, is *not* asserting the existence of the instantiation of certain natures or essences. On the contrary, he is to be understood essentially, as saying something more like Leibniz's "a figure of a constant relation to some one point exists" than like Leibniz's "a man liable to sin exists." The point could, provisionally but not quite accurately, be put by saying that in asserting the existence of extended substance or of God Spinoza is asserting the existence of a nature or essence itself.[21]

Quite evidently, this understanding of Spinoza runs completely counter to the usual one. We saw earlier how common is the idea that Spinoza's extended substance is to be identified with Descartes's extended substance, and we have just seen that Descartes's extended substance exists as the instantiation of a nature. We have just seen also that Descartes's God exists as the instantiation of a nature, and Bennett provides a pleasingly explicit example of the view against which I want to argue, that this is how Spinoza's God exists too. Referring to an earlier discussion of Frege's "third realm" (roughly, the realm of Cartesian and Leibnizian essences and natures), he says of Spinoza's God that it is "a concrete object—something *other than* an inhabitant of the third realm" (*Study*, p. 70; my emphasis); then, a few pages later, he says that Spinoza's single substance is something which exists as the necessary instantiation of a nature (*Study*, pp. 73, 74).

There is considerable irony in the fact that, if I am right, Descartes's God is, as the instantiation of an essence, more like the extended world than Spinoza's is. But why should we understand Spinoza in the way I suggest? Surely, it might be objected, when he says that "[i]t pertains to the nature of a substance to exist", that "its essence necesarily involves existence" (E IP7 (CS 412)), and that God is something "to whose nature it pertains to exist, or (what is the same) from whose definition it follows that he exists" (IP19 (CS 428)), he means, along with Descartes, that the existence of substance or of God is as the (necessary) instantiation of a nature or essence. I will not reply to this directly, though I hope that what I have to say will encourage a fresh and sideways look at these remarks. Equally I will do no more than merely note that Spinoza sometimes puts what must be the same point in ways more obviously friendly to my suggestion that his God or substance are more like essences or natures themselves than like instantiations of them. He says, for example, that what "constitutes God's essence . . . constitutes his existence" and that "God's existence, like his essence, is an eternal truth."22 Furthermore, other than pointing it out I will take no advantage of Bennett's report (*Study*, p. 74) of the "minor nuisance" of ID1 that it speaks of substance as "'that whose nature cannot be conceived except as *existing*', when Spinoza must surely mean 'that whose nature cannot be conceived except as *instantiated*'," and of the "same mishap" in IP7 and elsewhere. Instead I shall consider what he says in various places where he warns us against falling into the supposition that the kind of existence substances have is the same as that of modes (which are, for him, instantiations of essences).

One such place is the letter of 1663 "On the Nature of the Infinite." Here Spinoza says that he "conceive[s] the existence of Substance to be entirely different from the existence of Modes" (Ep 12 (CS 202)). The suggestion I am going to make, as to how to read Spinoza as saying that modes exist as the instantiation of an essence or nature, while substances exist rather as essences or natures themselves do, certainly does not rule out that Spinoza has in mind what he later says in the *Ethics*, namely that substances exist in themselves and modes exist in substances.23 And it certainly does not rule out that he has in mind that substances exist necessarily and modes do not. On the contrary I think it is plain that he does have these things in mind. But the fact that these things, particularly the latter, have been read so as to be part of the usual idea that Spinoza's extended substance, is, like Descartes's, the instantiation of a nature, does not mean that they cannot be read so as to be part of my rejection of that idea.

The difference between the existence of substance and the existence of modes, as Spinoza explains it to his correspondent Ludwig Meyer, is connected with the difference between "eternity" and "duration." The way in which modes exist is explained by the notion of duration; whereas the way in which substance exists is explained in terms of eternity.

At the beginning of the *Ethics* "eternal existence" is said to be existence which "cannot be explained by duration or time, even if the duration is conceived to be without beginning or end" (ID8 (CS 409)). This clearly means that eternal existence does not entail and is inconsistent with existence of a finite limited duration. But does it further mean that eternal existence does not entail and is actually inconsistent with existence of an unlimited duration, one without beginning and end? According to Bennett it does not (*Study*, p. 204-5). He says that Spinoza does not mean that being eternal does not entail and is even inconsistent with being temporally unlimited or sempiternal; he means that being eternal is not *merely* being sempiternal. He means that being eternal is being *necessarily* sempiternal.[24]

Both in this same passage of the *Ethics* and elsewhere,[25] eternal existence, the existence which pertains to substance, is related to existence which follows from the definition of the thing. Bennett takes this to mean that eternally existing is "having a nature which absolutely must be instantiated" (*Study*, p. 204). This tesselates nicely both with his understanding of 'being eternal' as being necessarily sempiternal, and with his view that Spinoza's substance exists as the necessary instantiation of a nature.

Bennett concedes that in the explanation of God's eternity given in the *Metaphysical Thoughts* (CS 316f) Spinoza means by "eternity" not something which entails sempiternity but something which is not such as to afford a foothold for temporal concepts. I say he "concedes," for this, which Wolfson calls the Platonic conception of eternity, is of course the usual view of what Spinoza intends in the *Ethics* too.[26] But, just as his view of what Spinoza means in the *Ethics* by eternity is all of a piece with his understanding of Spinoza's substance as the (necessary) instantiation of a nature, so the usual view of Spinoza's eternity fits with my understanding of substance as akin to a nature or essence itself. Though I think its parts are wrong Bennett's account is a crafted whole which does not combine an understanding of Spinoza's eternal substance as atemporal with an understanding of it as the instantiation of a nature.

As a total picture, mine gets plausibility from the fact that in his explanation of eternity Spinoza explicitly says that the eternal existence which substance has, the existence which follows necessarily from the definition alone of the eternal thing is "conceived as an eternal truth", just "like the essence of a thing" is (ID8 (CS 409)). There are similar passages at IP19 and IP20C2 where God's existence and his essence are said to be eternal truths; and at IP17S where the essences of other things, such as a man, are said to be eternal truths. I take these to mean that the kind of existence God has is the kind that essences have. Even if they say that God necessarily exists or that 'God exists' is a necessary truth we don't (since 'exists' doesn't have to mean "exists as the instantiation of an essence") have to mean that God exists as the necessary instantiation of an essence.

So far I have borrowed a distinction, from Descartes and Leibniz, between the existence of essences and the existence of instantiations of essences; and I have gone a little way towards supporting the suggestion that when Spinoza says that extended substance and God exist he means they exist rather as essences do, certainly not as instantiations of essences. In effect, then, the distinction between the two kinds of existence has been brought to bear on Spinoza from the outside. So, besides needing to go further in supporting my suggestion, the direction in which it would be best to go is one which brings the distinction to bear on Spinoza from the inside. Any further evidence for my reading of Spinoza will be of greater weight if it shows Spinoza himself recognising the distinction Descartes and Leibniz made and giving the same kind of weight and significance to it that they do.

As a start of a move in that direction something more needs to be seen about the mode of existence of immutable natures and essences as understood by Descartes and Leibniz. Such essences, we saw, have an existence independent of any instantiation they might have in the corporeal world, and independent of the human mind; and we finally had a brief glimpse of the fact that, for Leibniz at any rate, the existence they have is in relation to God—they are, as he says, "divine ideas." We must now return to that briefly noted point.

In his *Objections* to the *Meditations* Gassendi questions Descartes about his immutable, eternal essences and natures and suggests, first, that "it seems very hard to propose that there is any 'immutable and eternal nature' apart from almighty God";[27] and second, that Descartes has no need of them. Our idea of a triangle, Gassendi suggests, is derived from our observations of certain existent things in the world and not from an immutable nature. To the second point Descartes replies that he doesn't agree "that the ideas of these figures ever came into our mind via the senses";[28] and to the first that "I do not think that the essences of things, and the mathematical truths which we can know concerning them, are independent of God."[29] And then, in writing to Mersenne, he says "The mathematical truths which you call eternal . . . depend on . . . [God] entirely no less than the rest of his creatures" (15 April 1630 (K 11)).

The theme of immutable natures and essences having an existence in relation to God carries through into Leibniz according to whom "God is the source not only of existences but also of essences, in so far as they are real."[30] But there are differences. For one thing, according to Descartes it is a matter of God's choice that eternal truths are as they are. "[J]ust as He [God] was free not to create the world, so He was no less free to make it untrue that all the lines drawn from the centre of a circle to its circumference are equal."[31] According to Leibniz, however, they depend on God's understanding only and not also on his will. "We must not . . .

imagine . . . that because the eternal truths are dependent on God, they are therefore arbitrary and depend on his will, as Descartes seems to have thought . . . . [N]ecessary truths depend solely on his understanding, of which they are the internal object."[32] As Leibniz rhetorically asks: "is it by the will of God . . . or is it not rather by the nature of numbers, that certain numbers allow more than others of various exact divisions?" (*Theodicy*, §21 of the appendix entitled, "Observations on the Book Concerning 'The Origin of Evil' Published Recently in London" (H 428))[33]

A further difference is that though it is clear that immutable essences and natures would have no existence were it not for God, and though it is clear that their existence is independent of the rest of creation, Descartes does not say *where* they exist. For Leibniz, on the other hand, it is clear that they exist *in* the divine mind: "the Understanding of God is the region of eternal truths or of the ideas on which they depend."[34]

Now this whole apparatus of a distinction between, on the one hand, essences or natures which exist independently of our ideas of them, independently of any instantiations they may have in the corporeal world, but not independent of God, and instantiations of those essences on the other, is there in Spinoza too. It occurs most clearly and explicitly in the *Metaphysical Thoughts* (1663) which, as an appendix to Spinoza's exposition of *Descartes's Principles of Philosophy*, may not report Spinoza's own wholehearted thought. But there is no doubt that it is there in the body of the *Ethics* too.

In the *Metaphysical Thoughts* [35] Spinoza distinguishes between the "being of essence," the "being of existence," and the "being of idea." The "being of existence" is the being of an instantiation of an essence; it is, says Spinoza, "attributed to things after they have been created by God." As to essence, there are, says Spinoza, certain questions usually raised about it: "whether essence is distinguished from existence? and if it is distinguished, whether it has any being outside the intellect?" To the first of these Spinoza replies that except in the case of God whose essence cannot be conceived without existence "in other things it [essence] does differ from and certainly can be conceived without existence." To the second, whether an essence is anything different from an idea, he replies that "a thing that is conceived clearly and distinctly, *or* truly . . . is something different from the idea."

What then is it? Given that it is different from an idea it "must surely be granted," says Spinoza, that it "has . . . being outside the intellect." But in what way has it being outside the intellect? "[I]t depends," says Spinoza, "on the divine essence alone, in which all things are contained. So in this sense we agree with those who say that the essences of things are eternal."

Less explicitly, but no less clearly, at IIP8 of the *Ethics* (CS 452) Spinoza makes a distinction between "formal essences" of modes which "exist . . . insofar as they are comprehended in God's attributes" and things which "exist ... also as they are said to have duration."[36] The same distinction is there at VP29S (CS 610) where things are said to be "actual in two ways:" first, "insofar as we conceive them to exist in relation to a certain time and place;" and, second, "insofar as we conceive them to be contained in God;" in this second way in which they are "true, *or* real" they "involve the eternal and infinite essence of God."

As I say, then, this line of thought about essences or natures which exist independently of our ideas of them, independently of any instantiation they may have in the corporeal world but not independently of God, is there in Spinoza too. But there is a crucial difference. At one point we saw Leibniz speak of essences as divine *ideas* and this draws our attention to the fact that for Descartes and Leibniz the dependency of essences on God is a dependency on a divine *mind*. It can only be so, because for Descartes and Leibniz that is all there is to God. God, for them, is a *thinking* substance.

But Spinoza's God is not only a thinking substance it is also an extended substance, it has the attributes of both thought and extension. So when Spinoza believes that the essences of geometrical figures are "contained" in God is he, like Descartes, thinking of them as dependent on a *thinking* substance? Is he, like Leibniz, thinking of them as contained in God's *mind*? Or is it his belief that they are contained in God insofar as he is *extended* substance? The second, given that the possibility of thinking it is open to Spinoza, is surely the more likely. (After all, it is as *extended*, not as thinking, substance that God, for Spinoza, is the cause of the extended world.) And I suggest that this is indeed what he does think. When he says that formal essences of geometrical figures are contained in the attributes of God he is surely going to mean, given that God has both the attributes of thought and extension, that these essences, these modes of extension, are contained in God as extended substance.

Of course, if one's conception of corporeal substance were like Descartes's, the instantiation of an essence, it would be absurd even to flirt with the idea that the *essences* of geometrical figures are in any way dependent on it. (Unless, like Gassendi, one thought our ideas of geometrical figures were derived from sense experience.) All that could be dependent on corporeal substance conceived in *that* way could be *instantiations* of those essences. For Descartes corporeal substance is the substrate and foundation of instantiations of essences of geometrical shapes. But if for Spinoza extended substance is the substrate and foundation not of instantiations of geometrical essences, but of those essences themselves, his extended substance can be nothing like Descartes's. Its existence can be nothing like that of the instantiation of an essence but must be more like that of the essences themselves of which it is the substrate.[37]

This will come out clearly in another yet-to-be-discussed passage from Spinoza (E IP8S2). But for the moment I want to pause to dwell on what seventeenth-century thought achieves with its idea that essences and truths about them are dependent on God.

Russell described Leibniz's thinking on this matter as "scandalous."[38] In Broad's view, though, Russell had "completely misunderstood," and suggests that what Leibniz had in mind was this:

Possibilities that do not actually exist, essences that do not have actual instances, and propositions which ap-

ply not only to the actual but also the merely possible,
are in some sense real . . . . [I]t seemed to Leibniz that
they could not just hang unsupported in the air; that the
being of possibilities, unexemplified characteristics,
hypothetical facts, etc., must depend in some way on
something actually existent.[39]

"The question of what kind of being should be ascribed to
mere possibilities and to purely hypothetical facts is a real
problem", says Broad, and Leibniz's idea that God is the
source of the reality of possibilities and essences is an attempt to solve it.[40]

Broad's description of possibilities as "mere" and of
propositions about the properties of geometrical figures as
"purely hypothetical" is unfortunate. They would go better
with a suggestion that there is no problem here than with his
sympathetic attempt to make plausible sense of Leibniz. But
apart from that I think his interpretation is basically right.

I think it is exactly this kind of thing that Descartes has in
mind when he writes to Mersenne that "the eternal truths . . .
*are true or possible only because God knows them as true or
possible*;" if God did not exist these truths would not be true
"for the existence of God is the first and the most eternal of
all possible truths and the one from which alone all others
derive" (6 May 1630 (K 13-14)). It is exactly this kind of
thing Leibniz has in mind when he says that "God is the
source . . . of essences, in so far as they are real, that is of
all the reality there is in possibility . . . . [W]ithout him there
would be nothing real in the possibilities,"[41] and that "God
himself, [is] the fount of all essence . . . . [T]hrough [him] . . .
the things that are possible have their reality."[42]

But I think that what is involved in these ideas needs to be
brought out more than Broad brings it. In one place Leibniz
imagines an opponent who has in effect adopted Broad's unfortunate description of possibilities as "mere" and propositions about the properties of geometrical figures as "purely
hypothetical," and who has suggested that "possibilities or
essences prior to or beyond existence are imaginary or fictitious." Leibniz replies to him that "neither the essences nor

the truths about them which are known as eternal truths, are fictitious."[43]

Now what this amounts to, I think, is the thought that if essences and eternal truths about them did not have a reality lent them by God (if, that is, they were "imaginary" or "fictitious"), it is not so much that it would be false that the external angle of a triangle is equal to the two internal opposites, as that it would be neither true nor false. There would simply not be, what there plainly is, such a figure as the triangle and such a thing as geometry. Thus Descartes says that Gassendi has to accept that there are real and immutable natures dependent on God "unless you are maintaining that the whole of geometry is also false."[44] Of course, as Leibniz says, "It is true that an atheist may be a geometrician." "But," he goes on, just as "without God . . . there [would] be nothing existent," so "if there were no God, geometry would have no object" (*Theodicy* §184 (H 243)).

I don't think there is much to be gained here by considering what might be said against Leibniz's claim that "[i]f there were no eternal substance, there would be no eternal truths."[45] What is of use, though, is to consider the position which accepts this claim and yet which asserts the antecedent, denies the existence of an eternal substance, and so denies the existence of eternal truths. This position with regard to the whole of geometry would be something like the position of Leibniz and Descartes with regard to fictitious ideas such as those of the regular decahedron. If there is no such figure as a regular decahedron there can be no study of it; similarly, if there are no figures at all there can be no such study as geometry. Someone who held this would have to say either that the so-called study of geometry has already dribbled away into the sand and that geometers are fooling themselves with meaningless sounds or a meaningless game, or that, sooner or later, they will come to see that this is all it is.

Such a person would, of course, be completely unable to accept Cartesian or Spinozan physics; he would have to confess that the corporeal world is completely unintelligible, or would have to come up with some completely different account of its principles and foundations. For, according to Cartesian physics, geometry is the study of extension and what the corporeal world is is a world of extended matter in motion. If there is no such thing as geometry then either the corporeal world is unintelligible, or its essence is not extension and something other than geometry is required to come to grips with it.

Can we find in Spinoza more evidence for the idea that extended substance is the foundation and substrate not, as for Descartes, of instantiations of geometrical essences, but of these essences themselves? Can we, that is, find more evidence for the claim that his extended substance is nothing like Descartes's? Can we find in Spinoza more evidence for the idea that if there were no extended substance there would be no object of geometry? The best passage is at IP8S2 (CS 412-14). The point of this scholium is to explain IP7 that "[i]t pertains to the nature of a substance to exist." Spinoza says that "I do not doubt that the demonstration of P7 will be difficult to conceive for all who judge things confusedly, and . . . do not distinguish between the modifications of substances and the substances themselves." He says, however, that "if men would attend to the nature of substance, they would have no doubt at all of the truth of P7."

So what is it about the nature of substance to which we must attend? At first sight it seems hardly exciting. We are given formulas with which every reader of Spinoza is familiar and which can be taken in the usual ways. We are reminded that substance is "what is in itself and is conceived through itself," whilst modes are "what is in another" and have concepts "formed from the concept of the thing in which they are." But in the next paragraph, Spinoza draws our attention to a certain something which these definitions of substance and mode enable us to explain or give an account of; namely, "how we can have true ideas of modifications which do not exist." Now an example of this is, I take it, how we could have a true idea of a triangle even were there not in the corporeal world any instantiations of triangles, any triangular things, or triangular configurations of things. And we know the account Leibniz would give of this: a true idea of a triangle is one which matches up to the divine idea of a triangle, one which matches up to the immutable nature or essence of a triangle which exists in God's mind. And we have already seen that a Spinozan answer might be that a true idea of a triangle is one which matches up to the immutable nature or essence of a triangle which exists in God as extended substance.

Exactly this is effectively his answer here. We can have true ideas of modifications which do not exist because "their essences are comprehended in another in such a way that they can be conceived through it." The "other" through which they are conceived is substance, of course (as the first paragraph of the scholium made clear); and I take this to be saying, what I have just said above, that the immutable essence or nature of a triangle exists in extended substance. So I take Spinoza's thought to be: we can think of and understand triangles because we understand them in terms of extension.

What then of extension or extended substance itself? As we know from the second paragraph of the scholium, substance exists in itself and is conceived through itself, and Spinoza says in the third that because of this "[t]he truth of substances is . . . in them themselves." That is to say, though we can understand a triangle in terms of extension there is nothing further back in terms of which extension is to be understood.

There is, at this point, an interesting variation in the Dutch version of the *Ethics*. Here, rather than that the "truth of substances is . . . in them themselves" we find that "the object of a true idea of substances can be nothing other than the substances themselves" (CS 414, n. 18). This says that while the object of the true idea of triangle is the immutable essence of a triangle, which is a modification of extended substance or of extension, the object of a true idea of extension is extension itself.

But, now, what is it to have a true idea of extended substance? It is, of course, what it is for Descartes to have a clear and distinct idea of extension. Roughly speaking, being in possession of geometrical knowledge is having a clear and distinct idea of extension. For Descartes one can do this without knowing that extended substance exists, and one could do it even if there were no extended substance—because for him extended substance is the instantiation of an essence. But for Spinoza, geometry would be impossible without the existence of extended substance because for him, unlike for Descartes, geometry is the study of extended substance. So, for Spinoza, to have a clear and distinct idea of (extended) substance is to know that extended substance exists.

He says exactly this in the next paragraph of IP8S2. From what has been said about the true idea of a substance it follows that "if someone were to say that he had a clear and distinct, i.e., true, idea of a substance, and nevertheless doubted whether such a substance existed, that would indeed be the same as if he were to say that he had a true idea, and nevertheless doubted whether it was false." This is to say, I think, that a necessary condition of our having a true idea of extension is that there is extended substance. To say that geometry is a going concern and a subject for intellectual investigation, is to say that extended substance exists. One might doubt that geometry *is* a going concern, and in so doubting might doubt that extended substance *does* exist. But if one has no doubt that geometry is a going concern, if, that is, one claims to have a true, a clear and distinct idea of extension, one can't doubt that extended substance exists. Extended substance, for Spinoza, is not the instantiation of an essence (as for Descartes). It is more like an essence itself; it is that on which essences depend and which makes them real. For Spinoza, to say that extended substance exists is to say that something on which formal essences depend exists. If extended substance did not exist neither would the essences which are geometrical figures; geometry would not be a going concern, and there would be no such subject for intellectual investigation, and no such subject for our physics to apply to the material world.

The point comes out again in Spinoza's next sentence. "[I]f someone maintains that a substance is created, he maintains at the same time that a false idea has become true. Of course nothing more absurd can be conceived. So it must be confessed that the existence of a substance, like its essence, is an eternal truth" (CS 414). That is, to say that extended substance might be created is to say that it might be the case at one time that geometry is not a going concern and that at another time it is.

Spinoza's proof that extended substance exists, that there is a substance with the attribute of extension, is not, as it is for Descartes, a proof that there are extended things or that the extended world exists; unlike Descartes's, his extended substance is not the extended world. It is a proof that the study of extension, which is geometry, is a *real* study; it is a proof that a world or things *could* exist *as extended*. As we have seen, Descartes and Leibniz too are interested in the reality of geometry and, despite his differences from them (as, for example, that his extended substance is not Descartes's) Spinoza's underpinning of it is, *in one way*, no different from theirs. For them its reality depends on God and so it does for Spinoza too—for *his* extended substance (though not the extended material world) *is* his God.[46]

# NOTES

1 *Principles of Philosophy* I.53 (CSM I, 210). Abbreviations are those adopted by the present volume.
2 *Discourse on the Method*, part 4 (CSM I, 129); *Principles* I.19, 23 (CSM I, 199, 200); *Objections and Replies*, set 2 (CSM II, 99).
3 Of course besides differing from Descartes in holding that a substance can have more than one attribute or principal property which constitutes its essence, he also differs from him in holding that there are attributes other than thought and extension .
4 H.H. Joachim, *A Study of the Ethics of Spinoza* (Oxford: Clarendon Press, 1901), p. 68.
5 *Ibid.*, p. 69.
6 Nicolas Malebranche, *Oeuvres Complètes,* 21 vols. ed. A. Robinet (Paris: J. Vrin, 1958-70), vol. 16, p. 25; vol. 17.1, p. 622; John Harris, *The Atheistical Objections against the Being of God: Eight Sermons* (London, 1698), 4th and 5th Boyle Lectures/Sermons (April and May, 1698), p. 31.
7 Samuel Clarke, *A Demonstration of the Being and Attributes of God* (1704), in Clarke's *Works*, 4 vols. (London: J. & P. Knapton, 1738), vol. 2, p. 532.

8   Frederick Pollock, *Spinoza: His Life and Philosophy* (London: C. Kegan Paul & Co., 1880), p. 164. It perhaps should be noted that Joachim and Pollock are uneasy about the identification of the material extended world with the one extended substance for they *also*, and inconsistently, identify it with the mediate infinite mode of that substance (Joachim, *ibid.*, p. 87; Pollock *ibid.*, pp. 164-65).

9   William Grant, *Much Ado about Nothing: Theories of Space and Vacuum from the Middle Ages to the Scientific Revolution* (Cambridge: Cambridge University Press, 1981), p. 229; see also p. 240.

10  Roger Scruton, *Spinoza* (Oxford: Oxford University Press, 1986), pp. 48, 50; see also Stuart Hampshire, *Spinoza* (Harmondsworth: Penguin Books Ltd., 1951), pp. 63-64: "the Universe as a system of extended or spatial things . . . [is one of] two attributes of the single substance." And Richard Schacht, *Classical Modern Philosophers: Descartes to Kant* (London: Routledge and Kegan Paul, 1984), p. 85: "The world for him [Spinoza] is not 'the aggregate of finite things' *as opposed to* God who created them, as it is for Leibniz (and Descartes). Rather, it is the one substance considered under the attribute of extension . . . . As such, the world cannot be considered God's *creation* . . . . Rather, the world *is* God himself, considered under the attribute of extension."

11  Jonathan Bennett, *A Study of Spinoza's Ethics* (Indianapolis and Cambridge: Hackett Publishing Company, 1984), here-after cited in the text as *Study*.

12  See Ep 43, W 241 (W=*The Correspondence of Spinoza*, trs. and ed. A. Wolf (London: Frank Cass & Co. Ltd., 1928), p. 241). R.J. Delahunty, *Spinoza* (London: Routledge and Kegan Paul, 1985) misreads this and says "[i]n his corre-spondence, Spinoza bluntly declares that 'the universe is God'" (p. 125; see also p. 127).

13  EIP18. So far as is possible all quotations from Spinoza are from CS.

14  As I discovered after coming to it, this view is at least verbally close to S. Paul Kashap's *Spinoza and Moral Freedom* (New York: SUNY Press, 1987). He says that "the meaning of the term 'exist' when Spinoza says 'God . . . exists' is entirely different from its meaning when existence is asserted of an individual or particular thing or object in . . . [what] Russell

calls 'the real world'" (pp. 14-15); and that "[i]t is quite clear that Spinoza's 'extended substance' is not the phenomenal world given to sense perception" (p. 42; see also elsewhere on p. 15, and pp. 16-24 *passim*, 27, 43). But Kashap also says "the precise sense in which God is actual or exists does not seem to be one that can be made intelligible by any argument" (p. 23), and I remain uncertain about the extent to which we are allied.

15  This interpretation is borne out by a related passage in the *Discourse on the Method* (CSM I, 129).

16  A. Kenny, *Descartes: A Study of his Philosophy* (New York: Random House, 1968), pp. 147-51.

17  *Objections and Replies*, set 1 (CSM II, 83).

18  "General Inquiries about the Analysis of Concepts and of Truths" (1686), in *Leibniz Logical Papers: A Selection*, trs. and ed. by G.H.R. Parkinson (Oxford: Clarendon Press, 1966), pp. 80-81; see also p. 115.

19  NE 268; see also NE 321.

20  *Principles* II.1 (CSM 1.223); see also Spinoza's *Descartes's Principles of Philosophy*, part 1, prop. 21 (CS 261).

21  More accurately, he is, as we shall see, asserting the existence of a "substrate" or "support" for natures or essences, something on which they depend for their existence.

22  IP20, IP20C1 (CS 428).

23  IA1, ID3, ID5.

24  See also A. Donagan, "Spinoza's Proof of Immortality," in *Spinoza: A Collection of Critical Essays*, ed. M. Grene (New York: Doubleday, 1973), pp. 241-8.

25  *Metaphysical Thoughts* (1663) (CS 310).

26  H.A. Wolfson, *The Philosophy of Spinoza*, 2 vols. in 1 (New York: Meridian Books, 1958), vol. 1, p. 358. Two examples of this reading are Hampshire, *loc. cit.*, p. 172, and Joachim, *loc. cit.*, pp. 297-8.

27  *Objections and Replies*, set 5 (CSM II, 221).

28  *Objections and Replies*, set 5 (CSM II, 262).

29  *Objections and Replies*, set 5 (CSM II, 261).

30  *Monadology* (1714), para. 43, (MP 185).

31  Descartes to Mersenne, 27 May 1630 (K 15); see also *Objections and Replies*, set 6 (CSM II, 291-92).

32  *Monadology*, para. 46 (MP 186); see also MP 77.

33  Here and below, 'H' refers to the English translation

*Theodicy*, trans. by E. M. Huggard (New Haven: Yale University Press, 1952; reprint, La Salle, Ill: Open Court, 1985), cited by page.

34  *Monadology*, para. 43 (MP 185).

35  Part 1, chap. 2 (CS 304-5).

36  This last is, at IIIP7 (CS 499), called "actual essence" or "given essence."

37  Awkwardly for my interpretation, there are passages where Spinoza says that essences of extended things exist in God in so far as he is *thinking* substance, e.g., at IP17S (CS 427) a formal essence (of an extended thing) is said to exist in God's mind.

38  B. Russell, *A Critical Exposition of the Philosophy of Leibniz* (London: George Allen and Unwin 1900, new ed. 1937), p. 178.

39  C.D. Broad, *Leibniz: An Introduction*, ed. C. Lewy (Cambridge: Cambridge University Press, 1975), p. 157.

40  *Loc. cit.*, pp. 157-8.

41  *Monadology*, para. 43 (MP 185).

42  "On the ultimate origination of things" (1697) (MP 140).

43  "On the ultimate origination of things" (1697) (MP 139-40).

44  *Replies and Objections*, set 5 (CSM II, 262).

45  "A Specimen of Discoveries about Marvellous Secrets" (c. 1686) (MP 77).

46  I am very glad to have had this opportunity to write in honour of Jonathan Bennett. As a graduate student I had the privilege to discuss Locke with him, and his work has always stood as an example of imaginative freshness and powerful clarity.

# DEFINITION, ESSENCE, AND UNDERSTANDING IN SPINOZA

*G. H. R. Parkinson*

## 1

Of the many questions raised by Spinoza's *Ethics*, perhaps the first that strikes the reader concerns the form in which the work is presented. What, one asks, does Spinoza hope to achieve by casting a philosophical work in geometrical form? The question may seem to have an obvious answer. Spinoza's *Ethics*, it may be replied, is clearly modelled on Euclid's *Elements*; now, just as Euclid establishes the truth of geometrical propositions by showing them to follow from his definitions and axioms, so Spinoza claims to prove the truth of philosophical propositions. Indeed (one may continue) if Spinoza is not offering proofs of the truth of what he asserts, then what is the point of offering a "demonstration" of each proposition of the *Ethics*?

There is much truth in this answer, though perhaps not the whole truth. But it has been argued that the answer, far from being even partly true, is entirely false. In his book *Spinoza*[1] Leon Roth drew attention to the fact that in 1663 Spinoza published a geometrical version of Descartes's *Principles of Philosophy*, while making it clear that he did not accept the truth of everything that is contained in the work. This means, Roth argues, that Spinoza could not have regarded the geometrical order of the *Ethics* as a method of proof. But this suggestion is not convincing. Roth has failed to distinguish between the validity of an argument and the truth of a conclusion that is established by a valid argument. Spinoza would doubtless claim that in his geometrical version of Descartes's *Principles*, as in his own *Ethics*, conclusions are validly derived from premises. But the mere fact that conclusions are validly derived from premises does not mean that the conclusions are true. Of course, if the premises are true and the conclusions are validly derived from them, then the conclusions must be true also. Spinoza would doubtless claim that this is the case in his *Ethics*; but where his geometrical version of Descartes is concerned, Spinoza is not obliged to say that the premises—or at any rate, all the premises—are true.

Why, then, did Spinoza present Descartes's philosophy in geometrical form? He could have intended simply to show the articulation of Descartes's system, irrespective of its truth or falsity. In this case, his intentions in writing the work would have been purely expository. However, Spinoza could have had a polemical aim; he could have been saying in effect, "Some at least of the propositions that Descartes declares to be true are in fact false. Now, *if* all the definitions that I have set out here were sound, and *if* all the axioms were true, then Descartes's philosophy would be true. As it is not, we ought to scrutinize these definitions and axioms more closely."

Just which of these aims Spinoza hoped to achieve by his geometrical version of Descartes is not clear, but it is clear that his use of a geometrical method in philosophy does not commit him to asserting the truth of every conclusion that is derived by such a method. There is, then, no reason to reject the immediate response to the geometrical form of the *Ethics*—namely, that Spinoza used this method to prove philosophical truths. For he is not just deducing conclusions from premises; he is deducing them from premises that he regards as true.

But there is more to Spinoza's use of the geometrical method in the *Ethics* than this. In the Preface to Part III of the work, Spinoza talks about his application of a geometrical method to human emotions. He contrasts his approach to the emotions with that of people who prefer to execrate and mock the emotions rather than to understand them (II/138).[2] Such people, he says, will find it extraordinary that he should try to investigate the vices and follies of men by a geometrical method, and should want to demonstrate with sure reasoning what they merely proclaim rhetorically. But, he goes on, human emotions follow from the same necessity and power of nature as other things do; "therefore they acknowledge certain causes through which they are understood, and have certain properties equally worthy of our knowledge as the properties of any other thing, the contemplation alone of which delights us." This indicates that the geometrical method is not just a means of establishing truths (though it is certainly that); it also enables one to *understand*, to *explain*.

The idea that explanation is deductive in form is by no means peculiar to Spinoza, but is shared by philosophers both before him and after him. For example, in his book *The Structure of Science*, Ernest Nagel writes:

> A type of explanation commonly encountered in the natural sciences, though not exclusively in those disciplines, has the formal structure of a deductive argument, in which the explicandum is a logically necessary consequence of the explanatory premises. Accordingly, in explanations of this type the premises state a sufficient (and sometimes, though not invariably, a necessary) condition for the truth of the explicandum. This type has been extensively studied since ancient times. It has been widely regarded as the paradigm for any "genuine" explanation, and has often been adopted as the ideal form to which all efforts at explanation should strive.[3]

In speaking of the study of deductive explanation in ancient times, Nagel doubtless has in mind Aristotle's account of explanation in *Posterior Analytics* I 13 (78 a38-b3). Here, Aristotle gives as an example an explanation of the fact that the planets shine steadily. He explains this fact by presenting the explicandum as the conclusion of a syllogistic argument:

> All bodies near the earth are bodies that shine steadily.
> All planets are bodies near the earth.
> Therefore, All planets are bodies that shine steadily.

We shall consider later (Section III) why Spinoza chose to present his explanatory system in geometric, rather than syllogistic form. For the moment, it is sufficient to note that the geometrical order has an explanatory function. Spinoza's claim is that the person who grasps the deductive system presented in the *Ethics* will not just know the truth of a number of propositions, but will have been presented with correct *explanations*: such a person will *understand* why things are as they are.

That this is Spinoza's view is made very clear by his use of definitions, which forms the topic of this paper. Since this use generates a problem of its own, it will be best to begin with the problem. Spinoza's definitions in the *Ethics* are nearly always of the form "By . . . I understand . . ." ("*Per . . . intelligo . . .*"). It is this that causes the difficulty. Spinoza says that he understands a term to mean such and such; that is, he proposes to take a term in such and such a way. In other words, his definitions seem to be of the kind that is commonly called "stipulative." Russell and Whitehead say of a definition of this kind that "it is not true or false, being the expression of a volition, not of a proposition."[4] The trouble is that this may seem to make of the *Ethics* a language game that is of no interest to anyone but the player. One may say of the book that if one uses terms as Spinoza does, and if one grants the truth of his axioms, then such and such conclusions will follow logically. But why should one use terms as Spinoza does? Why play his game, and not some other?

In seeking an answer to this question, the first thing to note is that Spinoza would have denied that his definitions are not true or false. On the contrary, he thinks that some definitions are true and some are false, and there is no doubt that he would have claimed that the definitions given in the *Ethics* are true. This view about definition is stated expressly in some of his letters (Ep 4, October 1661, IV/13; Ep 9, March 1663, IV/43) and implicitly in the *Tractatus de Intellectus Emendatione* (see TdIE §95, II/34), where Spinoza talks about "other people's errors" in definitions. These are all early works (the *Tractatus* was written about 1661); however, Spinoza seems to have begun work on the

*Ethics* as early as February 1663 (see Ep 8), and we may safely take these passages as evidence for the way in which Spinoza saw the definitions of the *Ethics*.

But how, one will ask, can Spinoza claim that his definitions are true? The answer is given briefly in Ep 9. Here, Spinoza distinguishes between two types of definition. A definition of the first type "explains a thing as it really is" (*prout est extra intellectum*), and such a definition ought to be true. One might (though Spinoza does not) call such definitions, using traditional terminology, "real definitions." Spinoza distinguishes definitions of this sort from those of another kind, which we might call "conceptual definitions." A definition of this type "explains a thing as it is conceived, or can be conceived, by us." Such a definition need not be true; all that is required is that it should be conceivable. Suppose, for example (IV/44) that one defines as "figurals" two straight lines which enclose a space. One is not asserting (Spinoza implies) that there *are* such lines; one is just forming the concept of a figural—much as (*ibid.*) one forms the concept of a non-existent temple. Now, the definition given is a good definition—i.e. figurals are conceivable—provided that one understands by 'straight line' what is normally understood by 'curve'. But if one understands by 'straight line' what is normally understood by that term, then the situation is inconceivable, and the definition is not a good one.

What concern us here are definitions of the first type. There is no doubt that, in the *Ethics*, Spinoza is claiming to explain things as they really are, and that he would say that the definitions contained in the work are true. Why, then, does he state his definitions in the form "By . . . I understand . . .", so giving the impression that they are merely arbitrary? It will be useful to consider what Spinoza is excluding when he states his definitions in this way. He is sometimes excluding what some (perhaps most) philosophers understood by the term defined, or perhaps even what people in general understood by the term. Spinoza is emphatic that his definitions do not describe other people's use of terms. As he says in No. 20 of the Definition of the Emotions in the *Ethics* (E III, at II/195), his intention is not to explain the meaning of words; it is to explain the nature of

things. Accepted usage, he implies, is not a guide to the nature of things; new terms must be coined, or old terms given
a new sense. The only concession that Spinoza makes to
standard usage (*ibid.*) is to give words a sense which is not
wholly remote from their usual meaning.

## 2

In sum, the definitions contained in the *Ethics* are explanatory in character; the test of a good definition is whether it
provides the inquirer with satisfactory explanations. A connection between definition and explanation is also present in
what Spinoza says about definition and essence, to which
we now turn. In Ep 9, which was discussed in the last section, Spinoza says briefly (IV/43) that a definition which
explains a thing as it really is "is concerned solely with the
essences of things." Light is thrown on this passage from
the *Tractatus de Intellectus Emendatione*, in which Spinoza
discusses the conditions of a good definition. As already
mentioned, the *Tractatus* is an early work; but the same view
about definition, and indeed the same example, is to be
found in Ep 60, written in 1675, i.e. only about two years
before Spinoza's death. A perfect definition, Spinoza says in
the *Tractatus* (II/34), must explain the inmost essence of a
thing, and must not substitute for this any of its properties.
For example (II/35), suppose that a circle is defined as that
figure of which the lines drawn from the center to the circumference are equal. "Everyone will see" (*nemo non videt*),
says Spinoza, that this definition is far from explaining the
essence of a circle; it merely explains one of its properties.
He adds that this matters little in the case of circles and other
"entities of reason,"[5] but that it matters very much in the case
of "physical and real entities," which interest him. "For the
properties of things are not understood as long as their
essences are not known; but if we neglect the latter, then we
necessarily destroy the order (*concatenationem*) of the intellect, which must represent (*referre*) the order of nature, and
so will stray from our end."
     This passage provides a further illustration of the impor-
tance that Spinoza's theory of definition attaches to the

achievement of understanding. A good definition must state
the essence of the thing defined, rather than any of its properties, because the properties of a thing are not understood as
long as its essence is not known. We now have to ask what
Spinoza means by 'essence' and 'property'. The language of
the passage just quoted ("everyone will see") suggests that
Spinoza thought that he was operating with familiar concepts, and indeed Spinoza's concept of a property is close to
the Aristotelian concept. For Aristotle, a property of $x$ is a
predicate that is peculiar to and convertible with $x$, but not
essential to it. For example, (*Topics* I 5, 102a 18-19) it is a
property of a human being to be capable of learning grammar. For if $x$ is a human being, then $x$ is capable of learning
grammar, and if $x$ is capable of learning grammar, then $x$ is a
human being. But being able to learn grammar is not the
essence of a human being. For his part, Spinoza seems to
think of properties, not in terms of hypotheticals ("If $x$ is a
human being, then . . ."), but in terms of what belongs necessarily to a thing. This emerges from what he says about
the properties of God in another early work, the *Short
Treatise on God, Man and his Well-being* (c. 1661). The
properties of God, he says, are such that without them, God
would not be God (KV I 1, note 4, I/18; KV I 3, note 1,
I/35)—in other words, the properties of God belong necessarily to God. But God is not God *through* them—a point
which the *Tractatus de Intellectus Emendatione* would make
by saying that they do not constitute his inmost essence.
Similarly, Spinoza would say, a property of a circle is not a
merely contingent feature of a circle. That the lines from the
center to the circumference are equal is a necessary feature of
a circle; nevertheless, this feature is not the essence of a circle.

It now has to be asked what Spinoza means by 'essence'.
Although his concept of a property is a standard one, his
formal definition of essence, to be found in E IID2 and in the
much earlier *Short Treatise* (KV II, Preface) is not, and
Spinoza knew this. That being so, it is somewhat surprising
that he should say that "everyone will see" the truth of what
he says about essence and property. We can perhaps best
make sense of the situation by supposing Spinoza to mean

that the term 'essence' has a nuclear sense that is generally accepted, but that there is room for disagreement about the best way to capture this sense in a definition. We will consider Spinoza's formal definition of essence in Section III; for the present, the topic will be what I have called the "nuclear sense" of the term. What, then, is this sense? Spinoza seems to have in mind something of the following sort: the essence of $x$ is that by virtue of which $x$ is what it is, or it is that which one must know if one is fully to understand the nature of $x$. One might put the point in the language of the *Short Treatise*—that the essence of God, for example, is that *through which* God is God.

Let us now look further at the passages quoted from the *Tractatus de Intellectus Emendatione* (II/35) and from Ep 60. In these passages, Spinoza rejects one way of defining a circle, on the grounds that it merely explains a property of a circle. In place of this definition (which is close to that given by Euclid, *Elements*, I, Def. 15) Spinoza proposes one which is borrowed from Hobbes (e.g. *De Corpore*, I, 1, 5). A good definition of a circle, Spinoza says (TdIE §96, II/35) would be: "That figure which is described by any line of which one end is fixed and the other is mobile." (Compare the definition given in Ep 60.) Spinoza says that this definition involves the "proximate cause" of the thing defined, and indeed he says that the definition of every "created thing" must involve its proximate cause (II/35). Spinoza does not define the term 'proximate cause', and one may take it that he uses it in the sense which was standard when he wrote:[6] a cause which produces its effects immediately, as distinct from a "remote cause," which produces its effect through intermediary proximate causes. In the *Tractatus de Intellectus Emendatione*, Spinoza says that it is only created things whose definitions must include the proximate cause; that which is "in itself" (*in se*), i.e. the "uncreated thing" must be understood through its essence alone (II/35). This may seem to be contradicted by Ep 60, which states that the definition of any thing whatsoever must include its "efficient cause"—a term which was commonly taken[7] to include both proximate and remote causes. However, there is no genuine contradiction here. Spinoza explains in Ep 60 that an efficient cause can be internal as well as external, and he implies that in the case of the "uncreated thing" the cause is internal. This is the same as saying, in the language of the *Tractatus de Intellectus Emendatione*, that such a being is to be understood through its essence alone. What the *Tractatus* excludes in this case is not a cause of any kind, but only an external cause.

We can now apply all this to the definitions contained in the *Ethics*, and ask in what sense they state the cause of what is defined. We will consider in turn the definitions of what the *Tractatus* calls an "uncreated thing" (namely, God) and of "created things." The reader unfamiliar with Spinoza's concepts may wonder how it is possible to state the cause of God, who is said by Spinoza to be the *first* cause (E IP16C3). Spinoza's answer is implicit in E IP7. The answer is that God, the one substance, is self-caused (*causa sui*); or, in the language of Ep 60, the cause of God is an internal cause. This is to say that God's existence is not a mere brute fact, but is to be explained through God's own nature; in short, God's existence is self-explanatory. Let us now consider the definition of God offered in E ID6. This runs: "By God, I understand a being absolutely infinite, that is, a substance consisting of infinite attributes, each of which expresses eternal and infinite essence." Spinoza comments on this definition in Ep 60. He says that the definition is to be preferred to the definition of God as "the supremely perfect being." (This, though Spinoza does not say so, is the definition given by Descartes: e.g. *Meditation* V, CSM II, 45). That definition, Spinoza says, does not express the efficient cause, and so one cannot derive from it all the properties of God. Descartes would doubtless reply that from the definition of God as a most perfect being he can derive the existence and all the other perfections of God—for example, God's infinity, eternity, immutability, omniscience and omnipotence (*Discourse on Method* IV, CSM I, 128; cf. *Principles of Philosophy* I.22, CSM I, 200). Spinoza does not defend his criticism of Descartes in Ep 60, but he might reply that one cannot derive from Descartes's definition the existence of what are called in the *Ethics* "attributes." These, he would say, are the key to the problem of the relations between mind and matter—a problem which Descartes failed to solve.

We come now to the definitions of uncreated things, of which the *Ethics* provides a wide range of examples. One definition is of particular interest, in that when he gives it, Spinoza refers expressly to the need for a definition to state the essence of the thing defined, and not just a property of it. In No. 6 of the Definitions of the Emotions that conclude E III, Spinoza defines love as "Pleasure accompanied by the idea of an external cause." In his explanation of this definition, he says:

> This definition explains the essence of love with sufficient clarity. That one given by authors who state that love is the will of the lover to unite himself to the object loved, does not explain the essence of love, but a property thereof: and as the essence of love has not been perceived sufficiently by the authors in question, they accordingly could not have any clear conception of its property, and accordingly their definition is considered by all to be exceedingly obscure. (II/192/20f)

The definition of love that Spinoza attacks here is offered by Descartes (*Passions of the Soul*, par. 79) as well as by other philosophers;[8] the question here is, why Spinoza should prefer his definition. Perhaps the answer is that that definition, unlike its rival, relates love to pleasure, which is one of the three fundamental emotions (*affectus*) of human beings (E IIIP11S). In other words, Spinoza's definition offers a genuine explanation of the nature of love; it explains love by reference to what is basic in a human being, and so instead of stating some property of love (which is all that the rival definition does) it states its essence.

### 3

After this discussion of Spinoza's account of the nuclear sense of the term 'essence', we now turn to the formal definition of essence given in E IID2. This definition (which, as already mentioned, is also given in the KV II, Preface, I/53) is stated in conscious opposition to another. This is, as Spinoza puts it, that "That appertains to the essence of anything without which the thing cannot either exist or be conceived" (E IIP10CS). This definition is to be found in some Scholastic manuals of Spinoza's time; it seems also to have been accepted by Descartes.[9] However, reason will be given later for thinking that Spinoza has the Scholastics primarily in mind. Spinoza says that what is wrong with this definition is that it is incomplete. Not only must one say that there belongs to the essence of a thing that without which the thing cannot exist or be conceived; one must also say that there belongs to its essence that which cannot exist or be conceived without the thing. So the definition offered in E IID2 is: "I say that that appertains to the essence of a thing which, when negated, the thing is necessarily negated; or that without which the thing, or on the other hand, which without the thing can neither exist nor be conceived." This is a cumbrous way of saying that, if $y$ is to belong to the essence of $x$, then not only must $x$ necessarily imply $y$ (which is all that the traditional definition asserts), but $y$ must necessarily imply $x$.

To clarify what is at issue here, let us first consider what was meant by those who defined the essence of a thing as that without which the thing cannot exist or be conceived. Take for example, the view that rationality is the essence of a human being. (Incidentally, this was not a view shared by Spinoza: cf. E IIP40S1. But this does not matter here.) Those who held this view, and also held the view of essence criticized by Spinoza, would say that a non-rational human being cannot exist; or, that one cannot really think of a non-rational human being. Take rationality away from a humanbeing, and what is left will not be truly human, even if it *looks* human. So much seems perfectly intelligible, but it would not satisfy Spinoza. He would say that if rationality belongs to the essence of a human being (in his sense of the term 'essence'), then not only is a non-rational human being inconceivable, but so also is a non-human rational being—a conclusion which would certainly be rejected by those who believe in the existence of a rational deity. But why should Spinoza define essence in the way that he does? The answer that he gives (E IIP10CS) is that if one uses his opponents' concept of essence when thinking about the relation between God and created things, one is faced with an unacceptable consequence. It is agreed (Spinoza says) that things cannot exist or be conceived without God; now, if one says that there belongs to the essence of a thing that without which the thing cannot exist or be conceived, then one must say that the nature of God belongs to the essence of created things. One may ask why one should not say this. Spinoza would reply that if one does, then (since God is a substance) one must say that a created thing such as man is a substance. But if man were a substance, then man would necessarily exist; but this is not the case (E IIP10, C).

This is not to say that Spinoza has the better of the argument. His opponents can reply that he has failed to distinguish between causal dependence and logical dependence. When it is said that things cannot exist or be conceived without God, what is meant is that they depend on God as their cause. But when it is said that a human being cannot exist or be conceived without rationality, the dependence that is asserted is not causal, but logical, in that it is being said that being rational is part of what is meant by being human. Spinoza would doubtless answer that there is no real distinction here, in that causal dependence is logical dependence. Given Spinoza's view of the nature of causality, this is a good answer; but it need hardly be said that this view has been severely criticized.

One can also make the point that the definition of essence given in E IID2 is not entirely consistent with the views about essence that were expounded above in Section II. It was remarked there that the *Tractatus de Intellectus Emendatione* states that a definition must express the "inmost essence" of a thing. Now, consider again the (Euclidean) definition of a circle that Spinoza rejects both in the *Tractatus* and in Ep 60—namely, that a circle is that figure of which the lines drawn from the center to the circumference are equal. This definition satisfies the criteria of essence laid down in the *Ethics*: for if $x$ is a circle, then (necessarily) the lines from the center of $x$ to the circumference are equal, and if $x$ is a figure such that the lines from the center to the circumference are equal, then (necessarily) $x$ is a circle. It seems, then, that if Spinoza is to exclude the Euclidean definition of a circle, then the definition of essence given in E IID2 must be elaborated in some way.

We have seen that, by defining essence as he does in E IID2, Spinoza avoids a consequence which he regards as metaphysically unacceptable. But there is more to the matter than this. Spinoza also thinks that his opponents' view of essence rests on a faulty methodology. When he explains the reason for his definition of essence (E IIP10CS) he says that those who held wrong views about essence, and so got into difficulties about the relation between God and created things, did so because they did not keep to "the order of philosophical argument" (*ordo philosophandi*). They treated the objects of the senses as first in the order of knowledge, and the divine nature—which should come first—they treated as last. Spinoza must be referring here to the scholastics; this remark is very similar to one contained in an account of the *Ethics* that was given to Leibniz by Tschirnhaus when Spinoza was still alive: namely, that the scholastics (the "common run" of philosophers, *vulgus philosophicum*) began from created things, Descartes began with the mind, whereas Spinoza began with God.[10] When Spinoza says, therefore, that those who did not follow the correct order of philosophical argument based the knowledge of created things on "fabrications," it is very probable that these "fabrications" are scholastic concepts. Spinoza does not mention the "fabrications" that he has in mind, but elsewhere in his works he criticises a number of scholastic ideas, such as transcendental terms and universal concepts (E IIP40S1), occult qualities (E VPref., II/279) and the method of definition by genus and species (KV II Preface, I/53).

It may be objected that Spinoza is unfair to the scholastics, in that the concept of deductive explanation, which plays such an important part in his own theory of definition, is also to be found in Aristotle, the main source of scholastic philosophy. (Cf. the syllogistic argument cited above in Section I.) Faced with such an objection, Spinoza would probably agree that the Aristotelian argument in question is an explanation of a sort, but he would add that it is far from satisfactory, in that it leaves much unexplained; for example, it does not say why bodies near the earth shine steadily. The objector may now ask why what is lacking in this explanation cannot be provided by further syllogisms; why, in short, Spinoza should present the *Ethics* in geometrical rather than in syllogistic form? Perhaps the answer is to be found in Spinoza's deep interest in the science of his time. For example, Descartes had declared (*Principles of Philosophy* II.64, CSM I, 247) that the only principles that he required in physics were those of geometry and pure mathematics, and Spinoza may well have thought that a method which was successful in physics would be equally successful in other fields of knowledge. Indeed, he would have done more than merely entertain this as a hypothesis. Even before he put his philosophy in deductive form in the *Ethics*, he argued that the connection that exists between physical things is the same as that which exists between their ideas (TdIE §41, II/16; cf. E IIP7). So he would say that a method which is successful in physics not only may be, but will be, successful in the study of the human mind as well.

## 4

A full account of Spinoza's theory of definition would also have to consider his view that the properties of the thing defined should follow from its definition alone. This was stated by him in the *Tractatus de Intellectus Emendatione* (II/35) and it continued to be his view. (It is defended in Ep 83, written in 1676.) However, this topic is not relevant to the main theme of this paper,[11] and I want instead to conclude by making some brief comparisons between the view of Spinoza set out here and that held by the philosopher whose achievements we are celebrating in this *Festschrift*. In his book *A Study of Spinoza's Ethics* Jonathan Bennett[12] has some characteristically acute and stimulating things to say about Spinoza's use of the geometrical method. He points out (*Study*, p. 17) that Spinoza doubtless believed that his definitions are correct, and his axioms true; nevertheless, he could hardly have expected them to be accepted without demur by someone who read them for the first time. So much, I believe, is perfectly true; as mentioned in Section

I of this paper, such a reader might well ask, when faced with Spinoza's definitions, "Why should I define terms in just this way?" Bennett's answer to this problem is that the *Ethics* is best viewed as a hypothetico-deductive system; "something that starts with general hypotheses, deduces consequences from them, and checks them against the data" (*Study*, p. 20).

Stated in an unqualified way, this thesis is by no means plausible. Spinoza did not regard the starting points of his system as merely hypothetical; on the contrary, he claims (cf. Section I) that the definitions of his system are true, and there is no doubt that he would say the same of the axioms. Bennett is well aware of this; he himself (p. 21) cites a passage from Ep 76 (1675) in which Spinoza claims that his philosophy is the true one. Bennett's thesis, however, is more complex than may at first appear. It is, that Spinoza's use of the hypothetico-deductive method is only propaedeutic; the method is, so to speak, a ladder which the reader can eventually cast away. "When the tutoring is completed the reader will see the starting points to be certain, indubitably true, beyond question" (*Study*, p. 21).

Let us grant, for the sake of argument, that Spinoza did use the geometrical method in this way. The next question to be asked is this. As Bennett points out, the definitions and axioms of a hypothetico-deductive system have to be tested against the data. Now, "against what data are we to test Spinoza's propositions?" (p. 23) I will consider one of the examples that Bennet gives, which will provide a good focal point for discussion. Bennett cites E IVP57, which states that a proud man hates the presence of the noble (*generosi*; also translated as "generous"). Bennett says of this proposition that it is answerable to empirical fact; it is relevant to check it "against the actual attitudes of people who are indisputably proud." So the overall pattern of argument in this case is as follows. Spinoza's definitions and axioms imply the truth of E IVP57; that proposition is discovered to be true by experience; therefore the axioms and definitions are confirmed.

Such is the interpretation that Bennett offers, and it is a plausible one. However, I would suggest another interpreta-

tion which is more in line with the general argument of this
paper. Bennett suggests that Spinoza expects his public first
to read the proposition that is E IVP57, and then check it
against experience. I suggest, on the other hand, that
Spinoza assumes that, before they read the *Ethics*, his readers already have some kind of knowledge of the truth of the
proposition. The proposition is a general one—it refers to
proud individuals in general—and one may take it that it is
based inductively on knowledge of the way in which a large
number of proud individuals behave. Now, Spinoza would
ask what kind of knowledge is possessed by the person who
has only inductive knowledge, and he would reply that it is
knowledge of the lowest kind, the sort that he calls knowledge of the first kind, or "imagination." (See especially TdIE
§20, II/10-11, which refers to our knowledge of the fact that
water extinguishes flame.) Spinoza argues that this kind of
knowledge is imperfect because it does not give an answer to
the question "Why?", and it is this kind of knowledge that
readers may have of the truth of E IVP57, before they have
worked through Spinoza's proof. But once they have
worked through the proof, then they know why proud people behave as they do, and the knowledge that they have is
of a higher degree.[13] In sum, my suggestion is that when
one considers Spinoza's use of a geometrical method in the
*Ethics*, one should bear in mind Spinoza's views about the
part that deductive arguments play in providing us with explanations, in enabling us to understand. Having said this, I
think it right to point out that I may have been developing a
hint that Bennett lets fall. For when he speaks of the hypothetico-deductive method, he remarks (*Study*, p. 20) that
"hypotheses must explain."

There still remains the question that Bennett has raised:
namely, how does Spinoza expect to win his readers' assent
to the definitions of the *Ethics*? It would be wrong to suppose that these definitions are intended to be provisional,
justified only by their success in providing explanations.
That may be the way in which a modern reader would prefer
to take them, but Bennett is surely right in saying that, for
Spinoza, their truth is known and unassailable. Perhaps one

might find an answer to the problem by first asking a different question: namely, why Spinoza's definitions are not accepted immediately by everyone. The same difficulty faced Descartes—as indeed it must face anyone who tries to build a philosophy on truths that will be accepted at once by any rational person. Descartes's solution was to blame the prejudices, or pre-conceived opinions, that his readers had already formed. (See, e.g., *Principles of Philosophy* I.71-2, CSM I, 218-20 and *Replies to Sixth Objections*, CSM II, 296-300.) Spinoza's solution is the same. For example, in the Appendix to Part I of the *Ethics* he says that he has attempted to remove any prejudices that might stand in the way of his readers' understanding of his propositions about God (GS II, 77), and there are many other references to prejudices and their removal (E IApp, II/78-80; E IIP40S1, II/120; E IVPref, II/206). But how does Spinoza hope to remove such prejudices? It is significant that the passages just quoted occur in the parts of the *Ethics* in which the argument is expressed informally—an appendix, a long note, and a preface. Perhaps, then, Spinoza would regard the removal of prejudices as the work of informal arguments of the kind that are found (say) in Descartes's *Meditations*. When these have done their work, then the reader can look back at the definitions of the *Ethics* and can see their truth. But the ultimate aim of the removal of such prejudices, like the aim of the definitions, is the achievement of understanding. And if the reader asks, "Why should understanding matter?" Spinoza would reply, "Because understanding makes you free."

## NOTES

1  Leon Roth, *Spinoza* (London: Benn, 1929) p. 24.
2  References to the Gebhardt edition are to volume and page; translations from Spinoza are my own,with the exception of the *Ethics*, which is cited here in the translation by A. Boyle, revised by G. H. R. Parkinson (London: Dent, 1989). All abbreviations are those adopted by the present volume.
3  Ernest Nagel, *The Structure of Science* (London: Routledge and Kegan Paul, 1961) p. 21.

4  Alfred North Whitehead and Bertrand Russell, *Principia Mathematica*, 2nd ed., (Cambridge: Cambridge University Press, 1927), vol. I, p. 11.

5  I have discussed "entities of reason" in my *Spinoza's Theory of Knowledge* (Oxford: Clarendon Press, 1954), pp. 151-56. Briefly, an entity of reason (*ens rationis*) has no real existence, but is a concept that we use in order to explain the nature of what exists. See especially Spinoza's discussion of the topic in his *Cogitata Metaphysica*, the appendix to his geometrical version of Descartes's *Principles of Philosophy*, I.1, 3 (II/233-34).

6  See, e.g., Heereboord, *Hermeneia Logica* (Leyden, 1650), pp. 58-9; quoted by H. de Dijn, "Historical Remarks on Spinoza's Theory of Definition," in J. G. van der Bend (ed.), *Spinoza on Knowing, Being and Freedom* (Assen: van Gorcum, 1974), p. 43.

7  See, e.g., Burgersdijck, *Institutionum Logicarum Libri Duo* (Leyden, 1626), cited in A. Wolf, trans. and ed., *Spinoza's Short Treatise on God, Man and his Well-being* (London: Black, 1910), pp. 190-92.

8  See H. A. Wolfson, *The Philosophy of Spinoza* (New York: Meridian Books, 1958) vol. II, pp. 76-77. Among those mentioned is the medieval philosopher Chasdai Crescas, cited by Spinoza in Ep 12, IV/61-2.

9  See, e.g., Suarez, a scholastic philosopher admired by Heereboord, *Disputationes Meaphysicae* 31.5, 13-15; cited by E. Gilson, *Index Scolastico-Cartésien* (Paris: Alcan, 1913), *s.v.* "essence." For his part, Descartes said that "If something can exist without some attribute, then it seems to me that that attribute is not included in its essence" (*Replies to Fourth Objections*, CSM II, 155). Compare Spinoza's geometrical version of Descartes' *Principles of Philosophy*, II, Axiom 2 (I/183).

10 Gottfried Wilhelm Leibniz, *Sämtliche Schriften und Briefe*, edited by the German Academy of Science (Darmstadt, Leipzig, and Berlin: Georg Olms and Akademie Verlag, 1923-), Series 6, Vol. 3, p. 385.

11 Tschirnhaus objected to Spinoza's view on the grounds that (Ep 82, 1676) it is contradicted by actual mathematical practice. He pointed out that in mathematics, we can always derive at any rate one property from the definition of a thing, but that

"if we desire several properties, we must refer the thing defined to others; then, if at all, new properties result from the conjunction of the definitions of these things." Spinoza answered (Ep 83) that what Tschirnhaus said may be true of "very simple things, or entities of reason—among which I include figures," but that it is not true of real things. He went on to claim that he derives several of the properties of God simply from the definition of a 'cause of itself' in E ID1. Yet if one looks at the way in which the relevant propositions are derived in the *Ethics*, it is easy to see that more definitions than ID1 are used.

12   Jonathan Bennett, *A Study of Spinoza's Ethics* (Indianapolis: Hackett Publishing Company, Inc., 1984). Abbreviated hereafter by *Study*.

13   It is probably of that kind which Spinoza calls knowledge of the second kind, or "reason". See G.H.R. Parkinson, "Language and Knowledge in Spinoza," in Marjorie Grene ed., *Spinoza: A Collection of Critical Essays* (New York: Doubleday, 1973), pp. 94-95.

# *ETHICS* IP5: SHARED ATTRIBUTES AND THE BASIS OF SPINOZA'S MONISM

## *Don Garrett*

Proposition 5 of Part I of Spinoza's *Ethics* states that: "In nature there cannot be two or more substances of the same nature or attribute."[1] This thesis, that substances cannot share an attribute, is crucial for the success of Spinoza's metaphysics. It is used explicitly in the demonstrations of IP6 ("One substance cannot be produced by another substance"), IP8 ("Every substance is necessarily infinite"), IP12 ("No attribute of a substance can be truly conceived from which it follows that the substance can be divided"), and IP13 ("A substance which is absolutely infinite is indivisible"). Moreover, it is the linchpin of his argument for substance monism at IP14D and IP14C1, an argument which reads as follows:

P14: Except God, no substance can be or be conceived. Dem.: Since God is an absolutely infinite being, of whom no attribute which expresses an essence of substance can be denied (by D6), and he necessarily exists (by P11), if there were any substance except God, it would have to be explained through some attribute of God, and so two substances of the same attribute would exist, which (by P5) is absurd. And so except God, no substance can be or, consequently, be conceived. For if it could be conceived, it would have to be conceived as existing. But this (by the first part of this demonstration) is absurd. Therefore, except for

God no substance can be or be conceived, q.e.d.
Cor. 1: From this it follows most clearly, first, that
God is unique, i.e., (by D6), that in Nature there is
only one substance . . . .

Is Spinoza entitled to assert that substances cannot share an
attribute? His demonstration of this proposition at IP5D may
be outlined in seven steps:

(1) "If there were two or more distinct substances,
    they would have to be distinguished from one an-
    other either by a difference in their attributes, or by
    a difference in their affections." [IP4]

(2) "If [two or more distinct substances are distin-
    guished] only by a difference in their attributes,
    then it will be conceded that there is only one of the
    same attribute."

(3) "[A] substance is prior in nature to its affections."
    [IP1]

(4) If two or more distinct substances are distinguished
    "by a difference in their affections, then . . . if the
    affections are put to one side and [the substance] is
    considered in itself . . . , one cannot be conceived
    to be distinguished from another." [from (3)]

(5) Substance "considered in itself [is] considered
    truly." [ID3, IA6]

(6) If two or more distinct substances are distinguished
    "by a difference in their affections, then . . . if the
    affections are put to one side and [the substance] is
    . . . considered truly . . . , one cannot be conceived
    to be distinguished from another." [from 4-5]

(7) "In nature there cannot be two or more substances
    of the same nature or attribute." [from (1), (2), and
    (6)]

The overall strategy of Spinoza's argument, at least, is
clear. IP4 states that two things can be distinguished from
one another only by a difference in attributes or by a difference in affections; and Spinoza proceeds to argue, at (2) and

(3)-(6) respectively, that neither alternative would be available in the case of substances sharing the same attribute. But as Jonathan Bennett has acutely argued in his landmark book, *A Study of Spinoza's Ethics*,[2] Spinoza's grounds for rejecting each of the two alternatives seem highly dubious. With respect to the latter alternative, Spinoza's argument at (3)-(6) seems to leave unexplained *why* the "priority" of substances over their affections should entitle us to "put to one side" all differences of affections in such a way as to preclude our *using* such differences to distinguish substances. In emphasizing this difficulty, Bennett is expanding on an objection also raised by Michael Hooker and explored by William Charlton.[3] And with respect to the former alternative, Spinoza's assertion of (2) seems to ignore the possibility of substances that share *some* attributes but are distinguished by their failure to share *others*. In emphasizing this apparent lacuna, Bennett is restating and reinvigorating an objection first made by Leibniz.[4]

If these two objections cannot be overcome with the definitions, axioms, and prior propositions at Spinoza's disposal, then the demonstration of IP5 must be judged a failure. And if it is indeed a failure, it threatens to be a most disappointing one; for his attempt to deduce his metaphysics geometrically will apparently have failed at a very early point indeed—and, moreover, a point on which much of what is most distinctive about his metaphysics depends. Furthermore, the threat of failure posed by the objections raises a serious problem for our very understanding of Spinoza. For surely he would not have offered the argument of IP5D unless he regarded it as providing rationally compelling grounds for its conclusion—and, moreover, grounds to which he had devoted considerable thought. Hence, if we do not know why he fails to address the two objections more explicitly and how—if at all—he himself would reply to them, then to that extent we do not fully understand the basis of his monism.[5]

In the first section of this essay, I consider two recent responses to the Hooker-Bennett objection to (3)-(6). I argue that neither response can fully overcome the objection on the basis of resources available to Spinoza, and also that neither provides a likely interpretation of Spinoza's own intentions with respect to (3)-(6). In the second section of the essay, I propose an interpretation that, I argue, does overcome the Hooker-Bennett objection, and also provides a likely interpretation of Spinoza's intentions. In the course of doing so, I also argue that IP1 is deducible from the definitions and axioms of Part I of the *Ethics*. In the third section of the essay, I survey five recent responses to the Leibniz-Bennett objection to (2). Once again, I argue that none can fully overcome the objection on the basis of resources available to Spinoza, and also that none provides a likely interpretation of Spinoza's own intentions with respect to (2). In the fourth section of the essay, I propose an interpretation that, I argue, does overcome the Leibniz-Bennett objection, and also provides a likely interpretation of Spinoza's intentions. In the course of doing so, I also argue that IP4 is deducible from the definitions and axioms of Part I of the *Ethics*. Since the two objections to IP5D can be overcome, and since IP1 and IP4 are the only prior propositions of the *Ethics* employed in IP5D, I conclude in the final section that IP5 is in fact a justifiable inference from Spinoza's definitions and axioms; and I comment briefly on the ultimate grounds of Spinoza's monism.

In the course of the essay, I consider several specific points and interpretive suggestions offered or described by Bennett, as well as points and suggestions due to others. But my debt to Bennett, in particular, goes far beyond his providing these specific objects of consideration. For the essay itself is largely inspired by the characteristically incisive way in which Bennett has rendered these issues about IP5 and its demonstration so unavoidable; and it is inspired, too, by what I regard as two of the most fruitful aspects of Bennett's overall approach to the interpretation of Spinoza. These are, first, the endeavor to do justice to Spinoza's thought by close attention to the actual content and logic of his arguments; and second, the use of "explanatory rationalism"— i.e., the thesis that whatever is the case can be explained—as a key to understanding Spinoza's arguments and motivations. For Spinoza's explanatory rationalism is derived, in part, from his thesis (embedded in his definitions and axioms) that whatever is, must be completely conceivable; and it is this latter thesis that constitutes, on my interpretation, the ultimate basis of Spinoza's monism.

## 1. The Hooker-Bennett Objection

Let us turn first to the Hooker-Bennett objection to (3)-(6). On the basis of IP1's claim that "a substance is prior in nature to its affections," Spinoza infers that if the affections of substance are put "to one side," so that substance is "considered in itself," then two substances cannot be distinguished by a difference of affections. But, he continues, "substance considered in itself" is (by ID3 and IA6) "substance considered truly"; thus, if we consider substance truly, we will not be able to distinguish two substances by their affections. This argument seems simply to trade on an ambiguity in the notion of "conceiving something in itself." ID3 requires that a substance be "in itself," in a sense opposed to "*in* something else"; hence, to conceive a substance as being "in itself" in that sense is—so far—to conceive it truly (especially since IA6 requires that "a true idea must agree with its object"). But Spinoza *seems* to infer from this that substance is truly conceived "in itself" in a different sense, a sense opposed to "*being with* something else." And this inference does not seem valid. For substance *also* truly has affections, and hence to conceive it *with* its affections is to conceive it truly; to conceive it as being *without* its affections, in contrast, as IP5D seems to ask us to do, would be to conceive it *falsely*. Unless IP1 entitles us to "set the affections to one side" in some other way when we attempt to distinguish substances, IP5D must fail.

Recent discussions of IP5 have yielded two proposals for justifying or explaining Spinoza's willingness to set the affections aside in (6). Before offering my own interpretation, I will discuss these two proposals, considering both their ability to overcome the objection with the resources available to Spinoza, and their plausibility as interpretations of his intentions. In doing so, I do not mean to imply that those who have offered or defended one of these proposals necessarily intended it to serve both of these purposes, or even that they were committed to its complete adequacy for *either* purpose. I am not, therefore, seeking to *refute* their authors. Nevertheless, both proposals do have a considerable degree of *prima facie* plausibility, both as ways of overcoming the objection and as interpretations of Spinoza's intentions; each is therefore deserving of consideration in both respects.

Bennett proposes an interpretation of Spinoza's willingness to set the modes aside which depends on their character as "accidental." He writes (using the term 'state' for 'affection' ['*affectio*']):

> The proposition that 'A substance is prior in nature to its states' [IP1] has been derived from the equation of 'substance' with 'what is in itself and conceived through itself' [ID3] and of 'state' with 'what is in something else through which it is conceived' [ID5]. If we take this to entail that any state of a substance is accident to it, i.e., that a substance could have lacked any of its actual states, then we get the following argument. Distinct substances must be unalike in respect of some properties which they cannot lose; for if they were unalike only in respect of their accidental properties they could become perfectly alike, and so, by the identity of indiscernibles, become identical. It is obviously intolerable to suppose that two substances could have been—or could become—one. So between any two substances there must be an unalikeness in respect of nonaccidental features, i.e., of attributes.[6]

While suggesting this argument as an interpretation of Spinoza, Bennett himself argues against its adequacy as a solution to the Hooker-Bennett objection, on the grounds that it is a modal fallacy to infer that "*x* and *y* could become exactly alike" from "*x* and *y* are unalike only in respect of their accidental properties." Edwin Curley, however, defends the proposed argument against Bennett's claim of fallacy, at least in a Cartesian context. Descartes' famous discussion of a piece of wax in his Second Meditation and his analogous discussion of a stone in the *Principles of*

*Philosophy* (II.11) strongly suggest that all of the mere affections (as opposed to the principal attribute) of a substance can change without altering or undermining the identity of the substance. But, Curley, argues, given these passages,

> . . . it is difficult to see how Descartes could block the possibility that two finite material substances might come to be exactly alike as regards their intrinsic properties (counting all the properties mentioned in the wax passage as intrinsic.)[7]

Furthermore, Curley continues, the two substances could not be distinguished by the "extrinsic" characteristics of their different locations in space, for Descartes *identifies* the extension which constitutes a body with the space that it is said to occupy; and his "relational" theory of space seems to imply that the distinction of substances is logically prior to the determination of their location.

Although these points are valid and important, they do not fully overcome the Hooker-Bennett objection with resources available to Spinoza from his definitions, axioms, and prior propositions (nor does Curley claim that they do). One problem lies in the fact that at IP5 Spinoza himself has not identified extended substances with the space they occupy, nor has he offered a relational theory of space; indeed, he has not even identified extension as an attribute. A second problem lies in the argument's reliance on a principle of the identity of indiscernibles for substances. I will argue in the fourth section of this essay both that IP4D embodies an identity of indiscernibles for substances, and that it can be justified from the axioms and definitions alone. The version of the identity of indiscernibles needed for the present argument, however, is stronger than the general principle that different substances cannnot be completely indiscernible; it requires that there not be even a *single time* for which they are indiscernible. It is not obvious how Spinoza could justify this stronger claim from his axioms, definitions, and prior propositions.

More fundamentally, however, even if we waive the possibility of distinctions of location, and grant the temporal version of the identity of indiscernibles, the apparent *difficulty* (especially for Cartesians) of blocking the possibility of two substances coming to have indistinguishable affections does not entail that the possibility *cannot* be blocked. And in fact, there are two ways in which the affections of two or more substances might prevent the substances from becoming indistinguishable.

First, substances might differ in affections that were necessarily permanent to them. As Curley points out in a footnote, Descartes himself is committed to the claim that the size of an extended substance is a necessarily permanent characteristic of it, Meditation II's discussion of the piece of wax notwithstanding. And nothing in the *Ethics* entails or implies that *all* of the affections of a substance can change. Quite the contrary, Spinoza later goes on to describe, at IP21-22, modes (i.e., by ID3, affections) of a substance that "have always had to exist and be infinite" in that substance. And although the interpretation I will later give of (3)-(6) rules out the possibility of substances *differing* in such "eternal and infinite" modes (as, of course, will the monism that Spinoza eventually derives in part *from* IP5D), nothing in the argument presently under consideration does so.

Secondly, even if substances did *not* differ in any necessarily–permanent affections, it might still be that each of two or more actual substances would give rise to a series of affections within itself in a way or order different from that in which any other substance gave rise to its affections, so that, although substances changed their affections, they would never become indistinguishable from one another. Furthermore, Spinoza's denial of contingency at IP29 and IP33 seems to imply that, if any two substances do not *in fact* become indistinguishable, then they *could not* have become indistinguishable. To be sure, the principle that substances with indiscernible affections are identical entails that any substances $x$ and $y$ are either identical or have discernible affections; but it does not say *which* of these alternatives must be realized. Leibniz, for one, was sufficiently confident of the plurality of substances that he inferred from the identity of indiscernibles the doctrine that each substance has a unique way of developing its affections. If Spinoza is fully to overcome the Hooker-Bennett objection, he must also have a positive way of refuting this Leibnizian alternative. But nothing provided by the argument presently under consideration does so.

Moreover, it is clear that Spinoza himself would not defend his "putting the affections to one side" in the way suggested by the proposal presently under consideration. For one thing, he could reasonably be expected to understand his own definitions and axioms sufficiently well to realize that they leave the argument open to at least one (if not more) of the objections just surveyed. Even more fundamentally, however, if the present proposal were to provide a plausible interpretation of Spinoza's language in IP5D, he would have to accept the argument's assumption that all affections *are* accidental to the substances in which they occur. And as we have seen, this is an assumption that he clearly does not make; on the contrary, his doctrine of "eternal and infinite modes" at IP21-22 clearly contradicts it. Hence, by the "priority" of substance over its affections, affirmed in IP1 and used to justify setting the affections to one side, he cannot mean the priority of substance over those of its characteristics that are accidental, as he would have to do if the present proposal were to serve as a plausible interpretation of his argument.

Henry Allison proposes another basis for setting the affections aside, based on Russell's discussion of the identity of indiscernibles as it occurs in Leibniz. Thus, Allison writes:

> According to Russell, the argument seems to be that, on the assumption currently under consideration [i.e., that substances are distinguished by their affections], the substances must be indistinguishable prior to the assignment of predicates (affections); however, the assignment of predicates cannot provide a basis for distinguishing otherwise indiscernible substances unless it is presupposed that they are numerically distinct to begin with. In other words, although we could certainly distinguish between the two Cartesian substances by referring to their distinct affections, we take

this to mark a distinction between two substances only because we have already assumed that the distinct affections must belong to numerically distinct substances. After all, the same . . . substance could certainly have two distinct affections, even simultaneously. Consequently, Spinoza could claim that it is really the Cartesian [who distinguishes more than one substance], not he, who is begging the question by refusing to set the affections aside.[8]

That is to say, the identity of indiscernibles entails that substances are not distinct unless they differ in predicates; but unless there is some other basis for distinguishing substances besides differences of predicates, any predicates— and hence any affections—can always be assigned to the *same* substance. This argument, however, cannot fully overcome the Hooker-Bennett objection, for two reasons. First, as long as it is established only that any set of predicates *can* be assigned to the same substance, both the "Cartesian," who distinguishes multiple substances, and the "Spinozist," who does not, will be *equally* begging the question. In order to avoid begging the question, the Spinozist would have to show not only that one *can* assign all of the predicates in question to one substance, but that one *must* do so; for otherwise, it will arguably remain equally true that one *can* assign them to *more* than one substance. Secondly, the claim that one *can* just as well assign all of the predicates to the same substance is itself a claim that stands in need of considerable justification. For although the same substance can have many different affections, it cannot have incompatible affections; hence, if there *are* incompatible affections, they will require us to distinguish two different substances. But there are many plausible candidates for pairs of incompatible affections. To take just one example from the attribute of thought: the predicate of presently feeling an intense pain is at least arguably incompatible with (i.e., cannot coexist in the same substance with) the predicate of presently believing that no intense pain is being felt.

Moreover, it also seems unlikely that Spinoza would intend to justify his putting aside of the affections by means of the argument Allison describes, for several reasons (and Allison does not state that he would). For one thing, if Spinoza wished to rely on the argument, he could reasonably be expected to foresee at least one (if not both) of the objections just described, and to do something to forestall them; but he does not do so. Furthermore, because the argument is concerned with *all* predicates, it applies, at least *prima facie*, to attributes just as well or as poorly as it does to affections. If, therefore, he thought that the argument would justify assigning all *affections* to one substance, he would presumably have thought that it would also justify assigning all *attributes* to one substance. In that case, there would be no apparent reason why he should have restricted himself to using it to justify (6) of IP5D, when it would equally permit an immediate inference to monism itself, in a way much less complicated than the argument for monism that he actually gives.

Thus, I conclude that neither of the two responses surveyed to the Hooker-Bennett objection fully overcomes the objection with resources available to Spinoza, and that neither provides a likely account of Spinoza's own intentions. Of course, we cannot simply assume that the objection can be fully overcome with Spinozistic resources at all, nor that he had any determinate intentions with respect to it. Similarly, we cannot completely rule out the possibility that, despite the objections raised to them as interpretations, one of the proposals does nevertheless correspond to his own intentions. Clearly, however, it is worth investigating whether a better response to the objection, and a more likely interpretation, are possible.

## 2. Differences of Affections

The Hooker-Bennett objection arises from the fact that IP5D seems, at (3)-(6), not to explain fully how the priority of substance over its affections, as asserted in IP1, can justify putting the affections aside in the attempt to distinguish substances. In order to see whether the affections might legitimately be put aside, therefore, let us focus on what is involved in the "priority" of substance over its affections.

The demonstration of IP1 reads simply: "This is evident from D3 and D5." Thus, the kind of priority involved should be a kind of priority immediately derivable from the definitions of 'substance' and 'mode'; and the "priority" involved in those definitions is, of course, the priority of "being in" and of "being conceived through." Can this kind of priority provide a justification for putting aside the affections in the attempt to distinguish substances?

It can if the "in and conceived through" relation requires that every affection be conceived through its substance in such a complete way that any *difference* of affections would have to be conceived through a *difference* of substance. For in that case, Spinoza would not be setting the affections aside on the (false) grounds that substances, as truly conceived, do not *have* them; rather, he would be setting them aside on the grounds that differences in affections must be understood through, and hence require, differences of substance. Since Spinoza argues in IP4D that differences of *substance* reduce, in turn, to differences of *attribute*, he would then be entitled to restrict the search for substance-distinguishing differences to differences of attributes, already considered at (2): for no differences of *affections* could occur *without* a logically or conceptually prior difference of *attributes*. Since Spinoza regards "being in" and "being conceived through" as parallel and mutually entailing relations (see note 24 below), it makes sense for him to add, at (5)-(6), that in treating substance as "in itself" or as prior to its affections, we are considering it truly.

Although this rationale for putting the affections aside requires that we construe the "in and conceived through" relation as a strong one, the construal is not unreasonable. For if substance $x$ differs in affections from substance $y$ *without* that difference being conceivable through a difference in the nature or essence of the substances themselves, then there will indeed be *something* about the affections of $x$ that cannot be completely understood solely through conceiving the nature of substance $x$: namely, the *reason or cause* (these notions are equivalent in Spinoza) why the affections of $x$ have that feature—whatever it might be—in which they differ from the affections of $y$. This in itself renders the strong construal of the relation at least somewhat plausible, aside from any other considerations. Furthermore, however, IA4 states that "The knowledge of an effect depends on, and involves, the knowledge of its cause"; and at IP8S2, Spinoza paraphrases the definition of substance as "what is in itself and is conceived through itself, i.e., that the knowledge of which does not require the knowledge of any other thing," thereby showing that he is willing to interchange "conceiving" and "having knowledge."9 IA4 thus entails that, if the reason or cause for some feature of the affections cannot be conceived through a substance, then that feature *itself* cannot be fully known or (by the equivalence employed at IP8S2) conceived through the substance.

Thus, Spinoza could argue, ID5 requires that the affections of a substance be completely conceived through their substance. But the affections cannot be completely conceived through a substance unless all of their features are fully conceived through that substance. By IA4, however, the features of the affections cannot be fully known or (by the equivalence from IP8S2) conceived without the knowledge of their cause. Now, to have knowledge of the cause of something is to have knowledge of something that determines it to occur rather than not. Hence, any feature in which the affections of one substance differ from the affections of another must be conceived through some difference in the substances themselves which accounts for the difference of affections.

Of course, this argument depends on an assumption about the meaning of ID5—namely, that ID5 requires that the affections of a substance be *completely* conceived through the substance, in a sense strong enough to entail that every feature of the affections be fully conceived through the substance. It also depends on two assumptions about the meaning of IA4: first, that knowledge of the cause, in the sense employed in IA4, requires knowledge of something that *determines* that the effect will occur, rather than not; and, second, that in using the term 'effects', Spinoza does not intend to limit the scope of IA4—or at any rate, to limit it in such a way that features of affections might not fall within it—but rather seeks only to emphasize the *correlation* between effect and cause. But each of these assumptions is a very plausible one in the context of Spinoza's philosophy. Each is individually compatible with, and even suggested by, what he says elsewhere in his writings—and, indeed, he treats the claim that *everything* has a cause as a truism (e.g., at IP11D). To be sure, the assumption about the meaning of ID5 renders it richer in content than it would otherwise be, and the assumptions about the meaning of IA4 render it more powerful. But IP5 is itself a strong claim, and hence if it is to be validly inferred from the definitions and axioms, the definitions must be at least somewhat rich, or the axioms somewhat powerful. The question is whether the definitions and axioms can be reasonably understood in such a way as to bear the deductive weight that must ultimately be placed on them; and in the present case, it appears that they can.

Still, it may be objected that the assumptions about IPD5 and IA4 required by the present proposal *jointly* entail that no substance could have had any affections other than the set of affections that it actually has, and that this conflicts with IP21 and IP28D, which require that finite modes do not "follow from the absolute nature of an attribute." Hence, it may be argued, at least *one* of those assumptions must be wrong. However, I have argued at length elsewhere[10] that the doctrine that no substance could have had any other affections is stated or entailed at a number of points of the *Ethics*—including IP16, IP29, and IP33—and is not contradicted anywhere. For although the finite modes do not follow from the "absolute nature" of the attributes, they do *follow* from the nature of the attributes (see IP16, IP17S, IP26D, IP33D, and IP33S1, plus IP29S); his distinction is thus not between following and not following from the nature of the attributes, but rather between two ways of following from the attributes. Although the relevant considerations are too lengthy to repeat here, if the distinction is properly understood, it will be seen not to conflict with the readings of IP5 and IA4 required by the present proposal.

Thus, it appears that the argument outlined above can overcome the Hooker-Bennett objection. Moreover, considered as an interpretation of Spinoza's intentions, the present proposal has three advantages. First, it does not require Spinoza to commit any errors of reasoning. Secondly, it takes the kind of "priority" mentioned in IP1 and employed in IP5D to be, quite straightforwardly, the kind of priority mentioned in ID3 and ID5, from which IP1 is derived. Finally, it makes good sense of the text of IP5D as it actually occurs. In the absence of any damaging objections to it as an interpretation, and in the absence of an equally plausible alternative, I conclude that it is a likely interpretation.

## 3. The Leibniz-Bennett Objection

Let us turn now to the Leibniz-Bennett objection to (2), the claim that if two or more distinct substances are distinguished "only by a difference in their attributes, then it will be conceded that there is only one of the same attribute." The claim seems plausible when applied to substances each having only a single attribute; for if their single attributes differ, then their attributes are not, after all, the very *same* attribute. But (2) *seems* less plausible when applied to substances having more than one attribute. For such substances, it seems, could share one attribute, with no difference of *that* attribute, and nevertheless be distinguishable as different substances on the basis of a *second* kind of "difference in their attributes"—namely, a difference in what *other* attributes the substances might have. For example, two substances might share attribute $A_1$, and yet still "differ in their attributes" because one substance also had attribute $A_2$ which the other substance lacked. Since Spinoza's use of IP5 in the demonstration of monism at IP14D and IP14C1 obviously depends on applying IP5 to substances of more than one attribute, Spinoza's use of (2) seems unwarranted.

Recent discussions of IP5 have yielded five proposals for justifying or explaining his use of (2). Before presenting and arguing for my own interpretation, I will discuss each of those proposals in turn, considering both their ability to overcome the objection with the resources available to Spinoza, and their plausibility as interpretations of his intentions. (Once again, in doing so I do not mean to imply that each proposal was intended by its author to serve both of these purposes, or even that its author was committed to its complete adequacy for either purpose; as before, I am not, therefore, seeking to refute their authors.)

One general strategy for overcoming the Bennett-Leibniz objection is to justify (2) by supplementing IP5D with a further premise to which Spinoza is entitled. Bennett himself offers, without insisting on, a suggestion of this kind. He writes:

> There may be a Spinozistic way of closing the gap. For example, Spinoza may be able to argue that if $x$ had only $A_1$ while $y$ had both $A_1$ and $A_2$, the demand of his explanatory rationalism to know why $x$ did not have $A_2$ as well could not be satisfied. (*Study*, p. 69)

If this suggestion is correct, explanatory rationalism—the doctrine that everything can be explained—would thus prohibit the possibility of substances sharing some but not all attributes, the possibility on which the Leibniz-Bennett objection depends. As I have indicated, I do believe that a thesis closely related to explanatory rationalism plays a crucial role in the demonstration of IP5. I do not believe, however, that explanatory rationalism can satisfactorily play the role suggested here, of directly prohibiting the possibility of the pairs of substances on which the Leibniz-Bennett objection depends. Since, by definition, nothing can exist without its essence, in order to explain why a thing has a feature that pertains to its essence one need only show that it *does* pertain to the essence of that kind of thing—as manifested in the thing's proper definition, which will capture its essence[11]—and then explain why *that* thing exists. For example, to explain why a particular circle is such that all of the points on it are equidistant from the center, one need only point out that this is of the essence of circles, as captured in the proper definition of the circle, and then explain why that *particular* circle exists. But a substance's attributes pertain to its essence. This is a consequence of ID4, and is also indicated by the fact that the only formal definition of a substance Spinoza gives, that of 'God' at ID6, is in terms of that substance's attributes. Hence, to explain why one substance has only attribute A1 while another substance has attributes A1 and A2, we need only to explain the *existence* of each.

Now, Spinoza seems to take IP7 ("It pertains to the nature of a substance to exist") to require that every possible substance exists necessarily, as his use of IP7 at IP11D strongly indicates.[12] Moreover, in IP11D he cites IP7 as showing that "the reason why a substance exists . . . follows from its nature alone." Thus, a potential explanation for $x$'s possessing only A1 while $y$ possesses both A1 and A2 seems readily available: it is in the nature of substance $x$ (as manifested in its definition as "the substance of attribute A1") to have only A1, and since $x$ is a possible (non-contradictory) substance, it necessarily exists from its own nature; at the same time, it is in the nature of substance $y$ (as manifested in its definition as "the substance of attributes A1 and A2") to have both attributes A1 and A2, and since $y$ is also a possible (non-contradictory) substance, it, too, necessarily exists from its own nature. Given the doctrine that substances exist from their own nature alone, it is not only possible but mandatory to suppose that the reason for the attributes and existence of every substance that exists will be found entirely within its own essence or definition in precisely this way.[13] Thus, explanatory rationalism alone cannot overcome the objection to (2) in the way suggested. Moreover, the doctrine that a substance's attributes are essential to it (required by ID4), and the doctrine that the reason why a substance exists must follow from its own nature (asserted in IP11D as a consequence of IP7, and also strongly implied by ID3), are both so central to Spinoza's thought as to render it unlikely that he would *believe* that the objection could be overcome in this way.

Bennett also reports a second suggestion for a supplementary premise, a suggestion due to Wallace Matson. IP2 states that: "Two substances having different attributes have nothing in common with one another." Bennett notes that this proposition can be read in two ways. On the weaker reading, it is equivalent to:

(IP2$_w$): Two substances which share *no* attributes have nothing in common.[14]

On the stronger reading, it is equivalent to:

(IP2$_s$): Two substances which differ in respect of *any* attribute have nothing in common.

If we adopt the stronger reading of IP2 (and assume that "$x$ and $y$ have nothing in common" entails "x and y do not share an attribute"), then IP2 will block the Bennett-Leibniz objection by ruling out the possibility of substances sharing some but not all of their attributes.

Which is the correct reading of IP2? Most commentators, including Bennett, find a weak reading more natural. Beyond the language of IP2 itself, there are two further sources of evidence about its meaning: Spinoza's employment of IP2 and his demonstration of it. Since the former is not definitive,[15] let us consider the latter. The demonstration of IP2 reads, in its entirety, as follows:

> This also is evident from D3. For each [substance] must be in itself and be conceived through itself, or [*sive*] the concept of the one does not involve the concept of the other.

The demonstration does not concern itself in any way with the question of whether "$x$ and $y$ have nothing in common" (and hence also "$x$ and $y$ differ in *all* attributes") follows from "$x$ and $y$ differ in *some* attributes," as the strong reading requires. This fact provides a powerful reason against supposing that the strong reading of IP2 is correct. Furthermore, it suggests that even if we do accept the strong reading of IP2 and, with it, Matson's proposed reply to the Leibniz-Bennett objection, we will only put the difficulty off one step: the objection that Spinoza has no basis for asserting (2) in IP5D will simply be replaced by the objection that he has no basis for asserting IP2 in the strong sense needed to justify (2).

However, not only does the demonstration make no apparent mention or use of the distinction between differing in some and differing in all attributes, it makes no *explicit* mention of the notion of sharing or differing in attributes at all. Hence it also makes no explicit use of the fact that the scope of IP2 has been limited to those substances "having different attributes" in *any* sense at all. For this reason it may seem, superficially at least, that the demonstration will prove the unrestricted conclusion that *no* two substances have anything in common with one another, precisely as well or as badly as it proves the stated conclusion that substances "having different attributes" have nothing in common with one another. And this unrestricted conclusion, of course, would entail IP5 directly. We must therefore ask why Spinoza did not draw the *un*restricted conclusion at IP2 and then proceed *immediately* to infer IP5 from it. Why did he restrict IP2 to substances "having different attributes," in *whatever* sense we take that phrase?

Presumably, Spinoza restricts the scope of IP2—and, implicitly, of its demonstration—to "substances having different attributes" because he doubts or denies that the demonstration would be *sound* in application to pairs of substances not meeting this condition. In linking "each must be conceived through itself" with "the concept of the one does not involve the concept of the other" by means of the term *'sive'* (which carries the sense of "in other words"), Spinoza implies that he regards these characterizations as simply equivalent. (The use of *'sive'* in IA5 also implies that "the concept of the one does not involve the concept of the other" is equivalent to "cannot be understood through one another.") Thus, IP2D involves only one real inference, that from:

(a)   Each substance must be in itself and be conceived through itself, i.e., the concept of one does not involve the concept of the other.

to:

(b)   Two substances are such that they have nothing in common with one another.

If Spinoza wishes to restrict the scope of this inference to substances "having different attributes," it can only be because he is concerned that, unless the substances in question "have different attributes," they might "have something in *common*" even though each is "in itself and conceived through itself" and (equivalently) "the concept of one does not *involve* the concept of the other." Such concern would be well-taken. For as its equation with "being conceived through" (at IP2D) and "being understood through" (at IA5) indicates, having concepts that "*involve*" one another is not merely a matter of two things having something in common; it requires that one thing have conceptual *priority* over the other. The possibility thus remains open that each of two substances could be understood without the *aid* of the concept of the other—and thus neither would have a concept *involving* the other—and yet when both were understood, it would nevertheless be seen that they had something (i.e., an attribute) *in common*. Hence, if the inference from (a) to (b) is to be valid, it must (at least) be restricted to substances that do *not* share any attribute; and IP2's phrase 'having different attributes' must be understood in that sense.

Thus, if Spinoza intends a restriction of scope on IP2D, it must be a restriction that requires the weak reading of IP2. For the only plausible rationale for a restriction is that just described; and this rationale requires restricting the inference in IP2D to substances that do not share even a single attribute. In contrast, no rationale can be given for restricting the inference in IP2D to "substances that differ in one or more attributes," as the strong reading of IP2 would demand. If the weak reading of IP2 is required, of course, then IP2 cannot be successfully used to justify (2) in IP5D. Moreover, if Spinoza intends a restriction of scope in IP2D, he would almost certainly be sufficiently aware of the rationale for his own restriction, and for the consequent weak reading of IP2 that the rationale requires, that he would not intend to use IP2 to justify (2).

Perhaps, however, Spinoza restricts the scope of IP2 to substances "of different attributes" *not* because he thinks that the demonstration *must* be so restricted, but simply because he has no need of the more general conclusion, since he prefers to demonstrate IP5 in another way. If this latter interpretation is correct, then Spinoza *would* regard IP2D as itself strong enough to warrant the strong reading. Nevertheless, appeal to IP2D still would not fully overcome the Leibniz-Bennett objection; for IP2D itself would be objectionable on the grounds that the inference from "two substances are in themselves and conceived through themselves" to "two substances are such that they have nothing in common" is valid only for substances that do *not* share any attribute. In other words, the proposed use of IP2D will be subject to the objection that Spinoza *ought* to have appreciated the rationale just described for restricting it, even if he did not actually appreciate it. Moreover, if Spinoza regards the restriction of IP2 to substances "having different attributes" as superfluous, then the fact that he nevertheless does not infer IP5 *directly* from IP2D would suggest that he does not *wish* to use IP2D in the derivation of IP5. If so, of course, then he would certainly not intend to justify premise (2) as a *part* of IP5D by appeal to IP2D.

A third proposal, suggested by Allison, is to supplement IP5 with the thesis that each attribute is identical with its substance.[16] Thus he writes:

> [F]or Spinoza, attributes are expressions of the essence, or nature, of substance. This allows him to claim that each attribute *is* substance, considered from a certain point of view or taken under a certain description, which, in turn, explains why he sometimes identifies substance and attribute. But if this is so, then it follows that attribute *y* of substance A is identical to attribute *y* of substance B, just in case they express the same nature or essence—that is, are descriptions of the same thing. . . . Consequently, it turns out on analysis that if the two attributes are really identical, then they cannot express the nature of two distinct substances. Conversely, if they do express the natures of two distinct substances, then the attributes cannot be identical.

The claim that Spinoza identifies a substance, not merely with the sum of its attributes, but with *each* of its attributes, is controversial. We need not decide its truth, however, in order to consider the proposal. For present purposes, the substance-attribute identity thesis cannot be understood only to claim an identity between a substance and its own *instance* of each of its attributes. For *that* thesis would not prevent the existence of the pairs of substances on which the Bennett-Leibniz objection depends: one substance might be identical with its own instance of attribute $A_1$, while another substance was identical with its own instance of $A_1$ and with its own instance of $A_2$.[17] Hence, the substance-attribute identity thesis must be understood to mean that for each kind of attribute, there is only *one* instance of it, identical with the substance that it characterizes. Then the thesis blocks the Bennett-Leibniz pairs of substances—but it is also an even *stronger* claim than IP5 itself, which it entails. As such, it is even *more* difficult to see how the identity thesis could be derived from Spinoza's definitions and axioms than it is to see how IP5 itself could be. Certainly, the identity thesis does not occur in the *Ethics* prior to IP5. Hence, the problem of justifying (2) in IP5D will simply be replaced by the problem of justifying the strong identity thesis. For this reason, the proposed supplement to IP5 does not fully overcome the Bennett-Leibniz objection. Moreover, it seems unlikely that Spinoza would rely on the strong identity thesis as a tacit premise of IP5D: for not only does he not state the thesis prior to IP5, but that thesis alone actually entails IP5, and would thereby render all the rest of his argumentation in IP5D entirely superfluous.

Alan Donagan suggests a related but different proposal, relying not on an identity of substance and attribute, but rather on the relation by which attributes "constitute the essence" of substances. He writes:

> The supplement Spinoza's proof needs to dispose of the objection is ready to hand. If the essences of the two substances differ because one is constituted by all the attributes that constitute the other, and by one more which the other lacks, then each of the attributes they have in common must constitute two different essences. However, the very idea of an attribute

constituting really distinct essences seems unintelligible; and if it is, Leibniz's objection fails. . . . Spinoza holds that an essence may be constituted by really distinct attributes, but nobody has seriously ascribed to him the inverse, that an attribute may constitute really distinct essences.[18]

In other words, from the proposed supplementary premise:

(a) No attribute can constitute two or more distinct essences.

together with the principle that:

(b) If the essences of two substances differ because one is constituted by all the attributes that constitute the other, and by one more which the other lacks, then each of the attributes they have in common must constitute two different essences.

taken together with the definition of 'attribute' given at ID4:

(c) By attribute, I understand what the intellect perceives of a substance as constituting its essence.[19]

it follows that:

(d) Two substances cannot share some attributes but differ in others.

But it is upon the possibility of substances sharing some attributes while differing in others that the Leibniz-Bennett objection depends; hence, if Spinoza is entitled to employ (a) and (b), the objection will be blocked.

'Distinct [or 'different'] essences' in (a) and (b) clearly means "qualitatively different essences" and not merely "essences of numerically distinct substances." For if it meant the latter, (a) itself would be highly controversial. Certainly, it would be disputed by any Cartesian who holds both that the essential attribute of all mental substances is thought, and that there is a multiplicity of such mental substances. Moreover, Donagan's mention of (b) would then be superfluous, since (a) and (c) alone would entail IP5 itself. Interpreting 'distinct essences' to mean "qualitatively different essences," however, does not remove all of the difficulties. For what, exactly, is the "constituting" relation? Does every attribute simply constitute its *own* essence of the substance which has it, or does every substance have a *single* essence constituted jointly by all of its attributes? If the first construal of the relation is correct[20], then the fact that substances of different attributes have *different* essences will not prevent them from also *sharing* some essences in common. Hence, if two substances which differ in some attributes share an attribute, that attribute will constitute the same essence for both substances—in which case (b) will not be true, and so pairs of substances that share some but not all attributes need not run afoul of principle (a).

Or suppose, on the other hand, that the second construal of the "constituting" relation is correct: each substance must have only a single essence, but may have multiple attributes, *each one* of which "constitutes" that essence. Then the precise nature of the "constituting" relation between attribute and essence will be sufficiently open that the truth of (a) will come into question. That is, it will not be obvious whether the same attribute *cannot* go to constitute different essences—in particular, by "constituting" the essence of two different substances which have different total sets of attributes but which have that attribute in common. IP11 ("God, or a substance consisting of infinite attributes, each of which expresses eternal and infinite essence, necessarily exists"), a proposition on which Spinoza's proof of monism depends, requires that at least one substance have multiple attributes; and Spinoza takes care to argue in IP10S that substances *can* have multiple attributes. The very question of whether the same attribute might *not* "constitute different essences" by belonging to substances with different sets of attributes is surely one of the first questions that any Cartesian who has been convinced by Spinoza's arguments at IP10S or IP11D will want to raise. *Prima facie*, the possibility of one attribute constituting different essences is no less intelligible than the converse possibility of two *distinct* attributes each constituting the *same* essence of a substance to which they both belong. And although (as Donagan rightly remarks) acceptance of the former possibility has never been ascribed to Spinoza while acceptance of the latter possibility has been, that may only be because the former possibility is obviously incompatible with IP5 itself, whereas the latter possibility is (on the second construal of the "constituting" relation) required by IP10S and IP11. It is *not* because the former possibility is obviously ruled out by any thesis or argument Spinoza provides *prior* to IP5 or IP5D.[21]

On neither construal of the "constituting" relation, then, can the use of (a) and (b) as supplementary premises fully overcome the Leibniz-Bennett objection. Moreover, it seems unlikely that Spinoza would suppose that they should. For if the first construal were correct, (b)'s falsehood would surely be evident to him. And if the second construal were correct, then (a)'s need for justification in the light of the possibility of substances with multiple attributes should be almost equally evident; since he does nothing to justify (a) prior to IP5, it seems unlikely that he would nevertheless intend to use it as a tacit premise of IP5D.

Not every response to the Leibniz-Bennett objection takes the form of proposing a supplementary premise. Thus, although Curley forcefully restates the objection, and observes that Spinoza himself asserts at IP10S that "it is far from absurd to attribute many attributes to one substance," he nevertheless makes two important points in Spinoza's (at least partial) defense. First, much of the metaphysics of the *Ethics* is developed against Descartes, and Descartes *himself* could not use the Leibniz-Bennett objection to refuse assent to (2), since Descartes holds that no substance has more than one attribute. Secondly, Spinoza's argument may also be effective for *us*, since to a large extent we share Descartes's intuitions about this matter. There is, Curley remarks,

> a real problem involved in explaining how it is that a being with two attributes would constitute one being rather than two. If we can have no conception of sub-

stance apart from its principal attribute, what are we saying of a substance when we say that it is one, yet has two attributes?[22]

These points are important and valid; nevertheless, they cannot overcome the objection. Certainly, if Descartes were to read the *Ethics*, he would not avail himself of the Bennett-Leibniz objection when (2) actually occurs in IP5D, since the objection depends on the possibility of substances with more than one attribute (or "principal attribute," in Descartes's terminology), a possibility which he rejects. However, Spinoza's argument for monism at IP14D and IP14C requires acceptance of *both* IP5 *and* IP11 (i.e., that God, the substance of all possible attributes, necessarily exists). And if the demonstration of IP11 were to convince Descartes, he would *at that moment* be forced to grant not only the possibility but the reality of substances with more than one attribute. If the demonstration of IP11 becomes effective for Descartes, in other words, the use of (2) in the demonstration of IP5 must apparently then *cease* to be effective, and so the demonstration of monism will not be effective for Descartes either. And what is true of Descartes will also be true of us: if, as readers, we cannot accept IP11 without giving up the grounds of our previous commitment to IP5, then Spinoza cannot convince us of either IP14 or IP14C1, which depend on both.[23] Thus, Descartes's (and our) initial intuitions in favor of the "one attribute per substance" doctrine do not provide considerations capable of overcoming the Leibniz-Bennett objection. Moreover, these intuitions must be overthrown by our acceptance of IP11; and since Spinoza shows himself in IP10S to be aware of the need to overthrow them prior to establishing IP11, it seems unlikely that he would nevertheless intend to appeal to them for the defense of IP5.

I conclude that none of the proposals surveyed provides a way of fully overcoming the Leibniz-Bennett objection on the basis of the resources available to Spinoza, and that none provides a likely account of Spinoza's own intentions. It is therefore worth investigating whether a better response to the objection, and a likelier interpretation of Spinoza, is possible.

## 4. Differences of Attributes

The Leibniz-Bennett objection arises from the fact that (2) seems to ignore the possibility of substances that differ by sharing some but not all attributes. In order to see how this possibility might legitimately be ignored, let us focus on what is actually involved in two substances sharing a particular attribute. One way of putting the question Spinoza faces is this: Given that there may be a multiplicity of what we ordinarily call "things" present under a given attribute, how can it be established how many genuinely distinct *substances* are expressed or represented? More specifically, given all of the affections of an attribute A1, how, if at all, could two substances $x$ and $y$ be expressed within the realm of that attribute? In response to this question, we may distinguish four alternatives.

The first alternative is that the two substances $x$ and $y$ will be distinct without any difference of affections or of attributes. Spinoza rules out this alternative, of course, at (1), by citing IP4 (to which I will return). The second alternative is that there will be a difference between the affections of $x$ and the affections of $y$. This alternative, however, is the subject of Spinoza's argument at (3)-(6), an argument which, I have claimed, can plausibly be interpreted as showing that, on his definitions and axioms, differences of affections can be set aside because they will always be due to some prior difference of attributes.

A third alternative is that there will be some difference of the attribute A1 itself—prior to any difference of affections— as it belongs to $x$ and as it belongs to $y$. But such a difference, Spinoza argues in (2) of IP5D, requires that "A1" in fact be two *different* attributes and so "it will be conceded that there is only one [substance] of the *same* attribute" (emphasis added). Thus, the argument stipulates a strict criterion for two instances of attributes to be instances of "the same" attribute; and it is because of this stipulation that the argument is able to rule out the possibility of different instances of "the same attribute" having an intrinsic qualitative difference that is prior to any difference of affections. The criterion itself, as a stipulation, does not require defense. It is not, however, an unusual criterion: in general, if two instances of characteristics differ *intrinsically* in some way, then they are instances of different characteristics. Furthermore, it is quite defensible: any way of trying to postulate an *intrinsic* qualitative difference between two instances of the same attribute would arguably amount either to regarding $A_1$ as a compound of two other attributes, and hence not itself an attribute; or to regarding the difference simply as a difference of the affections of the attribute, rather than of the attribute itself.

The fourth and remaining alternative is that the two substances will differ in attributes by differing not in the shared attribute $A_1$ but only with respect to some other attribute or attributes. This is, of course, the kind of attribute-sharing described by the Leibniz-Bennett objection. But rather than concentrating on the relation of $A_1$ to the *other* attributes of $x$ and/or $y$, let us instead consider for a moment how, precisely, $x$ and $y$ could share the given attribute $A_1$ with no *difference* of that attribute. Since attributes constitute the essence of substances (ID4), every affection of substance must (by ID5) be conceived through some attribute (Spinoza confirms the correctness of this inference at IIP1D). The affections *of* a particular attribute are thus simply those that must be conceived through that attribute. Since, as argued in Section II of this essay, any difference of affections must be due to and conceived through some difference of the attributes through which they are conceived, it follows from the assumption that $x$ and $y$ do not differ in *attribute* $A_1$ that $x$ and $y$ cannot differ in their *affections* of $A_1$ either. This leaves only two subalternatives: that the affections of $A_1$ in $x$ are *numerically* identical with the affections of $A_1$ in $y$; or that the affections of $A_1$ in $x$ are not numerically identical with the affections of $A_1$ in $y$ but are *qualitatively* identical with them in a way that results in no difference of affections of that attribute.

However, the principle that a given affection can only be in one substance is not only universally conceded, it seems to be implied by ID5 ("By mode, I understand the affections of a substance, or that which is in another through which it is also conceived"), IA1 ("Whatever is, is either in itself or in another"), and IA2 ("What cannot be conceived through another must be conceived through itself"); and Spinoza's later references to the substance/affection relation also seem to presuppose that each affection is only in one substance. If we read ID5 and IA1 as indeed requiring that no affection can be in more than one substance, then substances $x$ and $y$ cannot share numerically identical affections; and this leaves only the subalternative that they share A1 without any difference of A1 by having *qualitatively* identical but numerically distinct sets of affections.

But is it possible for two distinct substances to have qualitatively identical but numerically distinct sets of affections of an attribute in such a way that that there is no "difference of affections" between the two sets? ID5 states that: "By mode I understand the affections of a substance, or that which is in another through which it is also conceived." Yet if two sets of modes are qualitatively identical in such a way that there is no "difference of affections" between them, then it appears that they must be conceptually indistinguishable, i.e., conceived in exactly the same way. Hence, either *both* sets of modes can be conceived through a given substance or *neither* can be conceived through it. Accordingly, the supposition that two distinct substances have qualitatively identical sets of affections would lead to the conclusion that either both sets of affections can be conceived through both substances or neither set of affections can be conceived through either substance. But since the affections of substances are modes, which can only be conceived through exactly one substance (as we are interpreting ID5 and IA2), this will constitute a *reductio ad absurdum* of the supposition that two distinct substances can have qualitatively identical sets of affections.

This conclusion could be resisted only if qualitatively identical sets of affections with no "difference of affections" could be conceptually distinguished from each other by their different *relations* to things that are themselves conceptually-distinguishable. But, by IP4D, differences of substance reduce to differences of attribute; and two qualitatively identical sets of affections of the *same* attribute could not be distinguished by their being affections of *different* attributes. Furthermore, since they are conceived completely through their own attribute, their difference also cannot be conceived through any *other* attribute; and, indeed, any reason to conceive of one set of affections as related to another attribute would equally be a reason to conceive of the other set as so related as well. Since the two sets of affections are qualitatively identical, neither can be conceptually distinguished by its relation to the other; and since there is no "difference of affections" between them, they also cannot be conceptually distinguished by the relations among their members. Finally, they cannot be distinguished by their relation to affections of other attributes, either. For once again, since they are conceived completely through their own attribute, their difference cannot be conceived through their relation to affections of any *other* attribute; and any reason for conceiving of one set of affections as related to a set of affections of another attribute would equally be a reason to conceive of the other set as so related as well. But according to IP4D, there are only substances and their affections.[24] Hence, there cannot be two substances that share an attribute with no difference of affections of that attribute, as the fourth alternative would require. The Leibniz-Bennett objection is therefore blocked.

The argument just considered generates, in effect, a principle of the identity of indiscernibles for sets of affections. But this should not be surprising. For IP4D, on which IP5D partly depends, also embodies a principle of the identity of indiscernibles. It is instructive to compare them. IP4D may be outlined as follows:

(i) "Whatever is, is either in itself or in another . . ." (IA1)

(ii) "By substance I understand what is in itself and conceived through itself, i.e, that whose concept does not require the concept of another thing, from which it must be formed." (ID3)

(iii) "By mode I understand the affections of substance, or that which is in another through which it is also conceived." (ID5)

(iv) "[O]utside the intellect there is nothing except substances and their affections." [from (i)-(iii); see note 25 below]

(v) "[T]here is nothing outside the intellect through which a number of things can be distinguished from one another except substances . . . and their affections." [from (iv)]

(vi) "By attribute I understand what the intellect perceives of a substance, as constituting its essence." (ID4)

(vii) "Two or more distinct things are distinguished from one another, either by a difference in the attributes of the substance or by a difference in their affections." [from (v)-(vi)]

It may immediately be objected that (vii) does not follow from (v) and (vi) except on the further assumption that two or more distinct things must be distinguished by a difference of *something*; and this assumption is a version of the identity of indiscernibles. Could not two substances be distinct without being distinguished at all? A line of reasoning similar to that just considered in connection with affections is also applicable to substances: every substance must, by definition (ID3), be conceived through itself; but two indistinguishable substances are conceived in exactly the same way, and hence would either be conceivable through *both* substances or not conceivable through *either* substance. Since every substance must be conceived only through itself (ID3 and IA2), this constitutes a *reductio ad absurdum* of the supposition that there could be two indistinguishable substances.

Thus, I suggest that Spinoza neglects the Leibniz-Bennett objection because, for the same reasons that had already led him to assume the identity of indiscernibles for substances in IP4D, he also assumes the identity of indiscernibles for sets of affections of an attribute in IP5D. Indeed, because IP4 applies not merely to distinguishing substances but also to any "two or more distinct things," the version of the identity of indiscernibles tacitly employed in IP4D may itself be intended to have affections, and hence sets of affections, with its scope. Given the identity of indiscernibles for sets of affections, it follows that any difference between two substances sharing an attribute must manifest itself *within* that attribute, either as a difference of attribute or a difference of affections or both; for the situation envisioned by the Leibniz-Bennett objection would require two substances to have qualitatively identical sets of affections, which then could not be conceived uniquely through either substance. Hence, only differences manifested *within* an attribute need be addressed in IP5D.

Given the brevity of IP5D and the lack of any explicit consideration of the Leibniz-Bennett objection, it is not possible to say with absolute certainty how, or whether, Spinoza would have tried to refute the objection. Nevertheless, there are several reasons to suppose that the interpretation of IP5D just described is a plausible interpretation of Spinoza's own intentions. First, it allows Spinoza to reject the objection on grounds that do indeed follow from reasonable interpretations of his definitions and axioms, so that we need not ascribe to him any error about the consequences of his own axiomatic basis. Secondly, given the fact that Spinoza gives no explicit consideration to the Leibniz-Bennett objection in IP5D, interpretations which make his grounds for rejecting it simple and fundamental are to be preferred over interpretations which make his grounds complicated and derivative. On the present interpretation, his grounds are simple and fundamental, depending chiefly on the definition of a mode or affection as being in and (completely) conceived through a substance to generate an identity of indiscernibles for sets of affections. Thirdly, the grounds suggested by the present interpretation also provide, at the same time, a plausible explanation for Spinoza's tacit invocation of a principle of the identity of indiscernibles in the demonstration of the immediately preceding proposition, IP4; and the fact, if it is a fact, that Spinoza tacitly employs parallel considerations in IP4D would help to explain his willingness to do so also in IP5D. In the absence of any damaging objections to its adequacy as an interpretation, and in the absence of any alternatives of equal plausibility, therefore, I conclude that it is a likely interpretation of Spinoza's intentions.

## 5. Conclusion

In this essay, I have argued that Spinoza can overcome the Hooker-Bennett objection to IP5D by construing the relation of being "in and conceived through" strongly enough to require that any difference in affections must be conceived through some difference in the nature of the substances themselves, and hence in their attributes. For on that construal, all differences of affections between substances will require a prior difference of attributes, and the attempt to find differences of affections can be reduced to the attempt to find differences of attribute. I have also argued that, given this result, Spinoza can overcome the Leibniz-Bennett objection by taking the relation of being "in and conceived through" in such a way that each thing (and hence each affection) must be in and conceived through exactly one substance. For then, since two instances of attributes cannot differ intrinsically in any way without being instances of *different* attributes, two substances *sharing* an attribute could not (by the previous result) differ in their *affections* of that attribute either; but then neither set of affections could be conceived uniquely through only one of the two substances, contrary to the nature of the substance/affection relation. In addition, I have argued that it is plausible to suppose that Spinoza actually would have rejected the two objections for the reasons just described. Since the two objections can both be overcome, and since I have argued that the only two prior propositions employed in IP5D—namely, IP1 and IP4—are themselves legitimate inferences from the definitions and axioms of Part I of the *Ethics*, I conclude that we may regard IP5 itself as a legitimate inference from those definitions and axioms.

What then is the basis of Spinoza's monism, and how is it related to Bennett's explanatory rationalism? If a claim as strong as IP5 is indeed to be a legitimate inference from Spinoza's definitions and axioms, then those definitions and axioms must themselves have considerable content. On my view, much of that content is to be located in the "in and conceived through" relation, which requires both that affections be completely conceived through their substances (in a sense strong enough to entail that differences in affections can always be conceived through differences of substance), and that everything be in and conceived through exactly one substance. Because the definitions of 'substance' and 'mode' that employ this relation are therefore rich in content, the claim that something *is* a substance or a mode is a powerful claim. Accordingly, claims *about* substances and affections might have been expected to leave many things outside their scope. This outcome is prevented, of course, by IA1 ("Whatever is, is either in itself or in another") which, as we have seen in IP4D, Spinoza uses to infer that everything is either a substance or an affection of substance. (Spinoza repeats this use of IA1 in IP15D to infer from substance monism that *everything whatever* is in God; given the mutual entailment of "being in" and "being conceived through," IA2 ("What cannot be conceived through another, must be conceived through itself") would serve equally well for this purpose.) Thus, it is through IA1 (or, alternatively, IA2) that the ideal of complete conceivability which ID3 and ID5 apply to both substances and modes comes to be extended to everything whatever.

The requirement that each thing be *completely* conceived, when combined with IA4's requirement that everything be conceived through its cause (or reason), entails what Bennett calls explanatory rationalism: the thesis that whatever is the case can be explained. On my interpretation, the rejections of both the Hooker-Bennett objection and the Leibniz-Bennett objection depend on the thesis that any difference of affections must involve a difference of attributes; and to the extent that the argument for that thesis depends on IA4, to that extent, at least, Spinoza's monism depends on an application of explanatory rationalism. (In fact, the dependence is even stronger, since the second proof of IP11 also appeals to explanatory rationalism.) Bennett is therefore right to see

explanatory rationalism near the heart of Spinoza's metaphysics: it is an extension and application of his fundamental
commitment to the complete conceivability and intelligibilty
of all things. And it is that commitment, I suggest, that is at
the very basis of Spinoza's monism.

## NOTES

1  Quotations from Spinoza are taken from the Curley translation, CS. All abbreviations are those adopted by the present
   volume.
2  Jonathan Bennett, *A Study of Spinoza's Ethics* (Indianapolis: Hackett, 1984), Chapter 3, Section 17, pp. 66-70.
   Following others, I shall cite this work as *Study*.
3  Michael Hooker, "The Deductive Character of Spinoza's
   Metaphysics," in *The Philosophy of Baruch Spinoza*, edited
   by Richard Kennington (Washington, D. C.: The Catholic
   University of America Press, 1980), pp. 17-34; and William
   Charlton, "Spinoza's Monism," *The Philosophical Review*,
   vol. XC, no. 4 (October 1981), pp. 503-529. Bennett cites
   both works in his bibliography, and mentions Charlton in a
   footnote to his discussion of the objection.
4  The objection appears in Leibniz's reading notes (1678) to
   Part I of the *Ethics* (G I, 139-50), at L 198-99.
5  Partly for these reasons, perhaps, many commentators have
   sought to find a further Spinozistic argument for IP5 at IP8S,
   in a discussion which concludes that "there exists only one
   [substance] of the same nature." Although I cannot argue the
   point here, I believe that Spinoza's argument at IP8S does not
   and is not intended to establish a conclusion as strong as that
   of IP5. On the contrary, it establishes, and is intended to
   establish, only the weaker conclusion that no two substances
   can share the same total set of attributes. This weaker conclusion, of course, could not serve in place of IP5 in Spinoza's
   argument for monism.
6  *Study*, pp. 67-68. Similar interpretations occur in Charlton,
   *op. cit.*, pp. 514-15, and R. J. Delahunty, *Spinoza* (London:
   Routledge and Kegan Paul, 1985), pp. 113-14.
7  Edwin Curley, *Behind the Geometrical Method: A Reading of
   Spinoza's Ethics* (Princeton: Princeton University Press,
   1988), pp. 17-18 and 145.

8    Henry Allison, *Benedict de Spinoza: An Introduction,* revised
     edition (New Haven: Yale University Press, 1987), pp. 53-
     54. The reference is to Bertrand Russell, *A Critical Exposition
     of the Philosophy of Leibniz* (London: Allen and Unwin,
     1900), p. 59.

9    The importance of this paraphrase in applying IA4 to the def-
     inition of 'substance' is noted by Edwin Curley, *Spinoza's
     Metaphysics: An Essay in Interpretation* (Cambridge, Mass.:
     Harvard University Press, 1969), p. 15.

10   In my "Spinoza's Necessitarianism," presented at the first
     Jerusalem Spinoza Conference at Hebrew University in 1987,
     and forthcoming in the volume of the proceedings of that
     conference, edited by Yirmayahu Yovel (Philosophia Verlag,
     1990).

11   See Spinoza's TdIE §95, II/34/29 - 35/9, at CS 39. See also
     *Ethics* IP19D.

12   Specifically, Spinoza infers God's necessary existence from
     IP7 together with God's definition as a substance consisting
     of infinite attributes. For more discussion of the use of IP7 in
     IP11D, see my "Spinoza's 'Ontological' Argument," *The
     Philosophical Review,* vol. LXXXVIII, no. 2 (April 1979),
     pp. 198-223.

13   To be sure, this explanation could be blocked by IP5; for IP5
     entails that, contrary to appearances, $x$ and $y$ could not both be
     possible substances. But of course it is precisely the truth of
     IP5 that is in question; to appeal to it in this context would be
     to incorporate IP5 into its own demonstration and thereby to
     argue in a circle.

14   A slightly stronger but still weak reading—one that I prefer—
     would be, "two substances, insofar as they have different at-
     tributes, have nothing in common." For present purposes,
     however, nothing turns on the difference in scope between
     this weak reading and the one Bennett gives.

15   Spinoza explicitly employs IP2 three times in the *Ethics,* in
     IP6D, IP11D, and IP12D. IP6D and IP12D both use citations
     of IP5 to restrict the context in which IP2 is used to sub-
     stances that share *no* attributes. Thus, only the weak reading
     of IP2 is needed in these demonstrations. IP11D initially ap-
     pears to require the strong reading, but the weak reading suf-
     fices if it is combined with a tacit use of IP5 (which is, of
     course, available for use at this point of the *Ethics*). This tacit
     use of IP5 would not render the appeal to IP2 superfluous,

since the point Spinoza wants to make in IP11D is one about causation, and Spinoza always mediates points about causation between substances by means of the concept "having nothing in common with"—a concept that occurs in IP2 but not in IP5.

16  Henry Allison, *op. cit.*, pp. 52-53.

17  This version of the identity thesis does presumably entail by the transitivity of identity that, if there are any pairs of substances of the kind described by the Leibniz-Bennett objection, then a substance $y$'s instance of an attribute A1 would be identical with $y$'s instance of an attribute A2, whereas a substance $x$'s instance of attribute A1 would not be identical with *any* instance of attribute A2. It may be argued that this consequence would be difficult to allow, and hence that this version of the identity thesis does count against the possibility of such pairs of substances. The consequence does not, however, seem to be ruled out by anything Spinoza provides prior to IP5. Furthermore, the consequence is not obviously any *more* difficult to allow than a consequence *already* entailed by this version of the identity thesis together with the transitivity of identity: namely, that each instance of an attribute in any multi-attribute substance is identical to every instance of every other attribute of that substance.

18  Alan Donagan, *Spinoza* (Chicago, University of Chicago Press, 1988), pp. 70-71.

19  Donagan does not cite ID4 explicitly, but it is clearly required in order to guarantee that every attribute "constitutes the essence" of the substance to which it belongs.

20  This alternative is perhaps especially suggested by the original 1677 Dutch translation (*Nagelate Schriften*) of ID6, which states that each attribute of God expresses "an" eternal and infinite essence. The lack of articles renders the original Latin ambiguous. See CS ix-x and 405-407 for an account of the relation of the *Nagelate Schriften* to the Latin original.

21  Nor is it ruled out, as far as I can see, by the definition of 'constitute' that Donagan goes on to give later (Donagan, *op. cit.*, p. 88):

> It is now possible to state generally what Spinoza means both when he says that an attribute 'constitutes' the essence of a substance, and when he says that two really distinct attributes 'constitute' the same essence. ...

> Two or more attributes constitute the essence of the
> same substance if and only if it is a law of nature that
> whatever has either can neither be created nor de-
> stroyed, and that *it immanently causes modes both in*
> *the same order as whatever has the other, and with the*
> *same interconnections*, although insofar as it is consti-
> tuted by one, its kind is distinct from what is insofar as
> it is constituted by the other.

My uncertainty derives from my difficulty in interpreting the
phrase I have italicized.

It would, of course, be possible to build into the definition
of 'constitute' the requirement that no two attributes can
"constitute" the essence of the same substance unless every
substance having one of them also has the other, thus blocking
the Leibniz-Bennett objection. This would not be a satisfactory solution, however. For it would block the objection
only at the cost of rendering it difficult or impossible for
Spinoza to establish that any given characteristic *is* an attribute
(i.e., something that *constitutes* the essence of a substance).
In order to establish that a characteristic was an attribute, he
would first have to establish the following: that if *one* substance has both that characteristic and also some attribute $A_1$,
then *every* substance has either both of them or neither.
Furthermore, it would become debatable whether all or any
substances *had* attributes in this sense. Thus, such a definition
would only force the same difficulty to recur in a different
form.

22  Edwin Curley, *Behind the Geometrical Method, op. cit.*, pp.
    15-16.

23  The quotation from Curley cited above continues:

> In the special case of God, there may be a solution to
> that problem (see below, #11 [this refers to a later dis-
> cussion of IP10 and IP10S]). In the case of beings with
> some, but not all, attributes, I can see no such solution.

This may suggest to some a possible response to the difficulty
I have described: namely, to argue that, at IP10S (and hence
prior to IP11 and IP14), Spinoza shows that God is the only
possible *exception* to the general doctrine that there cannot be
substances of more than one attribute. The response would
not be sufficient, however, for two reasons. First, Spinoza's

declaration at IP10S that "it is far from absurd to attribute many attributes to one substance" is not directed towards an exception but is completely general, as are the grounds given for it. Secondly, and even more fundamentally, since IP10S does nothing of its own to rule out attribute-sharing, the admission of God as the sole exception to the "one attribute per substance" doctrine would itself be sufficient to allow the formulation of a version of the Leibniz-Bennett objection. The objection will now simply take the form of asking why God and a second substance could not share attribute $A_1$ and yet "differ in their attributes" in virtue of the fact that God has *all* other attributes in addition to $A_1$ while the second substance has *no* other attributes. This version of the objection is itself sufficient to undermine any version of IP5 that is strong enough to be useful in IP14D.

24   Spinoza deduces the claim that nothing exists except substances and their affections from IA1 ("Whatever is, is either in itself or in another") plus ID3 and ID5 (the definitions of 'substance' and 'mode'). It may be questioned whether the claim does follow, since it entails that something exists in itself if and only if it is conceived through itself, and that something exists in another if and only if it is conceived through that other. This suggests that Spinoza understands "a is in b" and "a is conceived through b" as mutually entailing, either through their own meaning, or through the mediation of one or more axioms. Such mediation may be supposed to occur either through IA4, in virtue of a relation between being "in" and being "caused by"; or it may be supposed to occur through IA6, on the assumption that the relation of being "in" is the relation that must hold between an object and the thing it is conceived through if true ideas are to correspond with their objects. In any case, given the fact that Spinoza seems to regard the inference from IA1, ID3, and ID5 to the claim that nothing exists but substances and modes as an obvious one, I take it as a constraint on the adequacy of the interpretation of the term "being in," that "being in" and "being conceived through" should somehow be mutually entailing. For discussion of the relation between being "in" and being "conceived through," see Curley, *Spinoza's Metaphysics, op. cit.*, chapter 1.

# NOTES ON A NEGLECTED MASTERPIECE (II): THE *THEOLOGICAL-POLITICAL TREATISE* AS A PROLEGOMENON TO THE *ETHICS*

*Edwin Curley*

*Bennett on the TTP*: Jonathan Bennett begins his *Study of Spinoza's Ethics* by observing that its central topic is "Spinoza's one indisputable masterpiece, the *Ethics*."[1] Before analysing that master work, he devotes the first section of his study, some ten paragraphs, to saying how the *Ethics* relates to the rest of the Spinozistic corpus. His sole reference to the *Theological-Political Treatise* comes in the following sentence:

> Setting aside Spinoza's grammar of the Hebrew language and his two works on politics, which I do not find helpful in understanding the *Ethics*, we are left with six substantial items. (*Study*, p. 7)

He then proceeds to discuss the *Short Treatise*, the *Treatise on the Emendation of the Intellect*, Descartes's *Principles of Philosophy*, the *Metaphysical Thoughts*, and the *Correspondence*. The *Ethics* itself is the sixth of his "six substantial items."

Now it's only natural, certainly quite reasonable, for a commentator on the *Ethics* to measure the importance of Spinoza's other works by the extent to which they shed light on the *Ethics*. Someone engaged, as I am, in a translation of the TTP may have a different perspective, may wish to press the TTP's claims to attention for its own sake, to emphasize its importance in the history of Biblical criticism,[2] or more generally, in the emerging Enlightenment critique of revelation as a basis for religious belief,[3] or its significance in the history of political thought, as a contribution to social contract theory and an argument for freedom of thought and speech. The TTP is not *just* a "political work." As its title suggests, much of it is devoted to theological issues. But it is *also* a political work. Nowadays historians of early modern philosophy tend to leave the history of early modern political philosophy to specialists in the history of political thought. Perhaps they think that in this area philosophy becomes too embroiled in empirical issues to be properly philosophical. Analogously, historians of political thought may find all that theology too remote from their concerns.[4] Perhaps it is not surprising that this masterpiece, as I shall presume to call it, has been quite generally neglected, at least among English language writers on Spinoza.[5] But I think that this neglect is a mistake, that proper appreciation of a systematic philosopher like Spinoza requires attention to the consequences he thought his metaphysics, epistemology, and psychology had for religion and politics.

In this paper I propose to make a case for the study of the TTP. But I shall try to make that case on Bennett's own terms. I shall not argue that the TTP is worth our attention for its own sake, as a substantial treatment of issues which are important, whether or not they fall comfortably within our current notions of what counts as philosophy. Rather, I shall restrict myself to arguing that a study of the TTP may illuminate the *Ethics* itself. In E IVP37S1 Spinoza claims to have shown what the foundations of the state are (II/236/25-26). But his treatment of politics in the *Ethics* is very sketchy. Presumably this is partly because he already had developed his views on politics to some extent in the TTP, and partly because he hoped to work them out more fully in the treatise on politics which he never lived to finish, the TP. At the very least the TTP gives us some leads to the consequences he thought his view of the world at large had for the world of human interaction in civil society. But we shall see that it also gives us some valuable hints for understanding his view of the world at large.

*Spinoza's purposes in writing the TTP*: One of the first things to recognize about the TTP is that it is a work with multiple agendas. Spinoza announces its primary purpose in the subtitle, when he claims to show in this work

> not only that freedom of philosophizing can be granted without harm to piety and the peace of the state, but also that it can not be taken away without taking away the peace of the state and piety itself. (III/3)

But when he writes to Oldenburg in Ep 30, he indicates a more complex set of objectives:

> I am composing now a treatise about my opinion regarding scripture. What moves me to do this are: 1) the prejudices of the theologians, for I know that they are the greatest obstacle to men's being able to apply their minds to philosophy; so I am busy exposing them and removing them from the minds of the more prudent; 2) the opinion ordinary people have of me; they never stop accusing me of atheism, and I am forced to rebut this accusation as well as I can; and 3) the freedom of philosophizing and saying what we think; I want to assert this in every way; here it is suppressed as much as possible because of the excessive authority and impudence of the preachers. (IV/166/20-29)

This is interesting in a number of respects. Of course the goal mentioned in the subtitle is mentioned here, but as the last of three, and with the additional information that, in spite of what he may say in the TTP itself, he does not really think the Dutch republic is one where people have complete freedom to form their own judgments and to worship God as they think best.[6] But the political goal of defending freedom of thought and speech is subordinated to two theological goals.

Spinoza's briefest description of the subject of the TTP, after all, is "my opinion regarding scripture." His first goal is to remove any theological prejudices which may prevent men from philosophizing, particularly, as the Preface will tell us, the notion that reason must be the handmaid of theology (§34), i.e., that in any conflict between reason and Biblical religion, reason must be subordinate. What scripture can teach us is how to conduct our lives; it cannot teach us to have a proper conception of God, since it records the thoughts of men who did not have one themselves (cf. ii, 31, III/37/10-18). So Spinoza's first theological goal is connected with his second: to defend himself against the ordinary person's claim that he is an atheist, he must try to convey a more correct conception of God, must try to persuade his reader that his own non-Biblical conception of God is sounder than the one the Bible offers.

There is a problem, though, about the intended audience of the TTP. Towards the end of the Preface, as he is concluding his summary of the main points of the work, he seems to be addressing the philosopher: "These, Philosophical reader, are the things I here give you to be examined . . ." (Preface, §33, III/12/3). But no sooner has he said that than he claims that the main points he will argue for in the TTP are already "more than adequately known to philosophers" (*philosophis satis superque nota*). On the other hand, in spite of what he says in Ep 30 about trying to correct the opinion ordinary people have of him, he says in the preface that he has no desire to commend his book to the non-philosopher. He does not seem to have much hope that non-philosophers can be saved from superstition. "I know that it is as impossible to destroy the superstition of the common people as it is to destroy their fear" (III/12/10-11). His intended audience, then, seems to be the person who aspires to being a philosopher, and who has some, imperfect knowledge of philosophy, but whose reverence for scripture gets in the way of his becoming a full-fledged philosopher, the person "who would philosophize more freely if he were not prevented by the thought that reason must be the handmaid of theology" (§34, III/12/17-18), someone like van Blijenbergh, who longs to know the truth, but regards scripture as a sounder guide to the truth on speculative matters than his own corrupted reason.[7]

Spinoza seems to have begun work on the TTP in 1665, at a point when he nearly had a complete version of the

*Ethics* ready to go to press. But he set the *Ethics* aside to work on the TTP. No doubt he had many motives for doing this, but I believe one of them must have been that he thought the time was not yet ripe for the *Ethics*, that his experience had persuaded him that people needed to be rid of their theological prejudices before they could give a sympathetic hearing to the *Ethics*.[8] In a similar way he had, some years earlier, set aside work on the *Ethics* to write his geometric exposition of Descartes's *Principles of Philosophy*, in the hope that this would create sufficient interest in his own work that people in power would see to it that he could publish it "without danger of inconvenience" (Ep 13, IV/64/6).

The TTP is a prolegomenon to the *Ethics*, not only in the sense that it is an attempt to remove a prejudice standing in the way of an appreciation of the philosophical argument of the *Ethics*, the prejudice that Scripture is an accurate revelation from God of the truth about speculative matters, but also in the sense that it is an attempt to present, in a less forbidding, non-geometrical form, and in a way which sometimes appeals to the very prejudices it wishes ultimately to remove,[9] many of the teachings of the *Ethics*. Sometimes those teachings need to be sifted out from a mass of material which has no obvious connection with the *Ethics*. Spinoza will anticipate important teachings of the *Ethics* in places where we might not expect it, as when a discussion of the doctrine that the Jews were God's chosen people leads to a treatment of predestination and arguments for determinism. But the sifting is worth the work. Not only does the TTP present certain teachings of the *Ethics* in a more popular form, sometimes it also suggests a way of reading the *Ethics* which can be illuminating. At the very least, we get to see what doctrines of the *Ethics* he wished to emphasize in this popular presentation. We may also get some insight into the reasoning processes which led to those conclusions—which are not necessarily the same as the reasoning processes Spinoza went through in the *Ethics*. If Spinoza thought there were alternate routes to the same conclusion, that's worth knowing. Again, since the TTP was written between the time Spinoza had completed, or nearly completed, a first draft of the *Ethics* and the time he completed the final version, it may offer some insight into his development. Finally, the way the doctrine is stated may suggest interpretations which make it more defensible.

A *thought-experiment*: To see what we can learn about the *Ethics* from the TTP I propose the following thought-experiment. Suppose the *Ethics* had never been published. Suppose that in a moment of despair, as he lay dying, Spinoza had committed the only existing manuscript of his masterwork to the flames, leaving behind just that brief table of contents which appeared on its title page:

I.   Of God

II.  Of the Nature and Origin of the Mind

III. Of the Origin and Nature of the Affects

IV.  Of Human Bondage, or of the Power of the Affects

V.   Of the Power of the Intellect, or of Human Freedom

Suppose also that all of Spinoza's correspondence relating to the *Ethics* had been destroyed, and indeed, all of his other works, apart from the TTP. How much of the teaching of the *Ethics* would we be able to reconstruct from the TTP? What is present there? What is absent? Why is what is present present, and what is absent absent? In what ways might our understanding of his views on these topics, if derived only from the TTP, be a misunderstanding? And are there any ways in which an understanding of Spinoza, constructed only on this base, might deepen our understanding of the themes the TTP has in common with the *Ethics*?

These are larger questions than I can hope to deal with thoroughly in this essay, but I do hope to make a beginning. To do that, of course, I will have to make use of the knowledge we are pretending not to have; we have to know what we are looking for to see how much of it we can find. But I think the exercise will be instructive.

# 1. Of God

Let's begin by noting a striking absence: the terms 'substance', 'attribute' and 'mode' rarely occur in the TTP, and when they do, they are normally not used in the technical sense they have in the *Ethics*.[10] So there is no hint in this work of such characteristic Spinozistic doctrines as IP5 ("there cannot be two or more substances of the same nature or attribute"), IP6 ("One substance cannot be produced by another substance"), IP7 ("It pertains to the nature of substance to exist"), IP8 ("Every substance is necessarily infinite") or IP14 ("Except God, no substance can be or be conceived"). Perhaps that is one reason why a commentator on the *Ethics* might feel this work held little illumination for him.

Nevertheless, in spite of this absence, Spinoza does manage in the TTP to affirm most of IP15 ("Whatever is, is in God, and nothing can be or be conceived without God"). In fact, on the title page Spinoza takes an approximation to the first part of IP15 as a motto for the whole work, in a citation of 1 John 4:13 ("By this we know that we remain in God and that God remains in us, because he has given us of his spirit"). I say only that the scriptural verse *approximates* the first half of IP15, partly because John presumably intends what he says to apply only to human beings, whereas Spinoza's proposition is more general. More critically, though, it's not obvious that the similarity between the passage in John and that in the *Ethics* is more than a superficial verbal one.

What John seems to have in mind, as appears from the context, is that, since God is love, insofar as we love one another, we participate in the divine nature, and so Spinoza construes the verse when he cites it again in TTP xiv, 17. Presumably this is something Spinoza *could not* mean by IP15, since he holds that God is without any affect of joy or sadness (VP17), and hence, strictly speaking, loves no one (VP17C). Spinoza anticipates these teachings of the *Ethics* in the TTP when he dismisses Scriptural attributions of a mind and of affects to God as examples of anthropomorphism, a concession Scripture makes to popular superstition (i, 35, III/25/25-30).

But in the TTP Spinoza does suggest a somewhat different sense in which we can be said to participate in the nature of God. Natural knowledge, he says, has as good a right as any other knowledge (such as prophetic knowledge) to be called divine, since "God's nature, insofar as we participate in it, and his decrees, as it were, dictate it to us" (i, 3). At this point, this is a mysterious claim, but as we proceed, I think we will be able to construct a theory as to what it means.

We might make a start by noting that Spinoza's commitment, in the TTP, to the second part of P15 is less equivocal. In ch. iv, he writes:

[10] . . . Since all our knowledge, and the certainty which really removes all doubt, depends only on the knowledge of God (both because nothing can either be or be conceived without God, and because we can doubt everything so long as we have no clear and distinct idea of God), it follows that our greatest good and perfection depend only on the knowledge of God, etc.

[11] Next, since nothing can be or be conceived without God, it is certain that all those things which are in nature involve and express the concept of God, in proportion to their essence and perfection. Hence, the more we know natural things, the greater and more perfect is the knowledge of God we acquire. (III/59-60)

It seems clear that Spinoza is doing some bridge-building here, as he had been earlier in appropriating the passage from John. Here the language is reminiscent of the Cartesian project of founding certainty in our knowledge of having been created by an omnipotent God, who could have no motive to deceive us. But the thought is not really that Cartesian.

Spinoza takes the latter half of P15—nothing can be or be conceived without God—as a premise in this argument, without having previously made any attempt to demonstrate it, indicating that this is a proposition he expects his proto-philosophical audience, whether Cartesian, or merely Jewish or Christian, to accept without argument. Perhaps he would be right in that expectation, and one conclusion we might draw from this is that when Spinoza demonstrates this proposition in the *Ethics* he is providing unusual grounds for accepting something his readers would accept without that (or any) argument. But §11 shows that it is supposed to be a consequence of this dependence of things on God that *everything in nature involves and expresses the concept of God*. It looks as though the theistic commonplace that nothing can be conceived [sc. as existing] without [being conceived as having been brought it into existence by] God is being read as entailing that we cannot even form a conception of any thing without in some way having the concept of God.

Now this is surely no Cartesian or Judaeo-Christian commonplace. Descartes held, as a good Christian, that *human beings* are created in the image of God, and justified the claim to similarity by arguing that the human will is infinite, other human mental capabilities being too limited to warrant the comparison. (Fourth Meditation, AT VII, 57) But he also held that all other created beings are merely material objects having no significant similarity to their creator. Even animals, for him, were soul-less machines. In this Descartes went to an extreme to which few of his contemporaries were prepared to follow him. But it *is* the teaching of Scripture that God made *man* in his own image (Genesis 1:26), and presumably it is this unique relationship to God which is thought to explain God's granting dominion to man over all the rest of creation. It would not, I think, be natural for a Jew or a Christian to say that everything in nature involves and expresses the concept of God. (Cf. TTP i, 15, which says that it seems quite contrary to reason for a created thing to express the essence of God. This may appear to introduce an inconsistency in the TTP, but I suggest that we should emphasize the *seems* there, and view Spinoza as arguing *ad hominem* in that passage.)

If we had the full doctrine of the *Ethics* available to us, it would be easy enough to offer an interpretation of this. Spinoza, we might say, understands by God a being absolutely infinite (ID6), a definition he takes to imply that God has all possible attributes, including both thought and extension (IIPP1&2). Insofar as man is a unity of mind and body (IIP13C), an individual capable of being conceived both as a mode of thought and as a mode of extension (IIP21S), conceiving him will presuppose having a conception of the attributes under which we conceive him. Since those attributes constitute the essence of God (IDD4&6), conceiving man presupposes having a conception of God. And since any finite thing must be conceived under one or the other of these divine attributes, any idea of any finite thing involves the concept of God (IIP45).

But most of the relevant doctrine of the *Ethics* is not available to the reader of the TTP. Spinoza does say (vi, 58, III/93) that God is an absolutely infinite being, in whom all the perfections are contained. But that statement by itself, not offered as a definition, is again one Spinoza thinks of as a commonplace: anyone who is even slightly more knowledgeable than the multitude knows *that* (and therefore knows that the language of the creeds—which suggests that God exists in a place and has a right and a left hand—must be taken metaphorically). Nowhere in the TTP does he make explicit that he takes it to be a consequence of this common conception of God that extension is one of his attributes. What is there in the TTP that a reader dependent on it alone could use to understand the thesis that everything in nature involves and expresses the concept of God?

Perhaps Spinoza felt that the text of the TTP left this thesis too mysterious, for in one of the notes he added to his work after its publication,[11] he offered the following explanation:

> For us to be able to conceive God's nature clearly and distinctly, it is necessary for us to attend to certain very simple notions which they call common, and connect

with them those which pertain to the divine nature. And then, for the first time, it becomes clear to us that God exists necessarily and is everywhere, and then at the same time, that all the things we conceive involve in themselves the nature of God and are conceived through it . . . . (III/252/30-253/6)

Now this is no more than a hint, but it seems a useful hint, particularly in the context of the TTP. First of all, what are these "very simple notions which they call common"?

In chapter vii of the TTP, arguing for his distinctive approach to the understanding of Scripture, Spinoza appeals to the analogy of the way we investigate natural things:

In examining natural things we strive, before all else, to investigate the things which are most universal and common to the whole of nature—viz., motion and rest, and their laws and rules, which nature always observes and through which it continuously acts—and from these we proceed gradually to other less universal things. (vii, 27, III/102/21-25)

The claim is that we ought to do the same in the interpretation of Scripture: proceed from the most universal to the less universal.

Now this is a fair description of the new science of nature, as practised by Descartes in the latter parts of the *Principles of Philosophy*. We establish universal laws of motion, laws obeyed by all bodies, and given our understanding of those laws, we try to work out how they will produce the effects they do in particular cases, where the bodies have a certain definite kind of structure. E.g., we try to explain the properties of a magnet in terms of the primary qualities (size, shape, location, motion) of its microstructure (cf. the *Principles* IV.133-83).

In the note added to the TTP Spinoza is telling us that we must connect these simple, common notions—motion and rest and their laws and rules—with the things which pertain to the divine nature, which is to say, in the technical language of the *Ethics*, connect them with the divine attributes.

In a certain sense, this was something Descartes had also claimed to do, insofar as he thought he could deduce the content of his fundamental laws of motion from the divine nature (cf. the *Principles* II.37). But he, of course, did not count extension as one of God's attributes. For him, deduction of the laws of motion from God involved thinking of those laws as like the laws a king might impose on his kingdom (cf. the letter to Mersenne of 15 April 1630 (K 8-12)). Their immutability and even their content was supposed to be a function of the immutability of his will.

This is a conception of God which Spinoza firmly rejects, both in the TTP and in the *Ethics*. It is a fiction of the multitude that God is related to nature as a king to his kingdom (TTP vi, 69, III/96; cf. E IIP3S). God is not a legislator (iv, 37, III/65). When we speak of his decrees, all we *can* mean, given that ascribing a mind to God is a form of anthropomorphism, are the laws of nature, conceived not as the commands of a personal being, but simply as certain regularities which hold necessarily in nature, and hence, hold throughout nature (cf. vi, 22, III/85; iv, 1, III/57). When Spinoza says that we must connect the common notions with the things which pertain to God's nature, he means that we must see motion and rest and the laws governing these phenomena as flowing necessarily from the nature of the attribute of extension.

Spinoza is cautious in the TTP about saying flatly that extension is an attribute of God, but his argument that we must not conceive God as a lawgiver presupposes that it is. The argument is contained essentially in three sections of chapter iv, sections which may seem to make some surprising concessions to popular opinion:

[23] We can easily deduce what must be maintained regarding [the question whether we can conceive God as a lawgiver, or prince prescribing laws to men] from the nature of God's will, which is distinguished from his intellect only in relation to our reason, i.e., in themselves God's will and God's intellect are really one and the same. They are distinguished only in rela-

tion to the thoughts we form concerning God's intellect. (III/62/27ff.)

Now the identity of will and intellect in God is a common
medieval doctrine, as I've noted elsewhere.[12] But so far this
argument has an *ad hominem* air about it, since attributing
any intellect or will to God seems impossible, if it is anthropomorphism to think of God as having a mind, a claim
Spinoza asserts dogmatically in the TTP and attempts to
prove in the E (cf. i, 35, and E IP31).
As the argument proceeds, however, Spinoza suggests
the possibility of an unusual interpretation of those notions:

[24] For example, when we attend only to the fact that
the nature of a triangle is contained in the divine nature
from eternity, as an eternal truth, then we say that God
has the idea of the triangle, *or* understands the nature
of the triangle. But when we attend afterwards to the
fact that the nature of the triangle is contained in the
divine nature in this way, solely from the necessity of
the divine nature, and not from the necessity of the
essence and nature of the triangle, indeed, that the necessity of the essence and properties of the triangle, insofar as it is conceived as an eternal truth, depends
only on the necessity of the divine nature and intellect,
and not on the nature of the triangle, then that very
thing which we called God's intellect we call God's
will *or* decree. (III/62/32-63/7)

One thing this passage is saying is that we *can* make sense of
ascribing an intellect to God, provided we understand that to
mean recognizing that the natures of finite things, like triangles, are contained in the divine nature.
Now I think a reader with some knowledge of traditional
theology, but ignorant of the *Ethics*, might well be puzzled
by that suggestion, since it seems to reverse the natural order
of things. For him the only sense in which God's nature
*contains* the natures of finite things like triangles is that
God's intellect contains ideas of those things. But here the

latter doctrine is the *analysandum*, not the *analysans*. We understand what it means to talk of God's understanding the nature of a triangle by interpreting it to mean that God's nature contains the nature of the triangle. Once the possibility of interpreting that latter formula in terms of there being an idea of the triangle in God's intellect has been excluded, it is difficult to see what this can mean, except that God's nature involves the attribute of extension and that the nature of extension explains the nature of the triangle, i.e., that the eternal truths which explicate the nature of the triangle follow from the eternal truths which explicate the nature of extension (or that the general truths we can formulate about triangles are deducible from general propositions about extended objects, the axioms, definitions and postulates of Euclidean geometry). The final sentence of the quoted passage confirms this reading by indicating that the eternal truths which state the nature and properties of the triangle are not self-explanatory, but rather are to be explained in terms of the nature of God.

Part, then, of what Spinoza means when he says that we finite things participate in God's nature is that, to the extent that we are material beings, we have properties, and act in ways, which exemplify necessary general truths about material objects, truths which are ultimately deducible from the nature of extension, via certain laws of motion and rest. I say that this is *part* of what is meant, to allow that our participation in God's nature implies also that, to the extent that we are thinking things, we exemplify necessary general truths about the properties and behavior of thinking things, truths which must, in turn, be deducible from the nature of thought, though how this deduction might work is more obscure in the case of thought than it is in the case of extension.[13] Understanding that God exists necessarily and is omnipresent is understanding that these eternal truths apply universally in nature (cf. note 6, III/252-53, cited above on pp. 118-19).

This conception of God and of his relation to finite things clearly commits Spinoza to a strong affirmation of determinism, and indeed, the determinism of the TTP was one of the things which most distressed its earliest readers.[14] Spinoza quite open about his determinism, though some of the formulas he uses to express it might easily be misunderstood if taken out of context, e.g.:

> No one chooses any manner of living for himself, nor does anything, except by the singular calling of God, who has chosen him before others for this work, or for this manner of living. (iii, 10)

Talk of God's choice, without further explanation, might suggest that God has a mind, a doctrine which at this point in the argument of the TTP has already been rejected as superstitious (cf. i, 35). But the context in fact provides the needed explanation: to say that no one does anything except by God's calling is to say that no one does anything except by God's "eternal guidance and decree," a concept which has just been defined in the following way:

> By God's guidance I understand the fixed and immutable order of nature *or* the connection of natural things . . . the universal laws of nature, according to which all things happen and are determined, are nothing but the eternal decrees of God, which always involve eternal truth and necessity. Therefore, whether we say that all things happen according to the laws of nature, or whether we say that they are ordered according to the decree and guidance of God, we say the same thing. (iii, 7-8)

This is not a claim that these expressions are equivalent in their ordinary use, which would be patently false, but an attempt at reductive analysis, which offers to translate the language of myth, unacceptable in its literal construction, into the language of sober 17th Century science.

Our participation in the nature of God, then, is to be understood in terms of God's being the ultimate cause of everything we are and do, not as a king ordains the actions of his subjects, but as a set of very general propositions entails less general consequences. This conception of God's causality, however, in turn implies that there is also a role in the explanation of events in nature for an appeal to finite things as (partial) causes of those events. God is the cause of all things in the sense that any event in nature owes its explanation to laws which are ultimately derived from the laws implicit in the divine attributes. A law of nature, as Spinoza conceives it, has the form of a generalized conditional, as in the example he takes as a paradigm:

All bodies, when they strike against other lesser bodies, lose as much of their motion as they communicate to the other bodies. (iv, 2)

We might paraphrase this by saying that in any particular case of collision between two bodies, if body $x$ strikes against a lesser body $y$, and communicates to $y$ a certain quantity of motion, $x$ itself loses the same amount of motion $y$ gains. Suppose some body, call it $a$, does collide with another lesser body, $b$, and does lose a certain quantity of motion. This law will explain $a$'s loss of that particular quantity of motion only in conjunction with the additional information that $a$ collided with, and communicated motion to, $b$. The form of the explanation requires some adversion to particular events in addition to the law of nature which connects the antecedent events with the one we are concerned to explain.

In the TTP Spinoza shows himself to be well aware of this implication of his conception of causality. So he argues in TTP iv, 3-4, that because the "universal consideration of fate and the connection of causes cannot help us to form and order our thoughts concerning particular things," we must explain such things by their proximate causes. What he means by this reference to proximate causes is illustrated in the discussion of miracles in chapter vi. Scripture, he has observed, tends to explain particular events by reference to the will of God, without mentioning intervening or particular causes (i, 8). Nevertheless, sometimes scriptural narratives do mention the particular or proximate causes by which God's will works, as when it mentions that Saul sought out Samuel because his servant had advised him that Samuel might help him find his lost asses (1 Samuel 9, discussed by Spinoza in vi, 40-41), or when it mentions that the increasing population of the Israelites resident in Egypt caused the Egyptians to fear their power, and hence to oppress them (Exodus 1:7-11, discussed in vi, 42). In each case there is some particular event—advice, growing population—followed by another particular event—seeking Samuel, fear and oppression. For Scripture the antecedent event is just a means a personal being deploys to work his will. For Spinoza talk of God's will is a mythical way of alluding to the connection between events which is governed by eternal laws of nature, in these cases, laws of human psychology.

The reader of the *Ethics* who approaches Part I with the TTP firmly in mind will not be surprised, then, when he finds Spinoza writing in IP28 that anything which is finite and has a determinate existence must be caused by something else which is also finite and has a determinate existence, and so on, *ad infinitum*. The causality of the finite by the finite is perfectly consistent with the causality of everything by God, because God's causality works by laws of nature which are of no effect unless there are particular events which, by satisfying the antecedents of the laws, enable them to produce the results they do. This is an understanding of God's causality which I think it would be hard for a reader dependent on the *Ethics* alone to reach, since the crucial concept of a law of nature is hardly mentioned in Part I of the *Ethics*. So it is no accident that my treatment of God's causality in *Spinoza's Metaphysics* made frequent reference to the TTP.[15]

Once we understand how finite things are related to God—that their existing in God (to use the language of the *Ethics*) or their participation in God's nature (to use the language of the TTP) is a matter of their being caused by God, in the sense that their properties and actions follow from God's nature, in conjunction with information about other finite things—then an interpretation of the mysterious infinite modes falls out rather easily. The laws of motion and rest, and the more specific laws of nature which follow from them, are the link between the most fundamental structural principles of the world (the eternal truths which express the nature of God's attributes) and the singular statements which describe the properties and actions of finite things. While we cannot, without the aid of information about the finite, expect any deduction of the finite from the infinite (of singular statements about finite things from the laws of nature unsupplemented by statements of antecedent conditions), we can expect deductions from the more general to the less general to be possible without the aid of information about the finite. That is why Spinoza says (E IP21) that the infinite modes follow from *the absolute nature of* God's attributes, i.e., from the nature of God's attributes *simpliciter*, without any further conditions being necessary.

## 2. Of the Nature and Origin of the Mind

If one of Spinoza's primary goals in the TTP is to wean people away from their incorrect, Scriptural conception of God to the correct, philosophical conception of God, then we would expect the TTP to be rich in anticipations of, and hints for the proper interpretation of, Part I of the *Ethics*. Spinoza's goals in the TTP do not require nearly so much anticipation of the other parts of the *Ethics*, and accordingly we cannot expect as much illumination from them. But they are not without their use, as I propose to show.

The TTP does not, I think, say much to indicate what Spinoza's own views of the relation of mind to body are. Indeed, to the extent that it says anything about that relationship, it seems somewhat misleading, insofar as a number of passages might suggest some allegiance to Cartesian dualism. E.g., in the course of defining his position on the nature and limits of the power of sovereigns, Spinoza notes that obedience is a matter, not so much of external action, as of the "internal action of the mind" (xvii, 8). The contrast between the internal actions of the mind (knowable only by the subject?) and the external actions of the body (knowable by anyone, including the sovereign?) may suggest a Cartesian theory of the mind, though the notion that our thoughts are private, whereas our external actions are not, is, I think, only a datum for the philosophy of mind, which any theory must reckon with. Behaviorism struggles to deny this datum, but unconvincingly.

More critical, I suggest, is the notion that the internal action is less under the control of the sovereign's commands and threats of punishment than external actions are:

[9] Although minds cannot be commanded as much as tongues can, nevertheless, minds are, in some manner, under the command of the sovereign, who can bring it about in many ways that most men, by far, believe, love, and hate, whatever he wishes. [10] Though these things do not happen by the direct command of the sovereign, still, as experience abundantly witnesses, they often happen by the authority of his power and by his guidance . . . . (xvii, 9-10, III/202/26-32)

The view here is that, while you can command someone else to *say* whatever you like, with good hopes of achieving your result, if you have the power, you cannot simply command someone else to *think* whatever you like, not with any hope of success, no matter how great your power, though you can, of course, bring it about indirectly that the other person believes (loves, hates, etc.) much of what you wish. Presumably Spinoza has in mind such indirect means as, say, controlling the information the person has access to, indoctrination, and so on.

The emphasis in xvii, 9-10, is on the *ability*, within limits, of one person to influence the thoughts of another. When Spinoza returns to the topic in ch. xx, however, his emphasis is on the *limits*:

[8] . . . no one can surrender his liberty of judging and thinking what he wishes, but everyone, by the supreme right of nature, is master of his own thoughts . . . . (xx, 8, III/240/15-17)

The idea, apparently embraced here, that the mind is immune to external influence suits the political conclusion Spinoza wants to draw: the sovereign cannot try to dictate what people say without unfortunate results; people will think what they like, no matter what they are forced to say; they will resent being forced to say what they do not think; if the

sovereign goes too far in trying to control their speech, he
will undermine his own power; since Spinoza identifies right
with power, this limitation on his power implies a limitation
on his right.

But is Spinoza, given his own view of the relation between mind and body, entitled to this happy conclusion? The
notion that the person is the master of his own thoughts suggests that man, insofar as he is (or has) a mind, is a kingdom
within a kingdom, with absolute power over his own actions. That is, it suggests the Cartesian view of man, rejected
in the Preface to Part III of the *Ethics*, not the view that man
is a part of nature, whose actions are necessarily determined
by the actions of other finite things in nature, according to
eternal and immutable laws (IVP2, IIIPref). Can we make
sense of the notion that the person is the master of his own
thoughts without assuming that a person is an immaterial,
thinking substance, exempt both from the causal influence of
its own body and from the influence other bodies might have
on it via their actions on its body? Again, is the claim that we
have an inalienable freedom to judge as we *wish* consistent
with the anticartesian account of judgment in IIP49S?

Someone may suggest that we have here another instance
of an all-too-common pattern in the TTP: Spinoza concealing
the extent of his radicalism by adopting conventional views,
in this case, mind-body dualism and freedom to believe as
we please. But though I think that pattern does exist in the
TTP, I'm not sure this is an instance of it. For the most part
the passage cited from xx, 8, is only a somewhat exagger-
ated version of the view Spinoza had expressed more carefully in xvii, 9-10. According to the latter passage, there is
much that a sovereign can do to influence the thoughts of his
subjects, but he cannot do it simply by commanding them to
believe certain things, and there will evidently be some people, at least, who are capable of resisting, to some extent at
least, the indirect methods he can use. I see no way this can
be made consistent with xx, 8, but I suggest that in the latter
passage Spinoza permitted his desire to reach a certain political conclusion to induce him to overstate his assumptions
about the limits of the sovereign's power.

As for the supposed freedom to judge as we wish, Spinoza may have been echoing, without intending it to be taken in a Cartesian sense, the title of ch. xx: "In a free state everyone may think what he wishes and say what he thinks." The title in turn is an allusion to a passage in Tacitus: "Rare happiness of the times, in which it is permitted to think what you wish and to say what you think" (*Histories* I, i, 4). In that context there is no question of a Cartesian ability to believe in the face of evidence to the contrary.[16] The issue is simply the desirability of being permitted to believe what seems to you to be true.

We can, I think, understand the claim that people have a certain control over their thoughts without giving in to the Cartesian fantasy of a mind insulated from the causal processes of the universe. The privacy of our thoughts, which I have claimed is a datum for any credible philosophy of mind, does offer us some protection against outside interference, as Spinoza's Marrano predecessors had learned during their persecution by the Inquisition, and as Spinoza himself no doubt experienced during the period when he maintained a merely external conformity to the practices of the Jewish community in Amsterdam.[17] If a person is prepared to feign the belief others wish him to have, he may free himself from unwanted attentions and go his own way, up to a point at least.

Spinoza does maintain in the TTP that man is a part of nature (iv, 3), but he does not explore the metaphysical basis for that doctrine. So far as I can discover, there is no hint of the doctrines that man is a mode of substance rather than a substance (cf. IIP10 and I/132/5-17), or that the human mind is the idea of the human body (IIP13). And there is just the barest hint of the doctrine that the human mind is part of the infinite intellect of God (IIP11C) in i, 5, where Spinoza writes that

Simply because our mind contains objectively in itself, and participates in, the Nature of God, it has the power to form certain notions which explain the nature of

things and teach us how to conduct our lives.
(III/16/10-13)

This passage, however, is more interesting from an epistemological point of view than from a metaphysical one. That
the mind participates in the nature of God might be taken to
mean merely that the human mind is like God in being a
thinking thing, not a very controversial doctrine. But that the
mind's power to form notions capable of explaining the nature of things depends on its containing within itself a representation of the divine nature is a more distinctively
Spinozistic doctrine, reminiscent (for those of us who know
the *Ethics*) of the account of the third kind of knowledge in E
IIP40S2. Why Spinoza should attribute this importance to
having an adequate idea of God's nature, he does not explain
in the passage cited, though an explanation does emerge
from the passages discussed in the preceding section of this
paper.
    On the whole, though, there is relatively little anticipation
of Spinoza's theory of knowledge in the TTP. He does have
some very suggestive things to say about the way we ought
to conduct ourselves in the quest for knowledge (notably in
vii, §§7, 13, and 27), things I found helpful once in making
the case that Spinoza has a valued place for experience in his
theory of knowledge.[18] There are some similarly interesting
passages dealing with problems we may encounter in communicating our knowledge to others (e.g., in v, 35-37, and
vii, 67). The former of these is particularly intriguing in its
implication that it is possible to understand our experience
clearly and distinctly, i.e., that knowledge involving experience is not inherently inadequate. But on the whole Spinoza
seems in the TTP to work with a simple contrast between the
intellect and the imagination (ii, 1 & 4), a contrast which
generally favors the intellect as a means of attaining knowledge. The division of knowledge into three kinds does not
appear.

## 3. Of the Origin and Nature of the Affects

Let us begin, again, by noting absences. Some of the most distinctive features of Spinoza's psychology are not antici- pated in the TTP. He does not, for example, draw any distinction between active and passive affects, and he does not undertake any reduction of complex affects, like love and hate, to simple ones, like joy and sadness.[19] Though he makes it clear that he regards human beings as a part of na- ture, subject to the laws of nature (iv, 2-3), and though his political arguments regularly appeal to those laws, there is no attempt to systematize them, to identify some as basic and derive others from them.

Still, there are a number of respects in which the TTP an- ticipates the psychology of the *Ethics*. E.g., Spinoza makes it clear that his psychology is strongly egoistic:

> It is a universal law of human nature that no one ne- glects anything which he judges to be good, except from the hope of a greater good, or from fear of a greater injury; nor does anyone endure any evil, except to avoid a greater one, or from the hope of a greater good. That is, of two goods, everyone chooses what he judges to be the greater, and of two evils, the one which seems to him lesser . . . . (xvi, 15, III/191/34- 192/4)

If it should be objected that this passage is not *clearly* egois- tic,[20] since it commits Spinoza only to the proposition that people necessarily choose *what seems to them best* (perhaps taking into account the interests of everyone affected by their action), and not necessarily *what it seems to them will be best for them*, I think the applications Spinoza makes of this law show that reading to be untenable:

> Suppose that without deception I have promised some-
> one that for a period of 20 days I will not taste food or
> any other nourishment, and afterwards I see that I have
> promised foolishly and that I cannot stand by my
> promise without the greatest injury. Since, according
> to natural right [*jus*], I am bound to choose the lesser
> of two evils, I can, with the greatest right [*jus*],[21]
> break such an agreement, and treat what I have said as
> if it had not been said. (xvi, 18, III/192/16-21)

It seems clear in this example that the calculation the
promisor is making is that it would be very damaging *to him*
to keep his promise, and that he is not claiming a freedom
not to keep it on the ground that it will be best *for everyone*
if he does not keep it.[22]

Again, commenting on the inevitable limits of the power
of the sovereign, Spinoza writes:

> It would be of no avail to command a subject to hate
> someone who has united the subject to himself by a
> benefit, to love someone who has done him an injury,
> not to be offended by insults, not to desire to be free
> from fear, or a great many other things of the same
> kind, which follow necessarily from the laws of hu-
> man nature. (xvii, 2)

This passage illustrates, what ought in any case to be obvious, that the egoism in question here is compatible with
people's having some interest in the interests of others. But
the view seems to be that such interests are derivative from
self-interest. If the sovereign had commanded me to hate
someone who had not won my good will by doing me some
good, I might obey. Not that hate can simply be commanded. As Spinoza makes clear in the *Ethics*, hate presupposes a belief that the person hated has harmed you. If
beliefs cannot be directly commanded, neither can affects
which essentially involve them. But if the sovereign can
manipulate his subjects' beliefs indirectly, then there will be
a sense in which he can command them to hate what he
wishes them to hate.

Each person has, of course, a variety of interests: e.g., in not being hated, in not being insulted, in being free of fear, and so on. But the *Ethics* makes one interest fundamental, the interest in self-preservation. Without attempting a systematic psychology, the TTP gives the same principle great prominence:

> Because the supreme law of nature is that each thing strives to persevere in its state,[23] as far as it can by its own power, and that not from consideration of anything else, but only of itself, it follows that each individual has a supreme right to this, i.e., to existing and acting as it is naturally determined to do. (xvi, 4, III/189/25-30)

I've translated the phrase *quantum in se est* here as I did in my translation of the parallel passage in the *Ethics* (IIIP6): "as far as it can by its own power," a rendering Parkinson has criticized as "seriously misleading," on the ground that it

> suggests that each particular thing has its own separate power, much as a Leibnizian monad has. But this was not Spinoza's view; the power that each thing has is a form of the power of God.[24]

Parkinson cites E IIP45S, according to which

> the force by which each [thing] perseveres in existing follows from the eternal necessity of God's nature.

Parkinson prefers the alternative translation which I had relegated to a footnote, according to which *(quantum) in se est* would be translated as it is in the definition of substance: "(in so far as) it is in itself."

Now it's an interesting question how much difference this makes. Much will no doubt depend on what you think *esse in se* means in the definition of substance. In an earlier article[25] I had contended that White's and Elwes' translation of this phrase, as it occurs in IIIP6—"exists in itself"—was "right in spirit," because I held a certain view about what the definition of substance means. "To exist in itself" is to exist independently of any external causes, to be *causa sui*[26] or to exist by one's own power (and not, say, to be an ultimate subject of predication). But I doubted whether the phrase, as used in IIIP6, was intended to remind us of the definition of substance, and I preferred a translation which seemed to me to pick up the resonances of Cartesian and Newtonian formulations of the principle of inertia. Someone who does not accept my understanding of the definition of substance, and who thinks that *esse in se* means the same thing in IIIP6 as it does in the definition of substance, owes us an explanation of how it can be that every finite thing *in some degree* satisfies the definition of substance (as *quantum* implies).[27]

However that gets sorted out, it seems to me that one thing we cannot say is that my translation is wrong because it suggests that finite things have a power of their own. No doubt it's true that Spinoza thinks the power each thing has to exist and act follows from the necessity of God's nature. I take it that the analysis of §1 of this paper explains in what sense that is true. But Spinoza also says quite plainly in the TTP that the power of the whole of nature, which he identifies with the power of God, is the sum of the powers of the individual things in nature:

> The right of nature extends as far as its power does, for the power of nature is the very power of God, who has the supreme right over all things. But because the universal power of the whole of nature is nothing but the power of all individuals together, it follows that each individual has a supreme right to do all the things it can do, *or* that the right of each thing extends just as far as its determinate power does.[28]

This is not, obviously, to say that each finite thing has a power *separate* from the power of God. But then I never said the power of finite things was *separate* from God's. Rather I think that the powers finite things display in their law-governed interactions with one another *are* the way God's power manifests or expresses itself (cf. E IIIP6D).

There are many other topics we might pursue here. A treatise on political philosophy is bound to make assumptions about human psychology. Perhaps this inevitable concern of political philosophy with matters we regard as empirical is one reason why (Anglo-American) philosophers tend to leave political philosophy to specialists in that subject. In any case, though Spinoza does not try to develop a systematic psychology in the TTP, we do hear the themes of the *Ethics*, reverberating in an environment whose acoustical properties give them a peculiar richness.

One the central concepts of Spinoza's psychology in the *Ethics* is our tendency to vacillate between contrary affects (cf. IIIP17S), a feature of human nature which prompts a rare and striking metaphor toward the end of Part III: "we are driven about in many ways by external causes, and . . . like waves on the sea, driven by contrary winds, we are moved to and fro, not knowing our outcome and our fate" (IIIP59S). This theme is given great prominence in the opening measures of the TTP:

> If men could manage all their affairs by a certain plan, or if fortune were always favorable to them, they would not be in the grip of any superstition. But since they are often reduced to such straits that they can bring no plan into operation, and since, from an immoderate desire for the uncertain goods of fortune, they generally vacillate wretchedly between hope and fear, for the most part their minds are eager to believe anything whatever. When they are in doubt, a slight impulse drives them this way or that; and this happens all the more easily when, torn by hope and fear, they are at a loss to know what to do; at other times they are too trusting, boastful and over-confident. (Pref, 1, III/5/2-9)

Spinoza had connected superstition with hope and fear in E IIIP50S, though not specifically with our vacillation between hope and fear. He had not, as he will go on to do in the TTP, given sacrifice and votive offerings or prayers as examples of superstitious behavior, though this is a natural enough consequence of his impersonal conception of God.

Particularly striking in this passage is the emphasis on our inability to control our futures by intelligent planning. You might have thought that Spinoza's determinism, his conviction that all human behavior is explicable in terms of invariable laws of nature, would lead him to think that we could predict the consequences of our actions well enough to plan sensibly for the future. After all, doesn't he, when he's casting about in the TTP for Scriptural passages supporting this determinism, cite Ecclesiastes: "There is nothing new under the sun" (1:9, cf. TTP vi, 67, III/95)?

But the laws of nature, as we have seen, do not by themselves explain any particular thing; they do this only in conjunction with information about the (often enormously complex) particular circumstances in which they are operating. If our knowledge of those circumstances is all too often inadequate, then all too often we will not be able to anticipate the consequences of our actions with any precision or confidence. Our desire for a certain outcome may drive us to try quite irrational strategies.

That human beings are prone to vacillate between contrary affects, and particularly between hope and fear, had been a theme of Spinoza's psychology as early as the *Short Treatise* (cf. KV II, ix). But some of the central motifs of the psychology of the *Ethics* appear neither in the *Short Treatise* nor in the TTP, raising the suspicion that they may represent conclusions Spinoza reached only after the publication of the TTP. Earlier (p. 112-13) I said that Spinoza "nearly had a complete version of the *Ethics* ready to go to press" in 1665, when he turned aside from that project to work on the TTP. It was not my intention to suggest that the *Ethics*, as Spinoza conceived it in 1665, differed from the *Ethics* published after his death *only* in that a long final part of what in 1665 was a three part work was subsequently subdivided into three parts, with the propositions merely renumbered, to produce the five part work we have today.[29] No one who has ever left a manuscript sitting on his desk for a long time would think that. A more reasonable hypothesis would be that Spinoza's preoccupation with politics in the writing of the

TTP and the TP considerably deepened his thoughts about human nature and human interactions, and led to a lengthening of that part of the work, which in turn required the subdivision.

Perhaps we have an example of this deepening reflection in the doctrine of the imitation of the affects which Spinoza develops in E IIIP27:

> If we imagine a thing like us, toward which we have had no affect, to be affected with some affect, we are thereby affected with a like affect.

Bennett calls IIIP27

> a cooler and more clinical version of the thesis on which Hume founded his moral psychology, namely, that people are linked by a universal, basic, instinctive tendency towards sympathy for one another's joys and sorrows. (*Study*, p. 279)

It seems an odd doctrine for an egoist to hold, as Bennett's allusion to Hume may remind us. Certainly I don't find anything quite parallel to it in the two psychologists who exercised the greatest influence on Spinoza, Hobbes and Descartes.[30] If it's a relatively late development in Spinoza's thought, that's an interesting fact about Spinoza's development.

The mere fact that the theory of imitation does not occur in the TTP does not by itself tend to show that Spinoza had not thought of it during the period when he was writing the TTP. As we've seen, there's a great deal of the doctrine of the *Ethics* which does not occur in the TTP. Much of what is absent from the TTP (such as the theories of substance and of the relation between mind and body, or the division of knowledge into three kinds) is demonstrably not something Spinoza only discovered later, since versions of these teachings occur in the *Short Treatise* or the *Treatise on the Emendation of the Intellect*. The theory of imitation is not in that category. Not only is that theory absent from the TTP and all earlier works, but its absence seems to have significant consequences for the political argument of the TTP, forcing Spinoza to adopt a contractualist account of the origin of the state, an account he will abandon in the TP, where his more sophisticated psychology permits him to give a non-contractualist explanation of the state. So, at any rate, Alexandre Matheron has argued, following up a suggestion by Christian Lazzeri.[31] To decide whether Matheron and Lazzeri are correct or not would take us beyond the bounds I wish to set for this paper. But it is certainly an intriguing hypothesis, well worth further investigation.

## 4. Of Human Bondage, or of the Power of the Affects

So far the titles of the parts of the *Ethics* have been pretty accurately indicative of the contents of those parts. Someone attempting to reconstruct the finished *Ethics* out of the TTP, using those titles as a guide, would have a fair idea of the kind of thing he was looking for. Part IV is different. It does, indeed, treat of human bondage, or the power of the affects, in its early propositions. But P18S marks a transition from that topic to the question of what reason prescribes, what affects do, and what do not, agree with the rules of human reason, a topic with which Spinoza is occupied for the remainder of this part of the *Ethics*, which is to say, for most of Part IV.

Now the TTP does not seem to me very helpful with respect to the first of these two topics. It does, of course, make it abundantly clear that Spinoza thinks *that* people are very prone to be governed by their passions, i.e., to act, from passion, in ways contrary to those which reason would prescribe:

> Everyone, indeed, seeks his own advantage, but people want things and judge them useful, not at all by the dictate of sound reason, but for the most part only from immoderate desire[32] and because they are carried away by affects of the mind which take no account of

the future and of other things. (v, 21, III/73/32-35; cf. xvi, 22, III/193/1-4)

But this does not go very far towards explaining *why* people are governed more by their passions than by reason. It suggests, of course, the commonplace thought that they are short-sighted. But I find no hint in the TTP of the deeper explanation the *Ethics* attempts, viz. that the knowledge of good and evil cannot restrain our passions simply in virtue of its truth, but only insofar as it has an affective component of its own (IVP14). Since I also don't find the *Ethics'* explanation in the relevant parts of the *Short Treatise* (II, xxi-xxii), I conjecture that the line of argument presented in the propositions leading up to IVP18S *may* be one of the things Spinoza worked out in the years following publication of the TTP. But this is only speculation. If it is correct, and if Bennett is right to suggest that Spinoza's explanation of this phenomenon in the *Ethics* is inconsistent with his "view that the emotions can be restrained through cognitive therapy" (*Study*, p. 286), then Spinoza's experiment with this line of thought may be a mistake. I leave this as a problem for future investigation.

With respect to the second topic—determining just what the dictates of reason are—the TTP seems to me to give a pretty fair picture of some, at least, of the main practical conclusions of Part IV. One of the central themes of Part IV is that to man nothing is more useful than man, i.e., than membership in a community with other men:

Man, I say, can wish for nothing more helpful to the preservation of his being than that all should so agree in all things that the minds and bodies of all would compose, as it were, one mind and one body; that all should strive together, as far as they can, to preserve their being; and that all, together, should seek for themselves the common advantage of all. From this it follows that men who are governed by reason—who from the guidance of reason seek their own advantage—want nothing for themselves which they do not

desire for other men. Hence, they are just, trustwor-
thy, and honorable. (IVP18S, II/223/9-18)

This scholium, foreshadowing an argument which culmi-
nates in P37, sums up the project very neatly: to show that
rational pursuit of their own individual interests requires
people to cooperate, to take thought for the interests of everyone (or at least everyone in their political community) and
to follow *most*, at least, of the requirements of traditional
morality.

Bennett finds the argument of the *Ethics* at this point to be
totally unconvincing: "I am afraid that Spinoza fails at every
step in his journey towards his collaborative morality"
(*Study*, p. 306). Others find the argument more persuasive.[33] To adjudicate between these commentators would
require more attention to the detail of the argument of the
*Ethics* than is possible within the confines of this article. But
I think it may be profitable to see how the TTP tries to
demonstrate the same thesis.

The general spirit of Spinoza's defense of cooperation in
the TTP is Hobbesian, at least in the emphasis it gives to
self-preservation and the consequent need to be a member of
a society with definite laws in order to "live securely and
avoid injuries from other men, and even from beasts."[34] In
the TTP Spinoza does not go so far as to claim that the state
of nature is a war of everyone against everyone else, but he
clearly thinks it's a highly dangerous place, and in the TP
(citing IVP34, without actually giving the reference) he is
more explicit about the reasons for this:

Insofar as men are torn by anger, envy, or some affect
of hate, to that extent they are drawn in different directions, and are contrary to one another; for that reason
they are more to be feared the more they are capable of,
and the more clever and astute they are than the other
animals. And because men are by nature liable to these
affects in the highest degree . . . , they are, by nature,
enemies. (ii, 14)

This implies, I think, that people are a threat to each other only to the extent that they are subject to certain antisocial passions, and would allow for the possibility that natural social passions, like the love of a man and a woman for one another, or that between a parent and a child, might permit there to be *some* generally harmonious relationships in the state of nature, and *some* limited cooperation.[35] But the antisocial passions are prevalent enough that the amount of cooperation which it is possible to maintain without the sanctions of the law is extremely limited. For the most part people in the state of nature must regard one another with suspicion and be prepared to anticipate the aggressive behavior of others with preemptive actions of their own. On this broadly Hobbesian picture of things, conflict will be rife and security a dominant concern. Without it people will not derive much benefit from the limited cooperation which their social passions make possible.

Spinoza differs from Hobbes, perhaps, in placing more emphasis on the economic advantages arising from the division of labor in an organized society, and less on security concerns:

A social order is very useful, and even most necessary, not only in order to live securely from enemies, but also to spare oneself many things. For if men were not willing to give mutual assistance to one another, they would lack both skill and time to support and preserve themselves as far as possible. Not all men are equally capable of all things, nor would each one be able to provide those things which, alone, he most needs. Everyone, I say, would lack both powers and time, if he alone had to plow, to sow, to reap, to grind, to cook, to weave, to sew and to do the many other things which support life . . . We see that those who live barbarously, without an organized community, lead a wretched and almost brutal life, and that it is still not without mutual assistance, such as it is, that they

are able to provide themselves with the few wretched
and crude things they have.[36]

Clearly Spinoza does not think it possible to live *well* without being a member of a political community. It may be
objected that we can still live, without living well. Survival
is possible in the state of nature. Insofar as Spinoza emphasizes these economic advantages, he is not explaining or
justifying the formation of a society strictly in terms of the
striving for self-preservation.

But this objection neglects two features of that striving,
features the *Ethics* is clearer about than the TTP. First, it is a
striving to continue in existence indefinitely (IIIP8). We
strive, not merely to survive for now, but to survive for as
long as possible. And it does seem that living well may be a
necessary condition for living as long as possible. By "living
well" here I mean, not living luxuriously, but living with a
dependable supply of varied and healthful food, adequate
protection from the elements and from predatory animals in
the way of clothing, shelter and weapons, adequate medical
care, and so on. Civilization no doubt has its discontents,
but until recently, at least, a shortening of the expected life
span has not been one of them. The second point is that the
striving is not merely a striving to survive, but a striving to
increase our power of acting (IIIP11). It's clear that the arts
and sciences which have developed within civil society, and
would seem to have been possible only within civil society,
have enormously increased our power of acting. That
Spinoza saw this connection seems evident from TTP iv, 12-
13 (III/60/20-28).

To the extent that we are rational, Spinoza contends, our
striving for self-preservation must lead us to strive to be
members of a social order. Because none of us is depend-
ably rational, to do this we must agree to establish a power
capable of making and enforcing laws, obedience to which
will serve our common interests, i.e., provide us with the
security and economic advantages we lack in the state of nature. By establishing that power we subject ourselves to it,
accepting constraints on the freedom of action we possessed
in the state of nature. Fearing what we would choose to do if

we were free of all restraints, we bind ourselves. Like Ulysses approaching the sirens,[37] we prevent ourselves from acting subsequently in ways which we now can see clearly would be contrary to our interest then. That is, we bind ourselves to rein in our appetite, insofar as it urges us to do something harmful to someone else, to do to no one what we would not wish done to ourselves, and to defend the other's right as if it were our own (cf. TTP xvi, 12-24, but particularly §14, III/191/26-32).

Bennett (*Study*, §69) questions whether, in the *Ethics*, Spinoza has really succeeded in getting such "enormously conservative conclusions"—e.g., adherence to the golden rule—from "a drastically radical premiss" —individual egoism. This is a fair question, and an absolutely crucial one. Spinoza's argument, as Bennett expounds it, certainly does not sound very convincing. But the attempt to make this argument convincing is as central to Spinoza's program in the *Ethics* as it is in the TTP. Can the TTP help us to understand the argument of the *Ethics*? Bennett seems to bar any such aid by his construction of the project of the *Ethics*:

> Spinoza [argues] that the thoughtful egoist will be led by his egoism to care as much for the welfare of others as for his own. Other moralists have said as much, but usually by appealing to civil society: the egoist is coerced by the thought that if he is not cooperative the state will make him pay. Spinoza agrees that this can be effective, but says that it involves the restraint of anger, greed, etc. 'by threats', whereas his argument shows how men can live 'by reason' [IVP37S2, II/238/13-15]; and I suppose he also prefers arguing through abstract metaphysics to relying on the historical fact that men have invented governments and prisons. (§69.1)

Similarly, after summarizing the argument for IVP31, "Insofar as a thing agrees with our nature, it is necessarily good," which he identifies as "the foundation of Spinoza's interpersonal morality," Bennett comments: "out of utter egoism flows a collaborative morality, without help from politics" (§69.3). So it would appear that he sees the project of the *Ethics* as fundamentally different from that of the TTP: to justify to an egoist the rationality of cooperative behavior without any appeal to political institutions.

Now certainly this much is true: Spinoza thinks that, in spite of people's egoism, the state would be unnecessary if all people were rational (IVP37S2, II/237/26-238/2). What makes the state necessary is the fact that people are generally subject to affects which overcome their reason. I take this to mean that if all people were rational, they would be able to cooperate to satisfy their needs without its being necessary for the state to coerce anyone with the threat of punishment.

There appear to be two ways Spinoza might think this conclusion justified. The *Ethics* sometimes suggests that a rational person, to the extent that she is rational, has, really, only one need: understanding things (IVP26). Since understanding is a non-competitive good, in the sense that one person's possession of it need not exclude anyone else from possessing it (IVP36), there is no reason for the interests of rational people to conflict. Understanding is not like apples. If I have some and share it with you, I do not thereby diminish what I have. No doubt there are transaction costs. It takes time and energy to impart understanding. But there are also compensations for those costs. The principle of the division of labor applies to intellectual matters in much the way it does to economic affairs. Each person's understanding may be aided tremendously if inquirers are part of a community whose members specialize and then share with one another the knowledge they have. And any teacher can testify to the gain in her own understanding which comes from trying to articulate it for someone else who does not yet understand.

The trouble with this line of thought is just that it is extraordinarily implausible to suppose that rational people, insofar as they are rational, have only that one interest, gaining understanding. This might be true of mythical creatures like angels, or even Cartesian minds. It is surely not true of Spinozistic human beings. The unity of mind and body which Spinoza claims to have demonstrated in Part II of the *Ethics* (P13&C, P21S) entails that the mind can never be free of the needs of the body. So we ought not to be surprised that Bennett finds Spinoza's argument for IVP26 woefully inadequate.[38]

The TTP suggests a different approach. We enter civil society both for security and for economic reasons. We derive great benefits from cooperative behavior, from each one's specializing in the production of certain goods and then peacefully exchanging his surplus for someone else's, from collaborating on projects which require the labor of more than one person, from the existence of a system in which people generally do not interfere with other people's possessions, and so on. These benefits would be sufficient to motivate a rational person to behave cooperatively if he could depend on other people being equally persuaded of the rationality of cooperation. We need the coercive power of the state to insure that irrational people will not try to exploit the cooperative tendencies of others by, for example, reneging on agreements which others keep. The state does this by giving everyone additional incentives to cooperate, making their calculation of their expected utilities abundantly clear. But the intervention of the state would not be necessary if everyone were rational and could depend on everyone else being rational. It's curious that the TTP, that political work, is as insistent about this as the *Ethics* is:

> If all men could be led easily by the guidance of reason alone, and could know the supreme utility and necessity of the state, there would be no one who did not absolutely detest deception; instead everyone would stand by their agreements without exception, with supreme honesty, from the desire for this supreme good, the preservation of the state, and everyone would practice honesty above all else, as the supreme protection of the state. (xvi, 21, III/192/30-35; cf. v, 20-21, III/73/27-35)

There's a paradox in this position, which we might bring out by the following paraphrase: if everyone saw that the state was necessary, the state would no longer be necessary. But Spinoza's point can be made without paradox: if everyone

saw clearly the advantages everyone derives from the cooperative behavior the state secures for them through its power
to coerce, and if everyone were capable of pursuing single-
mindedly the good he clearly saw, people would cooperate
without any need for coercion. The point of the state is not
that its coercive power makes reasonable behavior which
would not otherwise be reasonable, but that its coercive
power makes the reasonableness of cooperation so clear that
no one can fail to see it and that even weak-willed people
will be able to act on their perception of its reasonableness.
If this were not the case, then reason would not dictate the
creation of the state. Or so, I take it, Spinoza holds in the
TTP.

At the end of his discussion of Spinoza's attempt to derive
cooperation from egoism, Bennett writes:

> Any truth those theses [aligning harmony of interests
> with sameness of nature, and both of those with rea-
> sonableness] contain must depend on contingent facts
> about human nature and perhaps about societies; it
> cannot be derived in a few short steps from basic,
> abstract metaphysics, as Spinoza tries to do. (*Study*, p.
> 306)

Surely there is truth in *this* judgment. Certainly we need to
bring to our reading of E IVP18S-IVP37 some awareness of
the facts about human nature and human societies which underlie Spinoza's claims. We may not regard those facts as
contingent. I don't, and I don't suppose Spinoza would. But
an analysis of what man's situation would be like without
civil society, and of the advantages civil society can bring, is
essential to our understanding of the *Ethics*. Given his own
judgment of the flaw in Spinoza's argument in this part of
the *Ethics*, Bennett ought to have found the TTP, where
Spinoza conducts just the kind of analysis he calls for, helpful in understanding "Spinoza's one indisputable masterpiece."

Consider IVP31C: "The more a thing agrees with our
nature, the more useful, or better, it is for us, and conversely, the more a thing is useful to us, the more it agrees

with our nature." Bennett dismisses this corollary with the remark that "Spinoza cannot have seriously believed that only what is like me can be good for me" (§69.2). No doubt he can't. But is that what IVP31C says? Doesn't it rather recognize that things may be like us in varying degrees and claim merely that they will be useful to us in proportion to their degree of likeness. This is not to say that something very unlike me—some medicine, perhaps—may not, in appropriate circumstances, be useful to me. It is to say that, in general at least, something more like me will be more useful.

Generally speaking, other animals will be more useful to humans than inanimate objects. But what is most useful to a human is another human. The medicine I find useful— Zantac, as it happens—is useful to me because it was invented for a particular purpose—controlling the production of stomach acid—by human beings who were enabled by our general system of cooperation to specialize in biochemistry to the point where they could create this very useful thing. This is a modern example, but the point it illustrates is one the TTP shows Spinoza to be well aware of. A particular food may be useful to me, though unlike me. Other humans are more useful in that they make it possible for me to have a dependable supply of varied foods,[39] to determine what foods are most likely to be most useful for me, and so on.

Bennett writes that recognition of "one small point brings Spinoza's whole collaborative edifice tumbling down":

A thing's being a threat or a help to me depends not only on how it relates to my nature but also on other factors—e.g., on its spatial relation to me. However alike you and I are, the thing in question may relate to us . . . quite differently, and thus bear differently on our welfare . . . . Suppose that you and I are alike, that x could harm either of us, and that to avoid the harm what is needed is to keep at a distance from x; and suppose we cannot both do this—the floodwaters are rising in the mine and there is room for only one in the elevator which is starting up for the last time. Here the similarity between us is no help at all. And it can con-

tribute to conflict, as when we compete for limited
food: the rivalry would vanish if we didn't need the
same kinds of food . . . in [Spinoza's] collaborative
morality in Part 4 . . . the concept 'not enough to go
around' is conspicuously absent. (*Study*, §69.4)

Now I have no quarrel with the indented quote. What
Bennett says seems obviously right. But that's just the
problem. The truths Bennett reminds us of here are *so* obvious that it's hard to believe Spinoza was not aware of them,
particularly if we keep the TTP firmly in mind as background. How could the man who wrote so feelingly of the
wretchedness of savage life (v, 18-20: cf. above pp. 141-42)
fail to be aware that food is an important good, which may
be in short supply, and that a shortage of food can cause
conflict? So perhaps recognition of this one small point does
not bring the whole collaborative edifice tumbling down.
Perhaps Spinoza had something more complicated in mind.
   Suppose our common need for the same kind of food is a
necessary, but not sufficient, condition for conflict between
us over food. Equally necessary, though equally insufficient
by itself, is scarcity of food. Are these two necessary conditions jointly sufficient for conflict? In the state of nature,
where people are governed more by immoderate desire than
by reason, and where they are very much at the mercy of
fortune for the satisfaction of their basic needs (TTP iii, 13,
III/47/3-9), they probably will be. Certainly this is what the
Hobbesian analysis of the state of nature would suggest. But
the Hobbesian analysis of the state of nature also suggests
that its potential for violent conflict makes life in the state of
nature "solitary, poor, nasty, brutish and short," a judgment
with which Spinoza seems to agree. Reason, therefore, dictates that we seek safety, and a better life in general, in civil
society. One prominent way in which cooperation makes life
better is by taking advantage of the things we have in common.
   We share a desire for food, which, in certain circumstances, can lead to conflict. We also share a certain capacity
for dealing with the shortages which are an equally necessary condition for conflict. "Human guidance and vigilance

can do much to help us live securely" (iii, 14). Mere cooperation on such basic things as plowing, sowing, protecting
the crop against the depredations of other animals or the
weather, reaping, grinding, and cooking can do a great deal
to make more food available. Higher forms of cooperation—
the development of scientific agriculture, or the reclamation
of land from the sea, to take an example apt to come to the
mind of a Dutchman—can make an even greater difference.
All of these forms of cooperation would be impossible if we
did not have a great many things in common: common needs
to motivate us to seek ways of satisfying them, a common
capacity for understanding how nature works, a common
experience of the operations of nature, a common language
for communicating our desires and knowledge to one another, even a common, if somewhat limited, capacity for affection for other members of our species. To achieve these
benefits we needn't be "entirely of the same nature" if this
latter phrase means "indistinguishable from one another"
(*Study*, p. 306). Spinoza explicitly recognizes that not all
men are equally capable of all things (v, 19) and cites this as
a reason why the division of labor makes sense. But our
ability to be of benefit to one another clearly depends heavily
on what we have in common. I suggest that facts like these
are the sort of thing Spinoza had in mind in IVPP30-31. He
may well overstate these facts in those propositions, and he
may very well not argue persuasively for them in that context. But if we accept that these facts do underlie those
claims, then we ought not to feel that Spinoza's attempt to
make out an egoistic rationale for cooperation was a total
failure.

*    *    *

*Summing Up*: Some readers may, at this point, expect a section on anticipations of Part V of the *Ethics* in the TTP.
Reluctant as I am to disappoint such expectations, I think
there is not enough to say on that subject to warrant a special
section. (Other readers may now breathe a sigh of relief,
learning that a long article is coming to a close.) A reader of
the TTP, attempting to reconstruct the content of Part V,

armed only with its title, might be very much misled. What is the power of the intellect over the affects? How can the intellect lead us to freedom?

Well, the reader of the TTP might say, reason dictates to us that we strive to overcome our harmful affects by forming a civil society which will, in turn, alter our calculations of what is to our advantage by attaching special disincentives to antisocial behavior. Generally speaking, antisocial behavior doesn't pay, even if we set to one side any penalties the state may attach to it. An egoist seeking to guide his conduct by simple rules, without calculating his advantage anew on each occasion, might very well settle on the rules of traditional morality:

> As each one sows, so shall he reap. From evil deeds evils necessarily follow, unless they are wisely corrected, and from good deeds, goods necessarily follow, if they are accompanied by constancy of mind. (iv, 50, III/68/27-29)

But though the simple rules of traditional morality may well lead to happiness, if followed consistently, they admit sufficient exceptions that many egoists will require the threat of punishment to restrain their wayward desires. The intellect's basic solution to the problem of irrational desires is political: form a state which will alter the payoffs for different strategies so that they are more clearly in favor of cooperative behavior. Reason also prescribes the kind of state it would be best to form. Human freedom is best achieved by forming a civil society in which the people retain sovereignty, a democracy. Only when each citizen has an equal voice in the making of the laws by which all are bound, does she retain the freedom and equality of the state of nature (v, 22-25, III/73/35-74/32; xvi, 36, III/195/14-21).

All of this, no doubt, is good Spinozistic doctrine, even in the *Ethics*, but it is not what Part V is about. There Spinoza has quite different remedies for the affects in mind, and a very different conception of human freedom. There freedom is something the individual attains for himself by moderating his affects through coming to understand them and through practising certain maxims of life (cf. particularly VP10S & P20S); it is not, as in the TTP, a political condition present only in unusually fortunate states (TTP Pref, §12), but a condition an individual can strive for even in a bad state.[40] The remedies for irrational affects involve self-understanding, not political sanctions.

This is not to deny that many of the themes of Part V are sounded in the TTP, e.g., that the intellect is the better part of us (TTP iv, 10; E VP40C), that the more we know particular things, the more we understand God (TTP iv, 11; E VP24); that the mind's greatest satisfaction and blessedness come in the intellectual knowledge of God (TTP iv, 12, v, 40; E VP27); that blessedness is its own reward (TTP iv, 14-15; E VP42), etc. But I do not find in the TTP any hint of the doctrine in Part V which has caused interpreters the greatest difficulty: the eternity of the mind. So I don't find it helpful in illuminating the darkest passages of Part V. More's the pity.

So far in this essay I've concentrated on what (of the teaching of the *Ethics*) is present in the TTP and what is absent. I have not attempted to say very much about the reasons for these various presences and absences. Of course, any conjecture we make about the reasons for Spinoza's omissions must be highly speculative. But it should be evident from what I have said that the reasons must vary in different cases. For example, given that one of Spinoza's central purposes in the TTP is to correct popular misconceptions of God, it is only natural that this work should anticipate a good deal of the teaching of Part I of the *Ethics*. Given that his main intended audience is people who are not accomplished philosophers, it is natural that he should omit technical and abstract discussions of substance, attribute and mode. Indeed, it seems to me that one reason the TTP is so valuable is precisely that it tries to convey the fundamentals of God's nature and man's relation to God in less technical language.

Spinoza's purposes do not require him to reveal his theory of the relation of mind to body, and he avoids that topic. This may stem partly from a desire to avoid unnecessary complications—he has quite enough on his plate as it is—

and partly from a desire not to shock his audience more than absolutely necessary. As it is, the TTP already contains a great deal to offend Christians who are, by 17th Century standards, orthodox. To add that the mind and the body are one and the same thing, conceived in different ways, would be to pour gasoline on the fire.

The most interesting cases of presence and absence, though, come in the final three parts of the *Ethics*, the parts which I suggest that he altered most substantially between the draft of 1665 and the final version published in 1677, the parts which overlap most clearly with the TTP. That the psychology of the TTP should stress the principle of the striving for self-preservation is no surprise. The doctrine was present in the early *Short Treatise*. But in the *Short Treatise* it does not do any work worth mentioning, occurring only briefly in KV I, v, 1; its expanded role in the completed *Ethics* may be a product of the reflections Spinoza was engaged in during the writing of the TTP. The doctrine of the *conatus* may not have been so important in the 1665 draft of the *Ethics*. If that is so (and it is, I stress, only a conjecture), writing the TTP may have had an important influence on the development of Spinoza's psychology and ethics. Similar remarks apply to the doctrine of the imitation of the affects, Spinoza's explanation of the power of the affects, and his theory of the state. The virtual absence of any theory of the state in the *Short Treatise*, indeed, the apparent denial that the state is even necessary for man's well-being (KV II, xxiv, 6-8), is very striking. Whatever we may think of the primacy of the *Ethics* in the Spinozistic corpus, the TTP is, among other things, an important document for the study of Spinoza's development.[41]

# NOTES

1  In §1 of Bennett's *A Study of Spinoza's Ethics* (Indianapolis and Cambridge: Hackett Publishing Company, 1984), here-after cited in the text as *Study*. All abbreviations are those adopted by the present volume.

2  I have undertaken this in a paper presented at the Toronto Spinoza conference (April 1989), "Notes on a Neglected

Masterpiece (I): Spinoza and the Science of Hermeneutics," to appear in the proceedings of that conference.

3  See my paper on Hobbes' reaction to the TTP, "'I Durst Not Write So Boldly,' or, How to Read Hobbes' Theological-Political Treatise," in Emilia Giancotti, ed., *Hobbes e Spinoza: scienza e politica* (Naples: Bibliopolis, 1990).

4  A recent editor of selections from the TTP and the *Political Treatise* (TP) writes that the former work, in spite of its special interest as a defense of freedom of thought, "is little read because its philosophical content is embedded in a mass of biblical investigations. That content can, however, be excerpted and taken independently" (*Spinoza on Freedom of Thought*, ed. and tr. by T. E. Jessop (Montreal: Mario Casalini, 1962), p. ix). I would not concede that the "biblical investigations" lack philosophical interest, but I would also argue that it is not so easy to separate them from parts of the work which everyone should concede to be philosophical.

5  An exception to this generalization is Alan Donagan's *Spinoza* (Chicago: University of Chicago Press, 1989), which begins its account of Spinoza's philosophy with a reading of the TTP. It is more common, however, for French commentators to see the TTP as an introduction to the *Ethics*. See, for example, André Tosel's contribution to E.M. Curley and P.-F. Moreau, eds., *Spinoza: Issues and Directions* (Leiden: Brill, forthcoming) and the works cited there.

6  Cf. the Preface, §12: "Since, then, that rare happiness has fallen to our lot—that we live in a Republic where everyone is granted complete freedom of judging, and freedom to worship God according to his understanding, and where nothing is considered to be dearer and sweeter than freedom—I believed that I would be doing something not unwelcome and not without use if I showed that this freedom not only can be granted without harm to piety and the peace of the Republic, but also cannot be abolished unless piety and the peace of the Republic are abolished with it" (III/7/22-7). Spinoza undermines this praise of the Dutch Republic in the Preface itself (§17) when he complains about the ministers of religion who "persecute with such a hostile spirit those who disagree with them" (III/8/34-5).

7  Cf. IV/96-98 with Preface, §20, III/9/16-25. See also Leo Strauss, *Persecution and the Art of Writing* (Glencoe, Ill.: Free Press, 1952), pp. 162-63.

8  See my CS, pp. 349-50.

9  The very first sentence of the first chapter would be an example: "Prophecy, *or* revelation, is a certain knowledge of some
   thing, revealed to men by God" (III/15). Cf. this with the
   opening sentence of ch. xii: "Those who consider the Bible,
   just as it is, as a letter of God's, sent to men from heaven,
   will doubtless protest that I have committed the sin against the
   Holy Ghost, by maintaining that the word of God is faulty,
   mutilated, corrupted, and inconsistent, that we have only
   fragments of it, and finally, that the original of the covenant
   God made with the Jews has perished" (III/158). If the second statement does not completely undermine the first, it certainly forces us to consider in what sense the first can be true.
   I think the TTP also appeals to specifically Christian prejudices about Jesus and argue this in "*Homo audax*: Leibniz,
   Oldenburg and the TTP," to appear in *Studia Leibnitiana.*

10  So, for example, *substantia* is used twice in ii, 53, but in a
   sense in which it might be translated "chief point." So far as I
   can discover, it does not occur elsewhere. Similarly, *modus*
   seems to occur only in non-technical senses, as in vii, 50,
   where it means the mood of a verb. *Attributum* occurs more
   frequently (e.g., in ii, 31 and 41; iii, 22; iv, 30; and particularly xiii, 11-12), mainly in contexts in which Spinoza is
   denying that the prophets had any accurate knowledge of the
   divine attributes.

11  The note in question is the sixth of the 39 notes which
   Gebhardt prints in III/251-67. All of these notes seem to have
   been written as potential additions to a subsequent edition of
   the TTP (cf. Ep 68 & 69), though none of them are in any of
   the editions published in Spinoza's lifetime. The ms. sources
   vary, but the note quoted here is one of five Spinoza himself
   added to a copy of his book presented to Jacob Klefmann, and
   currently in the library of the Spinozaeum in Haifa.

12  See my "Spinoza on Miracles," *Proceedings of the First
   Italian International Congress on Spinoza*, Emilia Giancotti,
   ed. (Naples: Bibliopolis, 1985).

13  That Spinoza is thinking in these terms seems to be indicated
   by the fact that immediately after defining the concept of a law
   of nature in TTP iv, 1, he illustrates it (in §2) first with a law
   of physics, then with a law of psychology.

14  E.g., Oldenburg in Ep 74. I have analysed Spinoza's corre-
    spondence with Oldenburg regarding the TTP in *"Homo au-
    dax*: Leibniz, Oldenburg and the TTP."

15  See *Spinoza's Metaphysics* (Cambridge: Harvard Unversity
    Press, 1969), ch. ii. Bennett accepts my solution to the
    problem of finite causality in his *Study*, pp. 112-13, without,
    it seems, worrying about how he might textually justify
    introducing the concept of a law of nature into the argument of
    Part I. Arguably the concept is implicit in IP17, but the text
    offers little reason to identify the laws of God's nature spoken
    of there with the laws of nature which are so prominent in the
    TTP. Otherwise the concept of a law of nature does not ap-
    pear in the *Ethics* until the Preface to Part III.

16  For an analysis of the dispute between Spinoza and Descartes
    on metaphysical freedom of judgment, see my "Descartes,
    Spinoza and the Ethics of Belief," in M. Mandelbaum and E.
    Freeman, eds., *Spinoza, Essays in Interpretation* (La Salle,
    Ill.: Open Court, 1975).

17  On this see Yirmiyahu Yovel, *Spinoza and Other Heretics*,
    vol. I, *The Marrano of Reason*, (Princeton: Princeton
    University Press, 1989).

18  In "Experience in Spinoza's Theory of Knowledge," in
    Marjorie Grene, ed., *Spinoza: A Collection of Critical Essays*
    (Garden City, NY: Doubleday/Anchor, 1972).

19  The notion that some affects may be viewed as being com-
    posed of others does, however, appear briefly in xvii, 7.

20  I suppose Donagan might wish to object along these lines,
    since he apparently thinks that passages like E IVP18S are not
    egoistic: "Spinoza's principle [that everyone loves himself,
    seeks his own advantage, what is really useful to him, what
    will really lead *man* to a greater perfection, etc.], if it is egoist
    at all, cannot be egoist in the usual sense; for it asserts that
    you cannot will your own advantage without willing what will
    lead man (not just yourself) to greater perfection" (*Spinoza,
    op. cit.,* p. 164). I take it that, insofar as Spinoza holds that
    willing your own advantage entails willing the advantage of
    everyone, he holds this to be true only for those who under-
    stand the connection between their own advantage and the ad-
    vantage of all. Cf. IVP18S, II/223/14-18, IVP37.

21  The word *jus* can mean either *law* or *right*. The former
    meaning would seem more natural in the first occurrence here,
    but the second occurrence demands the latter translation and I
    have been reluctant to give that word two different renderings
    in the same context. Samuel Shirley adopts the same course
    (*Tractatus Theologico-politicus* (Leiden: Brill, 1989), p. 240).
    Wernham renders the first occurrence by *law* (Benedict
    Spinoza, *The Political Works* (Oxford: Clarendon Press,
    1965), p. 131). Elwes' solution was to give the first occur-
    rence a double translation *law and right*.
22  Cf. also xvi, 20, and TP ii, 12. Donagan, of course, is aware
    of these passages and cites some of them on p. 178 of
    *Spinoza, op. cit.* Why, then, does he question whether
    Spinoza is an egoist?
23  Note the difference in technical terminology from the state-
    ment of this principle in E IIIP6. What each thing strives to
    persevere in here is its state (*status*); in the *Ethics* it is its being
    (*esse*). On the possible significance of this see A. Matheron,
    "Le problème de l'évolution de Spinoza du *Traité théologico-
    politique* au *Traité politique*," in *Spinoza: Issues and
    Directions, op. cit.*, §3.
24  Review of CS in *Studia Spinozana* 2(1986): 419-23.
25  "Spinoza's Moral Philosophy," in Marjorie Grene, ed.,
    *Spinoza: A Collection of Critical Essays, op. cit.*, pp. 367-68.
26  See, for example, the *Treatise on the Emendation of the
    Intellect* §92: *si res sit in se, sive, ut vulgo dicitur,* causa
    sui . . . (II/34/10-13). In "Substance and Mode in
    Spinoza" (*Philosophia* 7 (1977):83-105) Charles Jarrett has
    argued that we should not take this passage at face value (i.e.,
    as supporting my interpretation of the definition of substance).
    The argument is too complex to go into in detail here, but I
    would note that the paraphrase of ID3 which Spinoza gives in
    IP8S2 (II/50/4-6) presupposes that he equates being *in se* with
    being *causa sui*. If what is in itself were not necessarily its
    own cause, then by IA4 knowledge of it might depend on
    knowledge of something else.
27  Arne Naess (in *Freedom, Emotion and Self-subsistence* (Oslo:
    Universitetsforlaget, 1976)) takes Spinoza to hold that being
    in something is a matter of degrees, that everything is in itself
    to some degree, though only one thing is completely in itself,
    citing E IIIP6 as evidence for this. I do not wish to reject that
    reading, only to suggest that if it is correct, we need some

explanation of the definition of substance which makes sense of that possibility. For discussion, see Charles Jarrett's review of Naess in the *Journal of the History of Philosophy* 16 (1979):345-48.

28  TTP xvi, 3-4, III/189/19-25. I think this view is also implicit in passages like TTP i, 44 (III/28/7-16), though a superficial reading may suggest that there Spinoza is reducing the power of nature to the power of God, rather than the other way around. Spinoza is not Malebranche.

29  *Pace* Parkinson, *op. cit.*, pp. 419-20. How could a careful reader of my work so misunderstand my intentions, given the things I say in various places? Cf., for example, my comments on the missing axioms in Part IV (CS 547n, 550n, and 561n). Parkinson reports that I regard "the book . . . as substantially complete by 1665." What I actually said was merely that "a substantial manuscript of the *Ethics* was in existence" by then. I granted that "we do not know how much revision the manuscript may have undergone in the next twelve years before it was published" (CS xiii). Later, discussing the composition of the *Ethics* (CS 404-06), I inferred from Akkerman's work on the *Nagelate Schriften* that Spinoza did not significantly revise Parts I and II of the *Ethics* after a date somewhere in the mid to late 1660s. This leaves plenty of room for significant revision of the material which in 1665 constituted Part III.

30  Hobbes identifies compassion with pity, defined as "grief for the calamity of another" (*Leviathan* vi, ¶46, p. 126 in the Macpherson edition) and explains it in terms of the subject's imagining that "the like calamity may befall himself." Descartes has a very similar account in *The Passions of the Soul* §§185-86. Spinoza's imitation of affects, like Hume's sympathy, is not so much a specific affect as a mechanism by which we come to have a wide variety of affects, which need not involve sadness. Cf. Jerome Neu, *Emotion, Thought and Therapy* (Berkeley: University of California Press, 1977), *passim*.

31  See §3 of the Matheron article cited above (n. 23). So far as I am aware, Lazzeri's work on this topic has not yet been published.

32  I render *libido* here by "immoderate desire." It seems to me to require a different treatment in the TTP than in the E or the TdIE. Cf. the note on "lust" at CS 644.

33  E.g., Donagan, *Spinoza, op. cit.*, pp. 165-66, following
    Matheron, *Individu et communauté chez Spinoza* (Paris:
    Minuit, 1969), pp. 258-77.
34  TTP iii, 13-14, III/47/3-12. Though Hobbes clearly thinks
    the state of nature a highly dangerous place, my impression is
    that he always emphasizes the danger from other human be-
    ings, and does not mention that from other animals.
35  In spite of Hobbes's famous dictum that the life of man in the
    state of nature is a war of all against all (*De cive* i, 12,
    *Leviathan* xiii, 8), it's arguable that this was a piece of rhetori-
    cal exaggeration, and that he intended to claim no more than
    what I attribute here to Spinoza. I discuss this in "Reflections
    on Hobbes: Recent work on his moral and political philoso-
    phy," *Journal for Philosophical Research* 15 (1989-90):1-81.
36  TTP v, 18-20, III/73/13-27. On the other hand, the emphasis
    in TTP xvi, 12-13 (III/191/11-26) is on security rather than
    economic advantages. Hobbes is aware of the economic ad-
    vantages, but sees security as a necessary condition for attain-
    ing them. Economic activity has no point if you have no
    security to enjoy its benefits. This comes out more clearly in
    *Leviathan* ch. xiii, ¶9, than in the parallel passage in *De cive*
    (i, 13).
37  For an exploration of this theme, see Jon Elster, *Ulysses and
    the Sirens* (Cambridge: Cambridge UP, rev. ed., 1984).
38  Cf. *Study* §69.7. Indeed, Spinoza's argument seems so weak
    on Bennett's construction of it that we may wonder whether
    he can possibly be interpreting the conclusion correctly. On
    his reading "What we strive for from reason is nothing but
    understanding; nor does the mind, insofar as it uses reason,
    judge anything else useful to itself except what leads to un-
    derstanding" comes out as "for reasonable people the only re-
    ally valuable thing is understanding" (*Study*, p. 304).
    Perhaps we might achieve a paraphrase which better repro-
    duced Spinoza's intentions if we gave more weight to the
    phrase "what leads to understanding," and acknowledged that
    many things having to do with the welfare of the body might
    lead to understanding in the sense that they are necessary but
    insufficient conditions for it. E VP39 or IVP45S or IVApp
    4,5,&27 might be used to support this interpretation. But
    while this move may make it more intelligible that Spinoza
    might accept IVP26, it will do so at the cost of making P26
    unusable to support the claim that fully rational people would

not need the state, since the goods of the body which it sup-
poses P26 to allow for will not, in general, be non-competitive in the way understanding is.

39 Spinoza seems to be quite keen on variety in the diet. Cf. E
IVApp27.

40 If Part V of the *Ethics* is a relatively late addition to the ms.,
written after the fall of the De Witts in 1672, then we might
find in this contrast confirmation of Lewis Feuer's suggestion
that in his later years Spinoza had given up hope of changing
the world to concentrate on seeking salvation for the individual
in withdrawal society. Cf. *Spinoza and the Rise of
Liberalism,* reprint edition (New Brunswick, N.J.:
Transaction Books, 1987), particularly pp. 38-40.

41 I would like to thank Charles Jarrett and Hermann De Dijn for
their comments on an earlier draft of this paper.

# LEIBNIZ ON MALEBRANCHE ON CAUSALITY

*Robert C. Sleigh, Jr.*

In the first section of this paper I outline the main ingredients of Leibniz's theory of the pre-established harmony and of Malebranche's occasionalism.[1] In the second section I consider Leibniz's most frequently articulated criticism of Malebranche's theory; I conclude that the criticism concerns an aspect of Malebranche's theory to which he could adjust with ease, were he to feel the need. In the third section I outline Malebranche's major arguments for his central thesis concerning causality, i.e., that God is the only real cause, and Leibniz's reactions thereto. I conclude that much of the real debate concerns the intelligibility of a doctrine of divine concurrence. In the fourth section I consider where the doctrine of divine concurrence fits in Leibniz's overall theodicean scheme, and make a preliminary stab at expounding some elements of Leibniz's conception of divine concurrence.

## 1

In the *Discourse on Metaphysics* Leibniz formulated an account of causality to which, to the best of my knowledge, he remained committed thereafter. The theory offered in the *Discourse* has four primary components: i) the thesis of spontaneity; ii) the world-apart thesis, and iii) an account of merely apparent causation (called "quasi-causation" hereafter); and iv) the thesis of concomitance (which Leibniz subsequently called "the pre-established harmony").[2]

According to the thesis of spontaneity every non-initial, non-miraculous state of every created substance has as a real cause some preceding state of that very substance.[3] According to the world-apart thesis no state of any substance has as a real cause some state of some other created substance. So, considering only created substances and leaving aside whatever causal contribution God may make in the case of non-initial, non-miraculous states of created substances, what we have is an affirmation of the ubiquity of real intra-substantial causality and the denial of inter-substantial causality.

Leibniz was aware of the obvious: spontaneity and world-apart are at odds with common sense and with most received seventeenth century philosophical wisdom. Much to Leibniz's credit (in my opinion), when he perceived his philosophical theses to be at odds with common sense and received opinion, he engaged in an effort to "save the appearances," i.e., to explain how the (mistaken) common sense view related to the underlying metaphysical reality posited by his theory. Spontaneity and world-apart fit the mold. Having supposed (for the sake of argument) that, for any human person S, S's mind is a distinct substance from S's body, Leibniz wrote in a draft for a letter to Arnauld:

> one particular substance has no physical influence on another.... Nevertheless, one is quite right to say that my will is the cause of this movement of my arm...; for the one expresses distinctly what the other expresses more confusedly, and one must ascribe the action to the substance whose expression is more distinct. (LA 71)

In this passage Leibniz began by asserting world-apart pure and simple, but then, drawing on his theory of concomitant adjustments on the confused/distinct perception scale among substances, he set out to formulate an account of quasi-causality in terms of features of the perceptions of substances.[4] Similar points are contained in a letter Leibniz sent to Arnauld, with the emphasis on the theory of concomitance.

> ... I do not at all object if minds are called occasional causes, and even *real* causes *in a sense*, of certain bodily movements; for with respect to divine decisions, what God has foreseen and preordained with respect to minds has been an occasion for his first regulating bodies in such a way that they would conspire among themselves according to the laws and forces that he would have given them . . . . God brings it about that there is a *real* connection in virtue of this general concept of substances which implies that they express each other perfectly although this connection is not immediate, being based only on what God brought about in creating them. (LA 95-96)

The first quoted passage contains Leibniz's "save the appearances" analysis. The idea is this: when we affirm that some state of created substance $x$ is a real cause of some state of created substance $y$ ($x \neq y$), what is really going on is a correlative alteration in the distinctness of relevant perceptions of $x$ and $y$. The idea is that the relevant perceptions of the alleged causal agent become more distinct, while those of the alleged patient become more confused. There is no real causality involved, just "quasi-causality." The second quoted passage purports to explain the mechanism whereby substances come to be related so that the relevant quasi-causal relations hold. The mechanism is this: God so programmed the created substances in the world that, although all real creaturely causality is intra-substantial, substances behave as if there were what there cannot be—real, intersubstantial causal relations.

No doubt there is more to say about Leibniz's theory of the pre-established harmony and his theory of quasi-causation. One comment on the latter. It is an example of what we might call a "replacement analysis," where the aim is not so much to analyze the meaning of causal statements in ordinary use, but rather to state what conditions obtain at the level of ultimate metaphysical reality when causal statements are employed. The aim here, as Leibniz put it, is ". . . to reconcile metaphysical language with practice" (DM §15), in effect, to *replace* a metaphysically muddled notion with a metaphysically correct concept. It should be noted that such replacement was required, according to Leibniz, only in cases of alleged inter-substantial causation. Cases of alleged intra-substantial causation need involve no metaphysical muddle, hence call for no replacement. For the sake of comparison with Malebranche's theory, I shall assume that Leibniz would regard real creaturely causes as quasi-causes as well.

Malebranche's account of causality covers pretty much the same ground as Leibniz's. No surprise, since Leibniz introduced the theory of the pre-established harmony with Malebranche's occasionalism very much in mind. In particular, Malebranche's theory like Leibniz's, contains both a positive thesis and a negative thesis concerning the distribution of real causes. The positive thesis is this: take any entity whatsoever such that its existing or obtaining is caused, then a real cause of its existing or obtaining is some volition of God. The negative thesis is this: there are no real causes other than volitions of God; further there could not be.

Malebranche, like Leibniz, was aware of the obvious—the claim that God's will is the only real cause is at odds with common sense and with most received seventeenth century philosophical wisdom. Malebranche too set out to formulate a notion of quasi-causality that obtained in those cases where common sense mistakenly held that real creaturely causality obtained. The notion involved is that of an occasional cause. Malebranche's primary motivation for introducing a notion of quasi-causality concerned explaining a distinction between two ways of acting open to God—acting by general volitions and acting by particular volitions. The distinctions are set out in Malebranche's *Treatise on Nature and Grace.*

> I say that God *acts by general volitions,* when he acts in consequence of general laws that he has established. For example, I say that God acts in me by general volitions when he makes me feel pain when I am pricked [by a pin], because, in consequence of the general and

efficacious laws of the union of soul and body that he has established, he makes me suffer pain when my body is ill-disposed.

I say, on the contrary, that God *acts by particular volitions* when the efficacy of his will is not determined by some general law to produce some effect— thus, supposing that a body begins to move without being pushed by another, or without changes in the will of some mind, or without some other creature who determines the efficacy of some general law; I say that God would move this body by a particular volition. (OM/5/147-48)

An examination of the various types of general laws to which Malebranche appealed in elaborating this scheme suggests that they all may be construed as having the following form—for any $x$ and $y$, if $x$ is f and bears R to $y$ then $y$ is g. To say that $x$'s being f and bearing R to $y$ is an *occasional cause* of $y$'s being g is just to say that $x$ is f, bears R to $y$, and that God has willed that the relevant law obtain.[5] Thus, according to Malebranche, when God acts by general volitions, he employs occasional causes; when he acts by particular volitions he acts miraculously. The distinction between these two modes of divine operation is crucial to Malebranche's theodicy. The notion of an occasional cause mattered to him, but basically as a component in his theodicean scheme.

As an ancillary feature of his total theory Malebranche organized the laws in accordance with which he claimed that God acts by general volitions into five distinct sets. Hence, he frequently mentioned five distinct types of occasional causes. Two sets concerning the operation of occasional causes in the realm of nature are particularly relevant to Leibniz's critique of Malebranche's theory: First, laws of the communication of motion, where the occasional causes are impacts of bodies and the effects are changes in the velocity of the bodies impacted; second, laws of the union of mind and body, where the occasional causes are thoughts or emotions or volitions in the soul and the effects are motions of matter in the body, or vice versa.[6] Note that laws of the second variety appear to allow the possibility of created minds "intruding" into the purely material realm, at least as quasi-causes. This feature generated Leibniz's most frequently articulated criticism of Malebranche's account of causality, to which we turn.

## 2

In a letter to l'Hospital (30 September 1695) Leibniz claimed that his own theory of the pre-established harmony should be viewed as an advancement, not an overthrow, of Malebranche's doctrine.[7] Leibniz went on to say that he owed to Malebranche ". . . my foundations on this subject."[8] As an example, Leibniz cited their agreement that substances of diverse natures, such as Malebranche took the mind and body to be, could not causally interact. But, of course, starting from these foundations Leibniz moved on to world-apart, as exemplified in the following gallingly enigmatic passage from a letter to DeVolder (21 January 1704):

> You [DeVolder] say that nothing prevents substances of the same nature from acting on each other . . . . But what prevents substances of diverse natures from acting on each other? When you have explained that, you will see that all finite substances are prevented from mutually influencing each other. Not to mention that all substances are of diverse natures, nor are two differing in number alone given in nature. . . . (G II, 264 (L 534-35))[9]

Leibniz concluded a summary of his indebtedness to Malebranche in the letter to l'Hospital as follows:

> We agree that the mind and the body have no influence on one another, and that all the perfections of things are always produced by the operation of God. I only add that what he produces in A, conforming to what he

produces in B, conforms also with its own laws that he has established for A, which has not been sufficiently considered. (GM II, 299)

The last sentence in this passage contains a reference to the aforementioned "intrusion" argument. Here is a more pellucid and strident form of it, contained in a draft for a letter to Arnauld. Writing specifically about causal relations between mind and body Leibniz noted:

It does not conform . . . to the hypothesis of occasional causes, as if God were to intervene ordinarily in any other way than by conserving each substance in its course, and as if God on the occasion of occurrences in the body aroused thoughts in the soul that would change the course that the soul would have taken without that. (LA 47)

What is the objection Leibniz had in mind here? Consider a case where Arnauld voluntarily raised his arm. Malebranche held that in such a case there is a sequence of quasi-causes, all physical, leading up to the arm raising, starting with an initial flow of animal spirits. Consider that initial flow of animal spirits. Malebranche would hold that it is an occurrence that required a real cause which, of course, must be some volition of God. Malebranche would also have held that this flow of animal spirits has a quasi-cause (an occasional cause), in this case Arnauld's willing to raise his arm. Furthermore, it is quite clear that Malebranche believed that there is no quasi-cause of the relevant flow of animal spirits other than Arnauld's willing to raise his arm.

What is Leibniz's problem with this scheme? Note that it cannot be based on a general rejection of mind-body quasi-causal relations. Leibniz himself said, ". . . one is quite right to say that my will is the cause of this movement of my arm . . ." (LA 71). Leibniz claimed that Malebranche's scheme was inconsistent with ". . . that great principle of physics that a body never receives a change in motion except by another body in motion that pushes it" (G VI, 541 (L 587)). Finally, we have a version of Leibniz's criticism in hand. It is this: Malebranche's belief that some physical events have as their sole immediate quasi-cause a mental event, is inconsistent with Leibniz's great principle of physics. Leibniz himself was not vulnerable to this criticism. He too held that some physical events have as *an* immediate quasi-cause a mental event. But, in virtue of spontaneity, his great physical principle, and the idea that every real creaturely cause is a quasi-cause, Leibniz was committed to the existence of an immediate physical quasi-cause for every non-miraculous physical event.

Is that a major criticism of Malebranche's theory? I can't see that it is. Suppose that Leibniz's great principle of physics is true. Probably Malebranche's beliefs about mind-body interaction were inconsistent with it. If so, this was an empirical failing on his part. If Leibniz were to convince him that he needed to adjust his beliefs about human physiology, he could easily adjust his system of occasional causes to reflect his newly acquired empirical beliefs. But need he? No. Malebranche's system of occasional causes was intended primarily as a catalog of the ways in which God acts by general volitions. Under certain conditions such a catalog may also serve as a catalog of laws of nature. But if there is quasi-causal over-determination, as Leibniz supposed, then a catalog of the ways in which God acts by general volitions might be complete, in the sense of accounting for every non-miraculous occurrence that has a cause, without being complete as a catalog of laws of nature.

There is, however, an aspect of Malebranche's philosophical theology to which Leibniz's criticism is relevant. Some of Malebranche's remarks suggest that he wished to affirm a certain hierarchy among various types of laws. In particular, various of his remarks suggest that he held that laws governing mind-body interaction take precedence over laws governing purely physical communication of motion. (See, for example, OM/3/74 (LO 580-81) and OM/3/97-98 (LO 594). At OM/3/74 Malebranche noted a point of philosophical theology connected with the hierarchy claim. He wrote of man before the Fall: "... man could on certain occasions suspend the natural law of the communication of motion . . . ." And at OM/3/97-98 (LO 594) Malebranche claimed that, although our powers of suspension of the laws governing communication of motion have withered in virtue of the Fall, they have not lapsed entirely. So the "intrusions" permitted by Malebranche's theory, which were so objectionable to Leibniz, play a role of some consequence in Malebranche's theory.

Why would Leibniz spend so much effort drawing attention to a purported failing of an ancillary aspect of Malebranche's theory? I think Leibniz's fundamental interest was in shoring up defenses around his own system. Here's what I mean. Suppose we accept the idea that all real creaturely causes are quasi-causes. I have suggested that Leibniz accepted this thesis; note that Malebranche would regard it as vacuously true. Suppose, in addition, that Malebranche's catalog of occasional causes is accurate and complete as a catalog of laws of nature, i.e., of creaturely quasi-causes. In particular, suppose that some physical events have mental events as their sole immediate quasi-causes and vice versa (i.e., some mental events have as sole immediate quasi-causes, physical events.) Putting these suppositions together has the consequence that Leibniz's thesis of spontaneity is a non-starter, because empirically false. But the conjunction of spontaneity and world-apart is the heart of Leibniz's account of the nature of individual substances, i.e., the ultimate individual entities of his ontology.[10]

## 3

Malebranche offered three major philosophical arguments for the thesis that God's will is the only real cause: the "to be powerful is divine" argument, the necessary connection argument, and the conservation argument. In the process of formulating replies to objections to some of these arguments, Malebranche utilized ideas from which we may construct yet another argument for the thesis that God's will is the only real cause; namely, what I call the incoherence of divine concurrence argument.

(i) *The "to be powerful is divine" argument.* Malebranche's initial formulation of a defense of the thesis

that God's will is the only real cause occurs in chapter three
of Part Two of Book Six of *The Search After Truth*. The
first argument presented comes to this: an entity is divine to
the extent to which it is powerful, i.e., can act as a real
cause. But nothing is in any way divine except God.
Therefore, only God can act as a real cause.[11] Malebranche's
main target here was the Scholastic's attribution of
substantial forms with real causal powers to created entities.
In the case of the Scholastics Malebranche wrote: ". . . if the
heart is Christian, at bottom the mind is pagan" (OM/2/310
(LO 446)).

The premiss that Leibniz rejected in this argument is the
premiss that connects divinity exclusively with power. We
have already noted that the thesis of spontaneity is at the
heart of Leibniz's account of the fundamental elements of his
ontology, i.e., individual substances. The thesis of spontaneity attributes real causal powers to created individual
substances. In *De la connaissance de soi-même* Lamy, taking up Malebranche's side of this particular debate, argued
forcefully that Leibniz's position is inconsistent with doctrines formulating the essential dependence of creatures on
God. Leibniz replied, utilizing unusually strong language by
Leibnizian standards:

> But you do not indicate why and in what respect my
> supposition is contrary to these doctrines. In order for
> a creature to be weak and dependent, must it be with-
> out any power? And in order for the Creator to be
> supremely powerful, must he alone be powerful and
> active? Because God is infinitely perfect, would he al-
> low no perfections in creatures? You would prove in
> the same way that because he is the supreme Being, he
> is the only Being, or at any rate the only substance. I
> agree that God acts on creatures at every moment by
> conserving them; but if he alone acts, what perfection
> has he given them? I really wish that you would spec-
> ify it, because you will find none that does not indicate
> some action. And if he has given them no perfections,
> his work would be unworthy of him. (G IV, 586-87)

ii) *The necessary connection argument.* Consider this thesis: $x$ is a real cause of E only if there is some state C of $x$ such that, necessarily, if C obtains then E obtains. That thesis was common ground among the Rationalists. A question is—what notion of necessity is involved? Malebranche took it that the relevant notion of necessity is metaphysical necessity.[12] With this thesis in hand, Malebranche argued as follows: a thorough review of alleged cases of causation reveals that the required connection occurs only in those cases where the alleged cause is God's will and the alleged effect is whatever he wills. Hence, God's will is the only real cause.

I have found only one passage where Leibniz undertook to refute this argument; it is a private reading note, not intended for publication. In it Leibniz wrote:

Malebranche's strongest argument for why God alone acts reduces to this in the end—a true cause is that which the effect follows from necessarily, but an effect follows necessarily from the will of God alone [therefore, etc.]. However, it should be noted that if the state of any entity is known perfectly, then the state of any other entity can be inferred *infallibly* (although not, I grant, *necessarily*, i.e., not in such a way that it could ever be demonstrated that the contrary implies a contradiction, since analysis goes on ad infinitum.) (ML 412)[13]

Here we find Leibniz employing his doctrine of infinite analysis to distinguish metaphysically necessary connections from those that are infallible, but not metaphysically necessary. This is just what we should expect, since Leibniz's writings are replete with references to a distinction between metaphysical and physical necessity, accompanied by the thesis that physical necessity is sufficiently strong for causal connectedness.[14] It is one thing to utilize a distinction between metaphysical and physical necessity, as Leibniz frequently did, and another thing to be entitled to its use. It is

notorious that there are components of Leibniz's metaphysics that create problems for his formulating a viable
distinction between the two.

iii) *The conservation argument.* Consider the following
two theses:

(a)  For any finite individual substance $x$ and time t, if
     $x$ exists at t then God brings it about in toto that $x$
     exists at t.

(b)  For any state of affairs $\alpha$ and time t, if $\alpha$ obtains in
     the created world at t and $\alpha$'s obtaining at t requires
     a cause, then God brings it about in toto that $\alpha$ ob-
     tains at t.

The locution 'God brings it about in toto that p' is meant to
imply that God is the total and exclusive and proximate cause
of its being the case that p and that an exercise of real divine
causal power via divine will is involved. Further, the locution is meant to imply that no entity other than God makes
any real causal contribution to its being the case that p.[15] By
a conservation argument I mean an argument intended to
establish (a) or intended to establish (b), by appeal to certain
alleged truths about the nature of divine conservation. By a
weak conservation argument I mean an argument intended to
establish (a); and by a strong conservation argument I mean
an argument intended to establish (b). It is no easy task to
uncover which (if either) of these theses leading Rationalists
accepted. One case is clear: Malebranche accepted both.[16]
Just as clearly Leibniz rejected (b); his attitude toward (a) is
not entirely clear to me.[17] In the sequel I concentrate on
Leibniz's rejection of various arguments for (b); I aim to do
so without ascribing the denial of (a) to him. And
Descartes's case is perhaps the most difficult to determine of
the three. In this discussion I put aside the question whether
Descartes meant to affirm (b) and, thus, the positive thesis of
occasionalism.[18] It is plausible to see Descartes as offering a
weak conservation argument and to see Malebranche's central contribution on this topic as an effort to augment
Descartes's argument so as to obtain a sound strong conservation argument.

I begin by considering a tepid instance of a strong conservation argument. We commence with some metaphysical suppositions. i) Finite individual substances with their properties constitute the basic elements of an acceptable ontology of the created world. In particular every state of affairs that obtains in the created world and that requires a causal explanation consists in either a) the coming to be, or continuing to be, or ceasing to be of a finite individual substance (or collection thereof); or, b) a finite individual substance's acquisition of, or continued possession of, or loss of a property (or collection thereof). ii) Finite individual substances with their initial properties come to be by creation and cease to be by annihilation. Now add the following theological suppositions. iii) Only God has the causal powers requisite to create or annihilate finite individual substances. Furthermore, creation and annihilation are brought about by God in toto, i.e., without any causal contribution of any kind from any entity other than God. iv) At any instant at which a finite individual substance exists subsequent to its creation that substance is conserved in existence with its then current properties by the causal powers of God. v) The causal powers required to conserve a substance in existence with its then current collection of properties at any non-initial instant of its duration are the same as those required to create it with its initial properties. vi) God's causal powers are always exercised through his will.

From these suppositions an adherent of a strong conservation argument might reason as follows. From iii) and vi) we may conclude: vii) God's will is the only real cause of the initial states of all finite substances in the created world. From iii), iv) and v) we may conclude: viii) God's will is the only real cause of all the non-initial states of all finite substances in the created world. And from i), ii), vii), and viii) we may conclude: ix) God's will is the only real cause of whatever requires a real cause.

This tepid version of the conservation argument has its problems, particularly, the inference to viii). First, one might suppose that although the causal powers required for conservation are the same as those required for creation, nonetheless, it does not follow in an obvious way that divine conservation, like divine creation, must be exercised without causal contribution from non-divine entities. Second, with respect to the states of substances, prima facie, there is a distinction to be drawn between producing a state and conserving a substance in a state. So even if God's will were the only real creative cause of the initial state of every substance and also the only real conservative cause of every non-initial state of every substance, still there may be room for creatures to function as real productive causes of non-initial states of substances.

An adherent of the conservation argument would claim that our version is too tepid, thus generating the two demurrals just noted. The claim is that were we to understand properly the thesis that divine conservation just is re-creation it would be obvious that divine conservation at some instant must be in toto as creation is, thus precluding non-divine causal contribution. Similarly, an adherent would claim that a proper understanding of the thesis would yield that conservation is as much productive causation as creation is.

I do not attribute the preceding tepid form of the conservation argument, or the two demurrals, or, the responses to the demurrals, to anyone. But I think consideration of the dialectic just elaborated will prove useful, because, roughly speaking, Leibniz's understanding of the thesis that conservation is continued creation places him on the demurrer's side of the issue; whereas, Malebranche's understanding of it places him on the adherent's side. Unfortunately (but typically) when we leave the purity of invented arguments, imagined demurrals and rejoinders—none attributed to anyone—and turn to the actual historical situation, the matter becomes complicated. My basic interest here is in Leibniz's response to the strong conservation argument for occasionalism. Leibniz's response is elaborated in the *Theodicy*, where the target is those versions of the argument presented by Bayle. In his presentation Bayle utilized all the help he could muster, including lines of reasoning to be found in Descartes as well as in Malebranche.[19] I begin with some comments on Descartes.

We may concentrate on a point that Descartes made on numerous occasions about the independence of non-overlapping temporal stages in the history of some contingent individual substance. Consider the following famous passage from the third meditation.

> . . . Since every lifetime can be divided into innumerable parts each of which in no way depends on the others, it does not follow from the fact that I existed shortly before that I must exist now, unless some cause as it were creates me again at this moment, i.e., conserves me. For it is quite clear to one who attends to the nature of time that entirely the same power and action are needed in order to conserve anything at each moment at which it endures, as would be needed in order to create it de novo, if it did not yet exist. (AT VII, 48-49 (CSM II, 33))[20]

Consider the first sentence in the quoted passage. The reasoning seems to go as follows. Let $t_n$ be some non-initial temporal segment in the history of some contingent individual substance $x$. Let $t_m$ be any other temporal segment in $x$'s history, provided $t_n$ and $t_m$ do not overlap and $t_m$ precedes $t_n$. Let $S_m$ and $S_n$ be, respectively, some state of $x$ during $t_m$ and some state of $x$ during $t_n$. Clearly it is metaphysically possible that $S_m$ obtains but $S_n$ does not, because it is metaphysically possible that $x$ exists during $t_m$ but not during $t_n$. So far, so innocent. Consider the following tepid conclusion from this innocent premiss: there must be some cause that brings it about that $x$ exists and is in $S_n$ during $t_n$. Surely, in virtue of his commitment to the principle of sufficient reason, Leibniz would have regarded this conclusion as correct. But Leibniz did not regard Descartes's reasoning here as innocent because of what he took to be implied by Descartes's way of stating his conclusion, i.e., ". . . some cause as it were creates me again at this moment . . . ." Consider Leibniz's critical remarks on article 21 of part I of Descartes's *Principles of Philosophy,* where Descartes formulated what appears to be the same line of reasoning as that just quoted from the third meditation. Leibniz wrote:

> From the fact that we exist now, it follows that we will still exist hereafter, unless a reason for change exists. Therefore, unless it is established from another source that we can not even exist unless by the support of God, nothing is settled concerning the existence of God from our duration; as if one part of this duration were completely independent of the others, which ought not to be conceded. (G IV, 360 (L 387))

Has Leibniz simply failed to grasp Descartes's point about the independence of non-overlapping temporal segments of an individual? Not at all. His point is the surely correct one that nothing follows about the causal independence of such segments from the fact that it is metaphysically possible for the earlier segment to exist even if the latter does not, unless we presuppose the main thesis of the necessary connection argument, i.e., that a connection is causal only if it holds of metaphysical necessity. Leibniz seems to me to have made just this point in §383 of the *Theodicy*, where he wrote:

> . . . it does not follow of *necessity* from the fact that I am, that I will be, but nevertheless it follows *naturally*, i.e., of itself, per se, if nothing prevents it.

But now we must consider what light is shed on Descartes's argument by his elaborations of it in his replies to objections to the *Meditations*. In reply to the first set of objections Descartes noted that the notion of causation relevant to his argument was a notion of efficient causation, where the natural light informs us that a state of affairs $\beta$ is a proximate efficient cause of a state of affairs $\alpha$ only if $\alpha$ and $\beta$ temporally overlap.[21] But this need not be troublesome to Leibniz. For even if $S_m$ existing during $t_m$, does not temporally overlap $S_n$ existing during $t_n$, still $S_m$ could be the proximate efficient cause of some state of affairs $\alpha$ which endures in such fashion as to overlap $t_m$ and $t_n$ and to be, in turn, a proximate efficient cause of $S_n$. In that case $S_m$ would be a remote efficient case of $S_n$, although they do not temporally overlap.

But when we turn to Descartes's reply to Gassendi's objections, it becomes clear that this maneuvering is irrelevant. Descartes wrote:

> When you deny that we require the continual influx of the first cause in order to be conserved, you deny something that all metaphysicians affirm as manifest, although the uneducated often do not think of it, because they only attend to the causes *of coming to be* [*causas secundum fieri*] and not however causes *of being* [*causas secundum esse*]. (AT VII, 369 (CSM II, 254))

Clearly Descartes's point is restricted to causes of being, e.g., to causes of the conservation of substance $x$ in state $S_n$ during $t_n$. With respect to such a series Descartes had tradition on his side for the following thesis: for any state of affairs $\beta$, if $\beta$ is a member of a series of conserving causes terminating in the conservation of $S_n$ during $t_n$ then $\beta$ obtains during $t_n$.

Note that nothing in this argument precludes finite individual substances from functioning as real productive causes, i.e., causes of states of substances coming to be. I take it that Leibniz intended to affirm such a position in the following passage from a letter to Bourguet:

> When I speak of the force and the action of creatures, I mean that each creature is at present full of its future state, and that it follows naturally a certain course, if nothing prevents it . . . . But I do not say on that account that the future state of a creature follows its present state without the concourse of God, and I am rather of the opinion that conservation is a continued creation with alteration conforming to order. (G III, 566)

In addition, nothing in Descartes's argument to this point rules out finite individual substances from serving as real partial conservative causes.

In fact Descartes did not accept the idea that created individuals might serve as real partial conservative causes. The argument of the third meditation seems to permit this possibility by allowing a finite regress of conservative causes each such series initiated by God.[22] But in response to the first set of objections Descartes put his cards on the table. He wrote:

> I will now add something that I have not written before; we do not even arrive at some secondary cause, for a cause that possesses such great power that it can conserve something outside itself must, a fortiori, conserve itself by its own power, and hence derive its existence from itself. (AT VII, 111 (CSM II, 80))

Here we need to distinguish two principles:

(c)   For any $x$ and $y$, if $x \neq y$ and $x$ conserves $y$ in toto, then $x$ is self-conserving, i.e., is God.

(d)   For any $x$ and $y$, if $x \neq y$ and $x$ causally contributes to the conservation of $y$, then $x$ is self-conserving, i.e., is God.

In this case, the relevant traditional view is this: Only God can conserve another being in toto, but a creature can contribute causally to the conservation of another creature.[23] However, Leibniz sided with Descartes against tradition in the case where the variables are taken to range over individual substances. This is a consequence of the thesis of spontaneity. But nothing in Leibniz's theory precludes one state of an individual substance from serving as a real partial conservative cause of another state of that same substance.

We may now turn to Malebranche's chief contributions to the subject. Let's begin with what is common ground between Malebranche and Leibniz, or, at least, what Leibniz was prepared to let pass without demurral for the sake of argument. They both accepted items i) through vi) of our tepid strong conservation argument. That means that Leibniz did not balk at Malebranche's use of (a) nor at Malebranche's use of the following restriction of (b):

(b') For any instantaneous state of affairs α, if α obtains in the created world at the first instant of creation and α's obtaining requires a cause, then God brings it about in toto that α obtains.

And, in virtue of accepting (iv) of our tepid argument, Leibniz and Malebranche agreed on the following:

(e) For any state of affairs α and time t, if α obtains in the created world at t and α's obtaining at t requires a cause, then God is a conservative cause of α's obtaining at t.

Some of the secondary literature seems to assume that Malebranche's chief strong conservation argument amounts to this: (e) tells us that God causally conserves every state of affairs requiring a cause that obtains in the created world. (b') tells us that in those cases where God's causal activity amounts to creation, God's causal activity is both productive and conservative, as well as being in toto in both respects. But the doctrine that divine conservative causation just is continued creation implies that God's conservative causation has the same intrinsic features as God's creative causation. Now the feature of being both productive and conservative, as well as being in toto in both respects, is intrinsic to God's creative causal activity. Hence, being both productive and conservative, as well as being in toto in both respects, is a feature of God's conservative causation. Hence, we may conclude that (b) is true, i.e., that God is the only real cause of whatever requires a cause.

I do not believe that this naive argument is to be found in Malebranche, nor in any other major figure in the relevant time period.[24] The best sources of the chief strong conservation argument based on (a), (b'), (e) that Malebranche did, in fact, offer are sections six through ten of dialogue seven of the *Dialogues on Metaphysics* (OM/12/155-160 (Doney 153-57)) and sections seven through eleven of the fifth meditation of *Meditations Chrétiennes et Metaphysiques* (OM/10/49-52). I concentrate on the latter text, where Malebranche set out to establish the following thesis:

(b") For any purely physical state of affairs α and time
t, if α obtains in the created world at t and α's obtaining
at t requires a cause, then God brings it about in toto
that α obtains at t.[25]

Let us say that a purely physical state of affairs α is a
rest/motion state of affairs just in case the propositional im-
port of α is to attribute to some individual substance either
the property of being at rest at some time t or the property of
being in motion with specified speed and/or direction at t. In
section eleven of the fifth meditation Malebranche brought
his commitment to mechanism to bear in order to establish
this thesis: if God brings about in toto every rest/motion state
of affairs that obtains in the created world and that requires a
cause, then (b") is true. With this lemma in hand,
Malebranche aimed to prove the following thesis:

(b"') For any rest/motion state of affairs α and time t,
if α obtains in the created world at t and α's obtaining
at t requires a cause, then God brings it about in toto
that α obtains at t.

Consider the following passage from section eight of the
fifth meditation (OM/10/50):

God can create a body only at rest or in motion. Now a
body is at rest because God always creates it or conserves it in the same place: it is in motion because God
always creates it or conserves it successively in different places. Thus, in order for a [finite] mind to move a
body at rest or stop a body in motion, it is necessary
that it compel God to change his conduct or action. For
if God does not cease to will, and consequently conserve a body in such and such a place, this body will
not cease to exist there; hence, it will be immobile. And
if God does not cease to conserve a body successively
in different places, no power will be able to stop it or
hold it in the same place. The moving force of bodies
is the all-powerful action of God, who conserves them
successively in different places: no [finite] mind is the
master of the action of God, no power can change it.

Hence, there is only God alone who can move bodies.[26]

A full treatment of this passage and Leibniz's attitude towards the theses contained within it would require extended
exposition, well beyond what is feasible in the present context. The point I want to emphasize is this: in this passage
Malebranche recognized the need on his part to rule out the
possibility that, in some cases, God exercises his will in a
causal manner by concurring with an exercise of real causality by some creature. In the passage Malebranche set out to
satisfy that need by offering an argument intended to show
that concurrence in causal activity between an omnipotent
agent and a finite creature is impossible. To the best of my
knowledge, Leibniz did not respond in writing to the specific
argument formulated by Malebranche in this passage.[27]
Malebranche also argued against the doctrine of divine concurrence on the grounds of ontological economy. He noted
that whatever God can bring about by concurring with the
real causal activity of creatures he can bring about without
their causal input; he concluded that ". . . it is useless to
multiply beings without necessity" (OM/3/24 (LO 679)). I
know of no written reply from Leibniz. He did respond in
the *Theodicy* to an argument of Bayle's intended to establish
the impossibility of the doctrine of divine concurrence, but
the reply is somewhat perfunctory.[28]
The fact is that Leibniz seems not to have been much
moved by particular arguments intended to establish the impossibility of divine concurrence. In contrast, he seems to
have been moved by considerations of the sort Malebranche
brought forth indicating that there was no coherent explication of the notion of divine concurrence.[29] In a draft for a
letter to Rémond (4 November 1715), Leibniz referred to Du
Tertre's *Réfutation de Malebranche*, and wrote:

. . . it seems that the author of the *Réfutation* has not
adequately answered the argument taken from continuous creation, which seems to deny all actions to creatures. I have responded to this argument in the
*Theodicy* in this manner . . . . God alone produces the

perfections in things, but the imperfection or new limitation annexed is a consequence or production of the preceding limited state of the creature, and thus there is truly what theologians call a concourse. (ML 479-80)

In this passage Leibniz indicated that his central reply to Malebranche's strong conservation argument consisted in an effort to provide a coherent explication of divine concurrence—one that is metaphysically and theologically adequate. In a letter of 5 February 1712 to Lelong Leibniz made plain what he thought was at stake here:

By the Force that I bestow on substances, I do not understand anything other than a state from which another state follows, if nothing prevents it. But I admit that one state does not follow another, unless God intervenes there by a continual production of perfections. And Force is one of the principal perfections, which were it destroyed, there would remain almost none of them, or rather, none of them at all. And I dare say that without Force, there would be no substance, and one will fall, in spite of oneself, into the view of Spinoza according to which Creatures are only passing modifications. Hence, it is necessary to say that God bestows force, and that he does not take the place of it, in order to conserve substances outside himself. (ML 421)

I have claimed that Malebranche saw the need to establish the impossibility of divine concurrence as an independent lemma in his strong conservation argument. Leibniz saw the challenge in Malebranche's claim that the doctrine of divine concurrence, involving shared exercise of real causality by creature and creator, is ". . . not even intelligible" (OM/7/545). Given the incoherence of the doctrine of divine concurrence, there is a simple argument for the conclusion that God is the only real cause of whatever requires a cause.[30] With respect to causality there are just three alternatives: either creatures go it alone or God sometimes concurs with creatures or God goes it alone. Malebranche and Leibniz agreed that the first alternative is theologically unacceptable. So, if divine concurrence is incoherent, the conclusion must be that God goes it alone. And, as the passage quoted above from the letter to Lelong indicates, Leibniz thought that if we are forced to the conclusion that God goes it alone we might as well throw in the towel and accept Spinoza's ontology.[31]

## 4

In the passage from the letter to Lelong, Leibniz affirmed that an ontology of created substances requires the attribution of real causal powers to created individuals. We might think of this as the basis for a metaphysical requirement on an acceptable account of concurrence—that it be consistent with creatures functioning as real causes. At the same time Leibniz aimed for an account of the nature of created individuals that was theologically orthodox in its account of the relations between creator and creature. Thus, Leibniz, like Malebranche, held that God's providence is total, i.e., as Leibniz put it, ". . . God determines all questions . . ." (Grua 312). Moreover, Leibniz, like Malebranche, construed God's omnipotence as implying God's ". . . independence from everything else, as well as the dependence of everything on him" (*Causa Dei* §4). We might think of this as the basis for a theological requirement of an acceptable account of concurrence—that it be consistent with the dependence of creature on creator. In connection with this requirement Leibniz formulated an adequacy condition in the second sentence of the following passage from *Necessary and Contingent Truths*:

> We must examine in what way contingent things, and especially free substances, depend in their choice and operation on the divine will and predetermination. My opinion is that there is as much dependence of things on God as is possible without infringing divine justice. (C 22 (MP 102))

In this passage Leibniz meant to associate himself with much of the theological motivation behind Malebranche's account of causality and to disassociate himself from the deist alter-

natives rampant in the seventeenth century.[32] But the phrase
"without infringing divine justice" indicates what Leibniz
took to be a barrier to accepting Malebranche's thesis that
God is the only real cause. Leibniz thought that only individual substances, persisting through changes are moral
agents, and, as such, fit objects of divine justice. And, as we
have noted, he believed that only individual entities that exercise real causal powers are individual substances persisting
through changes over time. But there is more to it than that.
In addition to satisfying a metaphysical requirement and a
theological requirement, Leibniz noted a theodicean requirement that an acceptable account of divine concurrence must
satisfy.

The basic idea of the relevant theodicean requirement is
this: an acceptable account of divine concurrence conjoined
with the facts concerning sinful creaturely behavior must not
imply that God is a cause of sin.[33] Now the vise tightens.
Leibniz took the theological requirement to imply that God
physically concurs in every action of creatures.[34] And
Leibniz was not one to use universal quantifiers willy nilly.
Thus, when he wrote that God concurs in every action of
creatures, he meant to include sinful actions. Touting the
virtues of the *Theodicy*, Leibniz wrote in its preface:

I show that God may permit sin and concur in it and
even contribute to it, without prejudice to his holiness.
(G VI, 37-8 (H 61))[35]

Surely it is no easy task to identify an otherwise adequate
notion of divine concurrence that satisfies the metaphysical,
theological, and theodicean requirements. Malebranche
aimed to disparage further the prospects of formulating a coherent notion of concurrence by noting that traditionally the
theological requirement was taken to have a consequence that
Malebranche put as follows:

Our action, considered as efficacious and capable of
producing some effect, is not different from that of
God; it is, as most theologians say, entirely the same
action. *Eadem numero actio.* (OM/3/242 (LO 679))

It is understandable that Malebranche and Bayle threw up their hands in despair. In truth, it is just the sort of intellectual challenge that Leibniz relished.

Here is a straightforward statement of Leibniz's account of divine concurrence from *Theodicy* §377:

> ... the concurrence of God consists in giving us continually whatever there is of reality in us and our actions in so far as it contains some perfection; but what there is therein of limitation or imperfection is a consequence of preceding limitations, which are originally in creatures.

The basic idea is obvious enough: in an action with respect to which God and some creature concur, God's causal contribution pertains to the perfections exhibited in that action, whereas the creature's causal contribution pertains to the limitations exhibited in that action. Surely without a detailed analysis of the notions of perfection and limitation, Malebranche could regard this account of divine concurrence as mere sloganeering on Leibniz's part.[36]

As is common in the case of the notion of divine concurrence, Leibniz presented many of his ideas concerning it by way of an analogy.[37] The analogy is this.[38] Imagine two boats of exactly the same construction and configuration, with one more heavily laden than the other, moving downstream under the influence of the same current, without means of propulsion other than the current. The current is the cause of the movement of each boat, but it is not the cause of the retardation of the more heavily laden boat relative to its less heavily laden sister ship. Consider the motion of the more heavily laden boat: We have a single action in which two causes concur, the current causing the positive aspects of that motion, its excessive of weight relative to its sister ship accounting for its retardation relative to its sister ship.

Now suppose that the retardation of the more heavily laden boat, due its greater inertia, is viewed in the context at hand as a fault of some kind. This fault—the lack of speed relative to its sister ship—would be due to what the ship and its cargo contribute to its velocity, not what the current contributes, since it makes the same contribution to both boats, one of which is tainted with fault, while the other is not. And, of course, this analogy serves to illustrate how, according to Leibniz, God can physically concur in a sinful action without any fault being assigned to God's contribution. God contributes whatever there is of perfection in the sinful action; the creature, in virtue of its limitations, contributes that in virtue of which the action is sinful.[39]

Still, analysis beats analogy any day. Ferreting out Leibniz's account of the notions of perfection and limitation is a daunting task, of the sort that historians, unfortunately, tend to shy away from, because the philosophical yield appears minimal. The texts are there. If my analysis of the dialectic of the Leibniz-Malebranche debate concerning causality is on target, the elucidation of those texts is crucial to a proper understanding of that debate. But it won't happen here.

## NOTES

1 Early versions of this paper were read at Wayne State University, the "Causation in Early Modern Philosophy" conference at the University of Wisconsin, Madison, and at the University of Notre Dame. I am particularly indebted to the following for helpful comments: the brothers Powers at Wayne State University, Jeremy Hyman at Madison, and Lynn Joy at Notre Dame. What I know about the doctrines of divine conservation and concurrence I learned from Fred Freddoso at Notre Dame.

The following abbreviations, used in citations, agree with those adopted by the present volume in all points of overlap:

AT        C. Adam and P. Tannery, eds. *Oeuvres de Descartes*. Paris, 1897-1913. Reprint. Paris: J. Vrin, 1964-1975. Cited by volume and page.

C         Louis Couturat, ed. *Opuscules et fragments inédits de Leibniz*. Paris, 1903. Reprint. Hildesheim: Georg Olms, 1966.

*Causa Dei*   G. W. Leibniz. *Causa Dei*. Cited by section number as given in G VI, 437-460; translated by Paul Schrecker in (ed.) Schrecker and Schrecker; *Leibniz: Monadology and other Philosophical Essays*. New York: Macmillan Publishing Co., 1985: 114-145.

CSM   *The Philosophical Writings of Descartes*. Translated by John Cottingham, Robert Stoothoff, and Dugald Murdoch. 2 vols. Cambridge: Cambridge University Press, 1985. Cited by volume and page.

DM   G. W. Leibniz. *Discourse on Metaphysics*. Cited by section numbers as given in G IV. Translated by Peter G. Lucas and Leslie Grint. Manchester: Manchester University Press, 1961.

Doney   Nicholas Malebranche. *Entretiens sur la metaphysique* (Dialogues on metaphysics). Translated by Willis Doney. New York: Abaris Books, 1980. Original French with translation into English.

G   *Die philosophischen Schriften von G. W. Leibniz*. Edited by C. J. Gerhardt. 7 vols. Berlin, 1875-1890. Reprint. Hildesheim: Georg Olms, 1965. Cited by volume and page.

GM   *G. W. Leibniz. Mathematische Schriften*. Edited by C. J. Gerhardt. 7 vols. Halle, 1849-1863. Reprint. Hildesheim: Georg Olms, 1963. Cited by volume and page.

Grua   *G. W. Leibniz. Textes inédits*. Edited by Gaston Grua. 2 vols. Paris, 1948. Reprint. New York and London: Garland, 1985.

K   *Descartes—Philosophical Letters*. Edited and translated by Anthony Kenny. Oxford: Clarendon Press, 1970.

L   *G. W. Leibniz. Philosophical Papers and Letters*. Edited and translated by Leroy E. Loemker. 2nd ed. Dordrecht: D. Reidel, 1969.

LA   Leibniz-Arnauld correspondence. Cited by page number in G II.

LO          Nicholas Malebranche. *The Search after Truth/Elucidations of the Search after Truth.* Translated by Thomas M. Lennon and Paul J. Olscamp. Columbus: Ohio State University Press, 1980.

ML          André Robinet, ed. *Malebranche et Leibniz: Relations personelles.* Paris: J. Vrin, 1955.

MP          *G. W. Leibniz. Philosophical Writings.* Edited and translated by Mary Morris and G. H. R. Parkinson. London: Dent, 1973.

OD          *Pierre Bayle—Oeuvres diverses.* Introduction by Elisabeth Labrousse. Hildesheim: Georg Olms, 1964--. Cited by volume and page.

OM          *Oeuvres complètes de Malebranche.* Edited by André Robinet. 20 vols., plus Index des citations and Index general. Paris: J. Vrin, 1958-1984. Cited by volume and page.

*Theodicy*   G. W. Leibniz. *Theodicy.* Cited by section number (indicated by '§' or 'section'), as given in G VI and the following English translation: *Theodicy.* Translated by E. M. Huggard. Hew Haven: Yale University Press, 1952. Reprint. La Salle, Ill.: Open Court, 1985 (=H). Occasionally, section numbers are not suitable, and citations are given by page numbers in G VI and H.

2  See DM §§14, 15, 16, and 33.
3  Here is a typical formulation of the doctrine: "Every present state of a substance occurs to it spontaneously and is only a consequence of its preceding state" (LA 47). Here is a much more careful formulation, which takes into account the case of the initial state of a substance and subsequent miraculous states (if such there be): "Everything happens in each substance in consequence of the first state that God gave it in creating it, and, extraordinary concourse aside, his ordinary concourse consists simply in the conservation of the substance itself, in conformity with its preceeding state and with the changes that it carries with it" (LA 91-92).
4  Roughly speaking, we may think of '*x* is a quasi-cause of *y*' as holding in just those cases where a well-informed, non-metaphysically inclined seventeenth century scientist would have regarded *x* as a cause of *y*, were he to have had an opin-

ion on the topic of whether a causal relation held between $x$ and $y$.

5  See OM/5/67.
6  For a presentation of the five sets of laws see OM/12/319-20 (Doney 321).
7  See GM/2/299.
8  *Ibid.*
9  I wish that Leibniz had answered the question contained in this quotation. Locating the ultimate source of Leibniz's denial of creaturely intersubstantial causation is a difficult task.
10  For more on this topic see chapter six of my *Leibniz and Arnauld: A Commentary on their Correspondence* (New Haven and London: Yale University Press, 1990). In the book, the role of Malebranche's thinking about our ability to suspend certain laws of motion in his theory is overlooked, unfortunately.
11  Lynn Joy drew my attention to this argument and to its significance for Malebranche.
12  See, for example, OM/2/313 (LO 448) and OM/10/63-64.
13  I found this passage difficult to translate; I appreciate Fred Freddoso's help.
14  See, for example, *Necessary and Contingent Truths* (C 16-24 (MP 96-105)).
15  The idea involved is clarified by Philip Quinn in his instructive paper "Divine Conservation, Secondary Causes, and Occasionalism," in (ed.) Thomas V. Morris, ed., *Divine and Human Action* (Ithaca and London: Cornell University Press, 1988): 50-73; see, especially, pages 52-53.
16  I assume that (b) entails (a); hence, that one who accepts (b) also accepts (a).
17  Sections 382 through 391 of the *Theodicy* contain a statement of Leibniz's mature view on this topic. At §391 Leibniz wrote:

> I agree . . . that the creature does not concur with God in order to conserve itself (in the manner in which conservation has just been explained), but I see nothing that prevents the creature's concurrence with God for the production of some other thing.

This sounds like an affirmation of (a) and a denial of (b), but the material in parentheses needs to be heeded. Section 386 commences with "Let us admit then in such a sense that con-

servation is continued creation. . . ." The entire discussion
may be hypothetical. Leibniz may have been saying—here is
the most favorable plausible interpretation of the doctrine that
conservation is continued creation from Bayle's point of view;
it is still too weak to establish (b). 'Conservation is continued
creation' is one of numerous slogans some translation of
which was uttered by most seventeenth century Christian
philosophers, but whose propositional content varied significantly from one philosopher to the next.

18  Some of Descartes's remarks suggest that he did accept the
positive thesis of occasionalism. Consider the following from
a letter of 6 October 1645 to Elizabeth: "God is the universal
cause of everything in such a way that he is in the same way
the total cause of everything; and thus nothing can happen
without his will" (AT IV, 314 (K 180)).
   There is some evidence that Malebranche thought that
Descartes accepted the positive thesis of occasionalism.
Consider the following passage from Malebranche's *Réponse
à la dissertation*. Referring to Arnauld, Malebranche wrote:

> He is too good a Cartesian . . . to doubt that God alone
> acts by his own efficacy, and that he communicates his
> power to creatures only because he makes for himself
> laws, according to which he acts unceasingly on their oc-
> casion. (OM/7/517)

Nonetheless, I am inclined to doubt that Descartes accepted
the positive thesis of occasionalism, particularly in its application to the causal activity of rational agents. On this score, I
have been influenced by Daniel Garber's insightful presentation at the University of Wisconsin conference on causality in
early modern philosophy.

19  OD/3/787-791.

20  Similar passages may be found in numerous texts of
Descartes. See, for example, AT VII,109 (CSM II, 78-79);
AT VII, 165, 168 (CSM II, 116, 118); AT VII, 369-70 (CSM
II, 254-55); AT VIIIA, 13 (CSM I, 200).

21  See AT VIII, 108 (CSM II, 78).

22  See AT VII, 50 (CSM II, 34).

23  The thesis that God's conservative causality is in toto, i.e.,
without causal contribution from other agents, is denied by St

Thomas—see *Summa Theologica*, Part I, Question 104, Article 2, Reply to Objection 1.

24 The argument noted involves a particularly unsophisticated reading of premiss v) from our tepid strong conservation argument. Some of Malebranche's writings, taken in isolation, may bring this reading to mind—see, for example, section seven of dialogue seven of the *Dialogues on Metaphysics* (OM/12/157 (Doney 153-155)). But note that the argument just formulated does not require an independent lemma ruling out the possibility of creaturely concurrence in the causation of non-initial states of the created world. Yet in his careful presentations of his chief strong conservation argument Malebranche always devoted attention to ruling out just this possibility—see, for example, OM/12/160 (Doney 157) and OM/10/50.

25 Special problems arise in the case of certain non-physical states of affairs, especially those that Malebranche called consentings, which are at the heart of his account of freedom of the will. I plan to discuss that topic in another place.

26 This version of Malebranche's chief strong conservation argument presupposes as already established that bodies have been ruled out as possible causes of motion. On this topic, see, for example, OM/2/313-14 (LO 448).

27 On the face of it, Malebranche's argument does not seem very powerful. Obviously, in a struggle between an omnipotent will and a creature's will, the omnipotent will wins. Just as obviously, if God wills with a final, consequent will that p, then p, no matter what a creature may will or not will. But if God chooses to act in a given case by concurring with a creature's will, then, just as obviously, what comes about depends in part on what the creature wills. The real issue is whether this latter idea makes theological and metaphysical sense. Leibniz thought so.

28 For Bayle's argument see OD/3/787-791. For Leibniz's response see *Theodicy* §388-392.

29 See, for example, OM/3/241-44 (LO 679-680).

30 See, for example, OM/7/545, where Malebranche formulated this argument.

31 For the sake of completeness it should be noted that there is a line of reasoning that Malebranche presented in section six, chapter two, Part two of *Traité de Morale* that both Bayle and

Leibniz saw as the heart of another strong conservation argument. There Malebranche wrote:

> There is only he who gives being, who can give modifications of being [*manieres de l' etre*], since modifications of being are nothing but the very beings in such and such a manner. (OM/11/160)

The idea is to convince us that a correct understanding of the ontology of accidents (modes) will lead us from (a) to (b). Bayle made much of this idea—see OD/3/788-89. Leibniz responded, somewhat derisively, at *Theodicy* §395, writing: "the production of modifications has never been called creation, and it is an abuse of terms to scare the world in this way." But in some of his "not for publication" writings Leibniz agonized for the relevant details, i.e., the correct account of the relation of an accident to a substance that, as we say, has that accident. See for example, Grua, 546-47. I plan to discuss this topic in another place.

32    See, for example, *Theodicy* §380, where Leibniz noted two influential seventeenth century works that argued for a mediate and general notion of concurrence, as opposed to the immediate and special notion Leibniz preferred. For Leibniz's understanding of concurrence as immediate and special, see *Causa Dei* §§11,12.

33    See, for example, Grua 308 and *Theodicy* §23.

34    See *Theodicy*, G VI, 37 (H 61). The term 'physically concurs' is used here in order to distinguish the notion of concurrence that concerns us here—physical concurrence—from the notion of moral concurrence, which pertains to yet another theodicean problem, according to Leibniz. (See *Theodicy* §§24-27, and §131.) Roughly speaking, agent S morally concurs in sinful action A just in case A is a sinful action that occurs such that S knew A was sinful and knew A would occur unless S prevented A from occurring and knew that S could prevent A from occurring without thereby failing to fulfill some overriding obligation. The relevant theodicean problem is to show that God does not morally concur in any of the sinful actions that occur in the created world.

35    See *Causa Dei* §68, where Leibniz explicitly asserted that God physically concurs in sinful actions, at least in a certain respect.

36  It is worth noting that Malebranche employed an analogous
    distinction to explain God's relation to our concupiscence—
    without, of course, committing himself to the doctrine of di-
    vine concurrence. Malebranche wrote:

    Thus, the formal aspect of concupiscence, no more than
    the formal aspect of sin, is nothing real . . . . Thus, it
    must be said that   God is not the cause of   concu-
    piscence . . . . Nevertheless, whatever there is that is
    positive and real in sentiments and impulses of
    concupiscence, God brings about. [OM/3/35-36 (LO
    557)]. ['Thus, it must be said that God is not the cause
    of concupiscence' is missing in LO.]

37  For example, St. Thomas used the analogy of agent and in-
    strument to explain the notion of divine concurrence. See, for
    example, *Summa Contra Gentiles*, Book Three, Part One,
    chapter seventy.

38  See, for example, *Theodicy* §30 and *Causa Dei* § 71.

39  See, for example, *Theodicy* §30 and Grua 316.

# LEIBNIZ AND LOCKE ON THE KNOWLEDGE OF NECESSARY TRUTHS

*Martha Brandt Bolton*

## 1

Locke's *Essay* is first and foremost an account of the grounds, extent and limits of human knowledge. It advocates an account of knowledge on which the extent of what we can know, by natural means, is significantly limited. This element of skepticism is surely an important motivation for the critique of the *Essay* developed in Leibniz's *Nouveaux Essais*. The latter is largely an attempt to defend metaphysical claims of a sort Locke holds are beyond the scope of human knowledge, e.g. that the soul is immaterial and indivisible. If he is to succeed, Leibniz must show that Locke's conception of knowledge is inadequate. He must offer an alternative conception which is, at the same time, free of the defects of Locke's account and less restrictive regarding the possibility of knowledge in metaphysics.

Such a strategy seems very much in evidence in the Preface and Book I of the *Nouveaux Essais*. There Leibniz contends that Locke was wrong to reject the doctrine of innate knowledge of speculative and practical principles. He singles out for particular attention Locke's account of knowledge of necessary truths. True propositions that are necessary and universal, such as theorems of arithmetic and geometry, were regarded in Leibniz's day as paradigms of what we know. Leibniz' strategy is to make knowledge of necessary truths a main case in point against Locke's conception of knowledge. If his opponent's account is inadequate in this case, then there is something fundamentally wrong with the Lockean view of knowledge.

I want to focus on the initial stages of this program: what is Leibniz's objection to Locke's account of knowledge of necessary truths? what is Leibniz's own innatist theory of knowledge? In spite of the central place these matters must have in the overall project of the *Nouveaux Essais*, there is no one place in the work where Leibniz clearly and fully explicates his position on them. Commentators typically conclude that he has no coherent theory of knowledge to oppose to Locke. In contrast, I will contend that Leibniz has a developed and, in some ways, attractive alternative to Locke's account of what it is to know a necessary truth. In order to discover it, however, we need to piece together widely scattered passages and continually to compare what Leibniz says with Locke's account of knowledge.

2

To begin with, then, what is the basic outline of Locke's account? His definition of knowledge presupposes a certain theory of what propositions are and what it is for a proposition to be true. On the first matter, Locke follows the line that was standard in his day. A mental proposition is a sort of mental act in which ideas (terms) are brought together in such a way that their combination is either true or false (see e.g. *Essay* 574: 8-12).[1] (A verbal proposition consists of words that signify ideas and an act of joining or separating them.) Ideas are joined, if the proposition is affirmative, and separated, if it is negative. As I interpret Locke's account of truth,[2] a (mental) proposition is true if and only if the ideas of which it consists agree or disagree in that respect in which they have been joined or separated in the proposition.[3] The ideas agree in a true affirmative proposition and disagree in a true negative one. There is more to be said about Locke's notion of ideational agreement and disagreement. But here the important point is that Locke *defines* a true proposition in terms of agreement and disagreement of its constituent ideas (*Essay* IV, v, 6).

Now Locke defines *knowledge* of a proposition as the perception of the agreement or disagreement of the ideas that constitute the proposition (*Essay* IV, i, 1). This needs to be spelled out. One consideration is that the definition of knowledge is in terms of *de re* perception. I assume Locke would say that if a person has perception *of* the agreement of certain ideas, then she perceives *that* those ideas agree. Another consideration is how to unpack the connection between perception and belief or, as Locke might put it, affirmation of a proposition. I suggest that Locke intends the definition to be filled out roughly as follows: a person knows a proposition just in case she affirms it as a result of perceiving the agreement or disagreement of its constituent ideas. There are three important features of this account. First, knowledge is assent to a proposition that is produced in a certain way, namely, by perception. Locke holds that we have the native ability to recognize what is true (e.g. *Essay* I, ii, 11); perception is an exercise of this ability. Thus, Locke thinks that perception issues in assent to true propositions, rather than false ones, because of the nature of perception. The second main feature is that the knower perceives the circumstance that constitutes the truth of the proposition known, namely, that the ideas comprising the proposition agree or disagree. Finally, Locke holds that we are conscious of anything that we perceive (e.g. *Essay* II, xxvii, 10). Putting these three features together, we can say that Locke's account implies that a person knows a proposition if and only if she assents to the proposition as a result of a process of a sort that non-accidentally issues in assent to propositions that are true and she consciously apprehends a content that has a specific evidential relation to the proposition; in particular, the content satisfies the definition of what it is for the proposition to be true.[4]

When a person perceives in this way, she has actual knowledge. Locke goes on to distinguish between actual and habitual knowledge. A person has habitual knowledge of a proposition, just in case she has perceived the agreement or disagreement of its ideas, she remembers having done so, and when the occasion arises she "embraces the right side, assents to [the proposition], and is certain of the Truth of it" (*Essay* IV, i, 8).

We should note that Locke uses 'perception' broadly, to refer to what we might call sensory, introspective, and intellectual apprehension; so, there is both empirical and *a priori* knowledge on Locke's account. Of course, we are interested in the way his account applies to the knowledge of *necessary* truths. He distinguishes knowable propositions into four types, two of which encompass Leibniz's main examples of necessary truths. These are: propositions that assert identity or diversity of ideas and propositions that assert a habitual and permanent relation among ideas (or their objects).[5] Propositions of the latter sort include the truths of mathematics, which are common among Leibniz' examples of necessary truths. According to Locke, we know propositions of these two types in either of two ways: intuitively or demonstratively. A proposition is known intuitively when there is immediate, unaided perception of the agreement or disagreement of its ideas. Immediate perception occurs with all identical propositions (e.g. 'A triangle is a triangle'), all negative identities (e.g. 'A triangle is not a circle'), and other simple propositions (e.g. 'A whole is greater than its part' and '2 + 2 = 4'). Demonstrative knowledge is perception of the agreement or disagreement of ideas aided or mediated by other ideas:

> Those intervening *Ideas*, which serve to shew the Agreement of any two others, are called *Proofs*; and where the Agreement or Disagreement is by this means plainly and clearly perceived, it is called *Demonstration*, it being *shewn* to the Understanding, and the Mind made to see that it is so. (*Essay* IV, ii, 3)

For example, the proposition that the sum of the interior angles of a triangle is equal to two right angles is known by demonstration. Locke describes demonstration in terms of apprehension of mediating ideas without availing himself of the notions of logical form or formal validity. Lockean demonstration is informally valid reasoning.

The role Locke assigns to particular propositions in the demonstration of general mathematical truths is not entirely clear. One passage indicates that general propositions are *in--ferred from* particular ones by the principle that the same ideas retain the same "habitudes and relations":

> Upon this ground it is, that particular demonstrations in Mathematicks afford general Knowledge. If then the Perception that the same *Ideas* will eternally have the same Habitudes and Relations be not a sufficient ground of Knowledge, there could be no knowledge of general Propositions in Mathematicks, for no mathematical Demonstration would be any other than particular . . . . (*Essay* 529: 27-33)

The picture is this: we prove the proposition 'Triangle A has angles equal to two right angles'; the ideas in this proposition are the same as the ideas in the generalization 'All triangles have angles equal to two right angles'; the same ideas "eternally have the same Habitudes and Relations"; therefore, the general proposition is true. It may be that Locke stresses the importance of particular propositions, here, to account for the role of diagrams in geometrical knowledge. Elsewhere, however, he indicates that we know general propositions by perceiving the agreement or disagreement of *general* ideas directly (*Essay* IV, iii, 31). He seems not to have settled his view on this question.[6] Nevertheless, we should note that neither view implies that our evidence for a general mathematical truth is simply that we have found it to hold in a number of particular cases.

## 3

We can turn now to the *Nouveaux Essais*. Before looking at Leibniz's attempts to refute Locke's account of knowledge, it is useful to consider what Leibniz means when he says that propositions are *innate* in our minds. This is well known to

be elusive.[7] My approach is to pursue in some detail
Leibniz's reactions to Locke's anti-innatist arguments.

Locke began his attack on innate principles by rejecting
the argument from "universal assent." Children and idiots do
not assent to the "two great speculative principles" which are
claimed to be innate, 'Whatever is is' and 'It is impossible
for the same thing to be and not to be'. Leibniz's spokes-
man, Theophilus, grants the point about universal assent
(NE 75-76). What then is the significance of the claim that
these principles are "engraved on the mind"?

Locke challenges the intelligibility of the answer that we
affirm the principles in some less than conscious way (e.g.
*Essay* 50:37-51:6; 59:36-60:6; 63:17-22). But Theophilus
also rejects this suggestion. When the Lockean Philalethes
argues that if there are innate propositions, there must be innate thoughts, Theophilus replies: "Not at all. For thoughts
are actions, whereas items of knowledge (or truths), in so
far as they are within us even when we do not think of them,
are tendencies or dispositions; . . . " (NE 86). Innate truths
are *not* in us as actions, but rather as dispositions. An unconscious affirmation of a proposition is an action (see e.g.
NE 53). So Theophilus's reply implies that when we are not
(consciously) thinking an innate proposition, we may not be
performing *any* action of affirming it, not even an
unconscious one.[8] This is further confirmed when Theophilus denies that innate truths are "in us" as *propositions*:
"[ideas and truths] are engraved [in our souls] not in the
form of propositions, but rather as sources which, by being
employed in particular circumstances, will give rise to actual
assertions" (NE 446). Affirmations, conscious or not,
would take the form of propositions.

Theophilus steers away from the unconscious-affirmation
view once again when explaining the way we "possess" innate propositions:

> Do not the Chinese have articulate sounds, just as we
> do? And yet, since they have adopted a different sys-
> tem of writing, it has not yet occurred to them to make
> an alphabet of these sounds. It is in that way that many
> things are possessed without the possessor's knowing
> it. (NE 84)

Leibniz surely does not mean to suggest that the Chinese un-consciously apprehend a written alphabet for their spoken language, but rather that they have an easily realized potential for devising one. For Leibniz, then, to say that we have an innate proposition is not to say that we constantly affirm it in an unconscious way, but rather that we are innately disposed to affirm it.

Leibniz associates an innate proposition with a variety of other dispositions.[9] It is especially important that in the case of Locke's "two great speculative principles," we are in-nately disposed to *use* them without actually thinking or af-firming them:

> . . . we use the principle of contradiction (for instance) all the time, without paying distinct attention to it; and the conduct of a liar who contradicts himself will be upsetting to anyone, however uncivilized, if the matter is one which he takes seriously. Thus, we use these maxims without having them explicitly in mind. It is rather like the way in which one has potentially [*virtuellement*] in mind the suppressed premises in en-thymemes, which are omitted in our thinking of the ar-gument as well as in our outward expression of it. (NE 76; also 83, 83-4)

What is it to *use* the law of contradiction without having it explicitly in mind? It has seemed to some commentators to mean that we perform acts of unconsciously or implicitly af-firming it.[10] But this is not clearly indicated in this passage. The simile of a suppressed premise may well be understood to indicate that the law of contradiction is altogether omitted, rather than unconsciously affirmed.

What Leibniz does seem to mean is that people constantly make inferences whose validity can be established by refer-ence to the law of contradiction even though they do not ac-tually recognize or assent to the principle (see especially NE 83). For instance, a child says that sugar is sweet; someone teases her by saying that sugar is *not* sweet; the child vehe-mently denies it. The child knows that sugar is sweet and in-fers that it is false that sugar is not sweet. Leibniz regards the propositional form, 'It is true that $x$ is A, so it is false that $x$ is not A', as an expression of the law of contradiction (NE 362). We can take this as an inference rule which shows the child's inference to be valid. Leibniz compares the law to the suppressed premise in an enthymeme and it is strictly inaccurate to say that the rule that licenses an inference is a suppressed premise. But Leibniz indicates that the one case is only "rather like" the other. The point of similarity is just that both contribute to establishing the formal validity of an argument.[11]

So far, Leibniz has indicated: (a) a proposition is innate in us if and only if we have an innate disposition to affirm it and (b) a general maxim (e.g. the law of contradiction) is innate in us if and only if we constantly use it without attending to it. Neither implies that we constantly affirm an innate proposition unconsciously.

But there is more to Locke's challenge. He insisted that an innatist is obliged to explain how an innate disposition to affirm a proposition differs from an innate capacity to understand and affirm that proposition. No one denies that we have an innate capacity to affirm every proposition we do affirm, as well as those we could affirm but don't (*Essay* 50: 20-32; I, ii, 22). In addition, unless this distinction is explained, it will follow that all propositions we affirm are innate. Locke assumes that an innate proposition, by hypothesis, is the foundation from which we prove and come to know other propositions.[12] And this is clearly false, if *all* propositions we affirm turn out to be "innate." These points challenge Leibniz's thesis (a).

An innatist might try to meet the difficulty by specifying conditions necessary and sufficient for a person to affirm an *innate* proposition. Locke considered two proposals: (i) a proposition is innate in a person if and only if the person affirms the proposition, when she comes to have the use of reason. And (ii) a proposition is innate in a person if and only if the person assents to it as soon as she understands it. Proposal (i) is untenable, Locke argued, because it implies that propositions we *learn* by the use of reason are innate (*Essay* I, ii, 6, 7, 9). Both proposals are inadequate, because they imply that propositions we cannot understand without *sense experience* are innate, e.g. 'Yellowness is not sweetness' (*Essay* I, ii, 16, 18). Also, the disposition specified by (ii) is nothing more than the capacity to perceive that certain propositions are true as soon as we think of them; it does not support the claim that such propositions are innate (*Essay* I, ii, 11).[13]

How does Leibniz respond to these arguments of Locke? Theophilus refuses to be led into stating the precise circumstances in which an innate proposition will be affirmed. He simply admits most of the points Locke had raised as objections to specific proposals.

Strictly speaking, Leibniz insists, all propositions we do and can affirm *are* innate. At the outset of the dialogue, Theophilus says:

> I believe indeed that all the thoughts and actions of our soul come from its own depths and could not be given to it by the senses. But in the meantime I shall set aside the inquiry into that, and shall conform to accepted ways of speaking, since . . . the outer senses can be said to be, in a certain sense, partial causes of our thoughts. I shall look into why, even within this framework, one should in my opinion say that there are ideas and principles which do not reach us through the senses, and which we find in ourselves without having formed them, though the senses bring them to our awareness. (NE 74)

All a mind's thoughts and perceptions are "innate," in the sense that none of them are caused by agents external to the mind. But for purposes of the dialogue, Theophilus is content to maintain that a proposition is innate if and only if it "does not reach us through the senses and . . . we find [it] within ourselves without having formed [it]" (NE 74). When Leibniz uses these expressions, he means to suggest that an act of affirming an innate proposition is neither causally nor epistemically grounded in sense experience (see below). This roughly conforms to Locke's requirement that nothing derived from experience should count as innate.[14]

But within this framework, Theophilus is not embar-
rassed to say with reference to *all* necessary propositions that
"their origin is in the understanding" (NE 75; also NE 77).
This is slightly misleading, because it later turns out that the
class of innate propositions does *not* include "hybrid conclusions," e.g. 'Yellowness is not sweetness' (NE 83). In
any case, all "truths of reason," including theorems of arithmetic and geometry, are innate (e.g. NE 77-78). Leibniz
does suppose that some innate principles are epistemically
primary, and that others are proved by them. But as he
proposes to use the term, both the principles and the derived
propositions are "innate" (NE 78). Neither is Leibniz
daunted by Locke's threat that propositions that are learned,
perhaps with difficulty, may turn out to be innate. Theophilus insists that it is so (especially NE 78; also 50, 84,
85).

Leibniz *should* be pressed to explicate his notion of innateness by Locke's point regarding propositions we assent
to on first understanding. Why should we think they are
innate in us, rather than simply thinking that our minds have
an innate faculty for perceiving that certain propositions are
true? When Philalethes (gently) raises this point, Theophilus
replies with one of his famous analogies:

> But what makes the exercise of the faculty easy and
> natural so far as these truths are concerned is a special
> affinity which the human mind has with them; and that
> is what makes us call them innate. So it is not a bare
> faculty, consisting in a mere possibility of understand-
> ing those truths: it is rather a disposition, an aptitude, a
> preformation, which determines our soul and brings it
> about that they are derivable from it. Just as there is a
> difference between the shapes which are arbitrarily
> given to a stone or piece of marble, and those which its
> veins already indicate or are disposed to indicate if the
> sculptor avails himself of them. (NE 80)[15]

The general picture is that what makes a mind's disposition
to affirm a proposition innate is that the mind has genuine
alternatives to affirm and inclines to one. It is not just that the

mind *does* affirm certain propositions, but that it does so
readily in the face of real options. But the analogy could be
spelled out in a number of ways. If Leibniz intended one in
particular, there seems no way of knowing which. Nevertheless, I think it is useful to consider one way of filling in
the picture, because it brings out an important way in which
Leibniz's position differs from Locke's. After that, we will
consider what ensues in the dialogue when Philalethes
pushes Locke's point that the propositions we find *most*
"easy and natural" are ones that cannot be considered innate.

The marble analogy suggests an innate proposition is one
the soul tends to affirm in circumstances in which it *could* do
otherwise. The case at issue is one in which the mind enter-
tains a proposition and finds it immediately evident. Suppose
we consider the proposition 'Red is red'. How "could" we
fail to affirm it? One suggestion is that we can understand
grounds on which we would deny that proposition or suspend judgement on it. What grounds? Leibniz holds that the
proposition is necessarily true, because it has the form of an
identity, 'A is A' (see below). But the proposition also instantiates a variety of other propositional forms, not all of
which are tautologous. We could overlook the proposition's
identical form and identify it as an instance of a non-tautolo-
gous form.[16] Then we would not have grounds to think the
proposition is necessarily true. So we can envision alternatives to affirming this proposition when we entertain it. But,
of course, we are naturally inclined to recognize it as an
identity and thus as necessarily true. This roughly specifies a
way Leibniz can make sense of the suggestion that a mind
has genuine alternatives when it considers an immediately
evident proposition, but naturally inclines to affirm it. But I
cannot claim it is just what Leibniz had in mind with the
marble analogy.

It is useful, nonetheless, because it does distinguish
Leibniz's position from Locke's. On Locke's view, a person
could *not* entertain a proposition such as 'Red is red' and fail
to affirm it. As Locke puts it: " . . . there can be no *Idea* in
the Mind, which it does not presently, by an intuitive
Knowledge, perceive to be what it is, and to be different
from any other" (*Essay* IV, iii, 8). For instance, if we have

in mind the idea of red and entertain the proposition that it is the idea of red, we must immediately affirm it. Otherwise we do not have *that* idea or *that* proposition in mind. Thus, the notion of a natural disposition to affirm an immediately evident proposition, rather than responding to it in some *other* way, has a purchase in the framework of Leibniz's theory of necessarily true propositions, which it does not have within Locke's. This suggests that it is an essential part of Leibniz's anti-Lockean innatism that necessary truths are necessary because of the logical forms they instantiate.

As suggested above, Leibniz's position is further revealed when Philalethes pushes the objection that the propositions claimed to be innate are *not* the ones we find it easiest and most natural to affirm. Theophilus has said that certain propositions are innate "*because* they are accepted as soon as they have been heard" (NE 76, emphasis added). He also said that when we affirm certain propositions "the exercise of the faculty [is] easy and natural" and "that is what makes us call them innate" (NE 80, just quoted). Philalethes eventually observes that we give *immediate* assent to propositions like 'Sweetness is not yellowness', just as we do to the proposition 'It is impossible for the same thing to be, and not to be [at the same time]'. Indeed, we find it easier and more natural to affirm the former than the latter. Isn't Theophilus committed to the untenable view that the proposition involving ideas of sweetness and yellowness is innate?

In response, Theophilus begins by saying that the general maxim is a principle and the proposition involving the idea of sweetness is an "application" of the principle (NE 82). In contrast to Philalethes, he prefers to express the general principle as a propositional form: 'A is not non-A'. But he backs off a bit from his previous statements about what makes a proposition innate:

> . . . the proposition that *The sweet is not the bitter* is not 'innate' in the sense we have given to the term 'innate truth'; for the sensations of sweet and bitter come from the outer senses, so that the proposition is a mixed conclusion (*hybrida conclusio*), in which the axiom is applied to a sensible truth. (NE 83)

Philalethes makes the correct response on Locke's behalf: "you seem to overlook the fact, sir, that these particular propositions are accepted as indubitable truths by people who know nothing of those more general maxims [which are looked on as innate principles]" (NE 83).

Theophilus' defense is to reiterate his earlier claim that we *use* the general maxim without *attending* to it, as in an enthymeme. We should understand this along the same lines we did earlier. In the present case, the particular proposition instantiates the general principle and we can appeal to the tautologous principle to establish that the instance is necessarily true. Theophilus goes on to say that such situations are pervasive:

> For general principles enter into our thoughts, serving as their inner core and as their mortar. Even if we give no thought to them, they are necessary for thought, as muscles and tendons are for walking. The mind relies on these principles constantly; but it does not find it so easy to sort them out and to command a distinct view of each of them separately, for that requires great attention to what it is doing . . . . (NE 83-84; also 91)

What turns out to be crucial to Leibniz's defense of his position against Locke is the thesis that we *must* use certain logical principles in all our thinking and we do use them *before* we have entertained and affirmed them.[17] This gives a robust sense to his claim that these principles are innate. Locke could agree that we use propositions without attending to them, when we have habitual knowledge. But Leibniz's contention is that we use propositions in this way long before we have habitual knowledge of them.

To conclude: Leibniz's notion of an innate disposition to affirm a proposition presupposes that propositions have logical forms. The innate dispositions to affirm indefinitely many propositions are encapsulated in an innate disposition to seek out and affirm propositions that have certain logical forms. Another crucial element in his innatist position is that we are innately disposed to *use* certain formal principles in affirming propositions and making inferences without (before) *attending* to those principles. That is not to say that we affirm the principles unconsciously. Rather, we are disposed to affirm propositions and to make inferences that conform to these logical principles.[18]

## 4

We are now in a position to consider Leibniz's objections to Locke's account of our knowledge of necessary truths. Philalethes faithfully states Locke's definition of knowledge as the perception of the agreement or disagreement of ideas. Theophilus responds:

> . . . it is true indeed that truth is always grounded in the agreement or disagreement of ideas, but it is not generally the case that our knowledge of truth is a perception of this agreement and disagreement. For when we know the truth only in the manner of empirics, through having experienced it without knowing how things are connected or what principles are at work in what we have experienced, we have no perception of that agreement or disagreement, unless you mean that we sense it confusedly without being aware of it. But your examples seem to indicate that you always demand knowledge in which one is aware of the connection or opposition, and that cannot be granted to you. (NE 357)

This is an objection to Locke's account of knowledge in general, but it also applies to Locke's handling of knowledge of necessary truths.[19] Leibniz agrees that we sometimes perceive the agreement or disagreement that grounds a necessary truth. But it is an assumption of Leibniz's program that all necessary truths are, or are reducible to, identities (NE 101, 361, 408, 414, 451, 452). So we have not penetrated to the agreement or disagreement of terms in a necessary truth unless we have perceived that the proposition *is* an identity. In the passage just quoted, Leibniz claims that we sometimes know a proposition even though we do not perceive the agreement or disagreement (e.g. identity) of its terms. He proposes to refute Locke's theory with a counterexample.

It is not promising. The argument is this: an empiric about a proposition knows that the proposition is true; she is not aware of the agreement or disagreement of ideas that grounds the truth of the proposition; so, Locke's account of knowledge is false. Someone is an empiric, if she affirms a general necessary truth and has noted cases that conform to it, but apprehends neither a proof of it nor the ground of its truth. For instance, a mathematician might have a technique for solving problems of a certain sort, which she has found to work in many cases, but cannot prove in general (NE 85, 369). The *claim* is that the empiric knows a proposition confirmed in this way. But a Lockean will simply deny that the empiric has knowledge, so the argument is blocked.

Moreover, it is far from clear why Leibniz himself should think that an empiric knows. The views of some commentators would suggest that we can fill out Leibniz's reasoning along lines such as these: an empiric does apprehend the grounds for the truth of the proposition in question and, for that reason, she knows the proposition; but she apprehends the grounds of its truth unconsciously or implicitly. Now it may be that Leibniz does think that the empiric subconsciously apprehends the agreement of ideas that grounds the truth of the general proposition. But this is not clearly expressed in the passage and, as I have argued, it is not implied by Leibniz's account of what it is for a proposition to be innate. In any case, it is not clear why Leibniz should think that a person who subconsciously proves a proposition *knows* the proposition to be true. She cannot produce the proof as evidence for the proposition, nor can she review the proof to check that it is correct. So, whether or not Leibniz thinks the empiric completes a subconscious proof, we are left with the puzzle why he should think that an empiric with respect to a general necessary proposition knows that the proposition is true. Let's look at another attempt to raise an objection to Locke's account of knowledge.

## 5

This is the most familiar of Leibniz's sallies against Locke:

> So you see, sir, that these people who [reject innate knowledge], able though they are, have failed to think through the implications of the distinction between necessary or eternal truths and truths of experience.... The fundamental proof of necessary truths comes from the understanding alone, and other truths come from experience or from observations of the senses. Our mind is capable of knowing truths of both sorts, but it is the source of the former; and however often one experienced instances of a universal truth, one could never know inductively that it would always hold unless one knew through reason that it was necessary. (NE 80; also 50, 75, 77)

Like the previous argument, this one seems to have no force against Locke. For Locke does *not* suppose that mathematical theorems are proved "inductively." And he thinks they are known *a priori*.

But there is more to the argument. Leibniz maintains, not just that the knowledge of necessary truths is *a priori*, but also that knowledge of this sort is impossible unless the proposition known (the act of affirming it?) comes from an inner source. Now the source of an affirmation is not irrelevant to the question whether the affirmation constitutes knowledge.[20] Recent discussions have brought out that there is some plausibility to the view that if a person knows a proposition, then she believes the proposition as a result of an appropriate cause. Roughly speaking, the cause should be of a sort that always, or at least usually, produces beliefs that are true and it should not be an accident that it does so.

Leibniz does suppose that the inner causal source of our innate dispositions non-accidentally causes assent to propositions that are true.[21] (However, I know of no place where he undertakes to *argue* for this.) But as far as I can see, the demand for an account of knowledge that posits this sort of causal ground is equally well met by Locke. For on Locke's account, a person knows a necessary truth only if she assents to the proposition as a result of an act of intellectual perception. And intellectual perception is a process that non-accidentally actualizes our innate capacity to recognize truth. Of course, the two philosophers differ over whether we have an innate disposition to affirm specific propositions or a more general ability to detect the agreement or disagreement of ideas. But this seems not to be brought into play in the passage above.

There might be a case to make against Locke, if Leibniz favored some sort of non-realist account of necessary truth. It has been suggested that he explains the necessity of propositions by the thesis that we are innately disposed to assent to them.[22] The passage just quoted might be taken to say that the mind is the source of the "necessity" of propositions (also NE 75, 84). But other passages show that Leibniz thinks innate propositions have a necessity grounded in something other than the workings of our minds:

> The ultimate foundation of truth [is] that Supreme and Universal Mind who cannot fail to exist and whose understanding is indeed the domain of eternal truths.... This is where I find the pattern for the ideas and truths which are engraved in our souls. (NE 447)

In sum, we have not found that Leibniz has a point about the inner, non-sensory source of knowledge of necessary truths that is a telling objection to Locke. So far, his arguments have not brought his innatism fully into play. Let's look at one that does.

## 6

At one point, Leibniz attacks the Platonists' version of innate knowledge:

> The Platonists thought that all our knowledge is recollection, and thus that the truths which the soul brought with it when the man was born—the ones called innate—must be the remains of an earlier explicit knowl-

edge. But there is no foundation for this opinion; and it is obvious that if there was an earlier state, however far back, it too must have involved some innate knowledge, just as our present state does: such knowledge must then either have come from a still earlier state or else have been innate or at least created with [the soul]; or else we must go to infinity and make souls eternal, in which case these items of knowledge would indeed be innate, because they would never have begun in the soul. (NE 79; also 86)

Prior vision of the Forms cannot account for knowledge *in* the prior state. This is the heart of Leibniz's claim against Locke, as well: without innate propositions, knowledge of necessary truths is *impossible*. What is the argument for this?

As we said earlier, the doctrine that we *use* certain logical principles *before* attending to them is central to Leibniz's claim that the principles are innate. The anti-Platonist argument requires a strong version of the innatist doctrine. What is needed is not just that we do use principles before attending to them, but rather that we *must* do so. But as far as I can see, Leibniz gives no clear argument for this strong innatist claim. Nor do I see a way of using materials he has provided to make a convincing case.[23]

We might turn to our speculative construction of the marble analogy to provide the argument. The idea would be that whenever we immediately affirm a proposition or construct proofs, we must have a natural tendency to recognize and use tautologous forms and valid rules of inference. This is the case, even if we begin by affirming basic logical principles; for we can *always* envision an alternative response. But this argument cannot be attributed to Leibniz with confidence. So I am unable to say for sure how Leibniz would argue for the thesis that if we have knowledge of necessary truths, then certain logical principles *must* be *innate*. Nevertheless, all is not lost. It seems Leibniz's reasoning will take this as a premise: if we are to have knowledge of necessary truths, then we must use certain logical principles.

We can finesse the problematic argument for innateness of the principles, because Locke rejects the premise.

Locke denies that recognition of logical form is essential to knowledge of necessary truths. Indeed, he maintains that recognition of the logical forms of propositions has no *epistemic* value.[24] His notion of the agreement or disagreement of ideas in a necessary truth is a connection specific to the ideas in that proposition due to their conceptual contents (e.g. *Essay* IV, iii, 29). The ideas joined in 'A triangle is a triangle' agree because the content of 'a triangle' is that of 'a triangle', *not* because the proposition is a formal identity (*Essay* IV, vii, 4). As mentioned earlier, Locke's notion of a demonstration that issues in knowledge is a notion of *informally* valid argument.[25] It is not that Locke does not recognize logical form in propositions and arguments, but rather that he denies that it has a significant role in the acquisition of knowledge.

Locke seems to be right that we can acquire knowledge by apprehending the connections between contents of the terms in propositions and by inferences that are informally valid.[26] On the other hand, he goes too far in thinking that there is no epistemic value in constructing a formally sound argument for a proposition. He considers nothing but syllogistic forms. His main argument is that a person must perceive the agreement or disagreement of the extreme terms *via* the middle term in order to understand that a syllogism is sound; so the formal structure contributes nothing to one's knowledge of the conclusion.[27] Leibniz is unwilling to grant that syllogisms have no epistemic use and he is well aware that there are many other valid forms in logic and mathematics (e.g. NE 478ff). To show there is a gap in Locke's theory of knowledge, Leibniz needs only to make out that there are some cases in which formal considerations contribute to our certainty. As he argues:

The [laws of logic] are nothing but the laws of good sense . . . . their being put in writing and made easier to take in all at once enables one to see them more clearly with a view to developing and applying them.

> For when natural good sense undertakes to analyze a
> piece of reasoning without help from the art [of logic],
> it will sometimes be in a little difficulty about the valid-
> ity of the inferences—finding for example that the rea-
> soning involves some [syllogistic] mood which is in-
> deed sound but which is not in common use. (NE 480-
> 81)

The general point is convincing.

Leibniz has exposed a weakness in Locke's theory, namely, that it does not acknowledge that considerations of logical form sometimes have epistemic value. But it seems to me that Leibniz does not show that formal considerations are *indispensable* for the acquisition of knowledge of necessary truths. So Leibniz's innatist argument (whatever its details) cannot accomplish all that Leibniz intends. It cannot show that knowledge of necessary truth is impossible without in- nate propositions. There is one further argument to consider.


## 7


Locke rejects innatism in the realm of propositions and ideas; but he admits that we have innate behavioral tendencies to seek what is pleasant, avoid what is painful, and the like. Theophilus seizes upon this. He argues that these tendencies correspond to practical maxims or truths which are felt in a confused way: " . . . the maxim [we should pursue joy and avoid sorrow] is not known by reason but by an instinct, so to speak" (NE 89; also 94). Further, Theophilus contends that just as we instinctively feel that some things are desir- able and others not, we *feel* that certain theoretical proposi- tions are true or credible, while others are false or unworthy of belief:

> . . . Nor do instincts always pertain to practice: some
> of them contain theoretical truths—the built-in princi-
> ples of the sciences and of reasoning are like that when
> we employ them through a natural instinct without
> knowing the reasons for them. You cannot avoid ac-

knowledging some innate principles, in this sense . . . .
(NE 90)

Leibniz's point is that we use principles of reasoning without
*learning* them. He seems to think this is obvious on empirical grounds and that his doctrine that logical principles are
innate is confirmed by this. But however that may be,
Leibniz is making another objection against Locke's account
of knowledge in this passage and others like it.

When we make inferences in everyday life, often they
conform to valid patterns but we do not think of the fact.
Leibniz wants to say that inferences of this sort have epistemic value, because they *are* valid and sound. We do not
need to know that the inferences are sound, in order to have
knowledge of their conclusions. Locke never considers the
question whether (informally) valid inferences issue in
knowledge in cases where the grounds of their validity are
not fully recognized. In such cases, we do not perceive the
relevant agreement or disagreement of ideas. But Locke's
response to these cases would be tempered by his notion of
habitual knowledge. He could say that a valid inference produces knowledge, *provided* the one who makes it has habitual knowledge of all the agreements of ideas required to
show the inference to be sound. But it seems clear that
Locke and Leibniz would differ over cases such as the following. A child is told that at her birthday party, one half of
the cake will be given to each of the three children present;
the child immediately protests that this is impossible. Leibniz
will say the child knows that it is impossible. She has "used"
an argument, without attending to it: e.g. there are exactly
two halves to a cake; three is greater than two, so there is not
a one-one correspondence between a set of two things and a
set of three things; so the halves of a cake cannot be dis-
tributed one-one to each of three people. Suppose she could
not formulate the argument, if asked. Still, she knows,
because her inference can be shown to be valid by principles
she has a disposition to use and assert. In contrast, Locke
will say that the child does not have knowledge, for she has
neither present perception nor the ability to remember the
connections among ideas that show the inference to be valid.

Now it seems to me that Leibniz is right to suggest that the child's assertion has some epistemic value. Locke's theory does not allow for it.

To sum up: we have considered several of Leibniz's arguments to the effect that Locke is unable to account for our knowledge of necessary truth. Some of them are problematic. But at least two of them seem right: Locke does not allow that recognition of logical form sometimes provides evidence for a proposition's truth and he does not assign any epistemic value to sound inferences we make when we do not (and at the time cannot) attend to everything needed to show that the inferences are sound.

## 8

We can now see the basic form of Leibniz's alternative to Locke's account of knowledge. Locke grounds knowledge of necessary truths in a perceptual process that guarantees, not only that the proposition affirmed is true, but also that the knower has conclusive evidence that it is true. In contrast, Leibniz thinks that affirmation due to a reliable cause (specifically, an innate disposition) is a necessary condition of knowledge and a sufficient condition of knowledge of a rudimentary type. He defines several other types of knowledge in terms of the necessary condition just mentioned and various types of evidence. On Leibniz's account, the causal ground of knowledge can be present without the evidential one; and when there is an evidential basis, in addition to the causal one, the evidence can be more or less conclusive. In this final section of my paper, I want to look at five of Leibniz's types of knowledge of necessary truths and some of the issues they raise.

The most rudimentary type of knowledge is innate knowledge of a proposition. A person has innate knowledge of necessary proposition P if and only if (i) she has a disposition to affirm P and (ii) the disposition is innate (thus, Leibniz assumes, it non-accidentally issues in affirmations of propositions that are true). Innate knowledge is only potential knowledge (*la connoissance virtuelle*). A person does not have actual knowledge (*la connoissance actuelle*) of a proposition until she actually affirms it (NE 86). I take it that if a person affirms an innate proposition, even if she has no evidence for it, she has a type of actual knowledge of it. This is due simply to the fact that the affirmation has a reliable cause.

Another type of actual knowledge is that of the controversial empiric, who knows that a general proposition holds in a number of particular cases, but has no proof that it holds in general. Of course, this is an inferior degree of evidence. As Leibniz says, an empiric does not perceive the agreement of ideas in the proposition she affirms, but we might say that she "senses it confusedly without being aware of it" (NE 357; also 91). The "confused sense" expresses the innate disposition to affirm the general proposition. In the absence of *that*, Leibniz maintains, a person who has merely inductive evidence for a general proposition falls short of knowledge of *any* type (NE 80, quoted above). Another type of knowledge we encountered above occurs when we make inferences without thinking of the principles that license them or, perhaps, without having the ability to do so at the time (the child's birthday cake example). Here again, one has incomplete evidence. Leibniz's reason for saying one has a sort of knowledge in such a case depends on his doctrine that one's affirmation comes from a reliable source.

Leibniz also recognizes (at least) two other types of knowledge of necessary truths. They are roughly analogous to Locke's intuitive and demonstrative knowledge. Leibniz says we have *intuitive* knowledge of a proposition, when its truth is "straight away apparent" and "immediate," and it cannot be proved by anything more evident than it is (NE 367). In marked contrast to Locke, Leibniz seems to think we have intuitive knowledge of a proposition if and *only if* it is an "identity" (NE 361). He takes some care to explain that "identities" include all instances of certain propositional forms: 'A is A', 'AB is A', 'Non-AB is non-A', 'If A is B, then A is B', and the like. The class of "identities" also includes the law of contradiction ('Every proposition is either true or false', as Leibniz states it) and propositions of the form 'A cannot be non-A', and the like. Finally, it is some-

what surprising to find that "identities" include the propositions Leibniz calls "disparities", e.g. 'Warmth is not color',
'Man and animal are not the same'. Leibniz thinks that disparities *can* be reduced to instances of the law of contradiction (NE 82, 363), but nevertheless he classifies (unreduced)
disparities as identities. Now all identities are intuitively
known, and accordingly Leibniz says that disparities are
known intuitively "when the ideas are well enough understood not to need any analysis at this point" (NE 362-63).[28]
   Leibniz's thesis that identities are the only propositions
known intuitively directly conflicts with Locke on the epistemic status of "very evident" propositions. These are non-
identical propositions that are nonetheless immediately seen
to be true, e.g. 'The whole is greater than its part', '2 + 2
= 4'. Leibniz maintains that by defining the terms that
express a "very evident" necessary truth, we can reduce it to
an "axiomatic identity." He admits that we sometimes have
difficulty discovering the definitions needed to carry through
the reduction (NE 370, 375, 429, 432, 451). In any case,
Leibniz maintains that a "very evident" proposition can be
reduced to an axiomatic identity which is *more certain* than
the original proposition. So our certainty is increased by the
proof.
   In contrast, as we said, Locke holds that the maxim about
the whole and the proposition about the sum of two and two
are *intuitively* known (e.g. *Essay* IV, vii, 10). That is, they
are self-evident and cannot be proved by anything *more* evident than they are. Theophilus brings out the controversy:

> . . . in view of the differences in degrees of evidence, I
> disagree with your distinguished author when he holds
> that all these truths—which he calls principles, and re-
> gards as self-evident because they are so close to the
> first indemonstrable axioms—are entirely independent
> of each other and incapable of deriving proof or illumi-
> nation one from another. For we can always bring
> them right back to axioms or to other truths closer than
> they are to the axioms, as you were shown by the truth
> that two and two make four. (NE 414; also 424)

This disagreement reflects several more basic points of conflict. For Leibniz, if we have not reduced a necessary truth to an explicit identity, we have not perceived the "agreement of ideas" that grounds its necessity. From Leibniz's point of view, Locke simply fails to understand what the "agreement of ideas" *is*. Leibniz charges that Locke is content to claim knowledge when he does not have conclusive evidence of necessary truth (NE 452, 361, 375, 408, 451).

For his part, Locke would reject the suggestion that the sort of reductive proof Leibniz envisions is possible. Leibniz's method is to replace the terms in a proposition by their definitions. This advances our knowledge, on the assumption that the definitions show the terms to have content that was not previously recognized. (Had it been recognized, the identity would have been apparent from the start.) But Locke rejects the view that ideas have contents of which the mind is not *immediately* aware (e.g. *Essay* IV, i, 4; IV, ii, 1). So, from Locke's point of view, Leibniz's program for proving very evident propositions rests on a misconceived notion of ideas.

But Leibniz seems to be right that often the terms of "very evident" propositions can be instructively defined. Still, there is a question about the epistemic value of Leibnizian reduction. Locke's claim is that a proposition such as '2 + 2 = 4' has such immediate evidence that no proof can increase our certainty. How does Leibniz argue that it does?

Leibniz notes that we *feel* that '2 + 2 = 4' is evident. But we sometimes feel that a proposition is self-evident when, in fact, it is false or dubious. Theophilus points this out on several occasions when Philalethes puts forward a proposition as immediately evident (NE 408-09, 412). So Leibniz mistrusts the feeling of immediate evidence. This leads him to say that we can be more certain of a proposition that feels very evident, if we can show that it is an identity. It does seem right that we are entitled to be more certain of a proposition that we recognize to have a tautologous form than one whose evidence is grounded only in the conceptual content of its terms. But even so, Locke will object, the reduction will increase our certainty of '2 + 2 = 4', *only if* the definitions by which the proof is given are *more* evident than the arithmetical sum. It is not clear how Leibniz can overcome this objection.[29]

It remains to look briefly at Leibniz's account of demonstrative knowledge. A person has demonstrative knowledge of a proposition just in case she apprehends a proof of it. Here, the proof need not be by definitions and axiomatic identities. A proof is any formally valid argument whose premises are, in some way, known to be true. Leibniz is careful in handling the question of the epistemic status of the premises. Locke's requirement, that each step of a demonstration be intuitively known, is rejected, because it would make demonstrations too wordy. Moreover, Theophilus notes that sometimes we accept axioms that we don't know how to prove, e.g. Euclid's axioms specifying straight lines (NE 369-70).

Leibniz is sensitive to the special epistemic problems posed by proofs that have too many steps to keep in mind all at once. Like Locke, he says we need to rely on sensible representations to record the successive steps. He goes beyond Locke, however, in claiming that a well chosen system of representation can offer a way of checking one's reasoning that increases the certainty of each step (NE 359-60, 410). Locke limits the use of ciphers to aiding memory (*Essay* 551: 15-552: 2). One further point on which Leibniz remarks is the use of diagrams in geometry. As we said, Locke sometimes seems to suggest that diagrams are essential to the demonstration of geometrical theorems. But according to Leibniz, they serve only as an aid in focusing our attention (NE 360-61).

At the outset, I said that Leibniz's strategy in the *Nouveaux Essais* must be to supplant Locke's restrictive account of knowledge with a more satisfactory and inclusive one. I have tried to show that Leibniz gives a probing critique of Locke's definition of knowledge and that he offers a coherent alternative. Although his epistemology is not without problems, there is elegance in Leibniz's separation of the causal and evidential grounds of knowledge and his differentiation of various sorts of knowledge. But of course it remains to be seen whether Leibniz's epistemology can support his metaphysics.[30]

## NOTES

1  Citations and quotations from Locke's *Essay* are either of the form "Book, chapter, section" or "page: line(s)" of the Nidditch edition.

2  Contrast Ruth Mattern, "Our Knowledge Which All Consists in Propositions," *Canadian Journal of Philosophy* 4 (1978), pp. 677-95; and Lorenz Krüger, *Der Begriff der Empirismus* (Berlin: de Gruyter, 1973), chap. 12. My reading of Locke does not agree entirely with that of either of these authors.

3  Ideas can be joined or separated in the following respects: (1) identity and diversity, (2) (permanent) relations or habitudes, (3) co-existence in the same subject, (4) real existence (*Essay* IV, i, 2). In effect, this is a catalogue of basic kinds of propositions based on different types of predication.

4  This is *not* to say that one knows the proposition by inference from the proposition that the ideas in the proposition agree or disagree.

5  It seems that affirmations of "identity or diversity" should be understood to claim that ideas (vs. their objects) are identical or non-identical. Locke says that all such propositions are intuitively known. It may be that we know intuitively, e.g., that the idea of a bat is not the idea of a bird, but we do not intuitively know that a bat is not a bird (see NE 363). In contrast, propositions Locke calls "relations" apparently should be understood to affirm permanent and habitual relations among the objects of ideas constitutive of the propositions.

6  If diagrams are essential in geometrical demonstration, then the evidence provided by such demonstrations comes, in part, from the senses. But if diagrams are an inessential aid and demonstration concerns the "relations and habitudes" of general ideas, then geometrical knowledge is *a priori*. In any case, there is no reason to question Locke's commitment to the view that knowledge in other branches of mathematics is *a priori*.

7  See e.g. David E. Cooper, "Innateness: Old and New," *Philosophical Review* 81 (1972), especially sec. II; Stephen Stich, "The Idea of Innateness", in Stephen Stich, ed., *Innate*

*Ideas* (Berkeley: University of California Press, 1975); Ian Hacking, *Why Does Language Matter to Philosophy?* (Cambridge: Cambridge University Press, 1975), ch. 6.

8  The following passage may *seem* to suggest that Leibniz at least sometimes associates an innate proposition with continual unconscious acts of affirming it: "This is how ideas and truths are innate in us—as inclinations, dispositions, tendencies, or natural potentialities [*virtualités*], and not as actions; although these potentialities are always accompanied by certain actions, often insensible ones, which correspond to them" (NE 52).

But here, again, Leibniz *denies* that propositions are innate in us as actions. That is, a proposition's being innate does *not* imply that we are continually performing acts of affirming it. Thus the unconscious acts that correspond to an innate proposition are not acts of affirming that same proposition. Presumably they are insensible perceptions of the universe (see e.g. NE 113-15, 118). Perceptions of this sort are prerequisites for our having any conscious thoughts, including those that actualize our dispositions to affirm innate propositions (see NE 77, 80). I am assuming that Leibniz does *not* analyze a soul's disposition consciously to do act *A* in terms of the soul's continually unconsciously doing *A*. Leibniz's treatment of dispositions is an important topic, but I cannot do justice to it here.

9  If a proposition is innate, the mind has the tendency to seek and ability to discover the grounds of its truth (NE 84). In the case of an innate *general* proposition, we have a disposition to affirm particular instances of it. Because the maxim that a whole is greater than its part is innate, we tend to observe that a hand is greater than its finger, a house greater than its door, etc. (NE 448-49). And an innate general proposition involves a disposition to perceive particulars as instances of that proposition and to regard them as confirming it (NE 51, 475-76). Leibniz also links the notion of innateness with the ability to apply rules and to recognize things as "the same" (e.g. NE 158, 142, 154). This is closely tied to his notion of innate ideas (vs. propositions). That aspect of his innatism will not be considered here.

10  See Margaret Wilson, "Leibniz and Locke on 'First Truths'," *Journal of the History of Ideas* 28 (1967), pp. 359ff; Nicholas Jolley, *Leibniz and Locke* (Oxford: Clarendon Press, 1984), pp. 171-75. Jolley maintains that although Leibniz sometimes

holds a merely dispositional account of innate propositions, he sometimes propounds an inconsistent account on which innate propositions are implicitly or subconsciously affirmed. A few passages suggest that we do sometimes subconsciously use propositions which happen to be innate (especially NE 424). But they do not imply that the notion of what it is for a proposition to be innate is to be explained in terms of unconscious or implicit acts of affirming it. As we saw, Theophilus repeatedly denies that innate propositions are in us as actions (vs. dispositions) and as propositions (vs. sources).

11   The child's inference could be shown to be valid as an instance of some other inference rule (e.g. 'P; therefore, not not-P', or 'P & T; therefore not not-P', where T stands for a tautology and is understood to be suppressed in the child's inference). Because Leibniz holds that all (thinkable) necessary truths are innate, I think he would not be averse to saying that the child *uses* every principle that expresses such a valid inference rule, provided that the child has a disposition to affirm the principle.

12   For the assumption that innate propositions are epistemically prior, see e.g. *Essay* 57: 3-4; I, ii, 19; 59: 16-19; IV, vii, 3; 595: 1-10; 596: 19-21). Locke's polemic proceeds on the assumption that many of the mathematical propositions we know are not innate.

13   This is not a complete summary of Locke's objections to proposals (i) and (ii). See *Essay* I, ii, 6-14 and 17-21.

14   The conformity is not exact. E.g. Leibniz thinks that 'I exist' is innate (NE 411), whereas Locke seems to think it is known on the basis of experience of the sort he calls "reflection" (*Essay* II, i, 4 and IV, ix, 3). As this shows, Leibniz holds that some *contingent* truths are innate (see also NE 86 and 90).

15   The marble analogy is repeated several times, see NE 52, 86, 87. Locke's argument is repeated and answered again at NE 84.

16   E.g. we could take it to have the form 'A is B' or 'A'. For purposes of the contrast with Locke, it is enough if 'could' means roughly that our taking the proposition in this way is consistent with our psychological capacities and the nature of propositions. But if we wanted to specify the possibility more precisely, we would not be forced to ascribe it to our psychological capacity for error. Instead, it could be ascribed to a

certain lack of acuity in spotting the logical forms of propositions.

17  It is not clear to me whether Leibniz thinks there is an *a priori*
argument for either or both these claims. He sometimes mentions facts that might provide some empirical evidence that we
use logical principles before we affirm them (e.g. the Swedish
prodigy, at NE 78). But this does not preclude the possibility
that he thinks the doctrine can also be established *a priori*.

18  John Harris, in "Leibniz and Locke on Innate Ideas," *Ratio* 16
(1974), suggests something like this as an account of what
Leibniz means by the claim that "the laws of logic are innate"
(p. 240).

19  I am not concerned here with Leibniz's reaction to Locke's account of knowledge of contingent truths. Leibniz thinks that in
a contingent truth, the agreement or disagreement of ideas is
infinitely complex and there is no prospect of our perceiving
it. Still, he thinks that we have knowledge of some contingent
truths. No doubt this is one of his motivations for holding (as
we will see) that there are a variety of types of knowledge that
come short of the conclusive evidence provided by explicit
perception of the agreement or disagreement of ideas.

20  This passage is sometimes cited as evidence of a tendency of
Leibniz to conflate psychological questions (the causal origin
of an affirmation) and logical ones (the truth of an affirmation); see John Harris, *op. cit.*, pp. 241f.

21  See e.g. NE 446, quoted below.

22  Anthony Saville, "Leibniz's Contribution to the Theory of
Innate Ideas," *Philosophy* 47 (1972), pp. 113-24.

23  It is tempting to appeal to the point we credit to Lewis Carroll
(C. L. Dodgson), that the inference rule that licenses an argument cannot be included as a premise in that argument. But I
do not see that Leibniz explicitly makes this point. And it
seems easy for a Platonist to avoid the conclusion that at least
one rule of inference must be innate, simply by supposing that
in the ideal prior state we first affirm the requisite rules of inference and then proceed to use them without thinking of them
at the time to make our proofs.

24  Perhaps he is not dogmatic on this point (*Essay* IV, xvii, 4;
678: 5-26). But he does maintain that it is easier to attain certainty without the repetitious apparatus of syllogistic than with
it (*Essay* IV, xvii, 4).

25  Wilson (*op. cit.*) brings out the contrast between Locke's anti-
    formalist account of knowledge and Leibniz's formalist one.
    But Wilson further maintains that "Locke has resolutely turned
    his back on the whole notion of a formal order. There is no
    aspect of a proposition which is in any way independent of the
    character of the ideas involved" (p. 354). (She says that
    nonetheless Locke's doctrine that all identities are trivial, be-
    cause they repeat the same idea, invokes a notion of logical
    form.) But Locke's notion of a proposition simply follows
    that of contemporary logicians, e.g. Arnauld and Nicole.
    Locke is not barred from recognizing propositional form
    although he does want to hold that it has no epistemic rele-
    vance.

26  E.g. 'Lacking an umbrella, she hit him for the first and last
    time with a baseball bat; so when she hit him, she had no
    umbrella'. The example is due to Bruce Aune.

27  *Essay* 674: 1-6 and 16-38. In addition, Locke argues that
    syllogisms can have no evidential relevance for those who do
    not understand which moods are valid and why (*Essay* 670:
    25-671:4 and 674:9-16). And one needs to rely on the
    (informal) agreement of ideas in order to understand why cer-
    tain moods are valid (*Essay* 672: 1-4).

28  The fact that disparities *can* be reduced to instances of the law
    of contradiction and nevertheless are known intuitively gener-
    ates a tension in Leibniz's position. He says that a proposition
    is known intuitively if it cannot be reduced to one that is more
    certain than it is. So he must suppose that the reduction of a
    disparity produces an identical proposition that is *not* more
    certain than the disparity itself. But, as we will see, he also
    holds that propositions that are very evident (e.g. '2 + 2 = 4')
    can be reduced to identities that *are* more certain than they are.
    Thus he assigns a different epistemic status to two sorts of
    propositions that seem equally evident and are (allegedly) both
    reducible to identities. Perhaps the problem should be located
    in Leibniz's decision to include disparities among "identities";
    presumably he does so, in order to maintain that all *necessary*
    propositions are explicit or implicit identities.

29  It hardly seems plausible to maintain that propositions Leibniz
    regards as "very evident" (e.g. '2 + 2 = 4') are *less* evident
    than the definitions of their terms (e.g. '2 = 1 + 1', which

Leibniz takes to be the definition of '2'). Further, Leibniz seems to say contradictory things about the epistemic status of definitions. On the one hand, an instructive definition is not an explicit identity, and it seems clear that the former cannot be as evident as the latter. This view is supported by the fact that Leibniz sometimes indicates that only axiomatic identities are *intuitively* known (NE 361). On the other hand, Leibniz also says that an "adequate definition" is intuitively known (NE 367; also see 429, 432).

30 Support for work on this paper from the Institute for Advanced Study and Mr. and Mrs. J. Richardson Dilworth is gratefully acknowledged. A version of this paper was read to the Leibniz Society and I am grateful to the audience for their comments. It was also read at the Conference on Early Modern Philosophy, University of Massachusetts, Amherst. The discussion there was helpful and I am especially grateful for the well-argued comments prepared by Bruce Aune.

# BERKELEY AND MALEBRANCHE ON CAUSALITY AND VOLITION

*Nicholas Jolley*

"Strange impotence of men. Man without God. Wretcheder than a stone or tree, he having onely the power to be miserable by his unperformed wills, these having no power at all" (PC 107).[1] As this passage from the *Commentaries* shows, the young Berkeley seems to have been attracted to a form of occasionalism; in other words, he seems to have felt the pull of the doctrine that creatures are causally powerless and that God alone is a true cause. Yet, as is well known, unqualified occasionalism is not Berkeley's mature philosophical position, at least not officially. On the contrary, in his published writings Berkeley maintains that, in addition to God, finite spirits are true causes; they exhibit genuine causal activity in both imagination and voluntary physical movement. In the *Commentaries* Berkeley had signalled his departure from occasionalism with a significant late entry: "We move our Legs our selves. 'tis we that will their movement. Herein I differ from Malbranch" (PC 548).

Berkeley's departure from strict occasionalism is something of a puzzle, for in terms of philosophical consistency, it seems to represent a change for the worse. The claim that finite spirits are causally active in willing is important to Berkeley, but it is a source of serious strains in his mature system. For one thing, the claim is in tension with a residue of occasionalist assumptions concerning causality which is found even in the published works. More surprisingly, it sits uneasily with Berkeley's principal philosophical innovation,

227

namely immaterialism; indeed, immaterialism seems to push Berkeley in the direction of occasionalism. Thus Berkeley faces special problems in accommodating the claim that finite spirits are true causes. In the first part of this paper I shall set out the nature of the problem and examine the pressures towards occasionalism in Berkeley's metaphysics. In the second part of the paper I shall try to explain why Berkeley felt it necessary to depart from Malebranche's teaching concerning causality by insisting that finite spirits are true causes. This will require us to look beyond purely philosophical arguments to the theological concerns which underpin his metaphysics. But first of all, let us look briefly at the occasionalism of Malebranche.

## 1. Malebranche and Occasionalism

There are a number of routes to occasionalism in seventeenth-century philosophy; different philosophers were attracted by different arguments, or where they used the same arguments, they differed in the weight they gave them. Some philosophers argued that if Descartes's doctrine of continuous creation is thought through, then no room is left for secondary causes; all causal activity must be ascribed to God alone.[2] Such an argument seems to rely on the assumption that causal overdetermination is impossible. Others, such as Geulincx, made heavy use of the principle that if A is the cause of B, then A knows how to bring about B; as Geulincx puts it, "*Ego non facio quod quomodo fiat nescio* [I do not make (i.e. cause) what I do not know how to make (cause)]".[3] Here I am concerned only with what is perhaps the most interesting and powerful argument for strict occasionalism, namely the argument from the definition of true causality in terms of necessary connection. According to Malebranche, "a true cause as I understand it is one such that the mind perceives a necessary connection between it and its effect" (LO 6.2.3, 450). For Malebranche, God satisfies this definition of true causality, for God is, by definition, omnipotent, and in the case of an omnipotent being, it is logically necessary that what such a being wills should occur. Thus Malebranche seems to subscribe to the following principle concerning God:

Necessarily, for any logically possible state of affairs p, if God wills that p, then p.

In the case of finite substances, however, there is no logically necessary connection between those events which we take to be related as cause and effect. It is not logically necessary, for instance, that the linen should dry when placed near the fire. In the special case of the mind-body relation, it is not logically necessary that my arm should go up when I will to raise it; it is conceivable that I should be suddenly afflicted with paralysis. So Malebranche consistently concludes that my will is not the true cause of any of my physical movements:

Now it appears to me quite certain that the will of minds is incapable of moving the smallest body in the world; for it is clear that there is no necessary connection between our will to move our arms, for example, and the movement of our arms. It is true that they are moved when we will it, and that thus we are the natural cause of the movement of our arms. But *natural* causes are not true causes; they are only *occasional* causes that act only through the force and the efficacy of the will of God. (LO 6.2.3, 449)

Today of course it is natural to object that while genuine causal connections are indeed necessary, the necessity in question is not logical. But Malebranche's mistake, if it is one, is not a mere surface muddle; it is a mistake of a deep kind. Certainly, in the period before Hume there was nothing eccentric about Malebranche's analysis of the concept of true causality; and to many readers this argument for occasionalism must have appeared a powerful one. Indeed, as Loeb notes, if one grants Malebranche's definition of true causality in terms of (logically) necessary connection, the argument is even persuasive.[4]

## 2. Berkeley and Occasionalism

In the *Principles of Human Knowledge* Berkeley famously argues that many of the things we take to be causes are not causes at all:

> . . . the connexion of ideas does not imply the relation of *cause* and *effect*, but only of a mark or *sign* with the thing *signified*. The fire which I see is not the cause of the pain I suffer upon my approaching it, but the mark that forewarns me of it. In like manner, the noise that I hear is not the effect of this or that motion or collision of the ambient bodies, but the sign thereof. (*Principles* 65)

Such supposed causes as the fire are thus signs by which God communicates with us, and God himself is the true efficient cause in these cases. Thus, even in his mature philosophy, Berkeley remains something of an occasionalist; although he no longer holds that finite spirits are impotent, at least with respect to physical processes Berkeley continues to teach that true causality must be ascribed to God alone; he is also prepared to concede that the "signs," such as the fire, can be called occasional causes.[5]

Why does Berkeley hold this remarkable view of physical processes? Berkeley is not very forthcoming on this issue, but he seems to be in the grip of a Malebranchian argument; indeed, he appears to have in mind the argument from the definition of true causality in terms of necessary connection which we have just examined. In an earlier passage in the *Principles* Berkeley makes an explicit reference to necessary connection:

> That food nourishes, sleep refreshes, and fire warms us; that to sow in the seed-time is the way to reap in the harvest, and, in general, that to obtain such or such ends, such or such means are conducive, all this we know, not by discovering any necessary connexion between our ideas, but by the observation of the settled laws of Nature, without which we should be all in

uncertainty and confusion, and a grown man no more
know how to manage himself in the affairs of life, than
an infant just born. (*Principles* 31)

Berkeley thus stresses the contingency of the regularities
which we take to be causally related; as Bennett says, he
seems to want to highlight the inductive nature of our
knowledge about them.[6] It is natural to suppose, then, that
Berkeley is committed to the doctrine that genuinely causal
connections, by contrast, must be knowable *a priori*. But if
this is Berkeley's position, then it poses problems for his
differential treatment of bodies and spirits with respect to
causality; it seems to imply that the volitions of finite spirits
cannot be genuinely causal. For, as Hume was to observe,
we can no more have *a priori* knowledge of the effects of
volitions than of the effects of bodies; it is no more possible
for me to know *a priori* that my arm will go up when I will
to raise it than that the kettle will boil shortly after I light the
gas under it. The two kinds of cases are on a par; in each we
are dependent on experience:

> The influence of volition over the organs of the body
> . . . is a fact which, like, all other natural events, can
> be known only by experience, and can never be
> foreseen from any apparent energy or power in the
> cause which connects it with the effect, and renders the
> one an infallible consequence of the other. The motion
> of our body follows upon the command of our will. Of
> this we are every moment conscious. But the means,
> by which this is effected . . . must for ever escape our
> diligent enquiry. (*Enquiry* 52)

Jonathan Bennett has made an interesting attempt to defend Berkeley against Humean strictures. In other words, he
seeks to show that, on his own principles, Berkeley can
consistently claim that finite spirits are causally active while
denying that fires make kettles boil. Bennett suggests that,
despite appearances, Berkeley is not in fact committed to the
thesis that causal connections must be knowable *a priori*;
however, according to Bennett, Berkeley does deny that they

can be known only on an inductive basis. Bennett's way of combining these two claims is as follows:

> If I know that I am about to scratch my elbow, having just decided to do so, it is plausible to say that my knowledge—though not *a priori*, not knowledge of a logically necessary consequence of my decision—is not inductively based either. (LBH 202)

Following Hart and Hampshire, Bennett suggests that this knowledge about one's future actions is based on reasons, which is decision. Thus, in the eyes of Bennett, Berkeley is entitled to assert the asymmetry, in respect of causality, between arm-raising and boiling kettles.

This is a suggestive line of defence, but as Bennett admits, it faces textual difficulties (LBH 206-7). Berkeley says things in places which suggest that our knowledge of the relation between volition and upshot is inductively based after all; with regard to imagination, for instance, Berkeley writes: "I find I can excite ideas in my mind at pleasure, and vary and shift the scene as oft as I think fit. It is no more than willing, and straightway this or that idea arises in my fancy. . . . Thus much is certain, and grounded on experience" (*Principles* 28). Following Bennett, I believe that, on the most natural reading, this passage asserts that the relation between volition and upshot can be known only on an inductive basis. As Bennett puts it, "I find 'by experience' that certain volitions are attended or followed by certain upshots, and I trust (in God) that this correlation will continue to hold in future" (LBH 206). But in that case it looks as if, by Berkeley's lights, the relation cannot be genuinely causal. So it seems that Berkeley has difficulty maintaining the asymmetry between physical processes and the volitions of finite spirits. In spite of himself he gets pulled back into unqualified occasionalism.

Pressure towards occasionalism, at least with regard to voluntary physical movements, is also exerted by Berkeley's immaterialism. As we have seen, in the *Commentaries* Berkeley comes to insist, against Malebranche, that we move our limbs ourselves; and this claim is stressed not just in the

*Principles* and the *Dialogues* but also in later works (*De Motu* 215; *Siris* 161). Yet a little reflection on Berkeley's immaterialism suggests that he is not really entitled to make such a claim; to put the point another way, it is not clear that Berkeley is in any better position than Malebranche to attribute to the will causal power over the movement of our limbs. Consider how Berkeley must analyze the case of my raising my arm to scratch my ear. Berkeley will say that I perform a volition, and that the upshot of this volition is that my arm goes up. Now, for Berkeley, to say that my arm goes up is simply to talk about changes in the sensory state of myself and other perceivers. But this change in sensory state is not brought about by me but by God, for sensory ideas are causally independent of my will (*Principles* 29); God changes my ideas and those of other perceivers so that we have the appropriate sensations as of my arm going up.[7] But Berkeley is not in a position to say that my volition genuinely causes God to perform the appropriate actions; surely I cannot cause God to do anything. Rather, as Taylor says, my volition seems more like a signal to God to exercise his causal power in a particular way; in other words, my volition seems more like an occasional cause in this case.[8] Of course, as Berkeley says, "'tis we that will [the movements]"; it is indeed we who do the willing. But what is at issue between Malebranche and Berkeley is whether this willing is causally efficacious, and Berkeley, like Malebranche, is deeply committed to the view that it is not.

In fairness to Berkeley, it must be noted that immaterialism leaves the will sovereign in one sphere; the thesis that bodies are collections of ideas exerts no pressure towards an occasionalist account of imagination. Consistently with his immaterialism, Berkeley can say that we are causally active in imagining the Eiffel tower or pink elephants; not merely do we perform volitions, but these volitions are causally efficacious. Unlike sensory ideas, ideas of imagination are not causally dependent on the will of another spirit, God; they are causally dependent on our own wills. It may seem, then, that in imagination Berkeley has found a stronghold where he can take his stand against unqualified occasionalism; here, it seems, he has found a way of denying something that

Malebranche would accept. But the appearance is misleading. For, as we have seen, there is another force in
Berkeley's philosophy which pushes him towards occasionalism, and this does not discriminate between the cases
of voluntary physical movement and imagination. According
to Berkeley, it is by experience that we find that our ideas of
imagination appear when we will them (*Principles* 28). But
if this means, as I think it does, that the connection between
volition and upshot can be known only inductively, it seems
that, for Berkeley, it cannot be genuinely causal.

Berkeley is thus in great difficulties on the subject of volition. Officially, he is committed to the position that finite
spirits are causally active; unofficially, he is subject to pressures which make it difficult for him to maintain this anti-
Malebranchean stance. Why, then, does Berkeley revise
Malebranche's unqualified occasionalism in a way that
seems so unsatisfactory? It is of course tempting to say that
the answer, or part of the answer, is to be found in
Berkeley's concern with the defence of common sense;
Berkeley "sides in all things with the Mob" (PC 405), and
the mob believe that they move their legs themselves. But it
is difficult to know what role common sense really plays in
Berkeley's philosophy, and how much weight he attaches to
it. In any case the defence of common sense cannot be the
whole answer: it cannot explain Berkeley's differential
treatment of bodies and spirits with respect to causality, for
common sense presumably tells us that bodies are just as
much causally active as our wills. It is necessary, then, to
look for other reasons which Berkeley may have for attributing causal powers to finite spirits but not to bodies. Let us
begin by looking in the direction of theology.

## 3. Idolatry and the Image of God

Berkeley the theologian would surely insist that it is important not to put bodies and finite spirits on the same causal
footing. There are good theological reasons for trying to
show that bodies are not endowed with genuine causal powers; by contrast, there are no such reasons for trying to

establish the same thesis with regard to finite spirits. Indeed, Berkeley would want to go further than this; he would want to insist that good theology requires us to conceive of our minds as genuine causes. These theological ideas are not very intuitive today, and they therefore need to be explained.

First of all, we should notice an important area of agreement between Berkeley and Malebranche which has only recently begun to receive proper attention. In an early entry in the *Commentaries* Berkeley deplores the "rise of idolatry," and the discrediting of idolatry remained a major motive in philosophy for Berkeley as for Malebranche.[9] For both philosophers, the Aristotelian philosophy of nature was vitiated by a dangerous and fundamental error; indeed, in a well-known chapter of the *Search*, Malebranche describes it as "the most dangerous error of the philosophy of the ancients" (LO 6.2.3, 446). This error is the belief that nature is a realm of secondary causes, or entities endowed with genuine causal powers and forces. Such a conception of nature encourages idolatry by promoting the belief that bodies are endowed with god-like properties which make them worthy of worship; as Malebranche quaintly puts it, it encourages us to pay sovereign honour to leeks and onions (LO 6.2.3, 447). This view of nature might be understandable, and indeed is only to be expected, in a pagan philosopher such as Aristotle, but it is inexcusable in Christian philosophers who are informed by the Scriptures of God's immediate operations and of the total and direct dependence of all things on Him. It is thus important to show that this "nature this philosopher [Aristotle] has established is a pure chimera" (*Elucidation* 15, LO 668). Berkeley follows Malebranche very closely here; he too maintains that this conception of nature is a "vain chimera":

> But you will say, hath Nature no share in the production of natural things, and must they be all ascribed to the immediate and sole operation of God? I answer, if by *Nature* is meant only the visible series of effects, or sensations imprinted on our minds according to certain fixed and general laws, then it is plain that Nature taken in this sense cannot produce anything at all. But

if by *Nature* is meant some being distinct from God, as well as from the Laws of Nature, and things perceived by sense, I must confess that word is to me an empty sound, without an intelligible meaning annexed to it. Nature in this acceptation is a vain *chimera* introduced by those heathens, who had not just notions of the omnipresence and infinite perfection of God. But it is more unaccountable that it should be received among *Christians* professing belief in the Holy Scriptures, which constantly ascribe those effects to the immediate hand of God, that heathen philosophers are wont to impute to *Nature*. (*Principles* 150)

Berkeley even follows Malebranche to the extent of quoting scriptural passages as evidence of the "immediate and sole operation of God."

To ascribe causal powers to bodies, and thus to treat them as endowed with god-like properties, is, then, a thesis which encourages idolatry. By contrast, for Berkeley, no idolatry is involved in ascribing such god-like causal powers to human minds or finite spirits; indeed, far from being impious, such an attitude is actually required by the Christian religion; for according to Genesis, man is made in the image of God. Edward Craig has recently shown that the Genesis doctrine, as applied to the human mind, plays a central role in seventeenth-century philosophy; indeed, it motivates much that would be otherwise obscure.[10] In this respect Berkeley is very much of his age; he too gives a prominent place in his philosophy to the doctrine that the human mind is made in the image of God. In the *Dialogues*, for instance, Philonous remarks that "I have . . . though not an inactive idea, yet in myself some sort of an active thinking image of the Deity" (*Dialogues* III, 232). The Genesis text also seems to lie behind a remarkable passage in *Siris*:

In the human body the mind orders and moves the limbs; but the animal spirit is supposed the immediate physical cause of their motion. So likewise in the mundane system, a mind presides, but the immediate

mechanical or instrumental cause that moves or ani-
mates all its parts, is the pure elementary fire or spirit
of the world. (*Siris* 161)

Berkeley seems to be suggesting that our likeness to God is
exemplified in the analogy between the mind's power over
its body and God's dominion over the world. Like
Descartes, Berkeley may well believe that "it is above all in
virtue of the will that I understand myself to bear in some
way the image and likeness of God" (*Meditation* IV, CSM
II, 40).[11]
Here it is instructive to compare Berkeley's position with
that of Malebranche to whom he may well be replying.
Malebranche, like other seventeenth-century philosophers,
pays his respects to the Genesis doctrine; he even claims to
accommodate it in his own philosophy. In presenting his
case for vision in God, Malebranche claims that our minds
are united to God (specifically, the Word), and for
Malebranche, it is through "this union of our mind with the
Word of God . . . that we are made in the image and likeness
of God" (LO 3.2.6, 235). But Berkeley could plausibly
claim that Malebranche cannot really do justice to the
Genesis doctrine. All the emphasis in Malebranche's philosophy falls on the *disanalogy* between human minds and
God. For Malebranche, as we have seen, God is not merely
omnipotent; he is the sole true cause; finite beings, by contrast, including of course the human mind, are causally impotent. Moreover, as Malebranche himself insists, the doctrine of vision in God reaches parallel conclusions in the
epistemological sphere (LO 6.2.3, 449). According to the
doctrine of vision in God, God alone is the locus of ideas,
and these ideas are necessary for all genuine knowledge of
the world; the human mind is thus incapable of achieving
such knowledge unless it is related to the ideas in God. In
the metaphorical language of which Malebranche is so fond,
our mind is in a state of darkness unless it is illuminated by
divine light. Thus the human mind is not merely causally
impotent; by itself it is also, as it were, cognitively impotent.
Berkeley would be justified in claiming that, despite

Malebranche's lip-service to the Genesis text, his philosophy can give no real sense to the doctrine that the human mind is made in the image of God.

From Berkeley's perspective, then, Malebranche had mounted a powerful attack on idolatrous attitudes towards physical nature, but he had paid too high a price for his success; he had undermined idolatry at the cost of compromising the Genesis doctrine that the mind is made in the image of God. For Berkeley, it was important to re-establish the asymmetry between bodies and finite spirits for which Scripture provided warrant. For theological purposes, then, it was essential to discover an argument which drove a wedge between bodies and finite spirits with regard to causality. Such an argument should at least meet the desideratum of showing that bodies are causally powerless while having no such implications for the status of finite spirits. Now Berkeley's immaterialism seems to supply him with just such an argument. Bodies are collections of ideas, and ideas are "visibly inert, there is nothing of power or agency included in them," so bodies are powerless and hence not causes (*Principles* 25).[12] Possibly Berkeley himself was dissatisfied with this argument; certainly, as Bennett says, the second premise is "tremendously unclear" (LBH 199). Moreover, the argument seems to involve a fallacy of composition: from the fact that each individual idea is inactive, it does not follow that a collection of ideas is inactive. But whether Berkeley thought the argument was actually flawed or merely psychologically ineffective, he supplemented it with another, more Malebranchian argument for the thesis that bodies are causally powerless—one that did not depend on immaterialism. Unfortunately, this second argument, from the non-inductive basis of our knowledge of genuine causal relations, is not well-suited for Berkeley's purposes, for as we have seen, it tends to undermine the very asymmetry between bodies and finite spirits which, for theological reasons, Berkeley is anxious to uphold.

## 4. Causality and the Origin of Concepts

Berkeley also has more purely philosophical reasons for departing from occasionalism in the way he does, and these reasons take us to the heart of his philosophical quarrel with Malebranche. So far we have tended to emphasize Berkeley's affinities with Malebranche at the expense of his links with Locke, but we can no longer afford to ignore the Lockean side of Berkeley's inheritance. For Berkeley is committed to certain fundamental Lockean assumptions about concepts, and these assumptions are important for understanding his departure from unqualified occasionalism. In the first place, Berkeley follows Locke in regarding concepts as psychological items for which it is appropriate to seek a causal explanation; with respect to any concept, it always makes sense to ask how we acquired it, or more crudely, where it came from. So much Berkeley has in common with both Locke and Descartes, but he also makes the more distinctively Lockean assumption that the source of our concepts lies in our experience. It is this latter claim, in particular, which helps us to understand his philosophical reasons for insisting on the causal activity of the mind.

Consider, then, our concept of causality from a Berkeleian perspective. Berkeley cannot of course strictly say that we have an idea of it, for ideas, for Berkeley, are images, and we can form no image of causal power. But we do possess a notion of causality, and this notion is not only a psychological possession; it has its source wholly within our experience of volition. The concept of causality cannot indeed be abstracted from volition, and has no application beyond it. It is on the basis of our experience of volition that we form the notion of a being with unlimited causal power; when such a concept is suitably augmented by other perfections, we have the notion of God. Berkeley even provides an argument to show that our mind is the image of God, or rather, that our notion of God is made in the image of our mind:

> ... taking the word *idea* in a large sense, my soul may
> be said to furnish me with an idea, that is, an image or
> likeness of God, though indeed extremely inadequate.
> For all the notion I have of God, is obtained by reflect-
> ing on my own soul, heightening its powers, and
> removing its imperfections. I have therefore, though
> not an inactive idea, yet in my self some sort of an
> active thinking image of the Deity. (*Dialogues* III, 231-
> 2)

Thus Berkeley seems to be committed to the thesis that unless we experienced causality in ourselves, we should have
no concept of causality.

Berkeley's position is vulnerable on several grounds.
Suppose that, for the sake of argument, one were to accept
the empiricist programme of finding the source of concepts
within our own experience. It might still be claimed that an
empiricist account of our concept of causality is consistent
with the occasionalist doctrine that our minds are causally
impotent. Consider, by way of analogy, the case of our concept of infinity. Conceptual empiricists such as Locke and
Berkeley typically claim that we acquire this concept from
experience by suitably processing our concept of the finite.
In the same way a conceptual empiricist could claim that we
acquire the concept of genuine causality from experience by
suitably processing the concept of causal impotence which
we acquire from both sensation and introspection.[13] One
might also seek to criticize Berkeley from a more external
standpoint by charging that his derivation of the concept of
causality from experience is circular. We are supposed to acquire this concept by introspecting and noticing that our
mind exercises genuine causal activity in volition. But in
order to notice this it seems that we must already be in possession of the concept of causality.

Let us now consider two distinctive criticisms that
Malebranche would make of Berkeley's position. In the first
place Malebranche would insist that we must distinguish
between true and false ideas of causality. If what is in question is the idea of power, then Malebranche would claim
that, strictly speaking, we have no idea of this at all; for

Malebranche, the term 'power' is empty of all real content. The true idea of causality is the idea of a necessary connection between two events such that if one occurs, the other must occur.[14] Thus any serious philosophical enquiry concerning the concept of causality must be addressed to the concept of necessary connection.

This clarification of the concept of causality is only a preliminary move, however. For Malebranche has a deep reply to Berkeley which challenges his basic assumptions about concepts. For Malebranche, in contrast to Descartes and Leibniz, the empiricist programme does not simply give a wrong answer to a legitimate question about the origin of ideas; it goes wrong in a more fundamental way. The whole project of seeking to explain the origin of concepts is misguided in principle, for it involves something like a category mistake; it makes the assumption that concepts are psychological entities for which it is legitimate to seek a causal explanation. Malebranche may sometimes write as if he shares this assumption, but it forms no part of his considered position. Strictly speaking, for Malebranche, concepts are not psychological but, as we might say, abstract logical entities; such entities have a locus—God—but it makes no sense to suppose that they have a causal source. Thus to Berkeley's challenge: "Where could our notion of causality come from if not from experience?" Malebranche would reply: "It does not come from anywhere; it's not a psychological possession at all." This does not mean that Malebranche would similarly dismiss the question of how it is possible for us to think of causality; on the contrary, he would regard this question as legitimate, and he would seek to answer it in terms of our being related to concepts (ideas) in God. Thus to this question Malebranche would invoke his famous doctrine of vision in God. Berkeley of course insisted, and insisted rightly, that he rejected this doctrine.

We have seen, then, that Berkeley found it important for theological reasons to maintain the asymmetry between bodies and finite spirits with regard to causality. Sound theology requires us to attack the idolatrous philosophy of nature which is the legacy of the pagan Aristotle; to this extent Berkeley agrees with Malebranche. But sound theology also requires us to uphold the Genesis doctrine that the human mind is made in the image of God, and in Berkeley's eyes this doctrine is dangerously compromised by Malebranche's philosophy. As we have seen, Berkeley also has more purely philosophical arguments for departing from a strictly occasionalist position with regard to finite spirits. But unfortunately, in attacking the roots of idolatry Berkeley also helped himself to Malebranchian arguments which tended to undermine the causal asymmetry between bodies and finite spirits which he sought to defend. Moreover, Berkeley seems not to have noticed that even his immaterialism when thought through, tended in an occasionalist direction. We can see why Berkeley found it necessary to depart from Malebranche's unqualified occasionalism, but we cannot defend his departures on grounds of philosophical consistency. Berkeley's position on causality is at bottom incoherent. Even in his published writings Berkeley remains more of an occasionalist than he is willing to allow.[15]

## NOTES

[1]  I shall employ the following abbreviations, which agree with those adopted by the present volume in all points of overlap:

CSM          *The Philosophical Writings of Descartes*, translated by John Cottingham, Robert Stoothoff, and Dugald Murdoch.  2 volumes.  Cambridge: Cambridge University Press, 1985.

*Dialogues*   *Three Dialogues between Hylas and Philonous* (Works II).  George Berkeley.

*Enquiry*     *Enquiry Concerning Human Understanding*.  David Hume.  References are to the edition by L. A. Selby Bigge and P. H. Nidditch, Oxford: Oxford University Press, 1975.

LO           *The Search after Truth/Elucidations of the Search after Truth*.  Nicolas Malebranche.  Edited and translated, with philosophical commentary, by Thomas M. Lennon and Paul J. Olscamp.  Columbus: Ohio State University Press, 1980.

PC          *Philosophical Commentaries* (Works I). George
Berkeley.

*Principles*     *The Principles of Human Knowledge,* Part I (Works
II). George Berkeley.

*Works*        *The Works of George Berkeley Bishop of Cloyne.*
Edited by A. A. Luce and T. E. Jessop. 9 volumes.
Edinburgh, 1948-57.

References to PC are by entry number; to *De Motu* (Works
IV), *Enquiry, Principles,* and *Siris* (Works V) by section
number; to *Dialogues* by page. Page references to LO are pre-
ceded by book, part, and chapter of *Search* or by Elucidation
of *Elucidations.*

2 See, for instance, C.J. McCracken, *Malebranche and British
Philosophy* (Oxford: Clarendon Press, 1983), ch. 3, esp. pp.
93-4.

3 *Ibid.,* p. 105.

4 L.E. Loeb, *From Descartes to Hume: Continental
Metaphysics and the Development of Modern Philosophy*
(Ithaca and London: Cornell University Press, 1981), p. 205.

5 See Berkeley to Samuel Johnson, Nov. 25, 1729, *Works* II,
280.

6 Jonathan Bennett, *Locke, Berkeley, Hume: Central Themes*
(Oxford: Oxford University Press, 1971), pp. 201-2.
Subsequent references to this work, abbreviated hereafter as
LBH, will be given in the text.

7 In *Principles* 146 Berkeley seems to suggest that God is not
the causal source of all our sensations, but only of most of
them; this leaves open the possibility that our wills are the
causes of those sensations involved in our own voluntary
bodily movements. However, Berkeley does not develop this
suggestion. It is possible that Berkeley simply means to
allow for the fact that mental images are causally dependent on
our wills.

8 C.C.W. Taylor, "Action and Inaction in Berkeley," in J.
Foster and H. Robinson, eds., *Essays on Berkeley: A
Tercentennial Celebration* (Oxford: Clarendon Press, 1985),
p. 222.

9    On the concern with idolatry in Malebranche and Berkeley,
     see McCracken, *Malebranche, op. cit.*, pp. 211-17. For a re-
     markable use of the 'image of God' doctrine, which seems
     close in spirit to Berkeley, see Leibniz, *Principles of Nature
     and of Grace* 14.
10   E. Craig, *The Mind of God and the Works of Man* (Oxford,
     1987), esp. ch. 1.
11   It should be pointed out that Descartes makes this claim in the
     context of his discussion of the role of the will in assent.
12   See Bennett, LBH 199.
13   Berkeley might seek to counter this objection by pointing out
     that there is a disanalogy between the two cases: finiteness is a
     positive property whereas causal impotence is a negative one.
14   I owe this formulation to McCracken, *Malebranche, op. cit.*,
     p. 99.
15   I am grateful to Patricia Kitcher and Mark Kulstad for helpful
     comments on an earlier draft of this paper.

# REAL HUMEAN CAUSES

*Annette Baier*

## 1. Endorsing Rules for Causal Inference

Hume, towards the end of his long *Treatise* investigation of the causal relation, after repeating his earlier conclusion that, until we consult experience, all we can know is that "any thing can produce any thing,"[1] goes on to tell us how to consult experience, so that we can find out when objects that we suppose might be cause and effect "really are so" (T 173). He gives us eight general rules for our use in confirming or disconfirming causal claims, adding that these comprise "all the *Logic* I think proper to employ in my reasoning" (T 175). If we examine Hume's causal reasoning in subsequent passages, we will find him conforming to these rules, even if rarely citing them. As he notes here, their formulation "is not very necessary, but might have been supplied by the natural principles of the understanding" (*ibid.*). But what gives him confidence that conformity with these rules will enable us to recognise what "really" causes what? What gives his "rules by which to judge of causes and effects" their normative authority?

Suppose that a curious tracer of causes and effects, relying on "the natural principles of the understanding" made a little more reflective and self-conscious than usual, thought he could trace the following fairly long causal chain (where → indicates a causal relation), linking somewhat general and mixed "objects," some physical, some mental.

A   Nature, with her own habits (her constancies of conjunction of events);
↓

B   Human minds, experiencing some of nature's constancies, and sensitive to them;
↓

C   A union in the human imagination of the ideas of such events as have been experienced as constantly conjoined;
↓

D   An irresistible human tendency to infer the later of any such an event pair, given belief that the former has occurred, and a feeling of having no choice but to thus infer;
↓

E   An idea of causal determination or necessity, and a (resistible) tendency to project this back both into the subject-matter of the inference that caused it, and into the experienced natural constancy causing that;
↓

F   Puzzlement, in reflective minds, about the sources and truth-presenting power of this idea of causal necessity;
↓

G   Formulation of the causal hypotheses contained in the chain A - E, as genealogy of the idea of causal necessity, and concern about the truth of these hypotheses;
↓

H   Confirmation of these causal hypotheses, by finding no decisive counter-examples, and by finding analogous confirming examples (repetition-sensitivity in other living things, other cases of vivacity-communicating associative thinking, and other cases of human thinkers projecting the feeling of determination);
↓

I   Renewed attention to the natural constant conjunctions that affect both what we are and what we experience, and special attention to their perceptible effects on our habits of thought;

↓

J  New causal inferences (about our causal inferences), based on newly noticed constant conjunctions, and their newly noticed effects;

↓

K  Increasing self-consciousness of the causal conditions of human causal inferences, and of human awareness of nature's constancies;

↓

L  Increased self confidence in endorsing, as rules of causal inference, the habits of inference that have proved not just self-correcting (since experience-determined), but able to be turned without incoherence on themselves, thus giving us self-knowledge and promising us new possibilities of knowledge and of reliable inference.

The philosophical hunter for causes who traced such a sequence would have enjoyed a fairly extensive "stretch of thought" (T 449), once his beating about in neighbouring fields gave him scent of his prey. He would also have been led into an interestingly self-referential path. The habits of thought indulged in this mental exercise lead to their own self-examination, and to their self-endorsement. The hunters turn the hunt on themselves, catch themselves and find themselves fine game, "fit for the table" (T 451).

This causal chain is, of course, a reconstruction of Hume's findings in Part Three of Book One, the findings that are over-succinctly "collected together" in Hume's notoriously double "exact definition" (T 169) of cause, and completed in the two subsequent sections, "Rules by which to judge of causes and effects," and "Of the Reason of Animals." Hume endorses, in his rules, the very method which he has followed in the previous twelve sections, in his own long search for an answer to the question "why we conclude that such particular causes must *necessarily* have such particular effects; and what is the nature of that *infer-*

*ence* we draw from the one to the other, and of the *belief* we repose in it?" (T 78) Hume's enquiry into the causes of our attributions of cause ends in an endorsement of the "logic" of his own reasoning. Here he has a case of fairly refined reasonings that, when turned on themselves in more refined reasonings, establish themselves as rules (see T 268). Unlike the rationalists "reason," or pure intellect, which he turns on itself with fatal consequences within section VI of Part Three and in the first section of Part Four, causal reasoning as Hume has both described it and exhibited it in the whole of Part Three, triumphantly bears its own survey, so can endorse its own habits.

This sketch of an interpretation of Hume's account of causal reasoning is obviously one that utterly rejects Jonathan Bennett's charge that Hume "wrongly denies us reasons for our predictions."[2] Precisely the contrary: Hume shows us when, and why, the causes of our beliefs about the future count as *reasons*; when, and why, the natural principles governing our habits of causal inference count as a "*Logic*," to be depended on to determine what really causes what. Here I can only do a little to fill out the sketch, and make it plausible. Rather than show how, especially at step H, Hume does employ his eight rules, (since the text makes this fairly easy to do) I shall try to understand why Bennett saw Hume's achievement so differently, and address the question of how Hume's double definition of cause is best to be understood. But first some remarks about Hume's general treatment of norms.

Hume's endorsement of "some general rules, by which we ought to regulate our judgment concerning causes and effects" (T 149), and his reasons for this endorsement, are of a piece with his other normative endorsements in the *Treatise*. In one of his most often quoted and most often misunderstood passages, he says that any move from a recognition of what is the case to an endorsement of what ought to be the case is "of the last consequence," and should be "observ'd and explain'd" (T 469). He himself, fairly often in the *Treatise*, makes such moves, from describing habits to endorsing them. He nowhere, to my knowledge, formulates a general rule about what counts as a good reason for such a move, but a careful observation of when he makes such a move, and of what he says to explain it, gives us a pretty good basis for generalisation, for a general Humean rule for selecting which human habits can be established as rules.

Sometimes he appeals to what appear to be utilitarian or pragmatic considerations—we would "immediately perish and go to ruin" (T 225) did we not in our thinking make "the customary transition from causes to effects, and from effects to causes" (*ibid.*). The customs he refuses to endorse are ones that are "neither unavoidable to mankind, nor necessary, or so much as useful in the conduct of life" (*ibid.*). At other times he appeals to a more formal criterion, namely that no "contradiction" manifest itself when the custom in question is turned on itself. His sceptical conclusions about the rationalist's version of reason, in Part Four of *Treatise* Book One, are based on the failure of this version of reason to pass the test of coherent reflexivity, a test which the rationalists themselves had formulated and favored. Hume finds that deductive and calculative reason, when turned on itself, "must infallibly destroy itself" (T 184). This finding is reached in the first section of Part Four, immediately following Hume's completion of the successful turn of empiricist intelligent "animal" reasoning on itself in Part Three, a turn which led up to the establishment of the rules of its own successfully reflexive procedure as a sufficient logic. In Book Three, Hume uses the test of self-survey to distinguish advantageous from disadvantageous pursuits of advantage, pleasing from displeasing preferences or tastes in pleasure, sentiment-approved from sentiment-disapproved human sentiments and passions. At the end of that book he suggests that the moral sense or sentiment be directed not just on its normal subject matter, other human passions, but onto itself: "This sense must certainly acquire new force when, reflecting on itself, it approves of those principles from which it is derived, and finds nothing but what is great and good in its rise and origin" (T 619). The test is one of positive feedback. Morality will get new force from self-approval.

The pragmatic test, of what is life-preserving or life-enhancing for human beings, and the formal test, of what sur-

vives self-survey without self-contradiction, come together
in moral evaluation. Here the "principle of humanity"
(*Enquiry* 272) or "party of humanity" does the surveying.
Our concern as moral judges must be with what has utility
and agreeability for us, as our concern as properly reflective
moral judges is with the versions of utility and agreeability
that can bear their own survey. Pragmatic tests and the test
of coherent self-survey achieve unification in the endorsement of moral norms, as indeed do the various human faculties that moral judgement calls into play, widely-informed
self-correcting empirical reason, a lively imagination, calm
sympathy-enlarged passions. For moral judgment we need a
mind "all collected in itself" (T 270) sociable reason concurring with corrected sentiments. Its self-survey will collect
and perhaps correct the more piecemeal self-surveys that
Hume had conducted in Book One on more limited faculties—on rationalist reason and on causal reasoning, as it will
use the findings of Book Two about sympathy and contrari-
ety in human passions. The Book One findings about our
cognitive capacities are by no means Hume's last word on
them—the love of truth gets ironic self-application in Book
Two, and in Book Three our various habits of reasoning, re-
calling, forgetting, judging, joking, get classified as virtuous
or as vicious. The final authority of the normative rules advanced in Book One comes from the moral sentiment, a sentiment which observance of those very rules helped Hume to
discern and make fully reflective.

The general rules "by which we ought to regulate our
judgment concerning causes and effects," Hume writes, "are
form'd on the nature of our understanding, and on our experience of its operations in the judgments we form concerning objects" (T 149). We have to use our understanding on
our understanding, make and verify causal judgments about
our causal judgments, as Hume has been doing in all the
preceding sections of Part Three, before we can properly
form normative rules for the understanding. Hume indulges
his passion for reflexivity by noting that the role of the general rules he will later formulate is to correct for the influence
of other "unphilosophical" rules, ones that these rules will
condemn. Hume modestly or fake-modestly demotes his

own promised rules to the status of "unphilosophical probability," albeit at a higher or meta-level, since "the following of general rules is a very unphilosophical species of probability; and yet 'tis only by following them that we can correct this, and all other unphilosophical probabilities" (T 150).

This interesting Humean version of an older project of submitting would-be authorities to the test of coherent self-endorsement, this investigation into normative force, this search for rules that are reflectively rather than rashly formed, was neglected by Bennett in his discussion of Hume's analysis of causal inference. He attempted an "analytic salvage" of Hume's account of what a cause is. "Analytic" was contrasted with "genetic" and Bennett tried to "cleanse" (LBH 257) Hume's account from what he regarded as its unfortunate empiricist geneticism. The cleaned-up analytic account replaces Hume's talk of "habits" of inference with talk of "dispositions". As Hume makes clear, a habit cannot be acquired "by what was never present to the mind" (T 197) so the very term 'habit' has causal and genetic implications. A habit is a disposition only when it is acquired in a certain way, by repetitions in past experience. Bennett prefers to drop any implications about the causes of our inferential behavior, so prefers 'disposition', "a usefully clinical and non-genetic term" (LBH 305). Hume's insistence on trying in his philosophy to trace causes, and to give causal definitions, is seen to introduce dirt which clogs the wheels of an otherwise promisingly proto-Kantian philosophical invention namely "the Humean view" of causation, when this is interpreted as the thesis that sequences are cause-effect ones when they are instances of (contingent) laws. Bennett does not claim that "the Humean view" was Hume's own view—he allows that Hume's view is genetic. After an estimate of how much and how little of Hume's total account he with his analytic scruples has managed to "salvage," he guardedly concludes, "If the result is that Hume's total work on causation is more broken-backed than one had thought, so be it" (LBH 312).

Bennett never considers the possibility that the strength of Hume's account might lie precisely in its thoroughgoing and reflexive geneticism. Hume later said that the whole *Treatise* was juvenile or immature, even "defective" in places, but in his more mature *Enquiry Concerning Human Understanding*, the genetic account of our idea of cause is reproduced, there thriving and proudly presented. It was indeed a strange enterprise to try to improve the philosophical theory of the man the British library calls "David Hume, Historian" by an "impoverishment" (LBH 305) that rids it of its historical and natural-historical theses. As Donald Livingston has written of analytic or logical empiricist reconstructions of Hume's genetic version of empiricism, "As charitable reinterpretations they are, I think misplaced, for it is precisely the narrative imagery and past-referring character of the theory that makes it interesting."[3] This is especially true of Hume's account of our concept of cause. As Livingston notes, Hume's infamous double definition not merely specifies the empirical conditions for applying the concept of cause to the world, but is also "part of a causal theory that explains *why* we apply causal predicates to the world."[4] It is this twist, that Hume is "ready to convert my present reasoning into an instance of it" (T 169) (that is, of its own subject-matter), that gives his total work on causation what he calls its "subtility" (*ibid.*). This subtlety is lost on Bennett's reconstruction, and that is an impoverishment. Indeed to remove that self-referential element *is* to break the back of Hume's account.


## 2. Customary Transitions from Causes to Effects

Hume in the *Treatise* took thirteen sections, the bulk of Book One, Part Three, to get himself into a position to give his double definition, and it is misunderstood if the interpretation makes that long beating about in the neighbouring fields appear an unhelpful diversion.[5] An adequate interpretation of Section XIV of *Treatise* Book One, Part Three must both explain the long apparently indirect path Hume took, from Section II, in his "endeavour to discover" (T 75) the relation we call causal, and also explain the subsequent sections of Part Three, explain how Hume can go on to give us normative rules to improve our causal inferences, and why he thought it relevant to finish the book with a placing of our habits of causal inference in the context both of those of the higher animals, and in the context of other belief-fixing natural devices to be found in us and other animals.[6] Hume concludes that splendid section by assimilating all belief-fixers to "instinct," so that causal reasoning itself becomes an instinctive response to past experience, and, more generally, reason becomes "a wonderful unintelligible instinct in our souls" (T 179). (The word 'unintelligible' should here be taken strictly.[7])

Hume's first approximation to an explication of what a cause is came in Section II, and is repeated in Section VI. A cause is that from the perception of which we human beings infer another fractionally later existent. "The only connexion or relation of objects which can lead us beyond the immediate impressions of our memory and senses is that of cause and effect" (T 89). It is this clue about causes, elaborated in Section VI and both developed and applied in the following few sections, that Hume is recapitulating in the second version of his definition. Although second in the order of final exposition and "definition," it was first in the order of discovery. Bennett is surely right when he claims, "Hume bases his analysis of cause on his theory of why we predict" (LBH 295). To get to his own final analytic salvage, he starts with Hume's account of our predictive dispositions, drops its genetic component, then by a very swift two-stage transcendental move converts our disposition to expect effect, given cause, to "applying a rule to a case," and from that to treating a particular sequence as an instance of a law (LBH 306-7). I think Bennett is right to see Hume as expressing Kantian insights (LBH 303), although maybe those insights would more properly be called Humean. As Lewis White Beck,[8] Manfred Kuehn,[9] and others have pointed out, Hume's treatment of cause, and his account of the indispensable "fictions of the understanding," the fictions of duration without change, of the continuous mind-distinct existence of bodies, of their and our identity through time, do give us a sort of naturalistic preview of Kant's forms of intuition and categories, and of the antinomies produced when we misuse them, a Kantian world with the noumena exorcised, a common sense secular Kant and an abstruse and slightly spiritualised Hume (to continue Beck's balancings). Bennett is right to link Hume's account with Kant's, and obviously right to emphasise Hume's tracing of our idea of cause to our causal inferences. Hume begins his enactment of what I have labelled step G with a reverse tracing of the causal links A-E.

Bennett moves from a consideration and emendation of Hume's second version of his definition to an emendation of the first version, just as Hume himself, in "Of the inference from the impression to the idea," moves from D back to C, and then to B; from singular causal inference, to its background conditions, a union in the imagination that depends upon natural regularities of which the inferrer has had enough experience. (Whatever "enough" may be—Hume sometimes speaks as if one experience or "experiment" will suffice, as it surely usually does in cases like experience of how fire burns human skin and flesh, but his argument strictly requires that we should have experienced *repetition* of event sequences, "frequent" cases (T 87), to convince us of the constancy of the conjunction.) These earlier experienced cause-effect pairs are the "foreign objects" of the first version of Hume's definition. He originally encountered them by tracing back from the foreign object of the second version of his definition, the determination of the inferring human mind. He celebrates his encounter with them as a surprising discovery, and the reader who would understand Hume's account must try to recover the surprise. Like Flew's beginning student,[10] we find it trite to say that where we recognise causes there we recognise instances of regularities, and ones of which we have had prior experience. Flew himself takes Hume's "discovery" to be a great discovery of the obvious. But in the *Treatise's* narrative (or pseudo-narrative) account, the discovery of constant conjunctions, in the fields neighbouring on singular causal inferences, that is the discovery of the links I have represented as A-D, is hailed as a surprise, not as a discovery of the obvious. Hume writes, "Thus in advancing we have insensibly discover'd a new relation betwixt cause and effect where we least expected it, and were entirely employ'd upon another subject" (T 87). This is a touch disingenuous, but for Hume's first readers the relation of constant conjunction could have been "new" and unexpected, relative to their Cartesian and Lockean assumptions about causal dependency and its discernment. Only the Berkeleyans among them would be inclined, like Flew's student, to shrug and ask, "so what's unexpected?" We have to use historical imagination to see how Hume could expect his readers to least expect constant conjunction or regularity when they thought about causation.

We jaded post-Humeans and post-Kantians can take empirically verified causal regularities for granted—we take it that only if there are such known regularities are there any recognisable causes. It takes an Anscombe[11] to jolt us out of our dogmatic slumber on such an issue. As Hume would have said, there is flux and reflux, not steady "progress," on philosophical issues, and one generation's dream is another's rude awakening. Hume in Section VI of *Treatise* Book One, Part Three, and in his first *Enquiry* moves in Section IV, was jolting Cartesians and Lockeans out of their certainty that a single cause-effect dependency could be *a priori* intelligible when it was a change in primary qualities or other properties of which we supposedly had clear and distinct ideas. Hume is indeed sceptical about that natural light which Descartes supposed could, like an X-ray, show him the reality of the foetus effect there in the cause, waiting to be born,[12] the light that could elicit from Locke his rhetorical question of what sort of change a pestle could be expected to effect except an alteration of the texture of what it grinds (*Essay* II, viii, 20).

"All the operations of body *without exception* are known only by experience" (*Enquiry* 29, my emphasis). Not only can the color change of the ground almonds or the melted wax not be *a priori* expected, but our knowledge of causes of changes in shape, size, texture and position must also wait on experience. "The mind can never possibly find the effect in the supposed cause, by the most accurate scrutiny and examination" (*Enquiry* 29). Hume makes this claim for all causes and effects, mental or physical, and whatever sort of change is involved. So the mind cannot see *a priori* what the effect of a firm human intention will be, nor what it would take to produce a circular path, or a straight line, what it would take to move a body at rest, nor to arrest its motion. Repetition or custom in our past experience, not theological or geometrical insight or *a priori* statics and dynamics, give us what assurance we have in these matters.

> We are apt to imagine that we could discover these effects by the mere operation of reason, without experience. . . . Such is the influence of custom that where it is strongest it not only covers our natural ignorance, but even conceals itself, and seems not to take place, merely because it is found in the highest degree. (*Enquiry* 28-9)

Hume uncovered the self-concealed custom, succeeded in making it evident to such a degree that his own dramatics in the unveiling ceremony in the *Treatise* are now apt to surprise his reader more than what he then unveils. Constant conjunction of the thought of cause with the thought of constant conjunction has spoiled us for the role of a philosophical Adam who "least expects" constant conjunction in his path when he sets out to meet cause.

Hume's constant conjunctions are Berkeley's regularities between "natural signs" and what they signify. The only surprise that Berkeleyan readers of Hume would get would come when they find that these regularities are by a philosopher called "causal," for Hume's first version of his definition could serve as a definition of a Berkeleyan "sign." Hume levels Berkeley's distinction between true efficacious spiritual causes and mere signs, reducing all to the epistemological status of the latter, thus freeing the word 'cause' for what the vulgar call causes. Hume speaks with the vulgar, who take the fire to cause the painful burn, while he thinks with the reflective Berkeleyans that all we know about such causes are the regularities in which they have been observed to figure. Where his thought diverges from that of the Berkeleyans is where he adds "and all causes we can recognise *are* such causes." This is why he has to spend the amount of time and space he does eventually spend[13] in arguing against the view that Berkeley, Locke and Descartes all held, that we know our own wills as causes that are not mere signs, as causes in which, in any single case, the reality of the intended effect can indeed be found, without even too accurate a scrutiny and examination, there waiting in the prior intention cause.

## 3. Special Mental Effects

In the *Treatise* Hume tells us, briefly and with a "subtility" that is more difficult to comprehend than he claims, that psychological causes and effects, like other causes and effects, are known to us only by experience, that there is no superiorly intelligible "uniting principle" (T 169) to be found among our internal perceptions. The internal perceptions in question in this passage are our impression of an earlier event, our lively idea of its usual follow-up, and, notoriously accompanying them, our "impression of reflexion" of the mind's determination to pass from the one to the other. A "new determination" is felt, Hume says, when we change our point of view from considering "objects" and their effects to considering perceptions and their effects. Shifting our focus from mind-external objects to mental events gives us material for new constrained expectations, but introduces no "intelligibility" that would contrast with the "unintelligibility" or brute empirical contingency of non-psychological causes and effects. Psychological causes and effects, impressions of determination of the mind included, get no special or privileged treatment. (Their only privilege, if that is what it is, is to be what is naturally "spread" or animistically projected onto external objects.)

Hume also hammers this point home pretty directly in *Treatise* Book Two's discussion of liberty and necessity, where he neatly recapitulates his earlier account of causal necessity. Voluntary actions, he there writes, proceed from "some cause in the character and disposition of the person who performed them" (T 411) in the same contingently regular predictable way that other natural effects follow their causes. Human willings, defined as "the impressions we feel and are conscious of when we knowingly give rise to any new motion of our body or new perception of our mind" (T 399), take their place as part of the natural world, not some special spiritual intrusion into it. In the *Abstract*, Hume selects this part of Book Two for restatement, emphasizing that the "actions of the mind" are "on the same footing with matter" (T 660). What the Appendix and the *Enquiry* add to the original *Treatise* discussion of psychological causes in general, and exercises of the will in particular, is not that "the actions of the mind are, in this respect, the same with those of matter" (T 633), for this had been explicitly said in the Book Two passage quoted in the *Abstract*. What is new is an explicit formulation of the already implied claim that "no internal impression has an apparent energy, more than external objects have" (T 633). I suggest that the reason Hume adds this is to make it quite clear that his own references to the "determination of the mind" as the source of our ideas of necessity, and so of the ideas giving meaning to the "nearly synonimous" terms *efficacy, agency, power, force, energy, connexion, and productive quality* (T 157), are not to be confused with the idealist and in particular the Berkeleyan thesis that willings are paradigms of energy-displaying causes.

Did his early readers confuse his own positive account with Berkeley's and other idealist accounts? The reviewer in the *Göttingische Zeitungen von gelehrten Sachen* for January 7th 1740 both notes Hume's agreement with Berkeley about abstract ideas, and also writes that the author of the *Treatise* had "eine grosse Gabe, dasjenige was andere davon etwan deutlich gesaget haben, dunkel zu machen,"[14] going on then to give an unsympathetic but not really inaccurate summary of Hume's account of causal necessity. If this account was found not only obscure, but second hand, then it would be understandable that Hume would wish to clarify it, and to make quite clear how different his account is from Berkeley's. Even after Hume's attempted clarification in the *Enquiry*, careless or selective readers (like many of my students) have failed to see how the impression of reflexion of the determination of the mind in inference, to which Hume traces our idea of necessity, differs so greatly from that "consciousness of a power or energy in our own minds" (*Enquiry* 67) that he rejects as false consciousness.

If inference is construed as a controlled intentional process, as Bennett thinks that causal inference at its best should be construed (LBH 302), then the determination of the mind we experience in inference could, not implausibly, be taken as the consciousness of "knowingly giving rise" to a new perception of the mind, that is, an exercise of will. If the will is no more than the mind's consciousness of giving rise to a new motion or perception, then self-conscious inference exercises the will. Hume emphasises the unconscious as well as the irresistible form that causal inference often takes, when ingrained causal association works by "a secret operation" (T 104). Inference on those occasions will not involve the will as Hume has defined it. But once we become aware of our habits, the move to the inferred vivid idea will be "knowing," conscious, and so in Hume's sense voluntary. Hume regularly refuses to sharply separate the voluntary from the involuntary, and so he can recognise a continuum of cases going from unconscious inference to fully conscious and so fully voluntary inferring, where we know and endorse what we are doing. In every case there will be a "determination of the mind," a unique selection[15] of the next perception, but only in the self-conscious cases will this causal determination be accompanied by an *impression* of it, by that impression of reflexion from which Hume claims our idea of necessity is derived. If in addition to knowing that our mind is uniquely selecting its own next idea, we *endorse* its mode of operation, then a sort of epistemological approval will also be present, a "seconding" by the conscious mind of the determinations of the subconscious mind. This will be present in the inferrer who has followed and accepted Hume's account of causal inference, and of its norms, whenever she is aware that her inference conforms not just to her acquired habits, but to habits that have been endorsed, so made into norms. Scepticism ensues only in those cases where we can neither endorse nor change our habits, where our practice "contradicts" our reflective endorsements.

Hume gives us such a case in the "Conclusion of this Book" (that is, of Book One): "Very refin'd reflections have little or no influence upon us, yet we do not and cannot establish it for a rule that they ought not to have any influence; which implies a manifest contradiction" (T 268). The reason why we cannot establish it as a rule that refined reflections are to carry no weight is that we must use refined reflections to reach such a recommendation—we would be involved in a pragmatic contradiction were we to deny weight to the very reasoning leading to the denial. We get into such sceptical impasses, Hume believes, when we look into the more refined workings of our intellectual powers, into their inevitable attempts to move beyond "that narrow circle of objects which are the subjects of daily conversation and action" (T 271). Causal reasoning can get into such self-contradiction when it looks for an ultimate cause of order in the world, or when it attempts to give causal analyses of the perceived properties of material objects. But neither Hume's own analysis of our discernment of causal order nor ordinary causal inference about the subjects of daily conversation and action is involved in such "contradictions." It is ordinary causal inference about whether water will suffocate, bread nourish, that Hume is primarily concerned with in Part Three of Book One. Any limits to causal inference's proper domain are found later, in Part Four, when Hume looks at our various metaphysical ventures, and their various shipwrecks. And at the very start of his examination of sceptical systems, he makes the confident causal claim that the reason to be examined "must be consider'd as a kind of cause" (T 180).

It is inference which, on the Humean story, displays that determination of the mind the impression of which generates our idea of necessity, of what *must* be what. Any inference can generate it—mathematical or causal.

> Thus the necessity, which makes two times two equal to four, or three angles of a triangle equal to two right ones, lies only in the act of the understanding, by

which we consider and compare these ideas; in like manner the necessity or power, which unites causes and effects, lies in the determination of the mind to pass from the one to the other (T 166).

The feeling that the inference is constrained, even when it is fully self-conscious and so in Hume's sense voluntary, and the spontaneous conviction that it is the subject matter of the inference that does the constraining, leads us regularly to project that felt constraint back into the subject matter of our inferences, both mathematical and causal. Like the idealists, Hume focuses on an intentional human procedure as the key locus of our experience of an apparently necessitating cause. Unlike them, he picks not an intentional action that feels freely chosen, but inference, the least free-feeling, the most readily construed as rule governed, the most apparently constrained. The human will as effect, not the human will as cause, is what he singles out for the role of ancestor of our idea of causal necessity. It is our experience of our will being determined to one firm intention, as we intentionally draw the conclusion of our inference, rather than any experience of the will's role as determiner, that Hume fixes on to explain how we get our idea of necessitated fixed effects and so of necessitating determining causes.

The references to the mind's and "the thought's" determination, in *Treatise* Book One, Part Three, Section XIV, are not really ambiguous, and should not be obscure since they had been carefully prepared for in the preceding twelve sections—especially in Section VI and in Section IX. In this latter, "Of the effects of other relations and other habits", Hume contrasts the constraint we feel when causal association is at work in our causal inferences, with the "looseness" and "caprice" of our other associative thought moves, as we ourselves experience them. The mind, he says "feels the looseness of its actions and the weak hold it has on its objects," when association is by mere resemblance or mere contiguity, but

the relation of cause and effect has all the opposite advantages . . .each impression draws along with it a

precise idea which takes its place in the imagination as
something solid and real, certain and invariable. The
thought is always determin'd to pass from the impression to the idea, and from that particular impression to
the idea without any choice or hesitation (T 110).

The reader who has digested such passages will not be puzzled or misled by Section XIV's references to the mind's
determination, in inference.

Hume writes that the two versions of his definition of
cause differ only "by their presenting a different view of the
same object, and making us consider it either as a *philosophical* or as a *natural* relation, either as a comparison of two
ideas, or as an association between them" (T 170). Bennett
writes "One sees what he means, but the suggestion is better
ignored" (LBH 298). To see what Hume means, Bennett's
suggestion is better ignored. We need to see why the definition of the "compleat idea" (T 77) is double, and is disjunctive. Hume has converted cause into a philosophical relation
by his long controlled examination of it, but, by his own account, every substantive inference he, the scientist of human
nature, drew during that examination was guided by cause as
a natural relation, since "'tis only so far as it is a natural relation, and produces an union among our ideas that we are
able to reason on it" (T 94). Hume early in the *Treatise* had
called philosophical relations themselves the "remarkable"
*effects* of the unions which the natural relations produce in
the human imagination (T 13). Cause as a philosophical relation is, then, an effect of a series of inferences on Hume's
or other thinkers' part, all guided by cause as a natural relation. Those inferences are special reflexive ones, ones about
inferences. Cause as a natural relation has enabled Hume to
reason his way to the causes of our causal inferences, and so
to an idea of cause as a philosophical relation. Hume told us
fairly early in his account, "perhaps 'twill appear in the end
that the necessary connexion depends on the inference, instead of the inference depending on the necessary connexion" (T 88). Everything in Hume's story depends upon the
natural relation that guides the inference, and the first version
of his definition is arrived at only by depending on the sec-

ond version, on inferences to the more ultimate causes of such inferences.

Flew, in his most recent book on Hume, writes, "In so far as our interests are philosophical, Hume's account of causation as a natural relation has little to offer us."[16] This is to misunderstand the relation of philosophical to natural relations, and so to grossly undervalue Hume's "seemingly preposterous" (T 169) manner of proceeding, the "most violent paradox" (T 166) of which he was rightly proud. Bennett does not downplay either the importance or the cleverness of Hume's "preposterous" strategy, but on his cleaned-up version we lose both the dependency of knowledge of cause as a philosophical relation on the controlled workings of cause as a natural relation, and we also lose the dependency of the natural relation on the influence of nature's constancies, so lose the self-correcting character of Humean causal inference. Hume's double definition preserves and indirectly displays these generative causal dependencies. To understand cause is to grasp these two ancestral causal dependencies, that of our concept of cause on our consciousness of what guides our causal inferences, and that of our causal inferences themselves on nature's observed and not yet observed regularities (those exhibited in our own brains' workings) Hume shows us how our concept of cause can be coherently turned on itself, indeed turned on itself triumphantly, in such a way as to lead to the establishment of habits as normative rules.

## 4. Circularity and Reflexivity

Bennett preferred to purge Hume's account of its story about the idea of necessity, without purging it of its linking of the idea of cause with the human disposition to predict. Why did he want to effect this unnatural divorce? Was it because of an obscured view of what Hume means by "determines the mind" in the second version of his definition? Some commentators, such as John Passmore,[17] detect in Hume's explication of causation the same sort of "labyrinth" (T 633) that Hume eventually found in his explication of personal identity, the same inability to explain our belief in "real connexion" if real connexion is *nowhere* to be found in actuality. Passmore finds the phrase 'determines the mind' to introduce an apparent reference to necessary causal connexion into Hume's definition of causal connexion. The phrase either refers only to constant conjunction, or else introduces circularity or regress into the definition, leaving us, Passmore suggests, none the wiser about what more there is to causation than constancy of observed temporal conjunction. Bennett speaks of "the impression of being compelled or determined" (LBH 305), and also writes "I do not allege circularity . . ." (LBH 299-300). In a footnote he refers the reader to commentators who take "determines the mind" to refer to no more than the "introduction" of that impression of reflection, a feeling of constraint, that accompanies the move from knowledge of the earlier event to expectation of its usual successor. Then no compulsion, nor any actual constraint, nor any causal determination, but only the *feeling* of "the determination of the mind," need be seen to be involved in the second definition.

D.G.C. Macnabb[18] and Anthony Flew[19] are the commentators invoked by Bennett as support for his own non-committal non-allegation of circularity. Flew, agreeing here with Macnabb, writes:

> Certainly both determining and conveying look very like species of causing. But examination of the *Treatise* suggests that *determination* is to be taken not as a synonym either for *causation* or *necessitation* but as a special word for the alleged impression of habitual association from which the idea of necessitation is supposed to be derived. Without too much unscholarly charity *conveys* might perhaps also be construed not as a specifically causal word but as referring simply to an habitual associative transition (T 156-7, 165). But these nice questions are not important. Even granted that the definitions as they stand are circular, the obnoxious covert references to causation could fairly easily be excised.[20]

Flew's limited charity lets him consider the possibility of "covert" eliminable circularity in Hume's definition, but not to consider the possibility that the circularity might not be "obnoxious", and might most generously be kept in view.

I have already claimed that Hume's references to the mind being determined are references to unique selection or fixing. Is this fixing always a causal process? Is all determination causal determination? For Hume, I think, yes. (When determination of a conclusion is by "demonstration," rather than by causal inference, then "our reason must be considered as a kind of cause" (T 180).) If we take determination to be the unique fixing, by the cause, of a determinate effect, then the definition of cause as a natural relation will indeed employ a causal term. Only if we construe the determination of the mind as a causal process do we keep the subtlety of Hume's account, the result of his readiness to convert his subject matter, causal inference, into an occasion for it, to turn it on itself. I take Hume's use of "determine," in the second version of his definition of cause, to refer to that sort of causation of a mental event that fixes exactly what that event will be, without "looseness." So on this reading the second version of the definition of cause does employ a causative verb.

The whole of Hume's preceding account, which he says he is collecting together in his definition, had singled out for special emphasis one special case of causation, the causation of causal inference. His "violent paradox" that "the real power of causes" is placed in the inferring mind, which is also a necessity-projecting mind, is balanced by his claims about what we can reasonably infer concerning nature's part in producing our habits of inference, so his definition is double, to keep this balance. Not only can we infer that nature reliably gives us repetition-sensitive brains, but that she then repeats herself in other ways, providing the observable constant conjunctions that feed our appetite for regularities, and produce our particular habits of expectation. Our habits are formed by nature's habits, so that our thoughts about nature can go on "in the same train with the other works of nature" (*Enquiry* 54-5).

If Hume is right in thinking that only by causal inference
do we ever infer new matters of fact, then he must use causal
inference, and get us to use it, to "discover" his truths about
our use of causal terms, and about our causal thinking—
truths which are of course contingent. He ends Book One
Part Three pointing out that habit, learning by repeated experience, is only one of several belief-fixing instincts that we
can infer that nature employs in the animal kingdom. But if
Hume is right about us human animals, then our beliefs
about our concept of cause, as much as about any other
matter of fact not currently under observation, will be
reached by causal inferences. If cause is as fundamental a
guide to our thinking as Hume claims, then of course any
explication of it will have to employ it, just as any explication of "good reason" will employ good reasons, and any
justification of norms will apply norms.

The first version of Hume's definition of cause focuses
on constant conjunctions, themselves the cause of union or
association in minds that experience them. The second version of the definition focuses on inference, that mental effect
of experienced constancies. *A cause-effect pair is either a
instance of a special cause-containing cause, namely constant
conjunction, or the subject matter of a special effect-recog-
nising effect, namely causal inference.* Hume's definition is
disjunctive, because at this point in his meta-causal discourse
the sympathetic reader will be able to make her own inferences from either starting point to the other pole of the complete definition. The definition is "defective" only in its
extreme compression. Having for the whole of Part Three
used causal influence on causal inference, Hume now
"collects all the different parts of this reasoning" (T 169) in
what he optimistically calls "an exact definition," before
proceeding to endorse the habits of causal thought that led up
to the formulation of the definition and the rules. The
definition is not merely subtly and virtuously self referential,
it is understated, leaving some matters to be inferred by the
reader who comes to it after the long preparatory path. There
is, for example, no explicit mention of necessity in either
version of the definition, nor of the special impression of
reflexion from which the idea of necessity arises.[21]

But it was really necessary for Hume to say *again*, in the definition, that when the mind is determined by one impression or lively idea to form the lively idea of its customary associate, it tends to feel this determination, and displace it onto the subject matter of its inference, calling it "necessity"? The mention of inference, of the determination of the mind, is grounds for inferring an implied reference to the reflex awareness of this, and to its causal product, the idea of necessity.

Hume in his double definition presents us with the central case of a cause effect pair, nature's regularities and our mental habits. He shows us how they spawn the other cases of causes and effects, but he leaves it for us to draw a few more inferences, to note a few more implied causal connexions. The generative case of the causal relation is the metacausal relation between the "foreign objects" of the two alternative versions of the full double definition. Hume does not say this, but it is not so difficult to "collect" from his two alternative formulations, together with his commentary on them, and his lead-up to them. The two formulations are causal correlates. They make cause as a natural relation self-conscious of itself and its own causal history. This self-referential definition of cause is a philosophical achievement of which its author is properly proud. He refers to the extraordinariness of the sentiments he has arrived at, and "reposes" himself on them "as on establish'd maxims" (T 170). He boasts a bit about how "our present system" (T 177) can lead us on to fertile new generalisations about animal inferences, and the common features of all inferences. He has good reason for a bit of philosophical pride. He has turned causal inference on itself, seen its nature, seen what habits led to this successful self diagnosis, so discovered which of them should be maintained and strengthened by those who want to discern what really causes what.

Since natural regularities, as displayed outside human persons, are only part of the complete cause of human inference habits—we must add our own observing retentive repetition-sensitive minds and their limitations—then of course the extension of cause as a philosophical relation will be wider than or at any rate different from that of cause as a natural relation. Since some unions in the human imagination are acquired through the influence of prejudice, passion and through association by mere resemblance, then some determinations of the mind will not go on in train with the other works of nature, they will break the rules for judging of causes and effects. But in the normal case our inferences to expected natural effects will correspond with the past influence of natural regularities on our minds. It is "influence," not "determination," that we find between the foreign objects of the first version and that of the second, but it is a dependable influence, enabling us to make fairly a confident prediction that most of our predictions will prove correct.

The influence of our inference habits on our interpretation of their external causes, that is on our version of constant conjunctions in the rest of nature, is also fairly dependable— we usually project back the necessitation we feel in inference onto the subject matter of our inferences. This too is influence not determination. It may take a "sensible violence" to resist this urge to spread our mind on external objects, but Hume brought it off in his definitions, and surely expects at least some of us to be able to follow him. From those definitions, and our background knowledge of human nature, we can account for the belief in objective necessity, while ourselves avoiding it, at least in our armchairs. We will not avoid the *feeling* of determination, of being necessitated, for that is part and parcel of consciousness of inference. Nor will we avoid *determination*, for that is part and parcel of inference itself. But we may intermittently avoid projecting our feelings and the actions of our mind onto nature—we need not see nature as compelled to give each event its time-honored customary follow-up event. We will indeed expect nature to preserve its past "habits," including its habit of occasionally surprising us, but not because it must. When nature surprises us, we will adjust our views of its ways, trying to update our habits of expectations to keep them in train with the rest of nature. We will quite often and quite rightly change our minds about what really causes what. (Maybe also about what Hume really meant.)[22]

# NOTES

1  At p. 173 of David Hume, *A Treatise of Human Nature*, edited by L. A. Selby-Bigge and P. H. Nidditch, Oxford 1978, hereafter T. I shall adopt the convention of the present volume in citing passages from the Nidditch editions of Hume's *Enquiry* and Locke's *Essay*, using those abbreviated titles.

2  Jonathan Bennett, *Locke, Berkeley, Hume* (Oxford: Oxford University Press, 1971), p. 302. Subsequent references to this work, abbreviated as LBH, will be given in the text (e.g. LBH 302).

3  Donald W. Livingston, *Hume's Philosophy of Common Life*, (Chicago: University of Chicago Press, 1984), p. 106.

4  Livingston, *op.cit.*, p. 152.

5  Beauchamp and Rosenberg, in *Hume and the Problem of Causation* (Oxford: Oxford University Press, 1981), p. 79, rightly claim it as an advantage of their interpretation that it explains why Hume gives us his account of our probabilistic reasonings before he is ready to give us his definition of cause, and his account of causal necessity. They themselves, however, give little attention to Hume's account of what he calls "probabilities" rather than "proofs." See p. 53-55 for their discussion of Hume's sections on "the probability of chances" and "the probability of causes." For their criticisms of Bennett, see pp. 38-41, 54.

6  Robert Fogelin, in *Hume's Scepticism in the Treatise of Human Nature* (London: Routledge & Kegan Paul, 1985) insists on the need to look at "the complex dialectical development" (p. 39) in Part Three, but does not himself look beyond Section XIV. He finds scepticism about our inductive inferences in Part Three, where I find merely scepticism about rationalist versions of them, developed briefly within Section VI.

7  O.E.D.: *Intelligible 3 Philos.* Capable of being apprehended only by the understanding (not by the senses); objective to intellect. (Opp. to *sensible*.)

8  Lewis White Beck, "A Prussian Hume and a Scottish Kant," in *Essays on Kant and Hume* (New Haven: Yale University Press, 1978) pp. 111-29.

9  Manfred Kuehn, "Hume's Antinomies," *Hume Studies* 9 no. 1 (April 1983), pp. 25-45, and "Kant's Conception of

"Hume's Problem"," *Journal of the History of Philosophy*
Vol XXI, no. 2 (April 1983) pp. 175-93.

10   Anthony Flew, *Hume's Philosophy of* Belief, (London:
Routledge & Kegan Paul, 1961), p. 73. Flew's impatient student was reading the first *Enquiry*, not the *Treatise*.

11   See G. E. M. Anscombe "Causality and Determination," in
Ernest Sosa, ed., *Causation and Conditionals*, (Oxford:
Oxford University Press, 1975).

12   This is a bit unfair to Descartes, whose natural light operated
more likely a paternity test, detecting the father's genes in the
child.

13   Bennett says Hume was slow to "notice the threat" (LBH
208) to his own theory posed by the Berkeleyan view of voli-
tion-causes. But Hume's *Treatise* theory had itself
"threatened" *all* views that purported to find causes that wore
their efficacy on their sleeves.

14   See E. C. Mossner, *The Life of David Hume*, (Oxford:
Oxford University Press, 1980), p. 125-26, for a quotation of
these remarks, translated into English.

15   The O.E.D., to illustrate this standard usage, cites Hobbes'
famous statement, in *Leviathan* Ch. X that, as far as a man's
worth goes, "as in other things, not the seller but the buyer
determines the price." If we want a use closer in time to
Hume, the O.E.D. offers Samuel Johnson's (in *The Rambler*,
no. 141) that "the whole tenor of his life has been determined
by some accident of no apparent moment." Johnson in his
own dictionary gives "fix or settle" as the first sense of
"determine." In his entry for "determination" he cites Hale's
statement, in *The Origin of Mankind*, that "the proper acts of
the intellect are intellection, deliberation, and determination or
decision."

16   Anthony Flew, *David Hume, Philosopher of Moral Science,*
(Oxford: Basil Blackwell, 1986), p. 74.

17   John Passmore, *Hume's Intentions*, (Cambridge: Cambridge
University Press, 1952), pp. 74-83. Fogelin, *op. cit.*, p. 40
also speaks of the "bad infinite regress" that we are led to
when we take the second definition to introduce necessity into
causes, and take the first definition to need supplementation
by some necessity-introducers.

18   D. G. C. Macnabb, *David Hume*, (London: Hutchinson,
1951), p. 112-15.

19 Anthony Flew, *Hume's Philosophy of Belief*, *op. cit.*, ch. VI.

20 Flew, *op. cit.*, p. 122-23. Flew in his later book, *David Hume, Philosopher of Moral Science*, neither repeats nor revises this reading (see pp. 71-79), since as we have seen (p. 30) Flew no longer finds any philosophical interest in Hume's definition of cause as a natural relation. Beauchamp and Rosenberg (*op. cit.*, p. 22n) quote Flew's words in a private correspondence with them that he had always been "unhappy" with the above treatment of the circularity issue, and was still (1979) "uneasy." By his second Hume book, in 1986, it seems that uneasiness had been banished by boredom with the issue. So in what follows I may be beating a bored-to-death horse. I do so because Bennett seems to have been influenced by Flew's earlier expressed views.

21 Beauchamp and Rosenberg (*op. cit.*, p. 12) comment that "Flew seems to have confused the absence of a term with the absence of the term's meaning," but this is not quite right, since "the determination of the mind" does not, *pace* Macnabb and Flew, mean the same as "the feeling of the determination of the mind."

22 This paper was written with the help of an A.C.L.S. grant, and while enjoying the support and stimulating environment of the Wissenschaftskolleg zu Berlin.

# APPERCEPTION AND EPISTEMIC RESPONSIBILITY

*Patricia Kitcher*

## 1. Puzzles about Kantian Apperception

Kant's most famous proclamation is also one of his most confusing:

> That: *I think* must *be able* to accompany all my cognitive states (or their contents); otherwise something would be represented in me which could not be thought at all, which is the same as saying that: this state (or its content) is either impossible, or at least nothing for me. (B131-32)[1]

What does the deceptively straightforward expression, 'accompany'[*begleiten*], mean? Although it is clear what it means for one person to accompany another, it is not obvious what *I think* is supposed to be and what it means to say that it accompanies anything. One possibility is that Kant means to claim that whenever there is a cognitive state, there must also be a thinker, to which the state belongs. Following Jonathan Bennett, I will call this reading of B132 the "ownership" reading. It fits the cited text well and makes a central doctrine of the *Critique of Pure Reason* extremely plausible.

When we consider surrounding texts, however, further elements complicate this simple picture, and the ownership reading appears inadequate. The section is entitled the "Original Synthetic Unity of Apperception." 'Apperception' suggests that the topic is some kind of consciousness, perhaps self-consciousness; 'unity' implies an identical thinker through time. Both these elements are confirmed when Kant equates "apperception" with "self-consciousness" [*Selbstbewusstsein*] and when he describes a multiplicity of cognitive states as belonging to a single self-consciousness. He also characterizes *I think* as itself a content of a cognitive state and claims that it is produced by an act of spontaneity (B132). Together, these elements point in quite a different direction: Whenever there is a cognitive state, there is a consciousness of that state, a consciousness that includes the content that that state belongs with others to a single consciousness. More briefly, whenever there is a cognitive state, there is also a self-consciousness or some kind of consciousness of self. While this reading—the "self-consciousness" reading—seems to capture the implications of Kant's terminology, it faces a serious objection. Since the claim at B132 is meant to be perfectly general, it is obviously false. As Bennett, among others, has argued, a conscious being need not be self-conscious. Seemingly creatures could enjoy cognitive states that inform them about their environments and never think of themselves.[2]

Worse still, the self-consciousness reading seems to be repudiated in the text. First, Kant says explicitly that "all my cognitive states (*even if I am not directly conscious of them as such*) must conform to the condition under which they alone *can* stand together in one universal self-consciousness" (B132, my emphasis, amended translation).[3] That is, he acknowledges that we may have cognitive states and not be conscious of them as such. Second, he denies that we are conscious of an identical self: "Consciousness of self according to the determinations of our state in inner perception is merely empirical, and always changing. No fixed and abiding self can present itself in this flux of inner appearances" (A107; compare B134). Finally, he denies that any empirical consciousness that "accompanies" different cognitive states can establish the identity of a self through time: "For the empirical consciousness, which accompanies different cognitive states, is in itself diverse and without relation to the identity of the subject" (B134, amended translation). Thus he explicitly rejects all three pieces of the self-consciousness reading: We are not always conscious of cognitive states; we are not empirically conscious of an identical self at all; we are not conscious of an identical self in being empirically conscious of different cognitive states.

Bennett's way out of this morass has the substantial virtues of clarity and common sense. The heart of the doctrine of apperception is the ownership thesis. As for self-consciousness, although it is false that all cognitive states must belong to a self-conscious being, it is true that the only states that concern us are those of which we are conscious.[4] So he takes the doctrine of apperception to amount to the following:

> [A]ll suppositions about possible experience must concern experience which is owned and which is accompanied by self-consciousness. It is out of these modest but not trivial asseverations that Kant spins the argumentative thread of the Transcendental Deduction.[5]

He then notes immediately that Kant's point is not: Any cognitive state that you can worry about must belong to a self-conscious being. As he wryly observes, Kant's efforts are never directed toward curing philosophical neurotics of their anxieties.[6]

Although Bennett has been extremely effective in deflating the idea that Kant is trying to cure skeptical *Angst,* it is not entirely clear that he avoids this implication here. Kant's concerns are epistemological. His natural target would be all states that contribute to knowledge, that is, all cognitive states. So why should he restrict his attention to states of which we are conscious or self-conscious? I do not see how Bennett's account answers this question, and so resolves the puzzle about self-consciousness.

My aim is to preserve the ownership interpretation of B132, by uncovering the reasons that lead Kant to use a vocabulary that is much better suited to a thesis about self-consciousness. Only if we can achieve some grasp of these reasons can we ever say with confidence: Apperception is really about ownership, the elements that resist this interpretation reflect other concerns. Some of these reasons will turn out to be artifacts of eighteenth century psychology; however, others will reflect Kant's particular epistemological views, a presupposition of the enterprise of epistemology itself, and assumptions about the unique features of human beings. Thus, although I try to show that all these reasons are extraneous to the basic doctrine of apperception, some will turn out to be important, not to our consciousness of a self, but to our conception of ourselves and to epistemology. Before presenting these reasons, I will provide a more precise statement of the ownership thesis and explain why Kant holds it. This will enable us to see more clearly how various claims about consciousness might or might not be incorporated into the basic doctrine of apperception.

## 2. Apperception: The Core Thesis

Although I agree with Bennett's insight that the doctrine of apperception is fundamentally a thesis about the ownership of cognitive states, I do not accept his hypothesis about Kant's reasons for maintaining the thesis. Bennett surmises—this is not intended as exegesis—that Kant may have recognized the essentially adjectival status of mental or cognitive states. Such a state must be a state of someone.[7] Bennett acknowledges that there is a little more than this to the ownership thesis, because Kant refers to the "unity" of apperception. He is unwilling to follow Kant's reflections about the unifying or synthesizing of cognitive states necessary for cognitive experience, however, because he thinks such genetic psychology must lead to incoherence.[8]

I accept Bennett's point that Kant's genetic psychology leads to intractable incoherence when combined with other doctrines. Something has to give. It is not clear that it should be the psychology, however.[9] The problem with this move is that interpreting the doctrine of apperception without drawing on Kant's numerous discussions of the necessity of unifying cognitive states is building bricks out of straw. It just cannot be done. A central theme of the Deduction chapter is that cognitive states must be unified with each other. Throughout both the A and B versions of this chapter, Kant presses his case for the necessity of a synthesis of cognitive states. In order for us to represent an object (A105), or to perceive an object (A120, B134), or to apply a concept to an object (A103), or to make a judgment about an object (B141), we must synthesize or unify various cognitive states in a further cognitive state. That is, we must combine elements from diverse cognitive states in a resulting state which comprehends all those elements (A77/B103). All this synthesizing is necessary, because our senses present us with a vast and fleeting array of elements, elements that must be gone through, selected, and combined, if we are to going to be able to represent discrete objects and events in the world around us.[10]

The content of a cognitive state that is a perception or a judgment or any representation of an object is unified, because it was produced through a unification of elements from diverse states. Synthesis not only produces unified contents of cognitive states, however. It also produces a unity among cognitive states. States produced by synthesis are dependent upon states from which they were produced for their contents, and so for their existence as particular cognitive states. Here is the real connection among cognitive states that Hume despaired of finding, the connection that justifies the claim that diverse states belong together as states of one mind. As I have argued elsewhere, Kant explores the requirements of representing and making judgments about objects, in part to show that these very basic cognitive tasks require the kind of real connections among cognitive states that Hume denied.[11]

Synthesis not only produces a relation of real connection among cognitive states, it also presupposes a further relation among cognitive states. Some sets of cognitive states must be *connectable* by synthesis. It must be possible for their elements to be combined in the contents of a further state. When Kant says at B132 that it must be possible for '*I think*' to accompany all my cognitive states, he is asserting that any possible cognitive state must be connectable with a synthetically interconnected system of states. Otherwise, it could make no contribution to cognition and so would be impossible as a cognitive state. '*I think*' does not refer to some separate thing, a substance, which enters into various cognitive states, but to the synthetically connected system of states itself. Hence, he concludes the discussion begun at B132 with the observation that: "Synthetic unity of the diverse elements in intuitions, as generated *a priori*, is thus the ground of the identity of apperception itself, which precedes *a priori* all *my* determinate thought" (B134, amended translation).

The unification, or synthesis, required by cognitive tasks such as making a judgment about an object produces a real mental unity. Conversely, this unity of the contents of cognitive states is possible only because some sets of cognitive states are connectable by synthesis. There is a reciprocity between the unity involved in representing objects and the unity of apperception: Each makes the other possible (A107, B134). Thus, it is not a belief in an adjectival status for cognitive states, but his own distinctive recognition that cognitive states are and must be unified that stands behind the ownership thesis. Ownership and unity are not separate issues for Kant. Any possible cognitive state must be unified or unifiable with others—and so belong to an *I think*. Because this is the rationale behind the apperception doctrine, Kant characterizes the unity of apperception as "synthetic" (A116 and 116a, B131, section title), and "transcendental." The last epithet is warranted, because the synthetic connections among cognitive states that make them parts of one apperception are necessary conditions for various tasks that are essential for knowledge (A107).

As the attentive reader will have noticed, the denials of a consciousness of a self presented above mainly involve "empirical" consciousness. This may suggest that the doctrine of transcendental apperception posits, instead, some type of "transcendental" consciousness of a self. While this is correct, it can be extraordinarily misleading. A transcendental consciousness is no more a special kind of consciousness than a theoretical object is a special kind of object. To say that the unity of apperception is "transcendental" is just to say that this synthetic connection of cognitive states is a necessary condition for the possibility of knowledge that does not derive from any materials presented by our senses, and perhaps, that it is established by investigating the necessary conditions for knowledge. Kant does not and would not posit some non-empirical awareness of a self or anything else.

Henry Allison offers a useful suggestion for understanding B132 in discussing the first edition's version of this doctrine: "We are conscious *a priori* of the complete identity of the self in respect of all cognitive states which can ever belong to our knowledge, as being a necessary condition of the possibility of all cognitive states" (A116, amended translation). '*A priori* conscious' does not refer to a special way of being conscious. Rather, "this must be taken as Kant's rather clumsy way of referring to an awareness of something as necessarily the case . . . . what we are aware of is not numerical identity; it is rather the 'fact' that this identity must be presupposed as a necessary condition of knowledge."[12] Thus, the claim that *I think* must be able to accompany all cognitive states does not mean that there is a separate thing, a thinker, which has various states and it does not mean that we have any special awareness of a self at all. Rather, it asserts that any possible cognitive state must be connectable with a synthetically connected system of states and that anyone who theorizes about cognition must be cognizant of this fact.

In this way, we can deepen our understanding of the ownership thesis and also make substantial progress in removing the teeth from those elements of B132 that point towards the self-consciousness reading. Still, I think that there is something unsatisfying about the interpretive strategy I have been pursuing. If Kant's doctrine has nothing to do with self-consciousness, then why on earth does he use the terms 'apperception' and 'self-consciousness'? Further, even if this were an acceptable reading of B132, there are clear indications in other parts of the corpus that self-consciousness is very important to Kant, and somehow connected to his views about apperception. I will look at four key discussions to try to determine the basis of Kant's attraction to doctrines about self-consciousness. This will give us a better understanding of the prominent references to self-consciousness at B132.

## 3. Synthesizing and Inner Sense

Dieter Henrich makes one of Kant's more dramatic references to self-consciousness the critical text for his interpretation of the doctrine of the identity of the self.[13] A108 makes the following, seemingly unequivocal, claim:

> For the mind could never think its identity in the diversity of its cognitive states, and indeed think this identity *a priori*, if it did not have before its eyes the identity of its act, whereby it subordinates all synthesis of apprehension . . . to a transcendental unity, thereby rendering possible their interconnection according to *a priori* rules. (A108, amended translation.)

This is a remarkable claim. Kant seems to say that we have some special means of observing the mind's activities, a way so special that it informs us that we are watching a (numerically?) identical act. Further, it is from this privileged observation that we become aware of an identical self.

Henrich's reliance on this passage is somewhat surprising, because there are very good reasons for denying that it represents Kant's considered judgment. The most obvious is that no introspecting, however fancy, could ever establish that a claim is necessary or transcendental, but the doctrine of apperception is plainly intended to have both of these properties. Second, although Kant does refer to our ability to watch ourselves synthesize, he also backs off the claim that we are conscious of such acts (A104). Finally, this position is dramatically modified in two passages in the second edition. At B158-9, Kant claims only that "I exist as an intelligence, which is conscious solely of its power of combination." Here, Allison's reading seems forced. How can one be conscious of a power of combination, unless this means only that one is aware of the fact that one has this power? B133 contains a claim that is clearly meant to be a more careful statement of A108:

> Only in so far, therefore, as I can unify a diversity of elements of given cognitive states in *one consciousness*, is it possible for me to represent to myself the *identity of the consciousness across these cognitive states*. (A108, amended translation, original emphasis.)

Here there is no question of being aware of particular acts of synthesis or of any unifying activities. Rather, it is the fact that a unification of cognitive states is possible that grounds the claim that these states all belong to one mind, or that makes the content '*I think*' possible.

Although Kant makes a substantial retreat from his claims for self-consciousness at A108, this passage illustrates one way in which he is tempted into such claims. From his analyses of the prerequisites of various cognitive tasks, he knows that we must engage in acts of synthesizing. However, he also accepts Locke's notion of an inner sense through which we are aware of our own inner states. Locke believed that we were not only aware of the contents of states, however, but of different operations, thinking, willing, and so forth. It is the presence of inner sense that explains how we have ideas of these mental operations.[14] If we have the ability to be aware of our mental activities, and if we must engage in synthesizing, then it would follow that we are aware of acts of synthesis. Further, Johann Nicolaus Tetens, a committed Lockean, whose major work Kant read with care, suggested that we are aware of various feelings that attend the progress of our thinking from one idea to another.[15] Given these strong influences, it is not surprising that Kant was inclined to think that we must be aware of our own synthesizing. Ultimately, however, he rejects this position, both in the passages already considered, and at B134:

> The thought that the cognitive states given in intuition one and all belong to me, is therefore equivalent to the thought that I unite them [and their contents] in one self-consciousness, or can at least so unite them, *and although this thought is not itself the consciousness of the synthesis of the cognitive states, it presupposes the possibility of that synthesis.* (B134, amended translation, my emphasis.)

While A108 and its Lockean inheritance offer some insight into why Kant was once inclined to strong claims about self-consciousness, it does little to explain the persistence of this theme in B132. Despite Henrich's belief in the importance of this discussion, it seems clear that by the time of the second edition, Kant had abandoned any ideas about synthesis-watching.

## 4. Comparison and Attention

Another striking reference to the need for self-consciousness occurs in Kant's discussions of recognition in a concept. At A103, he claims that:

> If we were not conscious that what we think is the same as what we thought a moment before, all reproduction in the series of cognitive states [or their contents] would be useless. For it would in its present state be a new cognitive state which would not in any way belong to the act whereby it was to be gradually generated. The diverse elements in the content of the cognitive state would never, therefore, form a whole since they would lack that unity which only consciousness can impart to them. (A103, amended translation.)

Much of the motivation for this claim is the same as that which stood behind A108. Since we, as theorists, must recognize a synthesis of the contents of cognitive states, and since we (all) have an inner sense, then we must be aware of the gradual generation of a cognitive state by synthesis. He immediately backs off the claim of synthesis-watching, however, and stresses a somewhat different point:

> The word 'concept' [*Begriff*] might itself suggest this remark. For this unitary consciousness is what combines the diverse elements, successively intuited, and thereupon also reproduced, into one cognitive state. This consciousness may often be only faint, so that we do not connect it with the act itself . . . but only with the outcome. But notwithstanding these variations, such consciousness, however indistinct, must always be present. (A103-4, amended translation.)

I take Kant's point about the word '*Begriff*' to be twofold. '*Begriff*' comes from the verb '*begreifen*' which can mean "comprehend" in the intellectual sense and also "comprehend" in a literal physical sense of "include" or "contain." So '*Begriff*' itself implies that the application of concepts is somehow analogous to gathering up and containing diverse elements. The act of recognizing in a concept also involves consciousness, however; a *Begriff* is a conscious or mental grasping. Putting these two aspects together, Kant's point seems to be that, when we recognize an object before us under a particular concept, then we are (and must be) conscious that the cognitive states that form the basis of our recognition involve a particular diversity of elements, even if we are not conscious of the synthesizing of these elements in the resulting conceptual state.

Why? While Kant's position is reasonably clear, the rationale offered is little more than a restatement. Without consciousness, the diverse elements would lack unity and never form a whole. "If [for example] in counting, I forget that the units, which now hover before me, have been added to one another in succession, I should never know that a total is being produced through this successive addition of unit to unit, and so would remain ignorant of the number" (A103). Part of Kant's point is relatively straightforward. For a pre-

sent cognitive state to include a diversity of elements from
other states (as is necessary in representing an object, as he
is about to explain: A104 ff), then it must unite those elements in itself. So a synthetic connection of cognitive states
and a unity of apperception are required, but why consciousness?

This point is clarified in a later discussion of recognition.
The passages we have been considering occur as Kant is
preparing the reader for the formal presentation of his views
in section III of the first Deduction chapter. In section III, he
offers the following account of recognition:

> . . . [A]pperception [represents appearances] in the
> empirical consciousness of the identity of the repro-
> duced contents of cognitive states with the appearances
> whereby they were given, that is, in recognition.
> (A115, amended translation.)

When we recognize a presented object in a concept, we
somehow compare the conceptual content of the cognitive
state we have synthesized, with the elements that were included in the cognitive states that were the basis of our synthesizing, the appearances. That is, we have some type of
awareness that the diverse elements in the cognitive states
that form the basis of our conceptualization, are identical to
the diverse elements that are included in the concept.
Otherwise, we would have no grounds for applying the concept. This consciousness, or awareness, of the identity of
elements across cognitive states is empirical. The ability to
have such consciousness is transcendental, however, since it
is a necessary condition for the possibility of recognizing
objects in concepts, and so of cognitive experience.

Once again, Kant's account appears to be shaped by
trends in eighteenth century psychology. Judging and conceptualizing were widely regarded as being a matter of comparing the contents of cognitive states to determine identity
or difference. Many theorists recognized the existence of
unconscious cognitive states. In applying concepts and in
judging, however, the usual assumption was that the subject
attended to the contents of cognitive states and then com-

pared them.[16] Kant's account of the processes involved in conceptualization in the *Logic* indicates substantial agreement with this picture.[17] Further, since any account of concept application must advert to comparing a present cognitive state with others in some fashion, and since we are (allegedly) aware of our mental activities, it would follow that we are conscious of the requisite comparing.

The strange feature of this account of conceptual recognition is not that it reflects widespread contemporary views, but that it is inconsistent with Kant's later discussion of concept application in the Schematism! In that section, he is perfectly clear that, in applying a concept to an object, we do not compare the (perceptual) image of a presented object with previously experienced images; rather we compare the procedure that the imagination carried out in constructing the present image with "a universal procedure of the imagination in providing an image for the concept [the "schema" of the concept] . . . ." Since he goes on to say that the use of schemata is an "art concealed in the depths of the human soul . . . [that is never likely to] lay open to our gaze" (A140/B179), it follows that we are not conscious of the activities that permit concept application. Alternatively, it follows that the activities that permit concept application are not conscious activities. Of course, A104 hedges: we may not be conscious of mental activity, but only of the outcome. So even with the schematism doctrine, perhaps Kant feels that we are conscious of the outcome. If that is all we are conscious of, however, then it is far from clear how we can engage in conscious comparing. He may have come to appreciate this inconsistency, because the comparison account of recognition also disappears from the second edition.

## 5. Spontaneity

Although the *Critique* includes many references to spontaneity, the clearest statement of the link between spontaneity, apperception, and self-consciousness occurs in a note to the *Anthropology*:

If we consciously represent two acts: the inner activity (spontaneity) that makes a *concept* (a thought) possi-

ble, or *reflection*, and the receptiveness (receptivity)
that makes *perception*—that is, empirical *intuition*—
possible, we can then divide our self-consciousness
(*apperceptio*) into the self-consciousness of reflection
and the self-consciousness of *perception*. The first is a
consciousness of understanding, *pure* apperception;
the second is a consciousness of inner *sense, empirical*
apperception. So it is wrong to call the first of these
inner *sense*. In psychology we investigate ourselves
according to our ideas of inner sense; in logic, according to what intellectual consciousness presents us
with.[18]

While this doctrine is complex, some points are clear.
Spontaneity is necessary for the use of concepts. What Kant
means by this is that we cannot achieve conceptual recognition of objects if we merely repeat the data of sense in the
order in which they arrived, as suggested by the Empiricist
Law of Association. Rather, to recognize a presented object
in a concept, we must combine the data of sense according to
rules that are not themselves given in sense, but that come
from the constitution of our minds.[19]

In the passage, Kant does not claim that we are conscious
of this spontaneous activity, but that we consciously represent [*mit Bewusstsein vorstellen*] this act. This would occur
when, for example, we analyze our capacity for recognition
in a concept. It follows from the doctrine of spontaniety,
however, that when we are aware of our conceptual representations, we are aware of something that is the product of
the spontaneous activity of the mind itself.

The items that we are aware of in being conscious of the
contents of our minds are therefore of two sorts: perceptions
caused in us by outer objects and conceptual states that reflect our own spontaneity. The first sort is merely empirical.[20] In the second case, however, what we are aware of is
the product of a pure (that is, not derivable from the data of
sense) combination of elements that were given in sense. In
psychology, we try to discover whatever laws govern the
transition from one cognitive state to another, as those states
appear in inner sense. In what Kant calls "logic" and we

would call "cognitive psychology," we study our ideas insofar as they indicate our own spontaneous activity.[21] That is, we try to determine which aspects of our cognitive states cannot be traced to the data of sense. The self-consciousness of reflection involves consciousness in two different ways: We consciously represent the synthesizing activities that we are indirectly conscious of in being conscious of our conceptual states.

Both parts of the interpretation of this note are confirmed in discussions in the *Critique*. In the Amphiboly, Kant explains that "*Reflection* . . . is that state of mind in which we first set ourselves to discover the subjective conditions under which [alone] we are able to arrive at concepts. It is the consciousness of the relation of given cognitive state or its content to our different sources of cognition . . ." (A260/B316, amended translation). That is, in reflection, we represent the sources of our cognition [which include spontaneity.] The second part is supported by the discussion of inner sense versus apperception:

> Apperception and its synthetic unity is, indeed, very far from being identical with inner sense. The former, as the source of all *combination*, applies to the diverse elements of *intuition in general*, and in the guise of the *categories*, prior to all sensible intuition, to *objects in general*. Inner sense, on the other hand, contains the mere form of intuition, but without combination of the manifold in it . . . . (B154, amended translation.)

Inner sense is merely the faculty of being aware of the contents of our cognitive state [in time]. 'Apperception' [or 'spontaneity'] refers to the combination that is necessary for those cognitive states to come into being. Through inner sense, we can be aware of the contents of cognitive states that reflect the synthesizing activities of our own minds (which Kant associates with the categories), and so can be indirectly aware of the pure synthesizing activities of our minds. Nevertheless, it is not the deliverances of inner sense that inform us that our cognitive states must be produced through synthesizing, and so that there is a necessary unity of apperception and a spontaneity that produces it. The necessity of synthesis, of apperception, and of spontaneity are all demonstrated through Kant's careful reflections on the mental equipment required for the cognitive tasks that we actually perform, such as representing and making judgments about objects. These claims are not the fruits of any empirical psychology, but of his own transcendental psychology: "which investigates the sources of our cognitions of objects, in so far as they can not be ascribed to the objects" (A55-56/B80, my translation). Inner sense discloses states that have been produced through spontaneity and whose existence thus presupposes synthesis and the unity of apperception, but it does not present the states as having those properties.

In this note, at A103 ("the unitary consciousness which combines"), and at B159 ("I exist as an intelligence which is conscious solely of its power of combination"), Kant virtually identifies apperception with the power of spontaneity that synthesizes cognitive states and so produces the unity of apperception. After brief consideration, however, it is clear that he cannot identify the unity of apperception, or the unity of a self, with some faculty of combination. For what could the identity of such a faculty consist in, except the identity of a substance? In both the Paralogisms and the B Deduction chapter, however, Kant denies that the unity of apperception rests in the identity of a substance. Spontaneity is essential to, but not identical with apperception. A thinking self is not just a system of synthetically interconnected states, for there must always be some faculty which synthesizes the states with each other. The unity, or identity, of apperception does not reside in this faculty, however, but in the connections that are or can be created by synthesis. It is a synthetic unity. When Kant says at B134 that cognitive states belong to a single consciousness only because I combine them, he is giving a synoptic version of a more complex claim: Cognitive states belong to a single apperception in virtue of the fact that some faculty in whatever material or immaterial form in which these states are realized creates synthetic connections among them.[22]

Although the apparent identification of apperception with spontaneity cannot be regarded as Kant's considered view, the links between spontaneity and consciousness persist and seem to explain some of the emphasis given self-consciousness at B132. When we follow Kant in reflecting on the sources of our cognitions, then we consciously represent a unity among our states, an '*I think*'. This content of a cognitive state is a product of spontaneity (since it is conceptual) and it is about the spontaneity and unity of cognitive life. Although this reflective consciousness is a kind of self-consciousness, it is, as he notes, very different from empirical apperception. It is not a faculty that reveals any particular contents of our minds. Rather, it is a "pure" and "transcendental" apperception, because it is a recognition of the nonsensorily based combination of cognitive states that is a necessary condition for cognition. Because we have the capacity to reflect on the sources of our own cognitions, we have a self-consciousness of reflection, a recognition of our own spontaneity and unity.

Let me add a final note about spontaneity, self-consciousness, and apperception. In Leibniz, apperception appears to be what distinguishes humans from other sentient creatures; in Locke, it is self-consciousness that makes us to be persons (as opposed to mere animals).[23] Both claims are repeated by Kant. At the beginning of the *Anthropology*, he claims that it is our ability to have a cognitive state with the content 'I' that makes us persons.[24] The Third Paralogism defines a person as that which is conscious of the numerical identity of itself at different times (A361). Yet, it is clear that he also regards spontaneity as that which separates us from the beasts. In his lengthy *Philosophische Versuche*, Tetens reviews various claims about the unique characteristic of the human race. He presents Reimarus as opting for the capacity for reflection, while he lays out the case for self-activity (or spontaneity) himself. Kant's discussion of the self-consciousness of reflection can be seen as a way to preserve the virtues of both accounts. Without spontaneity, our consciousness of ourselves would be restricted to an awareness of the passing show of our cognitive states provided by inner sense. On the other hand, Kant seems to believe that it is only because we can be conscious of our states, and so of states that are the product of our own pure synthesizing activities, that we could ever come to recognize our own spontaneity. So for us to be able to attach the '*I think*', to have this special content, we must be both spontaneous and (indirectly) conscious of our own spontaneity and unity.

## 6. The Necessity of Empirical Consciousness

A number of passages foreshadow the claim at B132 that a cognitive state to which *I think* could not be attached would be nothing to me (A120, A122). The most detailed is a note to A116:

> All cognitive states [or their contents] have a necessary relation to a *possible* empirical consciousness. For if they did not have this, and if it were altogether impossible to become conscious of them, this would practically amount to the admission of their non-existence. But all empirical consciousness has a necessary relation to a transcendental consciousness which precedes all special experience, namely the consciousness of myself as original apperception. The synthetic proposition, that all the variety of *empirical consciousness* must be combined in one single self-consciousness, is the *absolutely* first and synthetic principle of our thought in general . . . . Whether this content ['I'] is clear (empirical consciousness) or obscure, or even whether it actually occurs, does not here concern us. But the possibility of the logical form of all cognition is necessarily conditioned by relation to this apperception *as a faculty*.

Three different claims are made in this note, one about unity and two about consciousness. The claim about unity is one that we have already encountered in B132 and which was first made at A116, to which the note is appended. Any possible cognitive state, that is, any state that can contribute to cognition, must belong to a synthetically connected system of states. While this claim can be supported by Kant's analyses of representing and making judgments about objects (as I suggest above[25]), the key claim about consciousness is highly problematic. We must be able to be empirically conscious of all cognitive states. Were this granted, then the third claim would follow. If it is necessary for us to be able to be conscious of any cognitive state, then the ability to be so conscious would be necessary for cognition and we would have a transcendental faculty of self-consciousness.

There are, however, two serious problems with the claim about empirical consciousness. Although it is easy to say that we perform this or that cognitive task because we are conscious, it has proven extraordinarily difficult to find *any* task, cognitive or otherwise, that actually requires consciousness. This issue became pressing after Darwin. For if human mentality, including consciousness, evolved, then it seems that it must have some function that contributed to survival.[26] Darwinians from Sigmund Freud to Daniel Dennett have speculated about what that function might be. Whenever a proposal is put forward, however, it is but a matter of time before an opponent explains how the same function could be carried out by an unconscious mechanism. Thus, it seems unlikely that Kant had a sound argument for the necessity of empirical consciousness.

Second, Kant admits the existence of unconscious cognitive states in the *Anthropology*.[27] His reason is clear and compelling and derives from Leibniz.[28] When we see a man in a far off meadow, we are not conscious of seeing his eyes, nose, and so forth. Yet, since we see the man, we must have obscure [unconscious] ideas of these features. In this case, we are mediately [or indirectly] conscious of the ideas. Even in the note, he hedges. If we could not be conscious of a state, that would *practically* amount to an admission of its non-existence. Presumably he is allowing for cases of indirect or mediate consciousness. As in the example given, we may have reason to believe that a cognitive state occurred, because it was necessary to produce a state of which we are conscious.

What about a state of which we cannot be conscious and whose existence cannot be inferred from its contributions to conscious states? Is this a possible cognitive state? Seemingly, we could still infer its existence, from its effects on behavior. Kant considers this very possibility, for the case of animals, in a well-known letter to Marcus Herz:

> [Unless sense data conformed to the categories] They would not even reach that unity of consciousness that is necessary for knowledge of myself (as object of inner sense). I would not even be able to know that I have sense data; *consequently for me, as a knowing being, they would be absolutely nothing*. They could still (I imagine myself to be an animal) carry on their play in an orderly fashion, as cognitive states connected according to empirical laws of association, and thus even have an influence on my feeling and desire, without my being aware of them . . . . (Amended translation, my emphasis.)[29]

That is, denying that states can be admitted to consciousness does not amount to an admission of their non-existence, since they can be known through other effects.

Still, Kant claims that such unconscious states would be nothing for us as cognitive beings—a slight expansion of the phrase that occurs at B132 and A120. Here, I think we come to the heart of the matter. Why are cognitive states which can have no access to consciousness nothing for us as *cognitive beings*? This doctrine does not emerge from any particular arguments or analyses provided by Kant, I believe, but from the background assumptions of the epistemological tradition in which he was working.

Descartes offered the *Regulae* in order to improve our epistemic practices. While Hume's interest was largely in giving a naturalistic explanation of our cognitive lives, part of his purpose was to encourage intellectual house cleaning, as his famous advice about how to reduce the size of one's library makes clear. Although Leibniz ridiculed Descartes's epistemic advice, he offered plenty of his own, particularly on the subject of how the goodness of God was not to be defended. Kant's work is clearly in this tradition. The purpose of the *Dialectic* is to expose, and so protect us from, a variety of intellectual errors. Even in the Analytic and the Aesthetic, however, our attention is frequently drawn to potential cognitive missteps. The categories are supposed to be necessary conditions for the possibility of objective cognition, which must be carefully distinguished from claims that have mere subjective validity; rival theories of space and time err in positing non-entities [*Undinge*] (A40/B57).

While Kant expresses some concern that the *Dialectical* illusions can still fool us, even after we have uncovered them, in the main, he assumes (with the tradition) that pointing out cognitive mistakes will enable us to do better. How can the kind of epistemic advice provided by these philosophers be efficacious? Standing behind this entire tradition is the assumption that we have some mental mechanism that permits epistemic self-improvement. If we look at key discussions in Descartes and in Locke, then it is fairly clear that that mechanism is an ability to be conscious of one's own cognitive states.

When Descartes considers how certainty in knowledge is possible, he worries about long proofs.[30] The problem is that we cannot keep all the steps in mind. All we can do is check that each step leads to its neighbor and then claim that the last follows from the first. In short proofs, we can keep all the steps in mind—we can be conscious of the contents of the different cognitive states that are the premises and inferences of a proof. If we are careful and enumerate each of the intermediate steps, then nothing will escape us and we can catch any errors. Long proofs are problematic, because although we have this wonderful ability (which can be enlarged somewhat with practice) to scrutinize our own cogitations, it is limited and cannot encompass enough steps. Locke also draws attention to this ability and to its limitation. We can all be conscious that we think and of the contents of our thoughts.[31] However, "[Since] . . . the narrow mind of man [is] not . . . capable of having many ideas under view and consideration at once, it was necessary to have a repository, to lay up those ideas which, at another time, it might have use of."[32] Since we can be aware of the contents of our cognitive states, we can improve the quality of our reasoning, by checking our performance against the standards provided by epistemologists.

When Kant refers to the capacity to be empirically conscious of our cognitive states and their contents, I believe that this is what he has in mind. We can be aware of cognitive states in such a way that we can compare their contents and their sequence with standards of good reasoning, and so improve the course of our cognitive lives. If we could not have this complex consciousness of a state, then we would lack conscious control over it. The state might lead us to various activities, as in the case of animals, but we would have no epistemic responsibility for it. For, however diligent we were about following the rules of good reasoning, we would be unable to check the reasoning embodied in such states. Unconscious cognitive states would be nothing for us as cognitively, or epistemically responsible, beings.

Kant is never completely explicit about why empirical consciousness of cognitive states is necessary. However, in light of his acceptance of some unconscious states, his explicit contrast with animals,[33] and the epistemological tradition in which he worked, I think it is reasonable to believe that he took something like this rich empirical consciousness to be necessary and central to human cognition, because it allows us to be epistemically responsible and demarcates us from the beasts. As noted, reflection was a popular candidate for the distinguishing characteristic of human beings and the sophisticated empirical consciousness required for epistemic reponsibility would be a sort of reflection. Again, it is more than simple inner sense. Tetens had criticized Reimarus for fastening on reflection, on the grounds that, for all we know, animals might have a primitive capacity for comparing or relating the contents of their states.[34] The empirical consciousness that enables us to be epistemically responsible is, however, a more complex capacity of reflection. Through it, we can be aware of the contents of cognitive states in a way that permits evaluation against epistemic norms, something apparently beyond the beasts.

Kant's position on this issue is, I will argue, three-quarters right. He is right that we have a conscious capacity to check some cognitive states, right that this enables us to be epistemically responsible, and right that this special consciousness and epistemic responsibility are distinctively human capacities (as far as we know). Where he errs is in thinking that this special consciousness is necessary for epistemic responsibility. I start with the positive.

Although popular with Kant's contemporaries, the idea that we have a limited window of awareness of our own cognitive states should arouse suspicion. Both Descartes's and Locke's belief in this capacity clearly rest on the evidence of introspection, a notoriously unreliable source. This is particularly clear in Locke's presentation: "Every man being conscious to himself that he thinks; and that which his mind is applied about whilst thinking being the *ideas* that are there, it is past doubt that men have in their minds several ideas . . . ."[35] Perhaps we are not really aware of any thoughts running through our heads, even when we think we are reasoning consciously. We seem to be aware of thoughts, but then we seem to see the nose of a plane tilt downwards when we land at night, even though we are actually informed about the altitude of the plane by a change in pressure in the inner ear. And this is but one of a stable of examples of the illusory power of introspection.

In the case of a complex empirical consciousness that allows us to check our reasoning, however, there is significant experimental confirmation of the deliverances of introspection. As Locke noted, people store vast amounts of information in long term memory. He also seems right that, in addition, we have a limited "short-term" or "working" memory that holds items presently under consideration. In a classic paper, George A. Miller offered a battery of experimental evidence to suggest that we can keep about seven unrelated items "in mind" at once.[36] Studies also suggest that material that is in mind can be critically evaluated. I describe just one elegant experiment. Subjects are asked to generate (speak) random letters. Everyone can do this for a while, up to about 20 letters. Subjects are required to continue, however, at which point, they fall into patterns. The crucial point is that subjects' ability to do this surprisingly hard task depends on the time allowed. If a response must be produced every half second, or second, then sequences will be repeated. When subjects are given as much as four seconds, however, they perform quite well. These results are explained by the following hypothesis: As a subject is about to fall into a pattern, he is aware of what he is about to say and aware that he has already given that sequence, and so stops the response and generates another one.[37] Thus, we seem to have an awareness of our states and their contents that permits us to check and so improve performance. If we can catch ourselves falling into patterns, then presumably we could also catch ourselves as we are about to commit any number of epistemic mistakes. Many questions about short term memory are still open, including the firm separation between it and long term memory, so I do not wish to imply that the issue is settled. Still, on the basis of current evidence, this aspect of Kant's position seems correct.

Second, given this capacity, we can be epistemically responsible. Since we can monitor our states, we can check their sequence against principles of good reasoning. This need not mean that we are constantly on the alert for cognitive fault. Presumably the situation is the same as in moral responsibility. Normally we think and act without any explicit evaluation. We have principles and a capacity for self-monitoring, however, which enable us to recognize a false step when we are about to make one. The third part of Kant's view also seems right, for a reason given in Bennett's first book, *Rationality*. Although Bennett offers careful analyses of the necessary conditions for rationality and for language-use, his real quarry is the distinguishing characteristic of humans. He notes that, although animals may have internal maps that enable them to perform many tasks, they cannot criticize the internal states and processes they go through and this is a difference in kind, not degree, with the capacities of humans.[38]

A central project of the *Critique* is to determine the capacities necessary for cognition. People can engage in epistemically responsible cognition. If a critical empirical consciousness is necessary for this sophisticated achievement,[39] then the faculty that enables us to be empirically conscious of cognitive states would be a transcendental faculty of self-consciousness. This is, I believe, Kant's position. As I argue below, it is a major factor behind the prominence of self-consciousness at B132 and elsewhere. I doubt that it is correct, however, for the reason already given. If epistemic responsibility requires only the presence of some mechanism for checking our reasoning processes, then an unconscious mechanism will do. All that is needed is some internal gate that stops or redirects our reasoning processes when they exhibit certain patterns. Such a gate could even be produced by a careful reading of the *Regulae*!

A tempting reply in Kant's defense is that an unconscious mechanism cannot produce true epistemic responsibility, even though it enables us to check and so improve our epistemic performances. For this monitoring would be something that happens in us, but not something that we do. Like moral responsibility, epistemic responsibility is possible only when we are capable of voluntary and, therefore, conscious control. Even granting the parallel with morality, the reply fails. Voluntary control could be exercised at an earlier stage. Knowing its salutary effects, individuals could voluntarily decide to study the *Regulae*. In which case, their improved performance (or lack of same, if they knowingly forgo the work) would be the result of conscious choice. Epistemic responsibility may require conscious control and it may require a monitoring function, but it does not follow that it requires conscious monitoring. Again, the problem is that is it is very hard to discover any actual psychological function that can only be executed consciously.

## 7. Conclusion

The textual mystery that I have been trying to solve is why Kant expresses a doctrine about the necessary synthetic unity of cognitive states in terms that advert to self-consciousness. Although other influences are probably at work, the four issues considered suffice to explain the language of self-consciousness. On the basis of his own work and the hypothesis of inner sense, Kant assumed for a time that we were conscious of our own synthesizing activities and that this informed us of our identity or unity through time. Eighteenth century psychology also led him to believe that applying concepts required an awareness of the contents of our cognitive states. This would imply that we have a transcendental faculty of self-consciousness. Although these reasons for connecting self-consciousness with unity and with transcendental faculties both disappear from the second edition, they would make the vocabulary of 'transcendental apperception' and 'self-consciousness' apt, and the vocabulary does not change between the editions.

The other two issues carry more weight and, presumably, explain the decision to keep the vocabulary, even though important claims about self-consciousness have been dropped. Any representing or judging objects requires that our cognitive states be unified by synthesis, by a spontaneity that combines elements of cognitive states in ways that they were not combined in the senses. In doing epistmology, we therefore consciously represent states that are the product of our own spontaneous activity, and so are indirectly conscious of ourselves. Further, Kant believes that epistemically responsible cognition requires that we be conscious of the contents and sequence of cognitive states. Here, then, are reasons grounded in Kant's own epistemological concerns for giving pride of place to cognitive states that involve some type of consciousness or self-consciousness. For a cognitive state of which we could not be conscious would be nothing to us as cognitively responsible beings; a cognitive state that did not reflect our self-activity would be nothing for us as transcendental epistemologists, seeking the mind's own contributions to cognition.

To sum up: For cognition to be possible, our cognitive states must be connected and connectable by synthesis; we must have a spontaneous faculty that does the combining; and we must have a faculty that can monitor and correct the sequence of our cognitive states. Further, it is part of the doctrine of spontaneity that we can reflect on the sources of our cognitive states, and so consciously represent these spontaneous activities. Together, these four points produce the classic statement of the transcendental, synthetic, and original unity of apperception: I must be conscious of any cognitive state that can be anything to me as a cognitively responsible being; any such state must belong to a synthetically connected system of states; in reflecting on the sources of cognition, we recognize the necessary spontaneity and unity of mental life, and so produce the content, '*I think*'. Although necessary, the empirical consciousness of cognitive states is diverse and cannot inform us of our unity; rather we recognize our unity by recognizing the necessary synthesis of cognitive states.

This doctrine is laden with claims about self-consciousness, but there is no very close connection between unity and self-consciousness. Even if Kant were right that epistemically responsible cognition requires critical empirical consciousness, so that we have a transcendental faculty of self-consciousness, this cannot inform us of the necessary unity of apperception through time (although we may be aware of several diverse states in monitoring our reasoning). Further, the self-consciousness of reflection is a rather tenuous form of self-consciousness. We are not conscious of, but consciously represent, our synthesizing activities, when we reflect on the sources of our knowledge. Thus, despite the tremendous emphasis on self-consciousness in this passage, self-consciousness is not an integral part of the claim that any cognitive state must belong to the unity of apperception.

If this is right, then what accounts for the emphasis? In a sense, I have already answered this question, in laying out various issues that lead Kant to connect self-consciousness with unity, apperception, and transcendental faculties. I now want to cast this material in a different light. Earlier, I noted the connection between 'apperception' and the question of the distinguishing characteristic of human beings. I also noted that reflection and spontaneity were two contenders for this mark, and that Kant's view about the synthesis of reflection amounts to a 'synthesis' of these two characteristics. We can attach the special content, '*I think*', to our cognitive states, only because we are spontaneous, which we can recognize, only because we can reflect on the sources of our knowledge.

Tetens also discusses a third candidate, offered by Rousseau. The unique character of human beings is their perfectibility. Tetens objects that this is too vague, and can only mean the perfectibility of our intellectual power [*Denkkraft*], in which case Rousseau should really locate the mark in this power itself.[40] Against this background, Kant's discussion of apperception takes on a different significance. For critical empirical consciousness—the ability to monitor and correct our own cognitive states—is a unique human capacity, which can be understood as a kind of reflection and as standing behind the perfectibility (or at least the capacity for self-improvement) that is also apparently unique to us. The complex doctrine of apperception presented above thus appears to offer a synthesis of all three standard positions on our *Grundcharakter*. In particular, both doctrines of self-consciousness that are included in B132, the necessity of critical empirical consciousness and the capacity for reflective consciousness of the '*I think*', seem to indicate a preoccupation with the question of our uniqueness.

B132 is very confusing, because it presents a doctrine that is intended to be the simultaneous solution to two large questions: What are the fundamental capacities required for knowledge?; What are the unique characteristics of human beings? The first question is answered largely by those elements that stress unity, synthesis, and spontaneity; the second, largely by those that stress spontaneity, reflection, and self-consciousness. That cognitive states must belong to a spontaneously created synthetic unity is the fundamental discovery of Kant's investigation into the possibility of cognition. This is the first principle of his philosophy, from which all the rest flows. Not surprisingly, perhaps, he believed that his discovery also resolved the important contemporary controversy over the unique characteristics of human beings. He offers one grand solution to both outstanding issues, by incorporating all the elements noted above into the doctrine of the transcendental unity of apperception.[41]

# NOTES

1 My translation. While it is somewhat awkward, I translate *'Vorstellung'* as 'cognitive state' or the 'contents of a cognitive state', rather than following the usual practice of using 'representation'. 'Representation' has an obvious advantage, because it preserves the state-content ambiguity of *'Vorstellung'*. I avoid it for two reasons. Kant does not believe that all *Vorstellungen stellen vor* (A320/B376). So the standard translation would have nonrepresentational representations. Further, while 'representation' can refer to a state, rather than a content, this sense is not very strong. *Vorstellung* was the most general name for a mental or cognitive state in Germany at the time Kant was writing. While inelegant, my translation forces the essential ambiguity of *'Vorstellung'* on us in a way that the usual translation does not. I use 'cognitive' rather than 'mental' state, because the latter would include volitions and pleasures and pains and these are not dealt with until the later Critiques. The First Critique is only concerned with those inner states that make some contribution to knowledge.

2 Jonathan Bennett, *Kant's Analytic* (Cambridge: Cambridge University Press, 1966), p. 105.

3 Immanuel Kant, *Critique of Pure Reason*, trans. Norman Kemp Smith (New York: St. Martin's, 1965). All subsequent translations will be from this work, unless noted explicitly in the text. In citing passages from Kant's other writings, I also give the location in the Academy edition (*Kant's gesammelte Schriften, heraus gegeben von der Königlichen Preussischen Akademie der Wissenschaften*, 29 vols., Berlin: Walter de Gruyter, 1902-) by "AA", the voume and page numbers in parentheses. References to passages from Descartes, Locke, and Leibniz employ the abbreviations adopted in the present volume.

4 *Kant's Analytic, op. cit.*, p. 105.

5 *Ibid.*, p. 106.

6 *Ibid.*, pp. 102, 106-107.

7 *Ibid.*, pp. 103-104.

8 *Ibid.*, pp. 111-12.

9 In chapter 5 of *Kant's Transcendental Psychology* (New York: Oxford University Press, 1990), I argue that the fun-

damental conflict is between transcendental psychology and the doctrine of the ideality of time. Since the latter doctrine is extremely problematic on independent grounds, I suggest that be sacrificed rather than the psychology.

10  I discuss this issue at greater length in chapter 3 of *Kant's Transcendental Psychology, op. cit.*

11  See "Kant on Self-identity," *Philosophical Review*, XCI (1982): 41-72, and chapter 4 of *Kant's Transcendental Psychology, op. cit.*

12  Henry Allison, *Kant's Transcendental Idealism* (New Haven: Yale University Press, 1983), p. 140.

13  Dieter Henrich, *Identitätund Objektivität: Eine Untersuchung über Kants transzendentale Deduktion* (Heidelberg: C. Winter), 1976, p. 81ff.

14  John Locke, *Essay* II, vi.

15  Johann Nicolaus Tetens, *Philosophische Versuche über ioe menschliche Natur and ihre Entwicklung, Vol. I* (New York: Georg Olms Verlag, 1979), pp. 194-98.

16  See, e.g. Locke, *Essay* IV,xiv, 3 and 4, and Étienne Bonnot de Condillac, *An Essay on the Origin of Human Knowledge*, translated by Thomas Nugent (Gainesville, Fl.: Scholars' Facsimiles & Reprints, 1971), pp. 74-75. Tetens criticizes this view in *op. cit.*, vol. I., p. 361.

17  *Immanuel Kant's Logic*, translated by Robert S. Hartman and Wolfgang Schwartz (New York: Bobbs-Merrill), 1974, p. 100 (AA. IX: 94-95).

18  Immanuel Kant, *Anthropology from a Pragmatic Point of View*, translated by Mary Gregor (The Hague: Martinus Nijhoff, 1974), p. 15 (AA. VII: 134).

19  Kant's arguments in favor of spontaneity generally take the form of arguments about the inadequacy of the Law of Association. Such arguments do not show that patterns in the sensory data other than simple spatio-temporal contiguity are inadequate to explain conceptualization.

20  This presents Kant's position as somewhat neater than it actually is. For in places, he suggests that perception also involves intellectual elements, e.g. A124, B161.

21  For a more extended discussion of the relation between transcendental logic and cognitive psychology, see chapter 1 of *Kant's Transcendental Psychology, op. cit.*

22  I argue for this claim at greater length in chapter 5 of *Kant's Transcendental Psychology, op. cit.*

23  See section 4 of "Principles of Nature and Grace, Based on Reason," at L 637. But see Mark Kulstad, "Leibniz, Animals, and Apperception" (*Studia Leibniziana, XIII* 1981: 25-60) for a careful discussion of whether and in exactly what sense Leibniz may take "apperception" to be unique to human beings. See also Locke, *Essay* II, xxvii, 9. As Nicholas Jolley pointed out to me, Locke also takes the ability to abstract to be our distinguishing characteristic.

24  Gregor, *op. cit.*, p. 9  (AA. VII: 127).

25  See above, p. 275.

26  This view of evolution is too simple, since some traits can become fixed in a population in virtue of being coupled with others. Nevertheless, it is often *thought* that consciousness must have some function to have evolved.

27  Gregor, *op. cit.*, p. 16  (AA. VII: 135).

28  Kant's discussion in the *Anthropology* seems to repeat the reasoning offered by Leibniz in a passage about ocean roars in the Preface to the *New Essays*. See NE 54.

29  *Emmanuel Kant Philosophical Correspondence*, edited and translated by Arnulf Zweig, (Chicago: University of Chicago Press, 1967), p. 153-54  (AA. XI: 51-52).

30  See Rule Seven of the *Regulae*: CSM I, 25-27.

31  Locke, *Essay* II, i, 1.

32  *Essay* II, x, 2.

33  Although the letter to Herz was not intended for publication, Kant instructs Herz to forward it to Maimon. Thus its evidential status lies between the published work and private notes. I think that it is reasonable to use such material to clarify points made in the published work and I take it to be an expansion of Kant's enigmatic claim that cognitive states of which we are not conscious are "nothing to us."

34  Tetens, *op. cit.*, pp. 744-45.

35  Locke, *Essay* II, i, 1.

36  "The Magical Number Seven, Plus or Minus Two: Some Limits on our Capacity for Processing Information," *The Psychological Review,* 63 (1956): 81-96.

37  For a review of the recent literature on working memory and a more extended discussion of this experiment, see Alan D. Baddeley, *Working Memory* (New York: Oxford University Press, 1986).

38  Jonathan Bennett, *Rationality* (London: Routledge and Kegan Paul, 1964), p. 91.

39 It might seem more natural to cast this issue in terms of the standard analysis of knowledge—justified true belief. Then the claim would be that being justified requires knowing that you know, and the latter requires empirical consciousness. I choose the somewhat unusual formulation of epistemic responsibility for two reasons. It is not clear that Kant is committed to the KK principle, and the phrase "nothing for me" suggests that such states are not my responsibility.

40 Tetens, *op. cit.*, p. 734.

41 I would like to thank Nicholas Jolley and Manfred Kuehn for helpful comments on an earlier draft of this paper.

# NOTES ON CONTRIBUTORS AND EDITORS

Annette Baier is Professor of Philosophy at the University of Pittsburgh. She is the author of *Postures of the Mind* and *A Progress of Sentiments: Reflections on Hume's Treatise.*

Martha Brandt Bolton is Associate Professor of Philosophy at Rutgers University. She has published articles on a variety of topics in early modern philosophy.

J. A. Cover is Assistant Professor of Philosophy at Purdue University. He is the author of a number of articles in metaphysics and early modern philosophy and co-author of *Theories of Knowledge and Reality.*

Edwin Curley is Professor of Philosophy at the University of Illinois at Chicago. He is the author of *Spinoza's Metaphysics*, *Descartes Against the Sceptics*, and *Behind the Geometrical Method* and is the editor and translator of *The Collected Works of Spinoza.*

Don Garrett is Associate Professor of Philosophy at the University of Utah. He has published widely on topics in seventeenth- and eighteenth-century philosophy and is the editor of the forthcoming *Cambridge Companion to Spinoza.*

Nicholas Jolley is Associate Professor of Philosophy at the University of California, San Diego. He is the author of *Leibniz and Locke: A Study of the New Essays on Human Understanding* and *The Light of the Soul: Theories of Ideas in Leibniz, Malebranche, and Descartes.*

Patricia Kitcher is Professor of Philosophy at the University of California, San Diego, and a member of its Cognition Science Program. She is the author of *Kant's Transcendental Psychology* and a number of articles in the philosophy of psychology.

Mark Kulstad is Associate Professor of Philosophy at Rice University. He is the author of *Leibniz on Apperception, Consciousness, and Reflection* (forthcoming) and a number of articles in early modern philosophy.

G. H. R. Parkinson is Emeritus Professor of Philosophy at the University of Reading. His publications include *Spinoza's Theory of Knowledge*, *Logic and Reality in Leibniz's Metaphysics*, *Georg Lukács*, and (as general editor) *The Handbook of Western Philosophy*.

Robert C. Sleigh, Jr. is Professor of Philosophy at the University of Massachusetts at Amherst. He is the author of *Leibniz and Arnauld—A Commentary on their Correspondence*.

Margaret D. Wilson is Professor of Philosophy at Princeton University. She is the author of *Descartes* and many articles on early modern philosophy.

R. S. Woolhouse is Reader in Philosophy at the University of York. His publications include *Locke's Philosophy of Science and Knowledge* and *Locke*.

# INDEX OF NAMES AND TOPICS

Adam, C. xi, 186n
'absolute nature', of attributes 82, 126
Accident(s), Leibnizian (of individual substances)192
Accidental
modes/affections of substance as? 74, 76, 77
source of knowledge can't be 210-11, 216,
Accompany, Kantian relation of 'I think' to my cognitive states 273, 274, 277
Action
of God, by general vs. particular volitions 164, 165
internal vs. external 126-127
Affects (also Affections)
in Descartes 14, 17 (see also Emotions, in Descartes)
– in Spinoza 75, 131ff, 138ff
as accidental/changeable? 74, 76, 77
active vs. passive 131
'in and conceived through' something else 43, 74, 80-81, 96-98, 100, 101
incompatible 78
'put to one side' 70, 71, 73, 74, 77, 78, 79, 80
qualitative identity w/ numerical diversity 96, 97
relation to attributes 80, 82, 95-98, 101
relation to substance 97-98, 100, 101
substance prior to 70-71, 73, 74, 77, 79-80, 83
Affirm, disposition to, and Leibnizian innateness 200-208
Affirmation
and Lockean knowledge 197

unconscious, of p if p is innate? 200, 201, 202, 208, 209
Affirming (also attending), to p vs. using p 201-02, 207, 208, 215
Agreement/disagreement, of ideas in Lockean propositions
as basis of truth 196, 197
knowledge as perception of 197, 208-09, 213, 215, 219
Akkerman 157n
Allison, Henry 77, 79, 89, 104n, 105n, 279, 302n
Alston, William P. x
Analysis, 'replacement' (vs. meaning-reduction) 163, 164
Analytic, vs. genetic reading of Hume on causal inference 251-52, 253
Anecdotes: see Examples, Illustrations, and Anecdotes
Angel(s) 3, 144
Animal(s) 249, 253, 266
consciousness and congnition in 291, 292, 294, 296
soul-less 117
Animal spirit(s) 167, 236
Annihilation 173
Anscombe, Elizabeth 255, 291, 303n
Anthropology (Kant) 285, 291, 303n
Anthropomorphism 116, 120, 121
Apperception
in Leibniz 289, 291, 303n
– in Kant (see also Consciousness, empirical; Consciousness, self)
vs. inner sense 287-88
pure (vs. empirical) 286, 287

as ownership of mental states
    273, 275, 276
and spontaneity 285-90
transcendental 278, 298, 299,
    300
unity of 273, 274, 276, 278,
    284, 287-88, 300
*a priori* 255, 256, 278, 279, 280
    knowledge 198, 210, 221n,
    231, 232
Aquinas, St. Thomas 190-91n,
    193n
Archtype 31
Aristotelian
    explanation 51, 61
    philosophy of nature 235
    concept of property 55
Aristotle 51, 61, 235, 241
Arithmetic 204
Arm raised
    vs. kettle boiled 232
    upon willing 162, 167, 229,
    231, 232, 233
Arnauld, Antoine 1, 2, 5-11,
    162, 167, 187n
Association, Empiricist law of
    286, 292, 302n
Atheist
    as geometrician 41
    Spinoza as? 111-12
Attention: *see* Affirmation.
Attribute(s)
    in Descartes (*also* Principle
    property) 23, 24, 45n, 75,
    94
  – in Spinoza 24, 25, 38, 57
    not accidental in substance 85,
    89, 90
    relation to affections 80, 82,
    95-98
    constitute the essence of
    substance 90-93, 96, 105n,
    106n
    definition of 91, 99
    multiple instances of a single
    90, 95-96, 101
    multiple, in a substance 92,
    93, 105n, 106-07n
    no sharing 69- 70, 83-89, 91,

92, 103n, 104n
    substances differ in *all* vs.
    substances differ in *some*
    83, 84, 86-89
    substance as identical with its?
    89-90, 105n
Aune, Bruce 225n, 226n
Authority 127 (*see also*
    Sovereign; Obedience)

Baddeley, Alan D. 303n
Baier, Annette 305
Bayle, P. 174, 181, 185, 188n,
    190n, 191n
Beauchamp, Tom L. 269n, 271n
Beck, Lewis White 253, 254,
    269n
'*Begriff*' 283
Behaviorism 126
Being, in Spinoza
    degrees of 156n
    kinds of 37 (*see also* Spinoza,
    kinds of existence in)
'being conceived through'
    as a relation of affects to
    substance 80
'being in' 107n
    as a relation of affects to
    substance 80
Bennett, Jonathan vii, ix, xii,
    xiii, 48n, 243n, 244n,
    269n, 296, 301n, 303n
    on Berkeley 231, 232, 238
    on Hume 248, 251, 253, 254,
    262, 263, 264, 270n, 271n
    on Kant 273, 274, 275, 276
    on Spinoza 26, 32-35, 46n,
    62-64, 67n, 71-72, 74, 84-
    86 101-102, 103n, 104n,
    109, 137, 139, 140, 143,
    145-148, 152n, 155n, 158n
    (*see also* Hooker-Bennett
    objection; Leibniz-Bennett
    objection)
Berkeley, George 242n, 244n,
    257
    causal knowledge *a priori*, or
    inductive in? 231, 232,
    234, 238

and Hume, on causality 255-57, 258
his immaterialism 228, 232-33, 242
and Locke, on concepts as ideas and their origin 239
occasionalist strains in 227, 228, 230, 232, 233, 234, 238, 242
on finite spirits as causally efficacious (vs. bodies as not) 230-34, 234-38
and theological constraints on ascribing causal powers 234-39, 241
– and Malebranche 227, 228
on causal connection as necessary 230
on causal efficacy of finite spirits/volitions 227, 228, 232-24, 236-38, 242
on idolatry and ascription of causal power 235-38, 241, 242, 244n
on the origin of our concept/idea of causality 239-41
Beyssade, Jean-Marie 18n
Bible (*also* Biblical; Scripture) 110, 111, 112, 115-16, 119, 124-25, 126, 136, 154n (*see also* Scripture, reference to passages in, by Spinoza)
Blood
Thick and sluggish 15, 16
In the lungs 17
Boats 185, 186
Bodies 119, 124, 165, 167, 180, 181
in Berkeley, as causally impotent unlike spirits 230-34, 234-36, 238
in Malebranche, as causally impotent like spirits 234-38
in Spinoza, laws of motion and 119, 124
relation to extended substance 24
– human, relation to minds
in Berkeley 236-37
in Descartes 2, 12, 129
in Leibniz and Malebranche 162, 163, 166, 167, 168, 169
in Spinoza 118, 126, 128, 129, 137, 139, 144-45, 151-52
Body 32
and space, in Descartes and Spinoza 26, 75
Bolton, Martha Brandt 305
Bondage, human 138
Bourguet, L. 177
Boyle, A. 65n
Boyle lecturer(s) 25, 45n
'bring about in toto' 172, 173, 179, 180
Broad, C. D. 39-40, 48n
Brown, Mark x
Burgersdijck, 66n
Burman, Frans 4

Calhoun, Cheshire 21n
Calling (*also* Guidance), God's 123
Carroll, Lewis 224n
Cartesian 27, 74, 76, 77, 78, 91, 255 (*see also* Descartes)
certainty 116-17
doctrines and Spinoza's *TTP* 116-17, 119, 120, 126, 128, 129, 134, 137, 144
dualism 126, 128
physics 41-42, 62
Causal
chain 245, 247
dependence (vs. logical) 60, 255
determination 246, 259, 264, 265 (*see also* Determination of mind)
independence, of non-overlapping temporal stages 175, 176
inference 245-52, 253, 254, 259-62, 265, 266, 267, 268

judgment 250
ground of knowledge 210,
   216, 220
laws 251, 253, 254
necessity 171, 176, 229, 246,
   247, 257, 258, 259, 260,
   261, 264, 266, 268, 269n
overdetermination 168, 228
reasoning: *see* Causal
   inference.
account of representation 11
− power
   in created substance 162, 170,
      177, 178, 183, 184, 233
      (*see also* Berkeley, on
      spirits as causally
      efficacious)
   for creation vs. for
      conservation 173, 174
   conservative (i.e.,
      conserving) 177, 178, 179,
      190n
   God's 51, 169, 170, 172, 173
      (*see also* Divine will, as
      cause)
   or energy, denied by Hume
      258, 259
Causality, concept of 239-41
*causa sui* 57, 134, 156n
Cause(s)
   and effect 28, 56, 81-82, 228,
      230, 245, 249, 254
   efficient 56-57, 176, 230
   of ideas 11, 18n, 232-33
   immanent 28, 106n
   occasional 163, 165, 167,
      169ff, 228-29 (*see also*
      Occasionalism)
   productive 174, 177, 179
   proximate 124, 172, 176
   natural 229
   real 162, 163, 164, 167, 168,
      169, 170, 171, 173, 174,
      177, 183, 184 (*see also*
      Cause, in Leibniz, real and
      quasi-; Cause, in
      Malebranche, quasi-)
   secondary 178, 228, 235
   transitive 27-28

− in Berkeley
   concept/idea of 239-41
   finite spirits/volitions as 227,
      228, 230, 231, 232, 233,
      234, 236-38
   of ideas 232-33
   knowledge of *a priori*, or
      inductive? 231, 232, 234,
      238
   threat of occasional 230-34,
      242
   theological constraints on
      234-38
− in Descartes 176
   God as 27, 28 (*see also*
      Descartes, on creation and
      conservation)
   of ideas 11, 18n
− in Hume
   double definition of 247, 248,
      252, 254, 262, 263, 264,
      265
   and customary transition to
      effect 253-57
   and effect, mental events as
      257-63
   genetic vs. analytic notion of
      251-52, 253
   as natural vs. philosophical
      relation 262, 263
   rules for applying concept of
      245-52
− in Leibniz
   and causal necessity 171, 176
   finite substances (or states of)
      as 162, 170, 177, 178, 183,
      184
   against occasional 161, 166-
      69, 170, 171, 172, 175-78,
      181-83
   real and quasi- 161-64, 169,
      170, 188n
− in Malebranche
   conservative vs. creative 179-
      80
   God's volition/will as a 164,
      165, 167, 169, 170, 171,
      172
   as necessarily connected with

effect 171, 228-29, 241
occasional: *see* Cause,
    occasional.
quasi- 164, 167, 168, 169
- in Spinoza 105n, 107n, 156n
and definition(s) 56
efficient 56, 57
external 134, 135
finite things as (partial) 124-
    25
God as 27-28, 39, 57, 60,
    123-125
immanent 28, 106n
internal (vs. external) 57, 58
proximate 124
or reason 80-81
Certainty 116-17, 218, 219
Change
of affections 75
persistence through 184
Chanut, Hector-Pierre 17
Chappell, Vere 18n
Charlton, William 71, 103n
Chiliagon 20-21n
Chimera, the 'Nature' of
    philosophers as 235, 236
Choice, God's 123
Christian(s) 28, 117, 152, 154n,
    170, 190n, 235, 236
Circle 30, 36
definition/essence of 54-56,
    60-61, 84
Circularity, in Hume's definition
    of cause? 264-66
Clarke, Samuel 25, 45n
Clear and distinct 3, 4, 31, 43-44
Cognitive beings 292
Cognitive state(s)
all able to be accompanied by
    '*I think*' 273, 274, 277, 279
adjectival status of 276, 278
contents compared 284-85,
    294
various sources of contents of
    286, 289
synthesized (*also* unified) 277,
    278, 281, 282, 283, 284,
    287, 288, 297, 298, 299
rendering of '*Vorstellung*'

300n
Cold and heat: *see* Heat and Cold
Collision 124
Color 1, 3, 12, 14
Combination, and Kantian
    spontaneity 288
*Commentaries* (Berkeley) 227,
    232, 235
'Common' notions 118-120
Common sense
in Berkeley 234
deep metaphysics at odds with
    162, 164
Community, and cooperation in
    Spinoza 139-41, 145-46,
    148-49
Comparison, of contents of
    cognitive states 284-85
Conceivable 19n, 53
'Conceived...' (*also*
    'Considered...')
truly 73, 80
- through another
modes/affects as 43, 74, 80-
    81, 96-98, 100, 101, 109
- in/through itself
ambiguity of 73
substance as 43, 70, 73, 80,
    86-89
Conceiving, as knowing 81
Concept(s)
as abstract entities 241
origin of, in Berkeley and
    Malebranche 239-41
as psychological entities 239,
    241, 283
- in Kant 285, 286
'*Begriff*' 283
recognition in a 283-85, 286
Conceptual definition 53
Conceptualizing 284, 302n
Conclusion(s), hybrid 204, 206,
Concomitance (*also* Pre-
    established harmony) 161,
    162, 166
Concupiscence 193n
Concurrence
- divine 161,193n
incoherence of, argument (for

occasionalism) 169, 180-83
and the Leibnizian theodicy
183-86, 192n
Condillac, Etienne Bonnot de
302n
Confused
expression/perception, vs.
distinct 162
idea(s)/thought(s) 3, 9-10, 14,
16
'sense' of truth of *p* 208, 217
Connection 253, 258
necessary 169, 171, 176, 228,
229, 230, 241
Consciousness
*a priori* 279
of cognitive states 274, 274,
283, 284, 287, 290-97
of synthesizing of cognitive
states 280-82, 283, 287
of sponteneity 286
– empirical 274, 284, 290-94,
297, 300
and epistemic responsibility
294-97, 298
– self- 274, 275, 279, 281, 282,
286, 287
transcendental faculty of 291,
296-97, 298, 299
Conservation (*also* Conserve)
and/vs. creation 173, 174,
175, 176, 177, 178, 179,
180, 188n, 189-90n, 228
Conservation argument (for
occasionalism) 169, 172-81
'Considered in/through": *see*
'Conceived in/through'.
Constant conjunction 246, 254,
255, 256, 264, 265, 268
'Constitute(s)'
as relation between attribute
and essence of substance 24,
90-93, 96, 105n, 106n
Contain
and '*Begriff*' 283
in the divine nature 121-22
Contiguity 262, 302n
Contingency
of causal regularities 231,

257, 266 (*see also*
Necessity, causal)
in Spinoza 76
Continuous creation 174-75,
177, 190n, 228 (*see also*
Conservation, and/vs
creation)
Contradiction
in Hume, as a reflexive test in
causal inference 249, 260
law of 201, 217
Cooper, David E. 221n
Cooperation, and community in
Spinoza 139-41, 145-46,
148-49
Corporeal
substance 23 (*see also* Bodies;
Body; Extended Substance)
universe/world, and Spinoza
25-28
Correlation, between cause and
effect 82, 232
Cottingham, John xi, 187n,
242n
Count term (vs. mass) 24
Couturat, Louis 186n
Craig, Edward 236, 244n
Creation (*also* Create)
and/vs conservation 173, 174,
175, 176, 177, 178, 179,
180, 188n, 189-90n
continuous 174-75, 177, 190n
(*see also* Conservation,
and/vs creation)
of man, in God's image 117,
236, 237, 238
Crescas, Chasdai 66n
*Critique of Pure Reason* (Kant)
273, 285, 287, 296
Curley, Edwin xi, 74-75, 93,
103n, 104n, 106n, 152n,
153n, 154n, 155n, 156n,
157n, 158n, 305
Customary, transition: *see*
Hume, on customary
transition from cause to
effect.

Darwin, Charles 291

Decahedron 31, 41
de Condillac, Etienne Bonnot
    302n
de Dign, Hermann 66n
Deductive (*also* Deduction)
    form of explanation 51, 52,
    61, 64 (*see also*
    Hypothetico-Deductive)
Definition
    involves cause(s) of thing
        defined 56-57
    and Leibnizian innatism about
        necessary truths 218, 219,
        226n
    real 53
    in Spinoza 52-58, 60-61, 62,
        84
    stipulative 52
    true or false? 52-53
Deist 183
Delahunty, R. J. 46n, 103n
Demonstration, in Spinoza's
    *Ethics* 49 (*see also Ethics*,
    geometric form of)
Demonstrative
    knowledge, in Locke 198,
        213, 217, 221n
    mode of referential
        representation 11
Dennett, Daniel 291
Dependence
    causal (vs. logical) 60, 255
    of created things on God 60
        (*see also* Finite things, their
        relation to God)
    of essences/natures on God 31,
        36, 37, 38, 39, 40
Descartes, Rene  xi, xii, 1ff,
    23ff, 46n, 62, 187n, 239,
    241, 244n, 255, 257, 270n,
    295
    on creation and conservation
        175-78, 228
    on essences vs. their
        instantiations 29-31, 39
    on kinds of existence 29, 30
    on extended substance 23-26,
        31-32, 42-44, 75, 76
    existence vs. reality 5 (*see*

    *also* Ideas, objectless)
    on God 23-24, 26, 27-28, 31,
        36, 38, 40, 57, 120, 172,
        178, 190n
    on idea(s) 3, 18n, 29, 36 (*see
        also* Descartes, on
        Sensation)
    and knowledge 116, 292, 293
    compared with Leibniz 36, 37,
        175, 176, 177, 178
    on passive emotions 2, 12,
        14-17
    on principle properties
        (attributes) 23, 45n, 66n,
        75, 94
    his science 41-42, 62
    on sensation and
        representation 1ff
    compared with Spinoza 24-29,
        31-32, 34, 38-39, 42, 50,
        57, 62, 65, 75-76, 94, 116-
        17, 119-20, 137 (*see also*
        Cartesian doctrines and
        Spinoza's *TTP*)
    his voluntarism about
        eternal/necessary truths 36,
        40
*Descartes's Principles of
    Philosophy* (Spinoza)
    37, 49-50, 66n
Desire, immoderate 135, 138,
    148, 157n
Determination
    vs. influence 268
    of mind 254, 257, 258, 259,
        261, 263, 264, 265, 267,
        271n
Determinism, in Spinoza 113,
    122-23, 136
de Velthuyzen, Lambert 26-28
DeVolder 166
Diagram(s), a role in geometric
    knowledge 199, 220, 221n
*Dialogues on Metaphysics*
    (Malebranche) 179, 191n
Disagreement, and agreement of
    ideas: *see* Agreement and
    Disagreement.
'Difference'

applied to ideas 3, 19n
– in/of affections 70-71, 73, 76,
    80
  entails difference of attributes
    80-81, 95, 96
– in/of attributes 70, 83, 91, 95,
    107n
  two readings of 85-89, 104n
Dilworth, Mr. and Mrs.
    Richardson 226n
*Discourse on Metaphysics*
    (Leibniz) 161
Disparities, as a kind of
    Leibnizian identity-
    proposition 218, 225n
'Disposition', vs. 'habit' in
    analytic vs. genetic reading
    of Hume 251, 253
Disposition 257, 263
– to affirm *p*
  innate propositions as 200-
    208
  vs. capacity to affirm *p* 202-
    03
  vs. unconscious affirmation of
    *p* 200, 201, 202, 208
Distinct (*also* Different)
  affections, as basis for
    distinguishing substances?
    77-78
  essences 91-92
  qualitatively vs. numerically
    77-78, 91-92, 97
Divine
  concurrence 161, 181-86,
    192n, 193n
  conservation and/vs. creation
    170, 172-80, 228
  holiness 185
  ideas 37, 38, 43, 237, 241
  justice 183, 184
  power 51, 169, 170, 172, 173
    (*see also* Divine will, as
    cause)
Divine nature 61
  finite things participate in
    115-16, 119, 121, 122,
    125, 130
  as related to natural laws 119-

    20, 123-24
Divine will
  as cause 164, 165, 167, 169,
    172, 173, 174, 180, 181,
    228-29
  vs. intellect? 120-121
  kinds of, in Malebranche 164-
    65
  and natural laws 164, 165
  vs. understanding 36-37
Divisibility
  of substance 69
Doctrine of vision in God 237,
    241
Dodgson, C. L. 224n
Donagan, Alan 21n, 47n, 90,
    92-93, 105n, 153n, 155n,
    156n, 158n
Doney, Willis 18n, 187n, 189n
Dualism, Cartesian 126, 128
Duration 38
  and eternity 34
  of individual substance 173,
    176
Du Tertre 181

Ealick, Greg E. x
*Ecclesiastes* (of the Old
    Testament) 136
Economic(s) 141, 142, 145,
    158n
Effect(s) 28
  known through cause 56
  mental events as 257, 261
Efficient cause 56-57, 176, 230
Egoism 131-32, 143-44, 146,
    150, 155n
Egypt(ians) 125
Elster, Jon 158n
Elwes, R. H. 133, 156n
Emanate 7, 26-27
Emotions
  in Spinoza 50-51, 58 (*see also*
    Affects, in Spinoza;
    Passions, in Spinoza)
– in Descartes
  active 21n
  passive 1, 12, 14-17
Empiric(s) 208, 209, 217

Empiricism 252, 252
Empirical consciousness 274,
   284, 290-94, 297, 300
   and epistemic responsibility
   294-97, 298
Empiricist
   conceptual 240
   law(s) of association 286,
   292, 302n
Energy, or power (causal)
   denied by Hume 258, 259
*Enquiry Concerning Human
   Understanding* (Hume) 252,
   255, 258
Enthymeme(s), and valid
   inference in Leibniz's
   innatism 201, 202, 207
Entity of reason 54, 66n
Envy 15
Epistemology (*also*
   Epistemological) 130, 220,
   221, 256, 259, 275, 276,
   292, 294, 298
Epistemic
   advice 292, 293
   responsibility 294-97, 298
   value, of recognizing logical
   form 213, 214, 215, 219
Error
   in Descartes 3, 4, 6, 8, 9, 10
   in Kant 293
*Essay Concerning Human
   Understanding* (Locke) 195,
   221n
Essence(s) or Nature(s)
   their manner of dependence on
   God 31-40
   exist outside the intellect? 29,
   31, 37-38
   vs. ideas of them 29-30
   vs. instantiations of them 29-
   39
 – in Spinoza (*see also* Spinoza,
   on definition and essence)
   of substance, 'constituted by'
   attributes 24, 90-93, 96,
   105n, 106n
   compared with Descartes on
   32-33, 39

defined 56, 58-61
   expressed by definitions 54-
   56, 58, 84
   his God not an instantiation of
   32-33, 35
   vs. mere properties 54-56, 58
Essential, vs. existential 30-32
Eternal, existence 34
Eternal truths 35-37, 40 (*see also*
   Necessary truths)
   Descartes's voluntarism about
   36-37, 40
   Leibniz on 36-37, 41, 210
   in Spinoza 121-23
eternal and infinite modes 76,
   77, 126
Eternity 35
   vs. duration 34
*Ethics* (Spinoza) 37, 43, 82,
   104n, 109
   definition in 52-54, 57-58,
   61-62
   geometrical structure of 49-50,
   52, 62-64
   relation to *TTP* 110, 113-15,
   118-21, 125-26, 128-29,
   131, 135-36, 138-39, 142,
   145, 149, 151-52
Euclid (*also* Euclidean) 49, 56,
   60-61, 122
Evidence, as ground of
   knowledge 216, 217, 218,
   219, 210
Evident, immediately/self-/'very'
   218, 219, 225n
Evil 131
Evolution 291, 303n
Examples, Illustrations,
   Anecdotes
 – Descartes
   Amputated limb/phantom pain
   11, 21n
   Two ideas of the sun 7
   Wax 74-5, 76
   God and nature as King and
   kingdom 120
 – Kant
   man in a far off meadow 291
 – Leibniz

two heavily-laden boats 185, 186

chinese as having no alphabet 200-01

marble and shapes within it 204, 205, 212, 222n

- Spinoza
  promise of fasting 132
  Samuel and Saul's lost asses 124-25

Exhibit, what ideas do 6, 8

Existence
and essence 37, 38, 59
modes of (senses of 'exists') 28-37
vs. reality 5

Existential, vs. essential 30-32

'Exists in itself' 133-34

Explanation
Aristotelian 51, 61
deductive form of 51-52, 61, 64
in Spinoza 51-54, 58, 61, 64

Explanatory rationalism 72, 84, 85, 101-103

Expression (*also* Perception), in Leibnizian substance 162, 163

Extended substance (*see also* Extension)
- in Descartes
  corporeal bodies as parts of 23-24
  as basis for geometry? 41-44
  compared with Spinoza on 25, 28, 32, 39, 45
  as substrate of instantiated geometric shapes 39
- in Spinoza
  compared with Descartes on 24-26, 28, 32, 38-39, 44-45, 75

Extension (the attribute)
in Descartes 23, 75
in Spinoza 25, 38, 43, 45, 75, 118, 120, 122

External
action, of body vs. internal action of mind 126, 127

cause 57-58, 134, 135

Extrinsic, properties 75

Faculty
innate, to affirm certain propositions 204
transcendental, of self-consciousness 291, 296-97, 298, 299

Fabrications, scholastic concepts as 61

Fall, the (Adamic) 168, 169

Fallacy
of composition 238
modal 74

Falsity, material, of ideas 1, 3, 4-5, 11, 14, 18n

Fear 14, 132-33

Feeling 22n
of determination of mind 264, 268, 271n
of truth/credibility of $p$ 214, 219

Feuer, Lewis 159n

Fictions, of the understanding, in Hume 253

Fictitious, essences and truths about them as 40-41

Figural 53

Figure(s)
regular 30-31
- geometrical
  chiliagon 20-21n
  circle 30, 36, 54-56, 60-61, 84
  myriagon 20-21n
  triangle 29-30, 36, 42, 43, 121-22, 213

Finite
- spirits, in Berkeley
  as causally efficacious (vs. bodies as not) 227, 228, 230, 231-34, 236-38
  causally impotent, in early Berkeley 227
  theological constraints on the causal nature of 235-38
- individual substances, in Leibniz 173-4, 175, 176

causal efficacy in 162, 170,
177, 178, 183, 184
as moral agents 184
– things (*also* Modes), in
Spinoza 82
as (partial) causes 124, 125
their relation to God 117-19,
121-22, 124-25, 129, 133-
34
First cause 57
Flew, Antony 254, 263, 264,
265, 270n, 271n
his beginning student 254,
255, 270n
Fogelin, Robert 269n
'Follow from attributes', two
senses of 82
Force(s) 180
in Leibnizian substance 163,
177, 182
'Foreign objects', of Hume's
definition of cause 254,
267, 268
Form(s)
of intuition 253
logical 205, 206, 207, 213,
216
substantial 170
Formal
falsity 3
validity 19n
Foster, J. 243n
Freddoso, Fred 186n, 189n
Freedom
– in Spinoza 133, 142, 150,
153n
of thought and speech 110-11,
127-29
Freeman, E. 155n
Frege, Gottlob 32
Freud, Sigmund 291

Garber, Daniel 190n
Garrett, Don 104n, 305
Gassendi, Pierre 36, 41, 177
Gebhardt xi, 65n
General/logical principles (*also*
Maxims)
knowledge of required for

knowledge of necessary
truths 212-14
vs. particular applications or
instantiations of 199, 206-
207
used but not attended
to/affirmed 201-202, 207-
208
*Genesis* (of the Old Testament)
117, 236, 237, 238, 242
Genetic, (vs. analytic) reading of
Hume on causal inference
251
Geometric(al)
figures, essences of 39-40, 43,
44, 45-6, 60
method, as a form of
demonstration/proof 49-52
knowledge 199, 220, 221n
insight, not the basis of causal
judgment 256
structure of the *Ethics* 49-50,
52, 62-64, 71
Geometrician, atheists as? 41
Geometry 41, 204
Cartesian view of 42-44
Spinozistic view of 42-45
Gerhardt, C. J. xii, 187n
Geulincx, A. 228
Gewirth, Alan 18n
Giancotti, Emilia 153n
Gilson, E. 66n
God
'brings about in toto that *p*'
172, 173, 1
infinite 118, 129, 170
as necessary being 25, 31, 33,
35, 69, 92, 119, 122
omnipotent 181, 183, 228-29
omnipresent 122, 236
perfect 57, 236
as self-caused (*also* self-
conserving) 57, 178
– in Berkeley
relation of human mind to
236-38, 239, 243n
– in Descartes 120
as a cause (*also* creator,
conserver) 27-28, 172, 175-

78, 190n, 228
and eternal truths 36-37, 40
sense of 'exists' as applied to
    28-29, 31-32
as independent 23
as thinking, incorporeal
    substance 23, 38
compared with Spinoza on 24-
    28, 32, 116-17, 120
– in Leibniz 45, 170, 172
and divine concurrence 181-86
and eternal/necessary truths
    36-37, 41, 45
as guarantor of quasi-causal
    concomitance 163, 166-
    67
as source of existences and
    essences 36-37, 38, 39
– in Malebranche
as conserving cause 172, 179,
    180
and divine concurrence 181-84
and power as divine 169, 170
relation of human mind to
    237-38
volition/will of 164, 165,
    167-72
– in Spinoza 85, 92, 106n, 112,
    126 (see also Spinoza, his
    monism; Substance, in
    Spinoza; Divine nature)
and affects 115-16
anthropomorphism of 116,
    120, 121
as cause 28, 57, 123, 124-25
    (see also Power, in Spinoza,
    of God)
identified with corporeal
    universe? 25-28
compared with Descartes on
    24-28, 32, 45,116-17, 120
and determinism 122-23
essence and existence of 33,
    35, 57
sense of 'exists' as applied to
    28, 32
as extended 24-27, 45, 118,
    120, 122
knowledge of 116, 15

man's relation to 116, 117,
    118, 119, 122, 123, 129
relation to natural world and
    natural laws 27-28, 117,
    118, 119-20, 123-24
necessity claims about 25, 26-
    27, 32, 35, 69, 119, 121,
    122, 134
will of 120-21, 124-25
Good (vs. evil) 131
Gorovitz, Samuel x
Grant, William 25, 46n
Gregor, Mary 302n
Grene, M. 47n, 67n, 155n, 156n
Grint, Leslie 187n
Grua, Gaston 187n, 192n

Habit, of mind in causal
    reasoning 247, 248, 249,
    251, 252, 259, 264, 265,
    266, 268
Habitual knowledge 197, 207,
    215
Habitudes and relations 199,
    221n
Hackett, Frances x
Hacking, Ian 222n
Hampshire, Stuart 46n, 47n, 232
Harmful 15
Harmony, pre-established (also
    Concommitance) 161, 162,
    163, 166
Harris, John 25, 45n, 224n
Hart 232
Hartman, Robert 302n
Hatred (also Hate) 15, 127, 131,
    132, 133, 140
Heat
    and cold 1, 3, 4, 5, 6, 8, 9 (see
    also Privation, idea of
    heat/cold as)
    felt when in love 17
Heaven 3
Heereboord 66n
Henrich, Dieter 280, 282, 302n
Herz, Marcus 292, 303n
Hippogriff 30
History, of early modern
    philosophy vii, 110 (see

*also* Seventeenth century)
Hobbes, Thomas 56, 137, 141,
    153n, 158n, 270n
Hobbesian 140, 141, 148
Hooker-Bennett objection 71-
    79, 82, 101, 102
Hooker, Michael 71, 103n (*see
    also* Hooker-Bennett
    objection)
Huggard, E. M. xii, 48n, 188n
Hullett, James x
Human
    bondage 138
    minds, relation to God 236-38
    – will (*also* Volition) 117, 191n
        as cause of bodily movement?
            167, 227, 229, 231, 232,
            234, 243n, 257, 258
        it's role in causal inference
            257, 259, 261
        experience of, as source of idea
            of causality 239, 258
Human being(s)
    distinguishing/essential
        properties of 55, 59, 289,
        294, 296, 299, 302n
Humanity
    'principle'/'party' of, in Hume
        250
Hume, David xi, 229, 242n,
    269n, 292
    and Berkeleyan causality 255,
        256-57, 258, 270n
    Kantian elements in 251, 253-
        54
    on moral sense/judgment 249,
        250
    on self-survey and normativity
        248-50, 259, 263
    on the will 257, 259, 261
    – two definitions of cause 247,
        248, 252, 253
        their relation 254, 262, 263,
            265, 266, 267
        circularity in second? 264-66
    – on customary transition from
        cause to effect 252
        and the definition of cause 253
        as Kantian 253-54

a surprising discovery? 254-
    57
– on mental events as causes and
    effects
    treated just as external causes
        are 257-58
    and the nature of causal
        inference 259-63
– on rules for causal
    inference/judgment 245,
    247, 248, 268
    analytic vs. genetic reading of
        251-52
    as reflexive and normative
        245, 247-51, 252, 259, 263
Hybrid
    conclusions 204, 206
    aspects of Cartesian
        representation 8, 11
Hyman, Jeremy 186n
Hypothetical(s)
    claims about geometrical
        figures as 40
    properties understood in terms
        of 55
    Spinoza's definitions as 63
Hypothetico-deductive system,
    Spinoza's *Ethics* as 63, 64

Idealist 258
Ideas
    divine 37, 38, 43, 237, 241
    – in Berkeley
        causally impotent like bodies
            238
        causes of 232, 233
        concepts as, and their origin
            239-41
        of imagination vs. sense 232
    – in Descartes
        causes of 11, 18n
        clear and distinct 3, 4, 31, 43-
            44
        concept of 2-3
        confused or obscure 3, 9-10,
            14
        of things having true and
            immutable natures 29, 30,
            31

vs. judgments 3, 6
objectless 4, 5, 15, 16, 17
sensory, as representational 1-
    11, 13, 18n
– in Hume
comparison of, and necessity
    260-61
of constantly conjoined
    events 246
and impressions 254, 257,
    261-62, 267
– in Locke 205
agreement and disagreement of
    196, 197, 198, 208-09,
    213, 214, 219
as constituents of
    propositions 196ff, 221n
relations among, in necessary
    propositions 198, 199,
    221n
– in Spinoza 38
true 42-44
Identical
elements of synthesized states
    and concepts 284
self 274, 279, 280
Identity
axiomatic 218, 226n
and change 75-76
and diversity of ideas,
    necessary propositions as
    asserting 198
numerical 279
qualitative, of affections 96-
    97
qualitative, of attributes 91,
    95
qualitative (vs. numerical) 77-
    78, 91, 96
of substance and its attributes?
    89-90, 105n
– propositions
and Lockean ideas 198, 199
Leibnizian innate necessary
    truths as 205, 209, 217,
    218, 219, 225n
Identity of Indiscernibles
applied to affections 98-100
applied to substances 74, 75-

76, 77-78, 79
temporal version of 75-76
Idolatry, ascriptions of causal
    powers as? 235-38
Illustrations (anecdotes,
    examples): see Examples,
    illustrations, anecdotes.
Image(s) 285
confused 14
ideas as 3, 14, 239
thoughts as 12, 14
Image of God, man created in
    117, 236, 237, 238, 244n
Imaginary, essences and truths
    about them as 40, 41
Imagination
in Descartes 20n, 29
in Hume 246, 254, 262, 268
in Kant 285
in Spinoza 64
Immanent causality 28, 106n
Immaterialism
Berkeley's, and it's push
    toward occasionalism 228,
    232-33, 242
Immediate
vs. mediate perception of
    agreement/disagreement of
    ideas 198
affirmation/assent and
    immediately evident
    propositions 205, 206, 217
Immoderate desire 135, 138,
    148, 157n
Immutable and true nature(s)
ideas of things having 29, 30,
    31
of a triangle 43
Immutability 120
Impression(s)
in Hume 253, 254, 257, 258,
    259, 264
'in and conceived through' 80,
    101, 102, 107n
Incoherence of divine
    concurrence argument (for
    occasionalism) 164, 180-83
Incompatible, affections 78
Indiscernible (also

Indistinguishable),
  substances 74, 75, 76, 77
Individual substance(s) 173-4,
  175, 176
– in Leibniz 169, 170, 177, 178
  causal efficacy in 162, 170,
    177, 178, 183, 184
  as moral agents 184
Individuation 19n (*see also*
  Difference)
Inductive
  inference 269n
– knowledge
  in Spinoza 64
  in Berkeley, vs. *a priori*, of
    causal connection 231, 232,
    238
Inertia 134
Infallible, vs. metaphysically
  necessary connection 171
Inference
  causal, in Hume 245-52, 253,
    254, 259-62, 265, 266,
    267, 268
  valid, and Leibnizian innatism
    201, 202, 212, 214, 215,
    223n
Infinite (*also* Infinity)
  analysis and Leibnizian
    necessity 171
  concept of 240
  as applied to God 118, 129,
    170
  modes 76, 77, 126
  substance 69
  human will as 117
Influence
  causal, between finite
    substances? 162, 166
  vs. determination 268
'in itself'
  'conceived...', substance as
    70, 73, 80, 86, 87, 88, 90
  'exists...' 133-34
Innate
  behavioral tendencies, in
    Locke 214
  capacity to affirm *p*, vs.
    disposition to affirm *p* 202-

03
– propositions, Leibnizian 221n
  as dispositions to affirm *p*
    200-08, 222n
  easiest and most natural to
    affirm? 204, 206
  general principles/maxims as
    201, 202, 206, 207, 208
  necessary truths as 204, 206,
    210, 211
  have no origin in outer senses
    203-04
  against 'universal assent'
    argument for 200
  as unconsiously affirmed
    propositions? 200, 201,
    202, 208, 209, 222n, 223n
  use of vs. affirmation
    of/attention to 201-02,
    207, 208, 215, 223n
  vs. thoughts 200
– knowledge 195, 216-17
  evidence for in practical
    reasoning 214-16
  Leibniz vs. Locke on 208-16
  inner source of, properly
    reliable 210-11
  required for knowledge of
    necessary truths 211-14
Inner Sense 281, 283, 286, 287,
  288, 289-90, 294
Instance(s)
  of single attribute 90, 95-96,
    101
  of causal law/regularity 251,
    253, 254
Instantiation of true and
  immutable natures 30-31,
  35, 37, 39
  modes as 33
  substance as 34, 35
Instinct, in causal reasoning 253
Intellect 122, 150
  relation of essences to 29, 37-
    38
  God's, vs. His will 120-21
  man's, vs. immagination 130
Intellectual perception 211
Intelligible 253, 269n

Interest(s), self 133-34 (*see also*
    Egoism)
Internal
    action, of mind vs. external,
        of body 126-27
    cause 57
    perception 257, 258
'in toto'
    bringing about, that *p* 172,
        173, 179, 180
    conserving 178, 179, 190n
Intrinsic
    difference, between instances
        of an attribute 96
    property 75
Introspection 240, 280, 295
Intrusion argument (against
    occasionalism) 166, 167,
    168, 169
Intuition
    Kantian 282, 286
Intuitive knowledge 217, 218,
    226n
Invention
    of ideas 29, 31
Involve (*also* Involving)
    as relation between
        (Spinozistic) concepts 86,
        87, 88
Israelites 125
'*I think*', in Kant
    accompanies all cognitive
        states 273, 274, 277, 279
    and conscious unity of our
        states 289, 290
    as a synthesized unity to
        which any state must
        possibly belong 277, 278,
        279

Jarrett, Charles 156n, 157n,
    159n
Jessop, T. E. 153n, 243n
Jesus 154n
Jew(s) (*also* Jewish) 113, 117,
    129, 154n
Joachim, H. H. 25, 45n, 46n,
    47n
Jolley, Nicholas 303n, 204n,
    305
John, St. 115
    gospel of 115-16
Johnson, Samuel 243n, 270n
Joy, Lynn 186n, 189n
Judaeo-Christian 117
Judgment (*also* Judging)
    vs. idea in Descartes 3, 6
    Kantian 284, 298
'*jus*' 132, 156n
Justice, divine 183, 184

Kant, Immanuel
    and epistemic responsibility
        294-97, 298
    and Hume 251, 253-54, 277
    on inner sense 281, 283, 286,
        287, 288, 289-90, 294
    on knowledge: *see*
        Knowledge, in Kant.
    on recognition in a concept
        283-85, 286
    and representation 277, 284,
        286, 287, 298, 301n
    on spontaneity 285-90, 298,
        299, 300, 302n
– Apperception
    vs. inner sense 287-88
    as ownership of mental states
        273, 275, 276 (*see also*
        Kant, and the ownership
        thesis)
    pure (vs. empirical) 286, 287
    and self-consciousness 273-74
        (*see also* Kant, and
        consciousness)
    and spontaneity 285-90
    transcendental 278, 298, 299
    unity of 273, 274, 276, 278,
        287-88, 300
– and Consciousness
    *a priori* 279
    of cognitive states 274, 274,
        283, 284, 287, 290-97
    empirical 274, 284, 290-94,
        296, 297, 298, 299, 300
    self- 274, 275, 279, 281, 282,
        286, 287, 290-97
    of synthesizing of cognitive

states 280-82, 283, 287
of sponteneity 286
- 'I think' 281, 290, 299
  accompanies all cognitive
    states 273, 274, 277, 279
  and conscious unity of our
    states 289, 290
  as a synthesized unity to
    which any state must
    possibly belong 277, 278,
    279
- and the ownership thesis (of
    apperception)
  Bennet on 273, 274, 275, 276
  motivated by the adjectival
    status of congnitive states?
    276, 278
  the role of unity of cognitive
    states in 277-79
- and psychology 276, 302n
  empirical vs. transcendental
    288
  influence of Eighteenth
    century 276, 289, 293
  vs. 'logic' 286-87, 302n
- and synthesis (also unity) of
    cognitive states 290-91,
    299
  acts of, as conscious 280-82,
    283, 287, 297-98
  and conceptual recognition
    284-85
  and 'I think' 277-78
  necessary knowledge 278-79,
    300
Kashap, S. Paul 46n, 47n
Kemp Smith, Norman 301n
Kennington, Richard 103n
Kenny, Anthony xii, 18n, 29,
    47n
Kirklin, Dan x
Kingdom 120, 128
Kitcher, Patricia 244n, 301-02n,
    305
Klefmann, Jacob 154n
Knowing, as conceiving 81
Knowledge
  a priori 198, 210, 221n, 231,
    232

actual (vs. habitual) 197, 217
causal ground of 210, 216,
    220
definition of (Locke) 196
demonstrative 198, 213, 217,
    220
evidential ground of 216, 217,
    218, 219, 220
and God's ideas, in
    Malebranche 237
geometrical 43, 199, 220,
    221n
habitual 197, 207, 215
inductive 64, 210, 217, 231,
    232, 238
intuitive 217, 218, 226n
potential 216-17
of necessary truths: see
    Knowledge, in Leibniz (vs.
    Locke), of necessary truths.
- of causal connection
  in Berkeley 231, 232, 238
  in Hume 231, 255-56
- in Kant
  synthetic unity of cognitive
    states necessary for 278-79
    (see also Epistemic
    responsibility)
- in Leibniz (vs. Locke), of
    necessary truths
  empirics know without
    perceiving
    agreement/disagreement?
    208-09, 224n
  his five kinds of 216-21
  reliable source of, as
    inner/innate 210-11, 217
  requires innate logical
    principles 212-14
- in Locke
  a priori 198, 210
  actual vs. habitual 197, 198,
    207
  definition of, as perception of
    agreement/disagreement
    197, 221n
  empirical 198
  intuitive vs. demonstrative
    198

of necessary truths 198-99
  (*see also* Knowledge, in
  Leibniz (vs. Locke), of
  necessary truths)
– in Spinoza 64, 130
  of a cause 80, 81
  of God 61, 116, 151
  natural 62, 116
  'order of' 61
  prophetic 116, 154n
Kruger, Lorenz 221n
Kuehn, Manfred x, 253, 269n,
  304n
Kulstad, Mark A. x, 244n, 303n,
  306

Labrousse, Elisabeth188n
Ladd, Cathy x
Lamy, F. 170
Lara, Nydia 22n
Law(s)
  of association, Empiricist
    286, 292, 302
  of contradiction 201, 217
  kinds of, in Malebranche 165,
    166, 168, 189n
  of logic (*see also* Logical
    principles) 224n
Laws of nature 168, 230, 236
  suspendable by creatures? 168-
    69, 189n
– in Descartes
  as derived from the divine
    nature 120
  as universal and explanatory
    119
– in Spinoza
  man(kind) as subject to 131
  e.g. of motion and rest 119-
    20, 122, 124, 125
  their relation to the divine
    nature 119, 120, 123-26
  as universal and explanatory
    119, 122, 124, 125, 126,
    136
Lazzeri, Christian 138, 157n
Leibniz, G. W. xii, 29, 45, 47n,
  48n, 61, 66n, 76, 133,
  154n, 187n, 188n, 241,

  244n, 292
  on apperception 289, 291,
    303n
  on causality, real and quasi-
    161-64, 169, 170, 188n
  deep metaphysics of, vs.
    common sense 162
  on divine concurrence 181,
    182, 183, 184, 185, 186
  on essences as divine ideas 37,
    38, 42-43
  on essences as possibilities
    39-40
  on eternal truths 36-37, 41,
    210
  on senses of 'exists' 30-32, 35
  expression/perception in 162,
    163
  on God 163, 170, 177, 172,
    176, 177 (*see also* Leibniz,
    on divine concurrence)
  and the identity of
    indiscernibles 76, 77
  individual (finite) substances
    in 162, 170, 177, 178, 183,
    184
  and innate propositions: *see*
    Innate propositions,
    Leibnizian.
  and Kant 289, 291, 303n
  on knowledge of necessary
    truths: *see* Innate
    Knowledge; Knowledge, in
    Leibniz.
  on the mind's causal relation
    to the body 163, 166, 167,
    168
  against occasionalism: *see*
    Leibniz and Malebranche,
    on occasionalism.
  and pre-established harmony
    (*also* concommitance) 161,
    162, 163, 166
  and Spinoza (*see also* Leibniz-
    Bennett objection) 31, 71,
    76, 91, 103n, 133
  and the spontaneity thesis
    161, 162, 168, 169, 178
  and the world-apart thesis 161,

162, 169
- and Descartes
  on divine conservation and
    creation 175, 176, 177, 178
  on essences/eternal truths and
    God 36-38, 40
- and Locke 195-96
  on innate propositions 200-
    08
  on knowledge of necessary
    truths 208-16
  on kinds of knowledge 216-21
- and Malebranche 161
  on divine concurrence 181-84
  on divine conservation 172,
    174, 178, 179
  on mental-physical causality
    166-68
  on necessary causal
    connection 171-72
  on power as divine 170
Leibniz-Bennett objection 72,
  83-84, 86, 89-91, 93-94,
  96, 98-100, 101, 102,
  105n, 106n, 107n
Lelong, J. 182, 183
Lennon, Thomas M. xii, 188n,
  242n
l' Hospital, 166
Limitation (*also* Imperfection)
  185, 186
Livingston, Donald 252, 269n
Location, spatial 75
Locke, John xii, 221n, 255,
  257, 302n, 303n
  and Berkeley on the origin of
    concepts/ideas 239-40
  and consciousness of one's
    own cognitive states 293-
    94, 294
  and Kant 281, 289
- on knowledge (*see also*
    Knowledge, in Leibniz (vs.
    Locke), of necessary truths)
  actual vs. habitual 197, 198,
    207
  *a priori* 198, 210
  definition of, as perception of
    agreement/disagreement

197, 199, 221n
  empirical 198
  intuitive vs. demonstrative
    198
- and Leibniz 195-96
  on innate propositions 200-
    208
  on knowledge of necessary
    truths 208-16
  on kinds of knowledge 216-21
- on propositions
  mentral vs. verbal 196
  relation of general to
    particular 199
  truth of, as
    agreement/disagreement of
    ideas 196, 197, 208-209
  necessary, kinds of 198
Lockean 255, 282
Loeb, Louis 229, 243n
Loemker, Leroy L.  xiii, 187n
*Logic* (Kant) 285
Logic 213
  of causal reasoning, in Hume
    245, 248, 249
  laws of 213-14
  and psychology, in Kant 286-
    87, 302n
Logical form (*also* Propositional
    form)
  and innatism in Leibniz and
    Locke 205, 206, 207, 212,
    213, 225n,
Logical principles 224n
  innate knowledge of, required
    for knowledge of necessary
    truths 212-14
Long proofs 293
Love
  in Spinoza 58, 115, 127, 131,
    132
  and Hatred 15, 131, 132,
  sensual (*also* Sensuous) 17
  rational 17
Lucas, Peter G.187n
Luce, A. A. 243n
Lyons, William 22n

Macnabb, D. G. C. 264, 270n,

271n
Maimon, 303n
Malcolm, Norman 21n
Malebranche, Nicolas xii, 25,
    45n, 157n, 161,187n, 190n
  against causal powers in
    Nature 169-70, 235-39
  on creation vs. conservation
    179, 180
  on the finite mind's relation to
    God 237-38
  on God's volition/will (and its
    causal efficacy) 164, 165,
    167-71, 172, 191n
  on laws 165, 166, 168, 169,
    189n
– and arguments for
    occasionalism
  incoherence of divine
    concurrence 180-84
  conservation 172-74, 178,
    179, 180
  necessary connection 171-72,
    228-29
  'to be powerful is divine' 169,
    170
– and Berkeley 227, 228, 230,
    232, 233, 234, 235
  on causal connection as
    necessary? 230
  on causal efficacy of finite
    spirits/volition 227, 228,
    232-34
  on idolatry and ascriptions of
    causal power 235-36, 241,
    242, 244n
  on the origin of our concept of
    causality 239-41
– and Leibniz 161
  on causal necessity 171-72
  on divine concurrence 181,
    182, 183, 184
  on divine conservation 172,
    174, 178, 179, 182
  on mental-physical causality
    166, 167, 168
  on power as divine 170
Mandelbaum, M. 155n
Man(kind)

Cartesian view of 117, 128
  created in God's image 177,
    236, 237
– Spinoza on
  and civil society 129, 139ff
  relation to God 116, 117, 118,
    119, 122, 123, 129 (see
    also Finite things, in
    Spinoza)
  a part of nature 128-29, 131
Marble 204, 205, 212, 223n
Marrano 129
Markie, Peter 18n
Mass term (vs. count) 24
Material falsity 3-5, 11, 14, 18n
Mathematical truth(s) 36, 199,
    222n
Mathematics (also
    Mathematician) 66n, 199,
    209, 213, 221n
Matheron, Alexandre 138, 156n,
    157n, 158n
Matson, Wallace 85-86
Mattern, Ruth 221n
Matusow, Allen x
McCracken, C. J. 243n
Meadow 291
Meaning
  and definition in Spinoza 53-
    54
  and the 'nuclear sense' of a
    term 56, 58
Mechanism 180
  for epistemic assessment 293,
    297
Medieval 66n, 121
Meditationes Chretiennes et
    Metaphysiques
    (Malebranche) 179
Meditations on First Philosophy
    (Descartes)
  Second 74
  Third 1, 2, 7, 8, 12, 13, 14,
    17, 18n, 22n, 175
  Fourth 117
  Fifth 29
Memory 295, 303n
Mental
  acts, conscious of? 280-82

events, as causes and effects
    257-63
Mere possibilities 40
Mersenne, Marin 36, 40
Metaphysical
    necessity 171, 176
    possibility 175, 176
    requirement, of Leibniz, of
        Malebranche 183, 184
Metaphysics
    Berkeley's 228
    deep, at odds with common
        sense 162-64
    Leibniz's 172, 221
    Spinoza's 71, 103n, 104n
*Metaphysical Thoughts*
    (Spinoza) 34, 37, 66n
Meyer, Ludwig 34
Miller, George A. 295
Mind
    theologically-permissible
        causal ascriptions to, in
        Berkeley and Malebranche
        234-38
    relation to body, in Descartes
        2, 12, 129
    philosophy of 126, 129
  – in Leibniz
    causal relation to body 162,
        163, 166, 167, 168, 169
    innate faculty of, to affirm
        certain propositions 204,
        205
  – in Spinoza
    ascribed to God? 116, 120,
        121, 123
    relation to body 118, 126,
        128, 129, 139
    exempt from external causal
        influence? 127, 128
    human, relation to God 129,
        130
    under less control of sovereign
        than body 127
    as mode of thinking substance
        24, 118
Mind-body relationship 2, 12,
        118, 126, 128, 129, 139,
        144-45, 151-52, 162, 163,

    165, 166, 167, 168, 169,
        229, 236-37
Miracles
    in Malebranche, distinguished
        from non- 165
    in Spinoza 124
Misrepresent 1, 5, 20n
Mockery 15
Modal fallacy 74
Mode(s) 18n
    defined 42, 96, 98
    eternal and infinite 76, 77,
        126
    sense of 'exists' as applied to
        33-34, 38
    finite 82
Modifications (i.e. Leibnizian
    accidents)192n
Monism: *see* Spinoza, his
    monism.
Moral, sense 249
Morality
    Humean 249, 250
    Spinozistic 140, 143, 150
Moreau, P. -F. 153n
Morris, Mary xii, 188n
Morris, Thomas V. 189n
Mossner, E. C. 270n
Motion 167, 168, 180, 185,
        186, 191n, 230, 256
    and rest, laws of 119-20, 122,
        124, 125
Murdoch, Dugald xi, 187n, 242n
Myriagon 20-21n

Naess, Arne 156n, 157n
Nagel, Ernest 51, 65n
*Nagelate Schriften* (Spinoza;
    Dutch trans.) 105n
Narrow content 18n
Nash, Ronald A. 21n
Natural
    cause 229
    light 255, 270n
    relation (vs. philosophical)
        262, 263, 267, 271n
Nature, divine: *see* Divine
    nature.
Nature

laws of: *see* Laws of nature.
as philosophers have
    understood it, a chimera
    235, 236
Spinoza's God as 27, 28
Natures or essences: *see*
    Essence(s) or nature(s).
Necessary
    being 25, 31, 33, 35
    existence of Spinozistic
        substance 25, 33, 34-35, 85
    instantiation of a nature or
        essence 34
    relation between a thing and
        its essential properties 59
– truths
    as identities, in Leibniz 205,
        209, 217, 218, 219, 225n
    and infinite analysis, in
        Leibniz 171
    as innate 204ff
    knowledge of: *see* Knowledge,
        in Leibniz, of necessary
        truths.
Necessary connection 169, 171,
    176, 228, 229, 230, 241
    vs. infallible 171
Necessary connection argument
    (for occasionalism) 169,
    171, 176, 228-29, 230
Necessity 26
    causal 171, 176, 228, 229
    our idea of, in Hume 258, 259,
        260-61, 263, 266, 267
    logical 229
    metaphysical 171, 176
    physical 171
*New Essays on Human
    Understanding* (Leibniz)
    195, 199
Nicole, P. 225
Nidditch, P. H. xi, xii, 221n,
    242n, 269n
Non-thing 3, 5, 19n
Normative, character of Hume's
    rules for causal judgment
    245, 248-51, 252, 259, 263
Normore, Calvin 21n
Noumena 253

Nuclear sense 56, 58
Nugent, Thomas 302n

Obedience 126, 132
*Objections and Replies*
    (Descartes)
    First Set 18n, 176
    Third Set 21n
    Fourth Set 1, 7, 10
    Fifth Set 36, 177
Objective
    existence in the intellect 5
    reality 19n
Obscure idea(s): *see* Confused
    idea(s)/thought(s).
Occasional cause 163, 165, 167,
    168, 169ff, 228-29 (*see
    also* Occasionalism)
Occasionalism
    in Berkeley? 227-28, 230-34
    Cartesian weak conservation
        argument for 175, 176, 177,
        178, 190n
    in Malebranch 161, 164, 165,
        167, 168
– Malebranchian arguments for
    conservation 171
    incoherence of divine
        concurrence 169, 181, 182,
        183
    necessary connection 171
    'to be powerful is divine' 169,
        170
    Leibnizian responses to 166-
        69, 170, 171-2, 181-83
Occult qualities 61
Odor(s) 1, 12, 13
Oldenburg, Henry 27, 28, 111,
    154n, 155n
Olscamp, Paul J. xii, 188n, 242n
Omnipotence 181, 183, 228-29
Omnipresence 122, 236
Ontological
    argument 31
    economy 181
Ontology
    Leibniz's 169, 170, 183
    Spinoza's 183
'Order of the argument' 61

Ostens, Jacob 26-27
Overdetermination 168, 228
Ownership thesis (of
    apperception)
    Bennett on the 273, 274, 275,
        276
    motivated by adjectival status
        of mental states? 276, 278
    the role of unity of cognitive
        states in 277-79

Pain 11, 12, 164-65, 214
Parkinson, G. H. R. xii, 47n,
    65n, 67n, 133, 157n, 188n,
    306
Pasley, Victoria x
Passions 249
    in Descartes 2, 17 (see also
        Emotions, Descartes on)
    in Spinoza 138-39, 141 (see
        also Emotions, Spinoza on;
        Affects, in Spinoza)
Passions of The Soul (Descartes)
    1, 12, 15, 16
Passive emotions 1, 12, 14-17
Passmore, John 263, 264, 270n
Perception
    internal 257, 258
    in Kant 286, 302n
    in Leibniz (also Expression)
        162, 163
    in Locke, of propositions and
        their consituent ideas 197,
        198, 199, 205, 211
Perfection(s) 57, 116, 118, 170,
    182, 185, 186
Personal identity 253, 264
Philosophical Commentaries
    (Berkeley) 227, 232, 235
Philosophical, relation (vs.
    natural) 262, 263, 267
Physical necessity 171
Physics
    Cartesian 41-42, 62
    Spinozistic 62, 154n
Physiological state/condition
    15, 17
Pity 15
Platonic, concept of eternity 35

Platonists, their version of
    innate knowledge 211-12,
    224n
Pleasure 13, 58
Political Philosophy 110, 135
Politics and the state
    in Spinoza 110, 111, 127-28,
        131, 136-37, 138, 140,
        141, 142, 143, 144, 145,
        146, 149, 150
Pollock, Frederick 25, 46n
Positive idea or object of idea 5-
    7 (see also Privation)
Possibilities (also Possibles) 40
Possibility, logical 229
Posterior Analytics (Aristotle)
    51
Power
    causal, in Nature? 169-70,
        235-39
    divine 51, 169, 170, 172, 173
        (see also Divine will, as
        cause)
    or energy, denied by Hume
        258, 259
    – in Spinoza
        of finite things 133-34
        of God 133-34, 157n
        of sovereign 126, 127-28,
            132
Powers, the brothers at Wayne
    State University 186n
Pragmatic, basis for Humean
    normativity 249, 250
Predestination 113
Predicate(s) 77, 78, 79
Prediction, and Humean causality
    248, 253, 263
Pre-established harmony (also
    Concommitance) 161, 162,
    163, 166
Prejudice(s), Spinoza on their
    removal 65, 111, 113
Preordination (also
    Predetermination) 163, 183
Presentation and representation
    7, 9-10, 13-14, 21
Preservation, self- 133, 139,
    140, 142, 152

Primary/secondary quality 2, 119
Principle of sufficient reason
     175
Principle property 23, 45n, 75,
     94
Principles, innate
     general/logical
   evidence for, in practical
     reasoning 214-16
   vs. particular
     instance/application of
     206-07
   used, but not affirmed/attended
     to 201-02, 207-08, 212
   required for knowledge of
     necessary truths 212-14
*Principles of Human Knowledge*
     (Berkeley) 230
*Principles of Philosophy*
     (Descartes) 1, 2, 8, 12, 14,
     15, 16, 20n, 31, 74-5, 119,
     120, 175
Priority
   epistemic, of some innate
     principles over others 204,
     223n
   logical, of substances over
     their locations 75
   conceptual, of substance over
     affections 70, 71, 73, 74,
     77, 79, 80, 83
Private, mental events as 126,
     129
Privation(s) 3, 7
   cold/heat as 4, 5, 6, 9, 10, 11
Probability 269n
   unphilosophical 251
Productive cause 174, 177, 179
Promise 132
Proof 49
   and demostrative knowledge,
     in Locke 198
   and inference, in Leibniz's
     innatism about necessary
     truths 212, 218, 220
Proofs, long 293
Property, vs. essence in Spinoza
     54-56
Proposition(s)

general, vs. particular
     instances/applications of
     them 199, 206-07
   geometrical 49, 195
– innate Leibnizian 221n
   as dispositions to affirm *p*
     200-08, 222n
   easiest and most natural to
     affirm? 204, 206
   general principles/maxims as
     201, 202, 206, 207, 208
   necessary truths as 204, 206,
     210, 211
   have no origin in outer senses
     203-04
   against 'universal assent'
     argument for 200
   as unconsiously affirmed
     propositions? 200, 201,
     202, 208, 209, 222n, 223n
   use of vs. affirmation
     of/attention to 201-02,
     207, 208, 215, 22
   vs. thoughts 200
– Lockean
   mental vs. verbal 196
   relation of general to
     particular 199
   truth of, as
     agreement/disagreement of
     ideas 196, 197, 208-09
   necessary, kinds of 198
   negative and affirmative 196
Proximate cause 124, 172, 176
Psychological entities, concepts
     as 239, 241
Psychology
   in Spinoza 131, 136, 137,
     138
– in Kant 276, 302n
   empirical vs. transcendental
     288
   influence of Eighteenth
     century 276, 284, 293
   vs. 'logic' 286-87, 302n

Qualitative identity
   of affections 96-97
   of attributes 91, 95

vs. numerical 77-78, 91, 96
Qualities
    primary and secondary 2, 119
    sensible 1ff (*see also* Colors;
        Heat and Cold; Odors;
        Sounds)
Quasi-causality 161, 162, 163,
    164, 167, 168, 169, 170,
    188n

Rationalism (*also* Rationalist)
    171, 172, 248, 249, 269n
    explanatory 72, 84, 85, 101-
        103
Rational(ity)
    essential to humans? 59
    Spinoza on 142, 144-45
Real definition 53
Real existence/thing 18n
Real qualities (*also* 'real and
    positive') 4
Reality, in Descartes
    vs. existence 5
    more or less 9
    objective and formal 19n
Reason 138
    the handmaid of Theology 112
    (vs. passions) as guide to
        behavior 138-39, 144, 148
    of the rationalists, rejected by
        Hume 248, 249
Reason(s)
    or cause 80-81
    causes of beliefs as 248
    entity of 54, 66n
Reasoning
    causal 245, 247, 248 (*see also*
        Inference, causal)
    rules of good 294
Recognition, in a concept,
    Kantian 283-85, 286
Recollection, Platonist's innate
    knowledge as 211, 212
Referential, component of
    representation 7-11, 16
Reflection
    its role in causal reasoning
        245, 246
    in Kant 286, 287, 294, 299

*Regulae* (Descartes) 292, 297,
    303n
Regularity, causal/lawlike 120,
    231, 254, 255, 256, 26
Regular
    figure 30, 31
    solid 31, 41
Reimarus, Hermann Samuel 289,
    294
Relational theory of space 75
Relation, philosophical vs.
    natural 262, 263, 267
Remnant, Peter xii,
Remond, Nicolas 181
Repetition, of event sequences in
    Humean causality 245, 256
*Replies* (Descartes): see
    *Objections and Replies.*
Representation (*also*
    Representing)
    causal theory of 11
    demonstrative 11
    in Kant 277, 284, 286, 287,
        298, 301n
    and passive emotions 12, 13,
        14
    presentational vs.
        representational notions of
        7-11, 14, 16, 21n
    and sensation 1-5, 7-14, 16,
        18n, 19n, 20n, 21n
Resemblance 1, 261, 268
*res extensa* 25
Responsibility
    epistemic 294-97, 298
    moral 296, 297
Revelation, Biblical 110, 113,
    154n
Right (ie, a just
    entitlement/privilege) 132,
    133, 134, 14
    rendering of '*jus*' 132, 156n
Robinet, Andre 45n, 188n
Robinson, H. 243n
Robinson, Minranda x
Rosenberg, Alexander 269n,
    271n
Roth, Leon 49, 65n
Rousseau, Jean Jacques 300

Rules, for causal
   inference/judgment, Hume's
   245-52
Russell, Bertrand 39, 46n, 48n,
   52, 66n, 77, 104n

Sadness 15, 16
Samuel (of Old Testament) 124-
   25
'save the appearances',
   Leibnizian efforts to 162,
   163
Saville, Anthony 224n
Scepticism: *see* Skepticism
Schacht, Richard 46n
Schematism 285
Scholastic(s) 59, 61, 66n
Schrecker, Paul 187n
Schwartz, Wolfgang 302n
Schwerin, Alan x
Scripture (*also* Bible, Biblical)
   110, 111, 112, 115, 116,
   119, 124, 125, 126, 136,
   154n, 235, 236, 237
   references to passages in, by
   Spinoza 115, 124, 125, 136
Scruton, Roger 25, 46n
*Search After Truth* (Malebranche)
   170, 235
Secondary cause 178, 228, 235
Selby-Bigge, L. A. xi, 242n,
   269n
Self-survey/-application,
   Humean test of rules as
   normative 247-51
Self-consciousness
   in Hume, its role in causal
   inference/reasoning 247,
   250, 259
   in Kant's B131-32 passage on
   apperception 274, 275,
   279, 281, 282, 286, 287,
   289, 298
Self preservation 133, 139, 140,
   152, 249
Sempiternal(ity) 34
Sensation (*also* Sense[s]) 233,
   240, 243n
   – in Descartes

(vs. Gassendi) as source of
   ideas of figures? 36, 39
   internal vs. external 16
   representationality of 1ff
   positive: *see* Privation
   objects of, in Spinoza 61
Sense
   common 162, 164
   confused, of truth of a
   proposition 208, 217
   moral 249
   inner 281, 283, 286, 287,
   288, 289-90, 294
Sensible qualities 1ff (*see also*
   Colors; Heat and Cold;
   Odors; Sounds)
Sensory states, and Berkeleian
   physical objects 233
Seventeenth century 162, 164,
   184, 188n, 228, 236, 237
Shirley, Samuel 156n
*Short Treatise* (Spinoza) 55, 56,
   136, 152
Signs, of cause and effect in
   Berkeley 230, 256
Simultaneous, possession of
   distinct affections 78
Sin 30
   God's concurrence with 184-
   86, 192n, 193n
Singular causal inference 254
Siren 30, 143
Size, of extended substance
   essential to it? 76
Skepticism
   in Hume 255, 259, 260, 269n
   in Locke 195
Sleigh, Robert C. Jr. x, 189, 306
Smith, Norman Kemp 301n
Society (*also* Social) 140, 142,
   143, 145, 146, 148, 150
   (*see also* Cooperation, and
   community in Spinoza)
Solomon, Robert C. 21n
Soul: *see* Spirits; Union of soul
   and body.
Sounds 3, 14, 21n
Sovereign, Spinoza on power of
   126, 127-28, 132

Space (*see also* Extension;
    Extended substance)
and extended substance in
    Spinoza 25, 26, 75
relational theory of 75
Spatial location 75
Spinoza, Baruch xi, xii, xiii,
    46n, 47n, 48n, 153n
    on the nature and kinds of
        causes 27, 28, 56, 57, 123,
        124
    on definition and essence 52-
        58, 60-61, 62
    compared with Descartes 24-
        29, 31-32, 34, 38-39, 42,
        50, 57, 62, 65, 75-76, 94,
        116-17, 119-120, 137 (*see
        also* Cartesian doctrines and
        Spinoza's *TTP*)
    determinism in 113, 122-23,
        136
    on the emotions/passions 50,
        51, 58, 138-39, 141 (*see
        also* Affects, in Spinoza)
    on essence(s): *see* Spinoza,
        on definition and essence;
        Essence(s) and nature(s), in
        Spinoza.
    and the *Ethics*; *see Ethics*
    kinds of existence in 33-34,
        37
    and explanation 51-54, 58,
        61, 64
    God in 24, 25, 26, 27, 28, 33,
        34, 38, 55, 56, 57, 60, 82,
        92, 106n, 112, 115, 116,
        117, 118, 120, 121, 122,
        123, 124, 125, 126, 134,
        151 (*see also* Substance, in
        Spinoza)
    on knowledge 61, 62, 64, 81,
        130
    on man's relation to God 116,
        117, 118, 119, 122, 123,
        129
    his monism 24, 69-70, 71,
        72, 73, 79, 83, 94, 102-
        103, 103n
    on nature and laws of nature:

        *see* Laws of nature, Spinoza
        on.
    on politics and the state 110,
        111, 127-28, 131, 136-37,
        138, 140, 141, 142, 143,
        144, 145, 146, 149, 150
    on power of sovereigns 126,
        127, 128, 132
    and psychology 131, 136,
        137, 138
    on scripture and Biblical
        criticism 110, 111, 112,
        115, 116
    on Substance: *see* Substance,
        in Spinoza.
    temporal concepts in 34-35
Spirits
    animal 167, 236
    – finite, in Berkeley
        causally efficacious (vs.
            bodies as not) 227, 228,
            230, 231, 232, 233, 234,
            236-38
        causally impotent, in early
            Berkeley 227
        theological constraits on the
            causal nature of 235-38
Spontaneity (*also* Spontaneous)
    causal thesis of, in Leibniz
        161, 162, 168, 169, 178,
        188n
    in Kant 285-90, 298, 299,
        200, 302n
State(s)
    of created substances 162,
        171, 173, 174, 175, 176,
        177, 188n
    sensory, in Berkeley 233
State of nature 140, 142, 148,
    150, 158n
Stich, Stephen 221n
Stipulative definition 52
Stoothoff, Robert xi, 187n,
    242n
Strauss, Leo 153n
Suarez, Francisco 66n
Substance
    count vs. mass conception of
        24

extended: *see* Extended
   substance.
– in Descartes
   creation and conservation of
      175, 176, 177, 178
   extended (*also* Corporeal) 23-
      25, 28, 32, 34, 39, 42, 43,
      44, 75
   compared with Spinoza on 24-
      26, 28, 32, 34, 39, 75, 91-2
   thinking 23, 38, 91
– in Leibniz
   causal efficacy of 162, 170,
      177, 178, 183, 184
   no causal transactions between
      created 162, 166, 189n
– in Spinoza
   its relation to affections 97-
      98, 100, 101
   its relation to attributes 69,
      80, 85, 89, 90, 97, 105n
      (*see also* Attributes, in
      Spinoza)
   definition of 42, 98, 133
   compared with Descartes on
      24-28, 32, 34, 42, 43-44,
      75, 128
   sense of 'exists' as applied to
      33-34
   exists necessarily 25, 33, 34,
      35
   extended 24-28, 32, 34, 42,
      44-45, 75
   possesses multiple attributes
      83, 92, 93, 105n, 106n
   priority over its affections 70,
      71, 73, 74, 77, 79-80, 83
   thinking  24
Substantial form 170
Substrate, substance as 39, 42,
      47n
Sun 7, 20n
Superstition 112, 135-36
Suppressed premise, and valid
      inference in Leibniz's
      innatism 201, 202
Sweet(ness) 201, 204, 206
Syllogism 51
   vs. geometric demonstration

52, 61-62
and knowledge, in Leibniz and
   Locke 213, 214, 224n,
   225n
Synthetic unity of apperception
   ownership vs. self-
      consciousness reading of
      273-76
   apperception in, understood as
      ownership 276-80
   how self-consciousness is
      relevant to: summary 297-
      300; *see* Kant, Synthesis in;
      Kant, on Recognition;
      Kant, on Spontaneity

Tacitus 129
'*tanquam*' 18n
Tannery, P. xi, 186n
Tastes 3, 13
Tautology 205, 207
Taylor, C. C. W. 243n
Temporal concepts
   in Spinoza 34-35
   applied to created substances
      and their states 162, 172,
      173, 175, 176, 177, 179
Tendency, to infer effect given
      cause 246
Tetens, Johan Nicolaus 281,
      289, 294, 300, 302n
Thau, Stewart x
Theodicy (*also* Theodicean) 165,
      192n
   requirements (of) 184
*Theodicy* (Leibniz) 174, 176,
      181, 184, 189n, 192n
*Theological-Political Treatise*
   (Spinoza): *see Tractatus
   Theologico-Politicus*
Theology 168, 173, 191n, 256
   and Spinoza 110, 111-12
– requirements/constraints of, in
      ascribing natural causal
      powers
   Malebranche vs. Leibniz 182,
      183, 184
   Malebranche vs. Berkeley
      234-38

Thinking
  thing 122, 130
  substance 23, 24, 38, 128
Third realm 32
Thirst 17
Thought, as a principle property
    or attribute of substance 23,
    38
Thoughts
  confused 3, 9, 10, 14, 16
  in Descartes 2, 3, 12, 16
  external vs. internal control
      over 127-28
  as private 126, 129
  'to be powerful is divine'
      argument (for
      occasionalism) 169, 170
Topics (Aristotle) 55
Tosel, Andre 153n
Tractatus de Intellectus
    Emendatione (Spinoza) 137
  and Spinoza on definition 52,
    54, 60
Tractatus Theologico-Politicus
    (Spinoza)
  Bennett on 109
  and Cartesian doctrines 116-
    17, 119-20, 126, 128, 129,
    134, 137, 144
  and 'common notions' 118-19,
    120
  relation to the Ethics 110,
    113, 114, 115, 118, 119,
    120, 121, 125, 126, 128,
    129, 131, 135, 136, 138,
    139, 142, 143, 145, 149,
    151, 152
  on politics and the state 110,
    111, 128, 131, 136-37,
    138, 140-42, 143-46, 149,
    150
  Spinoza's purpose in writing
    the 111-13, 151
  and Scripture and Biblical
    religion 110, 111-12, 113,
    119, 124-25, 152, 154n
Transcendental 280
  apperception 278, 298, 299,
    300

epistemology 298
faculty of self-consciousness
    291, 296-97, 298, 299
psychology 288, 302n
Transitive cause 27-28
Treatise of Human Nature (Hume)
    269
  and causal reasoning/inference
    245, 247-52
  and customary transition from
    cause to effect 252-57
  and mental events as causes
    and effects 257-62
  and circularity in Hume's
    definition of cause 264, 266
Treatise on Nature and Grace
    (Malebranche) 164
Triangle 198, 199, 213
  essence or nature of 29, 121,
    122
  idea of 29, 30, 36, 42-43,
    122,
Triangular 29, 42
True and immutable nature(s)
  ideas of things having 29, 30,
    31
Truth, as
  agreement/disagreement of
    ideas in Locke 196, 197
Truth(s)
  eternal 35, 36-37, 40, 41,
    121, 122, 123
  purpose of Spinoza's Ethics to
    demonstrate? 49-50
  mathematical 36
  necessary: see Necessary
    truths.
Tschirnhaus, Ehrenfried Walter
    von 61, 66-67n

Unconscious
  affirmation/apprehension of
    p, and Leibnizian innatism
    200, 201, 202, 208, 209,
    223n
Understanding
  – in Spinoza 158n
  and definition 51, 55, 56, 64,
    65

Unintelligible, instinct 253
Union of soul and body
  in Descartes 2, 12
  in Malebranche 165, 166
  in Spinoza 118, 139
Unity, of cognitive states: *see*
  Synthesis.
Universal mind 211
Un-philosophical,
  rules/probability, in Hume
  250-51
Use, of *p* without
  affirming/attending to *p*
  201-02, 207, 208, 215,
  223n

Vacillation, between contrary
  affects 135, 136
Validity
  and demonstration, in Locke
  199, 213
  and inference, in Leibnizian
  innatism 201, 212, 213,
  214, 215, 223n
  and truth of conclusion 49-50
Value, epistemic, of recognizing
  logical form 213, 214, 215,
  219
van Blijenbergh, 112
van der Bend, J. G. 66n
van Inwagen, Peter x
Velthysen: *see* de Velthuysen
Vision, in God, doctrine of 237,
  241
Volition: *see* Will
Voluntary
  action 257
  hence conscious epistemic
  assessment? 297
  vs. involuntary, in Hume on
  exercise of will 259, 261

'*Vorstellung*' 301n
Vulgar, the (*also* the Mob) 234,
  255

White(ness) 4, 11
White, W. H. 133
Whitehead, Alfred North 52, 66n
Will (*also* Volition)
– divine 183, 191n
  and occasional causality 165-
  66, 167, 169ff, 229
  vs. intellect 120-21
  particular vs. general 164-65
  vs. understanding 36-37
– human 117, 191n
  as cause of bodily movement?
  167, 227, 229, 231, 232,
  233, 234, 243n, 257, 258
  experience of, as source of idea
  of causality 239, 258
  its role in causal inference
  257, 259, 261
  infinite? 117
Willing 167, 227, 257
  in Hume 257-58, 259
Wilson, Margaret 18n, 222n,
  225n, 306
Wolf, A. 46n, 66n
Wolfson, H. A. 35, 47n, 66n
Wonder 15
World-apart thesis 161, 162,
  169
Woolhouse, R. S. 306
Worship, leeks and onions
  worthy of? 235
Wretched 135, 141-42, 148
Yellow(ness) 204, 206

Yovel, Yirmayahu 104n, 155n

Zweig, Arnulf 303n